Discourse-Pragmatic Variation and Change

Discourse-pragmatic markers are central to everyday language, yet many aspects of their use and functions remain elusive or under-investigated. Bringing together a global team of leading scholars, this volume presents a representative showcase of work currently being conducted in the field of discourse-pragmatic variation and change, including investigations of features such as *uh/um*, *please*, sentence-final *is all*, and discourse-pragmatic features from a number of languages. The book emphasizes not only that researchers have answered the call to address complex issues such as cross-linguistic reliability, extending research across languages, and expanding and improving on methods and analysis, but that they continue to address perennial questions in the field of language variation and change. With sections on theoretical and methodological issues, innovative variables, and language contact situations, the volume offers a robust overview of best practices for both new and experienced researchers.

Elizabeth Peterson is a sociolinguist based in Finland. She is the author of numerous articles on pragmatic borrowing in Finnish and the 2020 book *Making Sense of "Bad English"*.

Turo Hiltunen works as a university lecturer in English at the University of Helsinki, Finland. He has authored several studies on corpus pragmatics, corpus compilation, phraseology, and the language of science and medicine.

Joseph Kern is an assistant professor in Spanish at the University of Virginia's College at Wise, USA. He is the author of several articles on discourse-pragmatic features in Spanish, especially in varieties of Spanish in contact.

Discourse-Pragmatic Variation and Change

Theory, Innovations, Contact

Edited by

Elizabeth Peterson
University of Helsinki

Turo Hiltunen
University of Helsinki

Joseph Kern
University of Virginia's College at Wise

CAMBRIDGE
UNIVERSITY PRESS

Shaftesbury Road, Cambridge CB2 8EA, United Kingdom

One Liberty Plaza, 20th Floor, New York, NY 10006, USA

477 Williamstown Road, Port Melbourne, VIC 3207, Australia

314–321, 3rd Floor, Plot 3, Splendor Forum, Jasola District Centre, New Delhi – 110025, India

103 Penang Road, #05–06/07, Visioncrest Commercial, Singapore 238467

Cambridge University Press is part of Cambridge University Press & Assessment, a department of the University of Cambridge.

We share the University's mission to contribute to society through the pursuit of education, learning and research at the highest international levels of excellence.

www.cambridge.org
Information on this title: www.cambridge.org/9781108799478

DOI: 10.1017/9781108864183

© Cambridge University Press & Assessment 2022

This publication is in copyright. Subject to statutory exception and to the provisions of relevant collective licensing agreements, no reproduction of any part may take place without the written permission of Cambridge University Press & Assessment.

First published 2022
First paperback edition 2025

A catalogue record for this publication is available from the British Library

Library of Congress Cataloging-in-Publication data
Names: Peterson, Elizabeth (Professor of linguistics), editor. | Hiltunen, Turo, editor. | Kern, Joseph, (Professor of Spanish), editor.
Title: Discourse-pragmatic variation and change : theory, innovations, contact / edited by Elizabeth Peterson, Turo Hiltunen, Joseph Kern.
Description: Cambridge, United Kingdom ; New York : Cambridge University Press, 2022. | Includes bibliographical references and index.
Identifiers: LCCN 2021026770 (print) | LCCN 2021026771 (ebook) | ISBN 9781108836203 (hardback) | ISBN 9781108864183 (ebook)
Subjects: LCSH: Discourse markers. | Pragmatics. | Language and languages – Variation. | Languages in contact. | BISAC: LANGUAGE ARTS & DISCIPLINES / Linguistics / Semantics | LCGFT: Essays.
Classification: LCC P302.35 .D584 2022 (print) | LCC P302.35 (ebook) | DDC 401/.41–dc23/eng/20210930
LC record available at https://lccn.loc.gov/2021026770
LC ebook record available at https://lccn.loc.gov/2021026771

ISBN   978-1-108-83620-3   Hardback
ISBN   978-1-108-79947-8   Paperback

Cambridge University Press & Assessment has no responsibility for the persistence or accuracy of URLs for external or third-party internet websites referred to in this publication and does not guarantee that any content on such websites is, or will remain, accurate or appropriate.

Contents

List of Figures	*page* vii
List of Tables	ix
Notes on Contributors	xiii
Foreword by Jan-Ola Östman	xix
Acknowledgments	xxvi
List of Abbreviations	xxvii

Introduction ELIZABETH PETERSON, TURO HILTUNEN, AND JOSEPH KERN	1
Part I Innovations in Theory and Method	13
1 Reflexes of Abruptness in the Development of Pragmatic Markers DEREK DENIS	15
2 Evaluation of Pragmatic Markers: The Case of *You Know* ERIK SCHLEEF AND BRADLEY MACKAY	40
3 Quotative Variation and Change in French with Additional Insights from Brazilian Portuguese and Italian STEPHEN LEVEY, LAURA KASTRONIC, SALVIO DIGESTO, AND MÉLISSA CHIASSON	61
4 Cross-Linguistic Variation in Spoken Discourse Markers: Distribution, Functions, and Domains LIESBETH DEGAND, ZOÉ BROISSON, LUDIVINE CRIBLE, AND KAROLINA GRZECH	83
Part II Innovative Variables in English	105
5 An Emerging Pragmatic Marker: Sentence-Final *Is All* DANIELA KOLBE-HANNA AND LAUREL J. BRINTON	107

Contents

6 "That Is Totally Not My Type of Film": Innovations in the Intensifier System of UK English   127
   KARIN AIJMER

7 *Uh*, What Should We Count?   150
   TIM GADANIDIS AND DEREK DENIS

8 Modeling Listener Responses   173
   MIRJAM ELISABETH EISWIRTH

Part III Language Contact Settings   191

9 *You Know* in L1 and L2 English   193
   CHLOÉ DISKIN-HOLDAWAY

10 General Extenders in Bilingual Speech   212
    JOSEPH KERN

11 The Diverging Paths of Consequence Markers in Canadian French   230
    HÉLÈNE BLONDEAU, RAYMOND MOUGEON, AND MIREILLE TREMBLAY

12 What Governs Speakers' Choices of Borrowed vs. Domestic Variants of Discourse-Pragmatic Variables?   251
    GISLE ANDERSEN

13 A Place for *pliis* in Finnish: A Discourse-Pragmatic Variation Account of Position   272
    ELIZABETH PETERSON, TURO HILTUNEN, AND JOHANNA VAATTOVAARA

Afterword: Future Priorities in Discourse-Pragmatic Variation and Change Research   293
HEIKE PICHLER

References   301
Index   329

Figures

1.1	Distribution of EP variants in EOE in apparent time	*page* 23
1.2	Distribution of EP variants by syntactic position in four age groups	25
1.3	Probability of *I think* (vs. all other EPs) by syntactic position over apparent time	27
1.4	Distribution of EPs by subject complement over apparent time	29
2.1	Significant scales and factors	54
4.1	Frequency and polyfunctionality of DM use in the French dataset	90
4.2	Frequency and polyfunctionality of DM use in the Spanish dataset	93
4.3	Frequency and polyfunctionality of DM use in the English dataset	96
4.4	Frequency and polyfunctionality of DM use in the Polish dataset	98
4.5	Cross-linguistic domain distribution of discourse markers	99
5.1	Distribution of ", is all ." in COCA per million words (pmw) across text types and time periods	114
5.2	Distribution of "that BE all ." in COCA per million words (pmw) across text types and time periods	117
7.1	Proportion of *um* per speaker, shaded by region	158
7.2	Proportion of *um* per speaker, shaded by gender	159
7.3	Proportion of *um* in apparent time	160
7.4	Proportion of *um* in apparent time, by gender	160
7.5	Proportion of *um* in apparent time, by position	161
7.6	Proportion of *um* in apparent time, by position and cliticization	161
7.7	Conditional inference tree for farmers	162
7.8	Conditional inference tree for interviewers	163
7.9	Proportional and normalized frequency of two hypothetical datasets, one where variants are trading frequencies – (a) and (b) – and one where one variant remains static and the other increases – (c) and (d)	165

7.10	Frequency of *uh* and *um* per 1,000 words	167
7.11	Frequency of *uh* and *um* per 1,000 words, by position	168
7.12	Frequency of *uh* and *um* per 1,000 words, by position and gender	169
8.1	Structural definition and sequential position of LRs	178
9.1	Average rates of *you know* per 1,000 words across four speaker groups	204
9.2	Frequency of *you know* by migrants' level of education in the Dublin corpus	204
10.1	Frequency of general extenders in Spanish and English per 10,000 words according to participant, gender, and language dominance	219
10.2	Percentage of general extenders that fulfill a referential function in English and Spanish according to participant, gender, and language dominance	227
11.1	Study design	237
11.2	Variant frequencies in the 1970s and 2010s in Montreal and Welland	239
12.1	Waveform and spectrogram with *please*	262

Tables

1.1	Distribution of Earlier Ontario English speakers	*page* 21
1.2	Mixed-effects logistic regression testing the fixed effects of YEAR OF BIRTH (centered, continuous), POSITION, and their interaction and a random intercept for SPEAKER on the realization of EPs as *I think*	27
1.3	Mixed-effects logistic regression testing the fixed effects of PERIOD, SUBCOMP, and their interaction and a random intercept for SPEAKER on the realization of EPs as *I think*	30
1.4	Mixed-effects logistic regression testing the fixed effects of PERIOD, SUBCOMP, and their interaction and a random intercept for SPEAKER on the realization of EPs as *I guess*	31
1.5	Cross-tabulation of period and grammatical person of complement clause subject in EOE and TEA, showing the percentage of negated EPs relative to all EPs	33
1.6	Summary of the probabilistic niches of *I think* and *I guess*	36
2.1	Overview of guises	46
2.2	Guise distribution across eight subsurveys	47
2.3	Twenty-nine scales presented to participants in the survey	48
2.4	Best models for the three factors. Reference levels are neutral guise, Bella, Sick Sam topic, female respondent, middle class, and *you know* user	52
2.5	Results from the mixed-effects ordinal regression models for scales on which the ratings of *you know* and neutral guises were judged to be statistically different. References levels are neutral guise, Sick Sam topic, female respondent, middle class, and *you know* user	53
3.1	Characteristics of the corpora	66
3.2	Variant distribution by age in three varieties of French	71
3.3	Variant distribution by age in Quebec and Acadian French	73
3.4	Two independent multivariate analyses of social and linguistic factors contributing to the selection of *être comme* in Quebec French and Acadian French (younger speakers only)	75

3.5	Two independent multivariate analyses of factors contributing to the selection of *être comme* in Quebec French and Acadian French (younger speakers only)	77
3.6	Variant distributions in Brazilian Portuguese by age	79
3.7	Variant distributions in Italian by age	79
3.8	Summary of major findings in relation to the rate of change exhibited by quotative innovations in French and Brazilian Portuguese	81
4.1	Taxonomy of domains and functions (Crible and Degand 2019b)	88
4.2	Distribution of DMs across domains and functions in the French dataset (dominant functions are highlighted)	89
4.3	Distribution of DM types over discourse functions in the French dataset	90
4.4	Distribution of DMs across domains and functions in the Spanish dataset	91
4.5	Distribution of DM types over discourse functions in the Spanish dataset	92
4.6	Distribution of DMs across domains and functions in the English dataset	94
4.7	Distribution of DM types over discourse functions in the English dataset	95
4.8	Distribution of DMs across domains and functions in the Polish dataset	97
4.9	Distribution of DM types over discourse functions in the Polish dataset	98
4.10	Cross-linguistic distribution of DM functions across discourse domains	101
5.1	Synchronic corpora used in this study	110
5.2	Sentence-final *(that) BE all* in COCA and SOAP (search string: "_vb* all .")	112
5.3	Sentence-final *is/was all* in COCA and SOAP (search string "vb* all ."; PM=pragmatic marker)	114
5.4	Co-occurrence of sentence-final *is all* with *just*	115
5.5	Co-occurrence of sentence-final *that's/is all* with *just*	118
5.6	Diachronic corpora used in this study	119
5.7	*That/this BE all* in Late Modern English	122
5.8	Expanded forms with *all* or *what* in CEN (free-standing and parenthetical forms)	124
6.1	Number of occurrences of *totally* used by speakers in each age group in the BNC2014S	133

List of Tables   xi

6.2	The frequencies of *totally* with different syntactic targets and functions in the BNC1994D and the BNC2014S	134
6.3	The frequency of *totally* with positive, negative, and neutral adjectives	135
6.4	Occurrences of *totally* as a modifier of scalar adjectives produced by male and female speakers in different age categories	138
7.1	List of speakers	156
7.2	Cross-community comparison	157
7.3	Organization of the data	166
7.4	Mixed-effects Poisson regression model on non-initial (UHM) counts	169
8.1	Cross-tabulation showing how often each participant takes the speaker and listener role, depending on the gender of their interlocutor	175
8.2	Cross-tabulation of raw token counts of LRs by listener and speaker gender across all interactions	175
8.3	Minimum turn length at which the first LR is predicted based on the zero-model	184
8.4	Predicted number of responses to a 100-word turn based on speaker and listener gender	184
8.5	Fixed effects of the zero-inflated Poisson model predicting how many actions listeners do based on which party has how much impact on the action from a qualitative perspective	186
9.1	Participants in the Dublin and Melbourne corpora	198
9.2	Proficiency levels from the Common European Framework of Reference for Languages (CEFR)	199
9.3	Functions of *you know* in the Dublin corpus	201
9.4	*You know* among L1 and L2 speakers	203
9.5	Breakdown of *you know* by function (House 2009): Dublin corpus	205
9.6	Mixed-effects regression output for *you know* as illustrator by L1 speakers (Intercept) and L2 speakers in the Dublin corpus	205
9.7	Mixed-effects regression output for *you know* to refer to shared knowledge by L1 speakers (Intercept) and L2 speakers in the Dublin corpus	206
9.8	Mixed-effects regression output for *you know* to invite response by L1 speakers (Intercept) and L2 speakers in the Dublin corpus	206
10.1	Frequency of general extenders in Spanish and English per 10,000 words according to participant, gender, and language dominance	218

10.2	Forms of general extenders in English and Spanish	220
10.3	Length of general extenders in English and Spanish regardless of function	222
10.4	Distribution of referential and non-referential functions of general extenders in English and Spanish according to participant, gender, and language dominance	226
11.1	Corpora	237
11.2	Influence of connector choice according to linguistic function in Montreal 1971 and Welland 1975	240
11.3	Influence of social factors in Montreal 1971	241
11.4	Influence of social factors in Welland 1975	242
11.5	Influence of connector choice according to linguistic function in Montreal 2012 and Welland 2012–2015	244
11.6	Influence of social factors in Montreal 2012	245
11.7	Influence of social factors in Welland 2012–2015	246
12.1	Corpora used in this study	255
12.2	Use of *please* and equivalent domestic polite expressions in requests (total corpus token frequency in parenthesis)	257
12.3	Use of *sorry* and equivalent domestic polite expressions in apologies (total corpus token frequency in parenthesis)	264
13.1	Preferred position of *pliis* and *kiitos* on a Likert scale of 0 to 3: Can you give me that?	277
13.2	Representative request types in Finnish (non-comprehensive)	278
13.3	Baseline (elicited) positions for *kiitos* in seven request types	280
13.4	Baseline (elicited) positions for *pliis* in seven request types	281
13.5	Most frequent request strategies in transit data + lexical politeness markers	284
13.6	Distribution of request types for *pliis* and *kiitos* in FinnishWaC	287

Contributors

Karin Aijmer is Professor Emerita at the University of Gothenburg, Sweden. Her research interests focus on pragmatics, discourse analysis, modality, corpus linguistics, and contrastive analysis. Her publications include *Conversational Routines in English: Convention and Creativity* (1996), *English Discourse Particles: Evidence from a Corpus* (2002), and *Understanding Pragmatic Markers: A Variational Pragmatic Analysis* (2013). She is the coeditor of *Pragmatics of Society* (2011) and *A Handbook of Corpus Pragmatics* (2014).

Gisle Andersen is Professor of English linguistics at NHH Norwegian School of Economics in Bergen, Norway. His research interests span topics in pragmatics (discourse markers, interjections, politeness, etc.), language contact, lexicography/terminology, and language for specific purposes. His recent work has focused on ways in which linguistic items that are inherently pragmatic in nature are borrowed across languages. He has studied cases of pragmatic and phraseological borrowing and investigated how the use of borrowed items is constrained by cultural, social, and cognitive factors.

Hélène Blondeau is Professor of French and Francophone Studies and Linguistics at the University of Florida, USA. Her research investigates language variation and change at the individual and community level. She has examined varieties of French in North America with a focus on the Montreal sociolinguistic dynamics.

Laurel J. Brinton is Professor of English Language at the University of British Columbia, Vancouver, Canada. Her research interests include grammaticalization and lexicalization, historical pragmatics, phrasal verbs and composite predicates, verbal aspect, and intensifiers. Her most recent publications include the edited textbook *English Historical Linguistics* (2017) and the monograph *The Evolution of Pragmatic Markers in English: Pathways of Change* (2017) as well as five readers in De Gruyter Mouton The History of English series (2017) coedited with Alexander Bergs.

Zoé Broisson was an MA student in Linguistics at the University of Louvain (UCLouvain), Belgium, at the time this volume was compiled. She has since left academia and is now active as a cofounder and linguist in an EdTech startup and UCLouvain spin-off, developing a mobile app that English learners use to boost their pronunciation using voice technology.

Mélissa Chiasson is a project officer in the Office of the Vice-President, Research, at the University of Ottawa, Canada. Her doctoral research targeted sociolinguistic variation and change in Acadian French, as spoken in northeast New Brunswick.

Ludivine Crible earned her PhD in Linguistics at the University of Louvain (UCLouvain), Belgium, in 2017 on the topic of discourse markers and disfluency in spoken English and French. She published several corpus-based papers on the functions and variation of discourse markers, including from a contrastive perspective. After a Marie Curie postdoctoral fellowship at the University of Edinburgh, she is now an assistant professor in French linguistics at Ghent University (Belgium).

Liesbeth Degand is Full Professor of General and Dutch Linguistics at the Catholic University of Louvain (UCLouvain), Belgium. Her research interests are oriented toward the discourse grammar interface, with special attention to the study of discourse markers, discourse segmentation, and clause combining in spoken language. From a methodological point of view, she combines (multilingual) corpus studies with elicitation tasks. She is currently involved in a European project on prediction and alignment in spoken interaction.

Derek Denis is Assistant Professor of Linguistics in the Department of Language Studies at the University of Toronto Mississauga, Canada. His research focuses on the sociolinguistics of innovation and change with special attention to discourse-pragmatic features. His current work investigates the emergence of a multiethnolect in Toronto: Multicultural Toronto English.

Salvio Digesto is a part-time professor in the Department of Linguistics at the University of Ottawa, Canada. His doctoral research addressed variation and change in Italian. He has additional interests in the sociolinguistics of French and English.

Chloé Diskin-Holdaway is Senior Lecturer in Applied Linguistics at the University of Melbourne, Australia, and Chair of the Discourse-Pragmatic Variation and Change (DiPVaC) research network. Her research expertise lies at the interface of sociolinguistics and second language acquisition. She is the (co)author of several articles, including "Going global and sounding local: Quotative variation and change in L1 and L2 speakers of Irish (Dublin) English" (2019) and "'Northmen, Southmen, comrades all'? The adoption of discourse like by migrants North and South of the Irish border" (2020).

Mirjam Elisabeth Eiswirt is a postdoctoral researcher at the Sociolinguistics Lab at the University of Duisburg-Essen within the DFG-funded project "Tracing Language Variation and Change across the lifespan in Tyneside English." Her research focuses on the relationship between interactional structure and language variation at different levels of linguistic architecture, as well as variation and change in the use of interactional strategies. Her work has been published in the *Journal of Pragmatics*, the *Journal of Sociolinguistics*, and with Cambridge University Press.

Tim Gadanidis is a PhD researcher in the Department of Linguistics at the University of Toronto, Canada. His research primarily focuses on language and the Internet, such as how the use and perception of the English discourse-pragmatic markers *um* and *uh* vary across spoken and online (instant-messaging) communication. Most recently, he has used qualitative and computational-linguistic methods to critically analyze discourse about climate change in online communities.

Karolina Grzech specializes in language documentation and description. She received her PhD from SOAS University of London, UK, in 2017 and worked as a postdoctoral researcher at Stockholm University, Sweden. Her main research interests are evidentiality, discourse markers, and analysis of interactive spoken discourse. She conducts fieldwork related to these topics on Quechuan languages in Ecuador. In 2021, she began a postdoctoral project on Quechuan discourse at the University of Valencia.

Turo Hiltunen is University Lecturer in English at the Department of Languages, University of Helsinki, Finland. His research concentrates on corpus linguistics and corpus development, grammar, phraseology, and the analysis of scientific discourse, past and present.

Laura Kastronic is Assistant Professor in the Department of French Studies at the University of Toronto, Canada. Her research interests focus on language variation and change, language contact, bilingualism, and the sociolinguistics of French and English.

Joseph Kern is Assistant Professor in Spanish at the University of Virginia's College at Wise, USA. His research focuses on discourse-pragmatic variation in Spanish, especially varieties of Spanish in contact with English and Portuguese, as well as intersections between sociolinguistics and second-language pedagogy. He has analyzed several discourse-pragmatic variables in Spanish, including discourse markers, quotatives, general extenders, and tag questions. He is on the steering committee of the Discourse-Pragmatic Variation and Change (DiPVaC) research network.

Daniela Kolbe-Hanna is a teacher and researcher of English Linguistics at Trier University, Germany, where she received her PhD, in 2008, after an MA in Freiburg in English, Scandinavian and Slavic Studies, during which she studied for a year at the University of Glasgow. Her main research interest lies in the constant variation and change of language. Her publications include the development of the complementizer *as*, variation in complement clauses, and comment clauses in varieties of English around the world.

Stephen Levey is Associate Professor in the Department of Linguistics at the University of Ottawa, Canada. His research interests focus on morpho-syntactic and discourse-pragmatic variation and change, as well as language contact and historical sociolinguistics.

Bradley Mackay is a research assistant in the Department of English and American Studies at the University of Salzburg, Austria. His research focuses on language, gender, and sexuality and he is currently writing his PhD on the sociophonetic variation found among people with divergent sexual identities.

Raymond Mougeon is Professor Emeritus of French Linguistics at York University, Canada. He has carried out extensive research on the evolution of Ontario-spoken French, the ethnolinguistic vitality of Ontario's French-speaking communities and the acquisition of French by Ontario's French immersion students.

Elizabeth Peterson is University Lecturer in the Department of Languages at the University of Helsinki, Finland. She conducts research on language contact and language attitudes and ideologies. She is the author of *Making Sense of "Bad English": An Introduction to Language Attitudes and Ideologies* (2020). She is on the steering committee of the Discourse-Pragmatic Variation and Change (DiPVaC) research network.

Heike Pichler is Senior Lecturer in Variationist Sociolinguistics at Newcastle University, UK. She is the author of *The Structure of Discourse-Pragmatic Variation* (2013), editor of *Discourse-Pragmatic Variation and Change in English* (2016), and founding chair of the international Discourse-Pragmatic Variation and Change (DiPVaC) research network. Her ongoing research focuses on discourse-pragmatic variation in narrative discourse and computer-mediated communication as well as on language variation and change in old age.

Jan-Ola Östman is Professor Emeritus in Scandinavian Languages at the University of Helsinki, Finland. He is the author and editor of books and articles on pragmatics, discourse, construction grammar, variability, language contact, dialects, socio-onomastics, minority languages, language policy, ideology, and responsibility. He is the coeditor of the John Benjamins book series Constructional Approaches to Language and International Pragmatics Association's *Handbook of Pragmatics*. He was President of the International Pragmatics Association in the years 2012–2017.

Erik Schleef is Professor of English Linguistics at the University of Salzburg, Austria. His research focuses on variation and change in dialects of the British Isles, the acquisition of variation, sociolinguistics and perception, and language and gender in educational settings. He is coeditor of *The Routledge Sociolinguistics Reader* (2010) and coauthor of *Doing Sociolinguistics: A Practical Guide to Data Collection and Analysis* (2015).

Mireille Tremblay is Professor of Linguistics at the University of Montreal, Canada. She specializes in language change, morphosyntactic variation, and history of the French language. Her most recent research focuses on the new language practices of Montrealers and documents the changes in progress in the community.

Johanna Vaattovaara is Professor of Finnish language at the Faculty of Information Technology and Communication Sciences at Tampere University, Finland. Her main research areas are linguistic variation and change, language attitudes, and language ideologies. Her PhD on the Tornio Valley (2009) was the first folk linguistic dissertation on the Finnish language. Her more recent work looks at language ideologies in Finnish and on awareness and attitudes toward English loans integrated into Finnish.

Foreword

Discourse, Pragmatics and Responsibility

In the late 1960s, many scholars within text linguistics in Europe and within generative semantics in the United States became increasingly dissatisfied with a seemingly exclusive focus on the form and structure of sentences in mainstream linguistics. There was a growing need to open up the subject to make it acceptable to talk about context, function and variation in relation to the study of linguistics. Words and sentences have different functions in different contexts.

This turn had already seen the light of day in philosophy (the "later" Wittgenstein, ordinary language philosophy, and finally the influential studies by Searle and Grice); in anthropology (in fact, ever since Malinowski); in translation theory (including Pike's 1954 [1967] magnum opus); and in ethnography. Even though cultural, social, cognitive, philosophical, and anthropological aspects of language had been actively taken into account in neighboring disciplines and in non-mainstream approaches to linguistics, the stronghold by structuralist and transformational-generative thinking seemed unbeatable: the quest by linguists to be(come) properly scientific had steered the development of linguistic thinking on a route that had taken the very concept of language away from language usage and language users' adaptability.

Gradually, things started to change in the 1960s: the initial attempt was to build context and function on top of what we already had, that is, adding extra "boxes" or "circles" or "trees" on top of, or around, the structuralist specifications of language as a system, coupled with intricate discussions about compositionality and native speakers' often very varied intuitions.

Text linguistics developed into discourse analysis, which today includes contextual, political, and multimodal analyses. William Labov (e.g., Labov 1972a) took variation seriously, establishing what we today know as sociolinguistics, and started his and his followers' search for contextual factors, that is, sociolinguistic variables that could explain linguistic variation: age, gender, race, education, class, among others, to begin with – and new variables are added and tried out constantly. Corpora needed to be gathered and built in order to make it possible for everyone to check everybody else's data. Generative semantics was for a time declared dead,[1] but it gradually developed into

---

[1] For elusive, entertaining, and informative accounts of Generative Semantics, see Lakoff (1989), McCawley (1994).

linguistic pragmatics, which in the 1980s increasingly merged with the European, broader approach to language function inspired by Charles W. Morris's three-way distinction between syntactics, semantics, and pragmatics and his view that pragmatics should deal with "all the psychological, biological, and sociological phenomena which occur in the functioning of signs" (1938: 108).[2]

What was soon realized as being more important than adding context and function as viable factors to be referred to – very often "when needed" – was the methodological, epistemological, if not ontological, idea that complementary approaches could be used as tools in the study of language. Once function, variation, and context were taken seriously, linguistic data could be understood and interpreted in very many additional ways. The very concepts of context and function had to be explicated and extended: What *is* context? What *is* function? What *is* variation? What *is* discourse? Context and function for what and for whom – in society, in culture? Further, what are their effects really on language structure and language use? How do language structure and language usage themselves affect context? Some scholars even gave up using the very words *language* and *linguistics* altogether because these had too many connotations relating to studies of explicit word-and-sentence structures of languages. Yet talking about, say, communication, interaction, collaboration, or even Malinowski's (1923) communion, only moved the question in another direction and required understanding and definition of these additional concepts.

In the development of a need to look at function, context and variation as such, pragmatics, sociolinguistics, and discourse analysis have joined forces. Investigations of what goes on implicitly in communication, between the lines of what is actually said as propositional content, have become central. As a result, and in order to tackle such issues, within context-enhanced, interactional, and usage-based approaches to language it has thus become more and more acceptable to see language *from different perspectives*, with each perspective contributing to our overall understanding of, precisely, language.

We consequently find research quests taking semiotic perspectives on language as well as cultural and anthropological perspectives, sociological and philosophical perspectives, cognitive and conceptual perspectives, interactional perspectives, and more. Different perspectives have developed into different models, the results of which have gradually added to our *understanding* of language.

The very concept of "understanding" is important, because ultimately most linguists and students of language working within the humanities and social

---

[2] This is reflected and reiterated in the mission statement of the International Pragmatics Association to represent "the field of pragmatics, i.e., the **science of language use**, in its widest interdisciplinary sense *as a functional (i.e., cognitive, social, and cultural) perspective on language and communication*" (see https://pragmatics.international/page/Mission; emphasis in original).

sciences rarely seek the ultimate truth but, precisely, understanding – understanding of the phenomenon of language; and we have learned that understanding is not easily achieved through deductive reasoning, by setting up a priori models to be applied to instances of communicative expression. Understanding is attained by looking at a phenomenon from different perspectives – ideally at the same time. In practical analyses, however, we take one perspective at a time while simultaneously trying to keep the big picture in mind.

One set of linguistic expressions that very early on challenged the established view that linguistics should first and foremost focus on positive, declarative, transitive, finite clauses with a preset toolbox of word class categories and grammatical functions was the frequently occurring phrases *you know*, *I guess*, *like*, *well*, *oh*, and similar difficult-to-define phrases in terms of predicate logic. Even though school training did its utmost to obliterate these from the vocabularies of young children, the expressions kept occurring – even in adulthood among well-educated people. In fact, these are some of the most interactive features in language, and if linguistics is to deal with ordinary people's language – rather than, or at least in addition to, the written word, focusing on the language of classical authors – these "small words and phrases" had to be taken seriously; and so they have.

A prominent research network that has taken as its task to bring together scholars and promote research in this field is the Discourse-Pragmatic Variation and Change (DiPVaC) network, with a specific focus on, precisely, discourse-pragmatic features like the discourse markers or pragmatic particles already mentioned, which have as their main function to express interpersonal, (con)textual, and affective functions in communication. The present volume brings together an exciting collection of chapters by members and collaborators of this network.

Yet the road traveled to where we are at the moment has not always been an easy and navigable one. Robin Lakoff's (1972) article was an early attempt at getting scholars' attention to turn to context and language function, and since it was published in the journal *Language* it was not completely marginalizable, albeit that it was published at a time when language function and the very field of pragmatics were often scorned by mainstream linguists.

Lakoff's article may have opened the eyes of the English-language community of linguists to what she called pragmatic particles, but there had indeed been much earlier studies of (pragmatic) particles, in other languages, especially in (literary versions of) earlier forms of languages, and in languages that had not been previously described, where particles and clitics were a permanent challenge to the anthropologically minded linguist (see, e.g., Denniston 1934 on Greek particles; Kinkade 1976 on Interior Salishan particles). German particles received attention very early on – probably because many of the German particles also functioned as conjuncts, and the task was to explicate the differences in meaning and function of these linguistic expressions (cf. Arndt 1960; Schubiger 1965; Kriwonossow 1966). In fact, in the 1960s and 1970s, there was constant debate about whether the particles were grammatical and syntactically specifiable (as modal particles, as attitudinal adverbs, as conjunctive or connecting particles, or, for example, in the case of Japanese, as subject or topic particles) or whether their function was better described as more pragmatic.[3]

Even though the study of conversation analysis had started to make an appearance as early as in the mid-1970s (with Sacks et al. 1974 being the major article that reached the general linguistics audience – also published in *Language*), and although there were MA theses and PhD theses written on particles in different languages, a more intensive and specific research focus on pragmatic particles as expressions with different interactional functions did not properly start until the early 1980s. This was also the time when scholarship in pragmatics as a field of study on a par with phonology, morphology, syntax, lexicology, and semantics was beginning to become established – and with it not only the International Pragmatics Association but also book series in the field, notably the John Benjamins series Pragmatics and Beyond, as part of which I published one of the first studies that attempted to describe the intricacies of the pragmatic particle *you know* (Östman 1981): its use in interactions, in narratives, and in child language acquisition as well as differences in use with respect to gender.

It was important at the time to try to come up with a definition of the pragmatic particle I was investigating.[4] Thus, I suggested the following definition as the general, prototypical meaning of *you know*:

> The speaker strives towards getting the addressee to cooperate and/or to accept the propositional content of his[/her] utterance as mutual background knowledge.
>
> (Östman 1981: 17)

The definition is a product of its time (e.g., with regard to gender), but one of the most crucial indications to support and validate this definition was the data for "the same story" being told twice by the same teller to the same addressee. In the first telling of the story, that is, when the story is new to the addressee, the teller uses an abundance of *you know*s, striving to check the level of understanding of the addressee, pleading for cooperation, and seeking to get the addressee to take for granted the tenability of what they are being told. In the second telling, however, when the teller knows that the addressee knows the story, the teller uses hardly any *you know*s.

---

[3] See Weydt's influential 1968 book on *Abtönungspartikel* (Ger. *Abtönung*, "shading, toning down").

[4] This is, of course, still important, but notions like particles being multifunctional and polysemous are much more readily acceptable nowadays.

Conversation analysts in their very detailed ethnomethodological analyses of everyday interaction, focusing on wanting to answer the question of "Why that now?" with respect to the occurrence of a linguistic item,[5] necessarily also paid attention to pragmatic particles as well as to silence, supportive elements, filled pauses, and the like – all of which are also at the center of interest for the DiPVaC research network. When John Gumperz, on the basis of his experiences in India and of language contacts in London, wanted to make sociolinguistics become more "discoursy," a new branch called interactional sociolinguistics came into being; and his new book series at the time, Studies in Interactional Sociolinguistics, published what became the standard reference book for studies in this field for a long time, Deborah Schiffrin's (1987) *Discourse Markers*. The term was in accordance with Gumperz's (1984) book *Discourse Strategies*, and the very term "discourse marker" has today become as frequent – if not dominant – as that of "pragmatic particle."[6]

The rest, as one says, is history.[7] These early studies effectively opened up a field of inquiry that is still extremely vibrant forty years later. This edited volume and the DiPVaC network build on these earlier and subsequent studies and are, in that sense, one of the follow-up outcomes of the early pioneers' work.

It is difficult to make any predictions about the future of this line of work. One thing is certain, though, and that is that, despite the multitude of books and articles on pragmatic particles, discourse markers, discourse-pragmatic features, and the variability and adaptability of human communication, there is still a lot to do. That is of course another good reason for having a network like the DiPVaC, which, according to their mission statement,[8] "provides a platform for the dissemination and discussion of new research findings, the formation of new research collaborations, and the promotion of the field within and beyond linguistics."

All scholars working in this field would agree that pragmatic particles/discourse markers do not partake in establishing or affecting the propositional content of expressions they are used in connection with; and there are, of course, other characteristics: they are usually short, they are inflexible (which is the definition of "particle"), and they modify, qualify (etc.) something else.

---

[5] This was in stark contrast to the transformation-generative grammarian's "Have you made a generalization today?".
[6] Schourup (1983) – another early study – used the term discourse particle. Other terms include IFIDs (illocutionary-force indicating device), discourse connectives, speech-act adverbials, interjections, and pragmatic markers.
[7] For an overview of publications, see Aijmer and Simon-Vandenbergen (2009), but any respectable journal dealing with language function publishes articles on discourse markers, and references in the chapters in this volume clearly also include more recent contributions.
[8] See the DiPVaC research network website: www.dipvac.org.

Various contextual factors and variables have laudably been suggested as influencing their function.

Are there more general characterizations we can make, though? In my own work (cf. Östman 1982, 1986, 1995), I have talked about pragmatic particles as having an implicit anchoring function, as being the implicit anchors of messages par excellence – they are the markers that let us see what goes on "between the lines" of what we say, the verbalized connections to the implicit communication we engage in whenever we speak: our connection to the background society and culture we take for granted, to the systems of politeness and turn-taking we utilize, to the involvement, affect and emotions we might not want to verbalize directly.

I would like to conclude with a few words about the last of the trinity in the subheading to my Foreword, viz. *responsibility* (cf. Popper 1987; Solin and Östman 2016). I want to do this to suggest one direction for future research on discourse-pragmatic features.

If we take the general function of pragmatic particles to implicitly anchor a message, and to communicate information about (1) cultural coherence, (2) interaction-politeness, and (3) affect-involvement, then they are the surface manifestations par excellence of the underlying, implicit aspects of messages. The definition of pragmatic particles that I have taken as a guideline in my own research runs as follows:

> Pragmatic particles are (verbal) elements in language that have as their primary function to implicitly anchor utterances vis-à-vis the communicative restraints of a culture and society, the demands of aspects of interactive politeness, and the prevalent types of affect and involvement.

To this, I offer the addendum that access to and employment of pragmatic particles are part of our competence – as is pragmatic information generally. That is, every expression that takes linguistic form is a crystallization of some structurally, cognitively and/or socially relevant factor (for human expression); and what joins these three perspectives together is precisely the understanding of how communicators handle responsibility in communication.

Indeed, I feel the expression – or rather, negotiation – of responsibility is perhaps the most salient common aspect of the function of pragmatic particles as communicating implicit, subconscious messages: you implicitly express what level and kind of responsibility you want to take, give, have, and so on with pragmatic particles.

For instance, and very briefly, if we take another look at the abovementioned narrative data and my definition of the function of *you know* from the point of view of responsibility, we could say that, in the first telling of the story (with an abundance of *you know*s), the responsibility of what actually took place in the story was solely the teller's; but, in the second telling, when the addressee also knew the story, the responsibility for the story was shared by the teller and the addressee.

In other words, the focus on responsibility as a tool would perhaps not add a completely new interpretation, but it does add an additional *perspective*; and having access to a multitude of perspectives is crucial in order to get "the full picture" – especially so in discourse-pragmatic studies.

I think the gist of doing discourse-pragmatic work is precisely to keep focusing on what has traditionally been talked about as the periphery, the margins, the fringes. Context is also a perspective on language – it is not something "outside of" language. This insight alone will give us a deeper understanding of the function(s) of language.

JAN-OLA ÖSTMAN

Acknowledgments

The editors of this volume are indebted to the contributing authors, whose expertise and dedication to creating high-quality research remained a chief motivator throughout the editorial process. Our sincere thanks also go to the reviewers of the chapters in this volume as well as the external reviewers of the book proposal and complete manuscript. Their care and attention to their task lifted the writing and reporting of our research to a different level. We thank our editor at Cambridge University Press, Helen Barton, for her enthusiasm and encouragement from the initial stages through to the end of the publication process. We also thank our editorial consultant, Isabel Collins, for tirelessly, effectively and promptly responding to our many questions, as well as the editing and Integra production team for their careful work during the final stages of the project. Most of the chapters in this volume emerged from presentations at the DiPVaC4 conference held in Helsinki, Finland, in 2018. For this event, we thank the University of Helsinki, the university's Faculty of Arts and the Federation of Finnish Learned Societies for their support. We likewise thank the audience and participants at DiPVaC4 for their comments and feedback on our work. Finally, our thanks to Heike Pichler for sharing her expertise and knowledge on several occasions throughout the crafting of this volume. Her work and example as a leader in the field continue to inspire us.

Abbreviations

AmE	American English
AP	adjectival phrase
AusE	Australian English
BLV	Belleville
BrE	British English
CA	conversation analysis
CEFR	Common European Framework of Reference for Languages
CI	credible interval
CMC	computer-mediated communication
CP	complementizer phrase
CRE	Constant Rate Effect
DiPVaC	Discourse-Pragmatic Variation and Change [network]
DM	discourse marker
DPM	discourse-pragmatic marker
ELF	English as a Lingua Franca
EON	Eastern Ontario
EP	epistemic parenthetical
F-INT	female interviewer
IrE	Irish English
L1	first language
L2	second language
LOESS	locally estimated scatterplot smoothing
LR	listener response
M-INT	male interviewer
MC	middle class
NIA	Niagara
NNS	non-native speakers
NP	noun phrase
NS	native speakers
PAF	principal axis factoring
PM	pragmatic marker (Chapter 5)
PM	politeness marker (Chapter 13)
pmw	per million words
PP	prepositional phrase
RL	recipient language
SES	socioeconomic status
SL	source language

SLA	second language acquisition
TCU	turn construction unit
TRP	transition-relevance point
UMC	upper middle class
WC	working class

Introduction

Elizabeth Peterson, Turo Hiltunen, and Joseph Kern

Work in the area known as discourse-pragmatic variation and change (see Pichler 2016b) occupies a natural position between linguistics and pragmatics and the interactional and structural aspects of language, making use of methods and concepts spanning several subfields of linguistics (see Östman, Foreword, this volume). Discourse-pragmatic features, by definition, are themselves multiplex, multifunctional, context-dependent parts of language. By *discourse-pragmatic features*, we refer to an unlimited but delineated set of features consisting of *discourse markers*, *pragmatic particles*, *discourse particles*, and so on but also other elements that fulfill pragmatic functions: epistemic parentheticals, quotatives, general extenders, consequence markers, politeness markers, intensifiers, and filled pauses – all of which are highlighted in the present volume. The volume offers a contemporary incarnation of a robust and thriving research area, showcasing the work of well-established experts along with a fresh slate of researchers, addressing perennial as well as newly encountered issues relating to discourse-pragmatic research.

In this introduction to the volume, we first contextualize the field of discourse-pragmatic variation and change and then move on to describe the format of the volume and some of its major contributions. We then offer a short overview of each of the volume's thirteen chapters. The introduction ends by presenting some of the major implications of the body of work in this volume, with comments about how work in the area can continue. In the Afterword to this volume, Heike Pichler examines in further detail how the field has expanded and continues to expand.

Background

The field of discourse-pragmatic variation and change picks up a thread of variation research that was lifted to scrutiny in relation to the groundbreaking work in variationist sociolinguistics in the 1960s and 1970s (notably, Labov 1963, 1966, 1972a, whose work is cited numerous times in this volume). As is now well established, variationist sociolinguistics tends to primarily be motivated by explorations of phonological and morphosyntactic variables. Many contributions of the late 1970s and early 1980s (e.g., Lavandera 1978; Dines 1980) were concerned with the inclusion of discourse-pragmatic features within the overall consensus of defining a sociolinguistic variable – which became established as "two or more ways of saying the same thing" (Weiner and Labov 1983: 30). Discourse-pragmatic features clearly do not fit neatly in this characterization because, among other issues, they are (arguably) optional elements – unlike, say, vowels or consonants.

As highlighted in Jan-Ola Östman's Foreword to this volume, the 1980s and 1990s witnessed a spate of research on discourse-pragmatic features from differing perspectives, different academic disciplines, and with even widely divergent basic definitions. For example, the 1980s and 1990s showed a wealth of contributions from researchers more oriented toward pragmatics and discourse (e.g., Östman 1981; Schourup 1983; Erman 1987; Schiffrin 1987; Fraser 1999), issuing important insights, for example, about the structural versus interactional functions of discourse-pragmatic features. At the same time, the field of conversation analysis made strides showing the interpersonal and turn-structuring aspects of discourse-pragmatic features (e.g., Sacks, Schegloff, and Jefferson 1974; Jefferson 1991; Sacks 1995; Schegloff 2007). During the same period, historical linguists traced how, for example, lexical items can grammaticalize into discourse-pragmatic features (e.g., Traugott 1982, 1995; Erman 1987; Tottie 1991; Brinton 1996; Aijmer 2002). Alongside all of these contributions were a small but steady band of variationist sociolinguists who continued to push the boundary of what was meant by "sociolinguistic variable," offering measured and convincing perspectives on various discourse-pragmatic features, including general extenders, quotatives, and intensifiers (among many other features; e.g., Cheshire 1981, 2007; Dubois 1992; Tagliamonte 2005; D'Arcy 2005; Buchstaller 2006).

Building on this wealth of perspectives and insights, Heike Pichler (see Afterword, this volume) founded the Discourse-Pragmatic Variation and Change (DiPVaC) research network in 2012 and hosted the first two conferences devoted to this research topic. Pichler's (2010, 2013, 2016a) research contributions – including advancing the cover term *discourse-pragmatic feature* – ushered in a holistic approach to how we approach and work with discourse-pragmatic variables, essentially bringing together the distinct strands that have contributed (and continue to contribute) to how we work with these aspects of language. Indeed, a strength of discourse-pragmatic research is its openness to methods, perspectives, and even the variables of focus. This volume demonstrates that researchers of discourse-pragmatic variation and change are able to operate in different modes but with complementary and equally valuable outcomes.

Introduction

Aims and Scope

This volume showcases contemporary research in the growing and thriving research area of discourse-pragmatic variation and change. A key aim of this volume is to demonstrate the multiple, integrative threads of research that contribute to the overall quality and robustness of the field. A look at the chapters reveals a number of perspectives, data sources, languages of analysis, areas of focus, and, importantly, breakthroughs and critiques with regard to method, analysis, and theoretical underpinnings. While the overall theme of the volume is rooted in discourse-pragmatic variation and change, scholars from a wide range of disciplines will find topics of interest in this book. These disciplines include, for example, sociolinguistics, pragmatics, conversation analysis, second language acquisition, corpus linguistics, and language contact.

In a departure from the bulk of the work done on discourse-pragmatic variation (see, e.g., Pichler 2016a), this volume offers a number of chapters making use of data from languages other than English – including Finnish, (several varieties of) Canadian French/French, German, Italian, Norwegian, Brazilian Portuguese, Polish, and Spanish – as well as language contact situations. While a few chapters focus on standardized, norm-providing varieties of English, several others use data from less mainstream varieties of English, including regional varieties of Canada, Ireland, Australia, and the UK.

The volume highlights a range of approaches to data, including corpora, conversations, elicitation tasks, and matched guise tests – and even diachronic perspectives. Chapter 11, for example, by Blondeau, Mougeon, and Tremblay, offers a forty-year overview on changes in the use of consequence markers in two different regions of francophone Canada. The collection of variable features explored in this volume is vast yet well-centered around the main theme, including now-classic features such as *you know* and quotatives, as well as advancing our understanding of elements such as *totally, is all, uh* vs. *um*, and *please* (the latter as an example of a borrowing into Norwegian and Finnish).

The methodological and theoretical concerns addressed in this volume cannot be understated. While Part I of the book is devoted specifically to innovations in theory and method, breakthroughs are not limited to the four chapters comprising this section. Subsequent chapters take on issues such as the Principle of Accountability (Labov 1972b; see also Gadanidis and Denis, Chapter 7; Diskin-Holdaway, Chapter 9; and Peterson, Hiltunen, and Vaattovaara, Chapter 13, this volume), the role of interactional turns in accounting for discourse-pragmatic variation (Eiswirth, Chapter 8), and the use of discourse-pragmatic features in a second language (Diskin-Holdaway, Chapter 9) and among bilingual speakers (Kern, Chapter 10).

Terminology

The title of this book, *Discourse-Pragmatic Variation and Change: Theory, Innovations, Contact* reflects that, importantly, the name used to describe this overall research effort is, in fact, discourse-pragmatic variation and change. We treat this as an umbrella term encompassing interrelated and complementary avenues of research (following Pichler 2016a, 2016b, and others). While the term *discourse-pragmatic feature* is considered an "alternative, conceptually more neutral label" (Pichler 2016b: 3) than previous more nuanced – and contested – terms, the editors of this volume did not instruct individual authors to adhere strictly to the use of the term *discourse-pragmatic feature* in their own writing (although some did). Authors were encouraged to utilize terms that best expressed the core meaning of their own focal point of investigation. Readers will notice a range of terms all falling under the general rubric of *discourse-pragmatic feature*, but in each instance the authors have defined and delineated their own perspective on the feature in question.

Organization and Overview

In many ways, this volume has the luxury of presenting key works in a field of research that is already flourishing; there was no need to lay out the basic principles, which have been treated in previous work (e.g., Pichler 2016a). The contributions to this volume have been selected around three main themes, to illustrate the growth of this thriving field. Part I of the book, titled "Innovations in Theory and Method," comprises four chapters that address, in turn, theoretical questions, methodological questions, and issues of reliability relating to claims about language change and cross-linguistic annotation schemes. In Chapter 1, Denis makes an example of epistemic parentheticals (e.g., *I think, I suppose*) to investigate claims about the constant rate hypothesis of language change. Chapter 2, by Schleef and Mackay, uses matched guise techniques as a perception test to investigate a relatively neutral feature, *you know*, enabling them to draw conclusions about its social versus pragmatic functions. In Chapter 3, Levey, Kastronic, Digesto, and Chiasson, in the only investigation of quotatives in this volume, explore data from three varieties of French in addition to Brazilian Portuguese and Italian, determining the supposed influence from English is not always confirmed – and thereby calling into question the role of intuition and assumptions made by researchers to explain change. Chapter 4, which rounds out this section, offers a perspective from Degand, Broisson, Crible, and Grzech, demonstrating a system for annotating and thereby comparing the functions and use of discourse markers in four different languages: French, Spanish, English, and Polish.

Part II of the book, "Innovative Variables in English," carries on the tradition of exploring discourse-pragmatic features in varieties of the English language but either focusing on those not often encountered in the literature or offering a new position on previously documented features. For example, the first chapter in this section, by Kolbe-Hanna and Brinton (Chapter 5), offers a corpus-based synchronic and diachronic overview of sentence-final *is all*, a feature chiefly noted in US English from the twentieth century onward. In Chapter 6, Aijmer offers the only study of intensifiers in this volume, focusing on the adoption of *totally* in UK English. Hers is largely a grammatical exploration, looking at the different contexts in which *totally* occurs. In Chapter 7, Gadanidis and Denis simultaneously offer an account of the distribution of *uh* and *um* in Canadian English, while using this description as a means of defending a normalization approach to counting discourse-pragmatic features. The final chapter of this section, by Eiswirth (Chapter 8), offers the most overt stance in the volume on the merits of employing interactional turns in conversation as units of analysis, including statistical analysis. In doing so, Eiswirth describes an underexplored feature: listener responses in interaction.

Finally, the Part III of the book offers insights into a research area not previously encountered in a dedicated fashion in the literature on discourse-pragmatic variation: "Language Contact." Here, the notion of language contact is broad enough in scope to account for at least four different phenomena: the (English) second language acquisition of immigrant communities, individual bilingual speakers of US Spanish and US English, long-standing community level contact between Canadian French and Canadian English, and, in the final two chapters of the volume, the remote language contact relationship of English with Norwegian and Finnish, respectively. In Chapter 9, Diskin-Holdaway looks at immigrant communities in two different English-speaking areas: Ireland and Australia. Her chapter is one of two in the volume that focuses on *you know*. Chapter 10, by Kern, offers an unusual perspective on so-called balanced bilinguals, meaning bilinguals who are equally proficient in two or more languages. He finds, much like Levey, Kastronic, Digesto, and Chiasson (Chapter 3), that influence from English is negligible in how general extenders are used in the Spanish discourse of the individuals he recorded. Chapter 11, by Blondeau, Mougeon, and Tremblay, is a rare study of the same communities – in this case French-speaking communities in Canada – over a span of forty years. Through their longitudinal study, the authors were able to confirm the hypothesis that synchronic variation from the 1970s offered insights into where the use of consequence markers was headed. In Chapter 12, Andersen offers the first corpus-based exploration of how English-sourced politeness markers are used in Norwegian. In the final chapter of the volume, Chapter 13, Peterson, Hiltunen and Vaattovaara demonstrate the limitations of using only one type of data for research on discourse-pragmatic features, especially an elicitation task. In their exploration of *pliis* "please" in Finnish, they underline the context-sensitivity of discourse-pragmatic features and the need for mixed methods.

In addition to thirteen chapters, the volume draws additional insights from the reflections of Östman (Foreword) and Pichler (Afterword). As a founding contributor to the literature on discourse-pragmatic features with his groundbreaking work on *you know*, Östman offers an informed perspective on the philosophies and intentions that led to the current state of the field. As a final note in the Foreword, Östman reminds us that discourse-pragmatic variation is imbued with speaker responsibility, which extends to us as researchers of these features. In the Afterword, Pichler identifies and elaborates on priorities for discourse-pragmatic variation and change research in the future, in addition to offering reflections and critiques of the chapters in this volume.

Descriptions of Chapters

While the previous section distilled some of the highlights of the different sections of the book, the following section offers a brief description of each of the volume's thirteen chapters. This was deemed a necessary tool for readers, given that the chapters comprise a relatively heterogeneous set of backgrounds and perspectives.

Part I: Innovations in Theory and Method

Chapter 1, by Denis, tackles the bold aim of investigating the observation that pragmatic markers primarily develop through the gradual grammaticalization of lexical items. Using data from Canadian English, Denis makes use mostly of epistemic parentheticals (e.g., *I think, I suppose, I guess*) to demonstrate that their grammaticalization process is not necessarily gradual but rather can be seen as a sequence of abrupt changes, mirroring the claims made by Kroch (1989, 1994) regarding morphosyntactic change in English. Based on these observations, Denis outlines a schematic conceptualization of systems of change that involve upward reanalysis (in line with Roberts and Roussou 2003). He proposes that the chief meaning of *I think*, from propositional to expressive, has been abrupt – not gradual. Denis tackles some evasive elements of what we know about variation and change, and he spins them in a new light, observing the measures of position, doxastic strength, grammatical subject, and time.

Chapter 2, by Schleef and Mackay, makes an important methodological contribution by demonstrating the use of an innovative audio matched guise experiment to investigate the perceptions of *you know* in the English spoken in the Manchester, UK, area. This chapter, one of two studies of *you know* in the volume, offers an additional methodological contribution in its aims to compare discourse without *you know* versus discourse with *you know*, thereby offering additional validity to previous claims about this particular discourse-pragmatic feature. The authors find that perceptions of *you know* are relatively weak, thereby making it an example of a pragmatic marker that does not elicit overtly negative biases. Likewise, *you know* is not associated with any particular social groups. Some findings from the study indicate that use of *you know* is associated with features such as lack of formality, untrustworthiness, and less precision, although the authors argue that interpretations of the social values of *you know* are best considered in its immediate discourse context. Because it does not vary socially, the authors pose that the chief task of *you know* is pragmatic.

The first of two corpus-based, cross-linguistic studies in the volume, Chapter 3, by Levey, Kastronic, Digesto, and Chiasson, focuses on three varieties of French, with additional insight gained from Brazilian Portuguese and Italian data. In light of the extensive amount of work on quotative systems, the authors address a pertinent and timely issue: the possibility that English is a source of cross-linguistic influence in the quotative systems of other languages. The authors conduct a comparison of the quotative systems of three varieties of French (Quebec, Acadian, and European) in addition to the two additional Romance languages. The results of the comparison essentially show that claims of widespread changes in quotative systems are overstated. The Quebec and Acadian French varieties show evidence of change that may be attributed to contact with English (namely, *être comme*), but the other languages and varieties investigated demonstrate a paucity of such evidence. Based on their evidence, the authors call into question the practice of linguistic researchers who rely on intuition to explain change rather than relying on empirical evidence.

Like Chapter 3, Chapter 4 is a cross-linguistic study, focusing on four different languages from three different language families. The authors, Degand, Broisson, Crible, and Grzech, take on the much-needed call to supply insights into reliable, cross-linguistically applicable discourse marker annotation schemes. They supply a validity test of a two-dimensional annotation scheme for the domains and functions of discourse markers across the four spoken languages (English, French, Polish, and Spanish). Their analysis shows that the model can be applied to all four languages in the sample and accurately depicts the polyfunctional behavior of discourse markers, allowing for fine-grained observations of polysemy (several functions) and polyfunctionality (several domains). The researchers found that all four languages made use of discourse markers to structure language, with differences in the frequency of discourse markers for interpersonal purposes. The main aim of the chapter is to offer insights and annotation schemes for other researchers to find the balance between methodological elegance and cognitive soundness. As they state in their introduction, "*how* we use DMs [discourse markers] is a crucial step in finding out *why* we use them."

Part II: Innovative Variables in English

Chapter 5, by Kolbe-Hanna and Brinton, offers an up-to-date analysis of the English discourse-pragmatic feature *is all*, a form that emerged in sentence-final position in early twentieth-century American English. Using corpus data, the authors demonstrate the main uses and meanings of this innovative form, showing that speakers seem to use *is all* to close a topic and to distance themselves from an unwanted interpretation of the preceding utterance, among other functions. In their historical overview of the form, the authors propose that sentence-final *is all* derives from processes of phonological reduction and deletion with subsequent reanalysis – not, as previous accounts have postulated, a shortening of a longer construction such as *that is all I say/ mean*.

In Chapter 6, Aijmer conducts a corpus analysis of the innovative emphasizer *totally* in UK English, with the hypothesis that its use has diversified in the past two decades. The purpose of this chapter is to establish a baseline of the syntactic, social, and pragmatic properties of a "new" *totally* in UK English in the 2010s, as demonstrated through the Spoken British National Corpus 2014 (BNC2014S) as compared to data from the original British National Corpus (BNC1994D). In addition to looking at structural properties, the chapter also reports on social factors such as age and gender, offering information on the social meanings of *totally*. Aijmer offers a comprehensive overview of *totally* across different grammatical settings, including as a modifier of adjectives, verbs, negatives, noun phrases, and prepositional phrases, and as a discourse marker. In fact, she finds that the most dramatic change taking place during the twenty-year period under investigation is the expansion of *totally* to the area of pragmatics and discourse.

In Chapter 7, Gadanidis and Denis investigate the use of *uh* and *um* as manifestations of filled pauses in Canadian English (the Farm Work and Farm Life Since 1890 oral history collection of the Earlier Ontario English Collection), using their investigation as a means of defending the use of normalization as an approach to gaining representativity in analyzing discourse-pragmatic features. Namely, like Eiswirth in Chapter 8, the authors propose that statistical methods including Poisson regression can disentangle social and linguistic constraints on variation. While the first stage of their analysis demonstrated a loss in proportional frequency of *um* compared to *uh*, a second stage of analysis, applying Poisson regression, enabled them to determine that *um* is weighted for utterance-initial use, while *uh* is used elsewhere.

Eiswirth's contributions in Chapter 8 provide a new perspective in applying conversation analysis insights to investigations of quantitative analysis of discourse-pragmatic features, in direct response to calls from, for example, Pichler (2013) to make use of conversation analysis principles. The features under investigation in this chapter are non-interrupting listener responses (*I see*, *mm*, etc.). Eiswirth's data set comes from recorded conversations of English-speaking participants in Edinburgh. She incorporated innovative aspects such as the number of words in a turn to establish that variation of listener responses in the conversations are more revealing as variables than the social parameters of the individuals involved. In her overview, Eiswirth returns to a well-known concern for variationists: the Principle of Accountability, showing that achieving this aim can be effectively rooted in the turn-by-turn unfolding of everyday interaction.

Part III: Language Contact

In Chapter 9, Diskin-Holdaway's study is the only in the volume that highlights the speech of second-language learners. Her analysis of the discourse marker *you know* looks at two native speaker varieties of English (Irish and Australian English) and two non-native varieties of English (Polish and Chinese migrants in Ireland). While she argues that the salience of *you know* contributes to the frequent use of this form in non-native varieties of English, especially among Polish migrants, Diskin-Holdaway uncovers important differences in the functions that *you know* fulfills across native and non-native varieties. The native Irish English speakers favored the use of *you know* for interpersonal reasons (i.e., "pragmatic" uses), whereas non-native speakers preferred to use *you know* for "coherence" (i.e., discourse/structuring functions).

Kern's study in Chapter 10 is unique in this volume in its expressed focus on simultaneous bilingual speakers. Kern analyzes the use of general extenders among Spanish–English bilingual friends from southern Arizona. It was expected that general extenders would be susceptible to borrowing in a language contact situation similar to other discourse-pragmatic features, but contact with English did not appear to influence the use of general extenders in Spanish in the speech of the same Spanish–English bilinguals. As the first study to analyze the use of general extenders in both languages spoken by the same bilinguals, these results underline the ability of bilinguals to both understand and reproduce the subtleties of the use of these features in the two languages they speak.

In Chapter 11, Blondeau, Mougeon, and Tremblay offer a rare investigation of speech communities spanning a longitudinal overview of forty years. In addition, their contribution makes a comparison of two different francophone populations in Canada. The focus of the authors' investigation is consequence markers, which they explore in two communities over two time periods: the French majority community of Montreal and the French minority community of Welland, using corpora from the 1970s and the 2010s. Their multivariate analysis permits them to assess the degree of convergence and divergence in the use of consequence markers between communities over a forty-year period. The majority and minority francophone communities were already diverging in the use of consequence markers in the 1970s, especially in the use of the English borrowing *so* in Welland, and this divergence further intensified in the 2010s. The authors conclude that the linguistic vitality of French plays an important role in the use of consequence markers in each of these communities.

The volume finishes with two chapters on remote language contact. In Chapter 12, Andersen assesses the use of domestic and borrowed discourse-pragmatic features to make requests and to apologize in Norwegian. His analysis demonstrates that domestic and borrowed forms are primarily used interchangeably (with the exception of *vær så snill* 'please') to show, among other functions, exasperation. Domestic and borrowed forms were used with both strong and weak commitment to the speech act they perform, although the illocutionary force of *please* in requests was stronger than that of similar forms in Norwegian, while the illocutionary force of *sorry* to apologize was weaker than that of its domestic counterparts.

Finally, in Chapter 13, Peterson, Hiltunen and Vaattovaara investigate the lexical politeness marker *pliis* 'please' as an example of a pragmatic borrowing in Finnish. As such, this is the only chapter in the volume to use data from a non-Indo-European language. Like Chapter 12, Chapter 13 is an investigation of remote language contact with English as a source language, considering the borrowed form *pliis* to be a variant of the heritage form *kiitos*. This chapter makes use of various data sources, including a so-called opportunistic corpus, in an attempt to offer a grounded and accountable picture of how the borrowed politeness marker, a relatively syntactically free element, is situated grammatically in Finnish, a typologically unrelated language.

Implications

Many insights are gained from the contributions to this volume, in terms of both application for future research in the area of discourse-pragmatic variation and change and our general understanding about how these features function in language and interaction. The work in this volume carries on established traditions, as well as introducing new topics for consideration.

There are several examples in this volume of following through on ongoing concerns in this field and related disciplines. One example treated in several chapters is the Principle of Accountability (Labov 1972b), which implies that the envelope of variation can be established only if researchers consider where a variable could potentially occur but does not. For decades, this notion has presented a dilemma for researchers working on discourse-pragmatic features. This volume, like the work preceding it, continues to not only address this concern but demonstrate how our work accommodates this concept. A second example treated in this volume is the multifunctionality of discourse-pragmatic features: their division of labor in simultaneously discourse structuring, cognitive processing, and interpersonal relations. A third exemplary notion is the validation of synchronic variation and perceived avenues of change through a long-term perspective.

Emergent concerns, too, have been addressed in this volume. Several chapters have emphasized the necessity of triangulation in methods and data, for example through turning to computer-mediated data as a potential source and the use of perception tests. Other chapters have explored the promising yet relatively under-investigated relationship between clausal position, pragmatic meaning, and variation (work on periphery notwithstanding; e.g., Traugott 2012). This volume has emphasized the key importance of conversation and conversational context in interpreting and identifying the functions of discourse-pragmatic features. Chapters have also demonstrated that using statistical methods to investigate conversational interaction offers novel insights. Finally, a major contribution of this volume is its emphasis on a spectrum of languages and of nonstandardized varieties in particular. Future work will benefit greatly from investigations in different kinds of multilingual settings and from lesser-investigated languages, varieties, and speakers.

A most important observation gained from this volume is the extent to which an interdisciplinary perspective contributes to the overall quality of our work. With its convergence of several subdisciplines, the research on discourse-pragmatic variation and change has succeeded in implementing best practices and applications from a number of different scientific traditions. These possibilities for breakthrough will only strengthen as the field of research continues to grow.

Part I

Innovations in Theory and Method

1 Reflexes of Abruptness in the Development of Pragmatic Markers

Derek Denis

1.1 Introduction

In this chapter, I describe how pragmatic markers can develop abruptly. I identify reflexes of this abruptness in subsequent patterns of variation and change. My argument is based on data from the reorganization of the epistemic parentheticals (EPs) system of Southern Ontario English through the twentieth century. The results are interpreted with respect to Kroch's (1989) Constant Rate Effect (CRE) and Roberts and Roussou's (2003) conceptualization of grammaticalization as abrupt reanalysis. Although many researchers argue for the gradual development of pragmatic markers and I argue that my results represent reflexes of abruptness, my broader conclusion is that researchers who approach pragmatic markers from different theoretical perspectives are essentially on the same page about the process. In particular, I draw a parallel between the present generative approach and Kaltenböck et al.'s (2011) theory of cooptation.

I begin with a discussion of gradualness in the grammaticalization literature and offer a generative theoretical framework for understanding the development of pragmatic markers. I then flesh out the details of the EP system in the Earlier Ontario English Collection and the Toronto English Archive (Tagliamonte 2006a; Denis 2017). I suggest that, over the course of more than 100 years of apparent time, this data shows evidence of Kroch's (1989, 1994) predicted outcomes of competing grammars: obsolescence and specialization. Finally, I conjecture that, while abrupt, lexical material does not develop a new pragmatic role out of the blue. Rather, lexical material that already triggers particular implicatures in particular syntactic positions is reanalyzed by speakers as belonging to a higher syntactic category and the implicatures that they trigger become conventionalized (cf. Brinton 1996; Waltereit 2002, 2006). Though the specifics differ, the development of pragmatic markers is just as Traugott (1995: 15) suggests: "syntax via pragmatic strengthening in discourse > syntax with a different function."

1.2 Theoretical Background

1.2.1 Gradualness and Grammaticalization

Grammaticalization is described as a diachronic process, summarized as a change from lexical to grammatical to more grammatical. Grammaticalization has also been argued to provide an explanatory account of how pragmatic markers develop (Thompson and Mulac 1991; Traugott 1995; Brinton 1996, 2008). Simply put, if we extend what is meant by "more grammatical" to include the expansion of pragmatic function, then if a form expands from having a strictly propositional meaning to expressing a textual or expressive meaning, it can be said to be grammaticalizing (e.g., Traugott 1982: 256; Brinton 2008: 52).

Grammaticalization is typically argued to be gradual (see Heine et al. 1991; Bybee et al. 1994). Brinton and Traugott's (2005: 99) definition of grammaticalization elucidates this. Grammaticalization is:

> the change whereby in certain linguistic contexts speakers use parts of a construction with a grammatical function. Over time the resulting grammatical item may become more grammatical by acquiring more grammatical functions and expanding its host-classes. (Brinton and Traugott 2005: 99)

In the development of pragmatic markers, lexical material gains textual or expressive functions.

As described, gradualness predicts that the acquisition of new functions happens sequentially rather than wholesale. As Traugott and Trousdale (2010: 23) put it, "gradualness refers to the fact that most change involves (a series of) micro-changes." This is similar to Bailey's (1973) wave model of change: as a new linguistic rule (or form) replaces an older one, it does so by gradually expanding its operation to more and more environments (or contexts). Bailey (1973: 82) assumes that the frequency of an innovation and the rate of change (from one rule or form to another) in different contexts correlate with the relative time that the rule (or form) began to apply in that context.

Following Kroch (1989), who provides counterevidence to Bailey's claim, I test the gradualness of the development of pragmatic markers.

1.2.2 Gradualness, Discreteness, and the Constant Rate Effect

In Kroch's (1989) model of change, the *process of transition* is gradual but the transition phase should not be confused with *grammatical change* proper, a situation in which a community of speakers have acquired a grammatical system that is different from the previous generation's. Through the regular process of intergenerational language transmission, a child's grammar ends up different than their parent's grammar (Roberts and Roussou 2003: 11). Thus, a change from one grammar to another is "necessarily instantaneous" (Kroch 1989: 201) because the grammar of one generation is either the same as or different from the previous one. Once a child acquires something new, a discrete change has occurred. Such a change is typically thought to be the result of REANALYSIS as triggered by some ambiguous context(s) (Roberts and Roussou 2003). Abstractly, the process of change in Kroch's (1989) model involves three discrete language states and two changes: state 1 with grammar A, state 2 with competing grammars A and B, and state 3 with only grammar B. Grammatical change is not gradual but involves two discrete changes: the addition of grammar B (i.e., state 1 to state 2) and the loss of grammar A (i.e., state 2 to state 3).

While the transition phase from state 1 to state 3 can occur over several centuries (as options exist in sociolinguistic variation), the two substantive grammatical changes occur abruptly. What changes gradually is the frequency ratio of the two options. Adger's (2007) schematic of a system that separates grammar and usage in (1) directly addresses the presence of variability within a generative framework.

(1) a. $G \rightarrow \{v_1, \ldots v_i, \ldots v_n\}$ (=PoV)
     b. $U(PoV, C) = v_i \in PoV$

In this schematic, grammar (G) is "a device that generates all of the grammatical sentences of a language and none of the ungrammatical ones" (Chomsky 1957: 13). However, Adger's (2007) system explicitly recognizes that the grammar of a language has ways of producing multiple options of saying the same thing. The set of these minimally different options is the pool of variants (PoV). This is the extent of the grammatical system proper. Variation arises in usage (U), a choice function that takes the PoV produced by the grammar and given the (sociolinguistic and linguistic) context (C) chooses a variant (v).

In contemporary generative approaches, competing grammars can be relativized to competition between minimally different functional heads (see Roberts and Roussou 2003; Biberauer et al. 2010). The generative approach holds that (1) the input to syntactic structure is lexical items, including functional heads, located in the lexicon; (2) lexical items are composed of a set of features; (3) features provide instructions to the syntactic derivation; and (4) syntactic operations are invariant, given the lexical items (i.e., their features and instructions). Cross-linguistic variation is a matter of differing properties of functional heads that reside in the lexicon (Biberauer et al. 2010). If the variation that accompanies linguistic change is a result of competition between two grammars within a single speaker, this requires multiple options within the lexicon of a single speaker: multiple functional heads, with minimally different properties. For example, a "T" functional head that triggers verb raising, like in French, and a "T" head that does not trigger verb raising, like in English, results in word order differences between these two languages.

Adger's schematic is essentially the same system as Kroch (1989): Adger's (2007) grammar (G) that produces multiple variants ($v_1 \ldots v_n$) can be thought of as Kroch's (1989: 202) "repertoire of grammatical knowledge" that contains a set of competing grammatical options. Both these systems place the probabilistic selection of variants/competing grammars in the usage component of language. The modularity of grammar and usage means that grammatical change is abrupt (additions or subtractions of options), while its consequences (the competition between multiple options in usage) proceed gradually.

The evidence for this modularity comes from the study of usage data and the CRE. A variant might be highly favored in some particular context or situation but much less favored in some other context. However, if the magnitude of these contextual factors is constant as one variant becomes more frequent than the other, we can assume that some single underlying change is responsible. Because any case of grammar competition is the result of a single underlying change (i.e., the addition of a new functional head that is minimally different from some older functional head in the language), the rate of replacement during the transition phase will be constant, regardless of widely varying probabilistic factors of context and situation. As Kroch (1989: 199) puts it, "[c]ontexts change together because they are merely surface manifestations of a single underlying change in grammar."

Evidence of the CRE, then, suggests a single abrupt change. The rate of change in different contexts is expected to be the same when the underlying change is abrupt, since the choice between two competing grammatical options is what is changing over time and the contextual effects (i.e., favoring/disfavoring environments) are external to such competition. Conversely, certain mechanisms of grammaticalization, particularly semantic-pragmatic expansion, are diagnosable by evidence of different rates of change across contexts as each "micro-change" occurs sequentially and independently.

1.2.3 *Pragmatic Markers and the Constant Rate Effect*

The CRE is a prediction about competing grammars (i.e., competing functional heads). While for many years pragmatic markers hovered along "the edge of grammar" (Massam et al. 2006: 191), receiving only minimal attention from generativists, a recent surge in interest has resulted in a growing understanding that pragmatic markers are syntactic objects proper (e.g., Massam et al. 2006; Bayer and Obenauer 2011; Wiltschko and Heim 2006). In traditional generative models, the highest layer of sentential structure, and the one that relates to the semantics of the whole proposition, is the complementizer phrase (CP). Since pragmatic markers tend to operate with scope over whole propositions, generative analyses consider pragmatic markers as functional heads (or in dependencies with functional heads) above CP.

Therefore, in the case of pragmatic markers, and in particular those that are undergoing increases in usage frequency relative to other competing forms, if the slope of the rise in frequency of innovative pragmatic markers is found to occur at different rates in different contexts, this can be taken as evidence for the gradualness of their grammaticalization. On the other hand, even in the face of differential frequencies/probabilities of innovating pragmatic markers in different contexts, if change is found to be happening at a constant rate in each context, this can be taken as evidence for a single abrupt change.

In Section 1.3, I discuss a case study that tests the gradualness hypothesis by examining changes to EPs in Ontario English and the rate of change context by context.

1.3 Epistemic Parentheticals in Ontario English

I treat the set of epistemic/doxastic,[1] complement taking, main verbs that co-occur with first-person pronominal subjects as a variable set of pragmatic markers that express a degree of speaker commitment to a proposition.[2] As exhibited in (2), EPs can occur in clause-initial position (2a, 2b), clause-final position (2c) or clause-medial position (2d).

(2)   a.   *I think* that they used to go in the winter as well. (BLV/F/1897)[3]
         b.   *I suppose* ∅ I hoed likely from the time I was big enough to hoe the hoe. (NIA/M/1898)
         c.   I can recall staying overnight one time too in an hotel *I think*. (EON/F/1914)
         d.   I done all those kind of things whichever a young person done *I guess* on the farm. (EON/M/1912)

Thompson and Mulac's (1991) analysis lays the foundation for subsequent analyses by setting out multiple, testable hypotheses about the development of EPs. Beginning with the argument that the (apparent) alternation between overt and null complementizers in English is "better understood as an alternation

---

[1] The literature refers to EPs as relating to epistemic modality ("what is known"). However, these features relate less to speakers' knowledge and more to their beliefs (i.e., doxastic modality).
[2] I exclude (semi-)factive verbs such as *know* and *realize*, which presuppose that their complement propositions are true, in order to focus on verbs that, themselves, may vary with respect to speaker commitment.
[3] Metadata is included after examples. NIA=Niagara Region, EON=Eastern Ontario, BLV=Belleville, TOR=Toronto; gender and year of birth of the speaker is also included.

between constructions like [(2a)], in which *I* and *think* are main clause subject and verb, with *that* introducing a complement clause, and constructions like [(2b), (2c), and (2d)] in which [the EP] is an epistemic phrase, [...] functioning roughly as an epistemic adverb such as *maybe* with respect to the clause it is associated with," Thompson and Mulac (1991: 313) propose that EPs have undergone a process of grammaticalization. Their strong hypothesis is that tokens such as (2b) are grammaticalized forms of tokens such as (2a), having grammaticalized from main clauses introducing complement clauses to epistemic adverbial phrases (Thompson and Mulac 1991: 317–318).

Their evidence is twofold: first, the subject and verb combinations that most frequently appear without *that* in contexts like (2b) are those subject and verb combinations that also most frequently appear in a position other than before the complement clause as in (2c); and second, the verbs that appear without *that* are epistemic. Thus, the cline of grammaticalization of EPs according to Thompson and Mulac (1991) is as in (3) (where P is a proposition).[4]

(3)   Stage i: [$_{CP}$ I think [$_{CP}$ that P]]
       Stage ii: [$_{CP}$ [$_{AdvP}$ I think] P]
       Stage iii: [$_{CP}$ P [$_{AdvP}$ I think]]

Thompson and Mulac (1991) propose that the grammaticalization of EPs is due to reanalysis. However, if such a change is reducible to some other well-established method of linguistic change, there is no need to appeal to grammaticalization (see e.g., Joseph 2001). Indeed, reanalysis is an abrupt linguistic change.

1.3.1   Methodology

1.3.1.1   Data   To investigate the gradual development of EPs, I use data from the Earlier Ontario English Collection (EOE) (Denis 2016, 2017) along with the Toronto English Archive (Tagliamonte 2006a). The EOE is comprised of two sets of oral histories. The first set is the Farm Work and Farm Life Since 1890 Oral History Project, a collection of oral histories housed at the Archive of Ontario in Toronto, Canada. Interviews were recorded in the mid-1980s with elderly farmers who grew up in five regions of the province of Ontario in Canada at the beginning of the twentieth century (Denis 2016). Two regions, Eastern Ontario and Niagara, are part of the EOE. The second set of oral histories is the Belleville 1975 Oral History collection, housed by the University of Toronto Language Variation and Change Lab under agreement

---

[4] Brinton (1996: 241) suggests an alternative diachronic development of EPs from a Middle English relative clause structure which itself developed from "syntactically complete clauses with an anaphoric demonstrative referring back to the preceding clause."

Table 1.1 *Distribution of Earlier Ontario English speakers*

Region	Men	Women	Range of Birth Years
Belleville (BLV)	7	6	1879–1914
Eastern Ontario (EON)	8	6	1891–1919
Niagara (NIA)	8	8	1895–1917
Total	23	20	1879–1919

with the Hastings County Historical Society (Tagliamonte 2007–2010). Interviews were collected in 1975 in an effort to capture narratives about the history of the city of Belleville and the surrounding areas. The first European settlers to all three regions in the EOE were United Empire Loyalists. The Loyalists were refugees of the American Revolution, born in the United States but who fled to British Canada (or in many cases were drawn there with promises of inexpensive land and opportunities). Linguists and dialectologists point to the English spoken by the Loyalists as the founding variety of Canadian English (Chambers 2006). Speakers in the EOE were born between 1879 and 1919. Thus, the data represents a vestigial Canadian English that can be traced backward through a line of language transmission to Loyalist English. Table 1.1 shows the distribution of speakers in the EOE by region, gender, and range of birth years. Interviews range in length from half an hour to more than two hours. Only the first hour of longer interviewers was transcribed and analyzed. The EOE contains more than 200,000 words.

The EOE data is compared with a contemporary dataset, the Toronto English Archive (TEA), which contains more than 200 sociolinguistic interviews and more than 2 million words (Tagliamonte 2006a). Interviews were conducted between 2003 and 2005 with speakers born between 1916 and 1992. Thus, together, the data considered in this chapter spans more than a century of apparent time. For the purposes of this chapter, the data will be collated together, meshing real- and apparent-time perspectives through the "longue durée" (D'Arcy 2012). This approach allows us to document change over time by taking year of birth, even across data collected at different periods, as a proxy for time.

1.3.1.2 Variable Context I treat the set of EPs as a sociolinguistic variable. I circumscribe the variable context in terms of an amalgam of structural and functional properties (Pichler 2010; Tagliamonte and Denis 2010). Functionally, EPs are pragmatic markers that express a degree of speaker commitment to a proposition. Following a strict functional definition, the variable context should include modal adverbials such as *maybe* and *possibly*.

However, these adverbials fall outside of the proposed structural definition of EPs. This structural schema used to delimit EPs is presented in (4).

All EPs consist, minimally, of a first-person, singular pronoun and a non-factive, epistemic/doxastic verb. EPs can optionally occur with a modal between the subject and the main verb except those with *say*, which require a modal, and *(as I) recall*, which disallow modals. EPs that contain either bare present tense verbs or modal auxiliaries are both included in the variable context. All main verbs of EPs can also be negated (with the exception of *as I recall*). Although some dialects allow *guess* EPs to be negated, there are no tokens of *I don't guess* in this data. I also include *it seems to me* in the dataset.

(4)

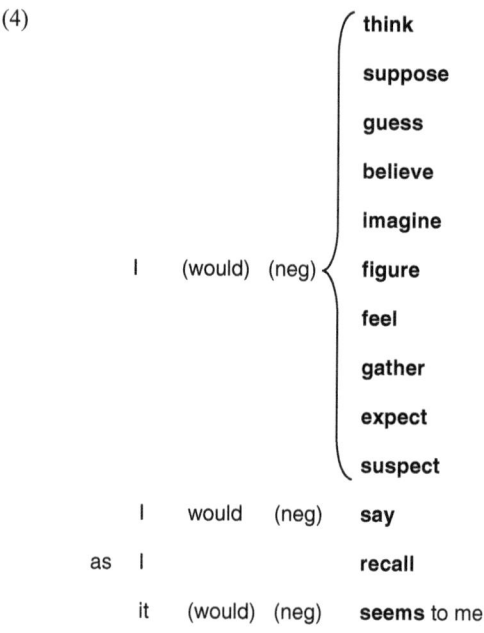

I now turn to a quantitative analysis of the development of EPs, concentrating on two factors that have been implicated in the grammaticalization of these pragmatic markers. I examine the distribution of variants across these factors and then assess the significance of patterns using mixed-effects logistic regression modeling.

1.3.2 Overall Distribution across Time

Figure 1.1 plots the overall distribution of the main variants *I think*, *I guess*, *I suppose*, and all other EPs across the longue durée. Speakers are grouped into

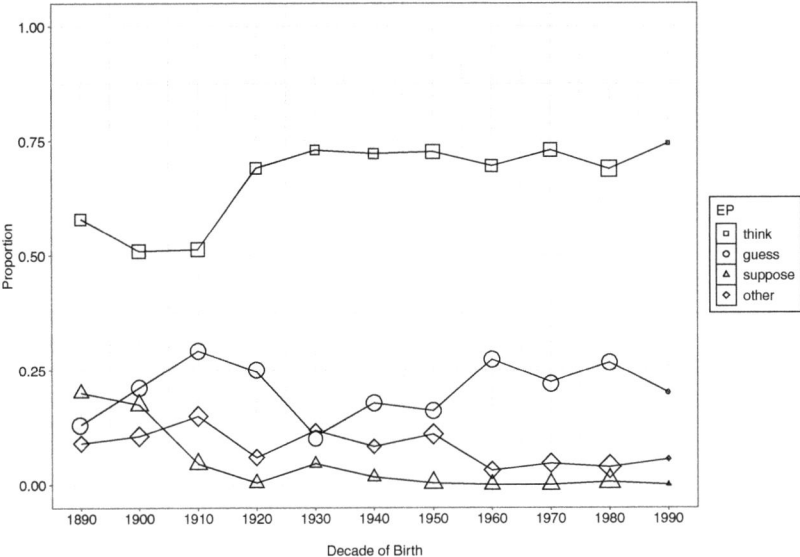

Figure 1.1 Distribution of EP variants in EOE in apparent time
Note. Size of data point represents *N*s in that decade. Think *N*=2,835; guess *N*=977; suppose *N*=470; other *N*=335. Total *N*=4,323.

the decade of their birth, except for those born before 1890, who are grouped with those born in the 1890s due to small *N*s.

I think has risen in frequency across the twentieth century, though after the 1930s stabilizes around 75 percent. In the same period, *I suppose* obsolesces from a maximum of 20 percent (and the second most frequent form) for those born in the nineteenth century to zero occurrences for speakers born after 1990. Although the initial obsolescence of *I suppose* seems to be at the expense of an increase of *I guess* rather than *I think*, once *I think* increases in earnest, *I guess* briefly recedes. After 1930, once *I think* stabilizes and while *I suppose* and the other variants decrease, *I guess* rises once again. For speakers born in and after 1960, the use of EPs is essentially a dichotomous variable.

To examine the gradualness of grammaticalization in the development of EPs, we must operationalize factors that have been implicated in their development as a series of linguistic constraints (Poplack and Tagliamonte 2001: 225). I consider two such constraints: syntactic position and doxastic strength.[5]

---

[5] Intervening material, which was examined by Rodríguez Louro and Harris (2013), was also considered but tokens with intervening adverbials (e.g., *I just think*) or modals (e.g., *I would guess*) occur only thirty-nine times (<0.1%).

1.3.3 Syntactic Position

The syntactic position of EPs has been used as a diagnostic of grammaticalization by several researchers (Thompson and Mulac 1991; Aijmer 1997; Kaltenböck 2013; Rodríguez Louro and Harris 2013). As Rodríguez Louro and Harris (2013: 424) put it, "[t]he looser the syntactic behaviour of [EPs], the more grammaticalized they are"; the more frequently an EP is used in non-clause-initial position, the farther along the cline of grammaticalization the EP is. Taking this hypothesis as a starting point, I test whether the variant that has been increasing over the twentieth century (*I think*) is becoming gradually "looser." Specifically, I operationalize the rate of change in two contexts – initial and non-initial – as a means of distinguishing abrupt change from gradual change. A statistically different rate of change across the two contexts would be indicative of gradual context expansion, while similar rates suggest an underlying abrupt change.

Following Rodríguez Louro and Harris (2013: 424), I coded every EP token for its syntactic position: clause-initial, clause-medial, or clause-finally. Many tokens were coded as being in clause-initial position, despite the EP not being the first element of the sentence. Several elements can occur in a syntactically higher position than a clause-initial EP including discourse-pragmatic markers (*so*, *well*), hesitation markers (*uh*/*um*), conjunctions (*and*, *or*), adverbials (*then*, *actually*), and attention/acknowledgment markers (*hey*, *oh*, *yes*) (Tagliamonte 2014). Extraposed topics can also occur to the left of an EP. The presence of a resumptive pronoun in subject position was the main diagnostic of whether or not an EP was in initial position but occurred after an extraposed topic or if the EP was in medial position. In practice, if an EP could be interpreted as functioning as a main clause, it was coded as being in clause-initial position. This was determined by whether or not a *that* complementizer could occur after the EP or not. So for example, a hypothetical token that includes an extraposed topic ("the corgi") with a resumptive pronoun ("he") as well as the discourse-pragmatic marker "well" as in (5a) would be coded as clause-initial but the example in (5b) would be coded as clause-medial.

(5)   a.   Well, the corgi$_i$, *I think* (that) he$_i$ wants a walk!
        b.   The yellow lab *I think* (*that) wants a nap.

Tokens with an overt *that* complementizer were coded separately and excluded from the analysis, on the assumption that they are grammatically functioning as main clauses and are not pragmatic markers (at least not parentheticals). Lastly, several EPs occur as independent or semi-independent clauses with a following *so* but these have been excluded from further analysis (N=202). Lastly, any tokens that were surrounded by incomprehensible speech, were part of a false start or were unclear for any other reason were also excluded from the analysis (N=99).

Abruptness in the Development of Pragmatic Markers

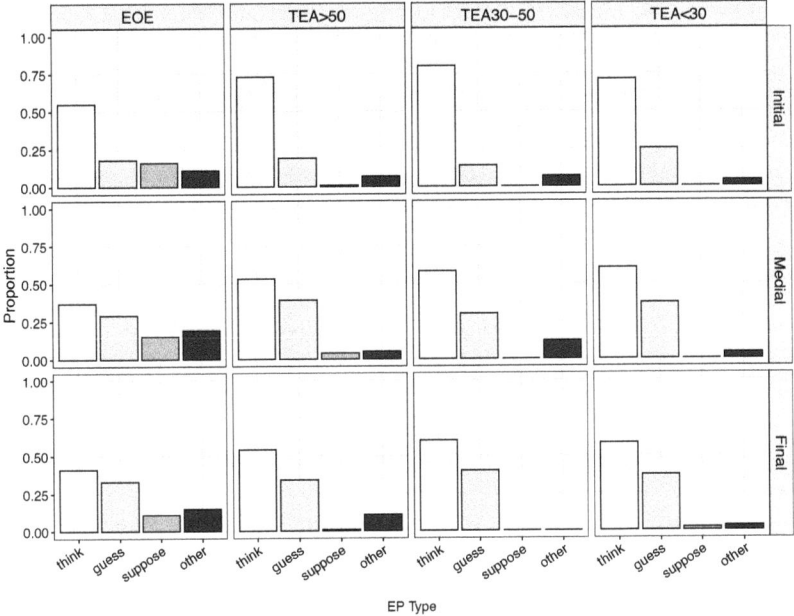

Figure 1.2 Distribution of EP variants by syntactic position in four age groups
Note. Cell Ns: EOE, Initial=723, Medial=105, Final=138; TOR>50, Initial=716, Medial=135, Final=102; TOR30–50, Initial=447, Medial=76, Final=40; TOR<30, Initial=1145, Medial=136, Final=135.

Figure 1.2 presents the distribution of *I think*, *I guess*, *I suppose*, and all other EP variants by the three main syntactic positions in EOE, collapsed across community and TEA, separated into three broad age groups.

Given that *I think* makes up the great majority of tokens, it is not surprising that this variant is the most frequent in all positions and age groups. However, the distribution of variants changes across contexts. In line with Figure 1.1, the frequency of *I think* increases in each subsequent age group and this is consistent across each position, with the exception of the youngest speakers, where *I think* is slightly less frequent in clause-initial and clause-final position than the middle-aged speakers in Toronto. Again, in line with Figure 1.1, *I guess* oscillates across age groups but, in all positions, is consistently more frequent with the youngest speakers in Toronto than with the speakers in EOE. The decline of *I suppose* is also apparent across positions. Comparing the distribution of different forms across positions, consistency across age groups is the norm.

Thompson and Mulac (1991) and Rodríguez Louro and Harris (2013) predict that more grammaticalized EPs will appear in non-clause-initial positions. From a diachronic perspective, ongoing grammaticalization should be evident as the gradual increase of syntactic mobility of grammaticalizing forms. EPs that are undergoing grammaticalization should exhibit an increased frequency in non-clause-initial positions and a decrease (or at least slower increase) in clause-initial position.

This hypothesis can be tested statistically. If the model suggests strong evidence for an interaction between syntactic position and time on the realization of an EP, we can interpret this as an indication that that EP has undergone gradual grammaticalization, having expanded contexts at some point and independently developing in that context. We might expect that the rise in frequency of *I think* evident in Figure 1.1 is the result of such context expansion. If there is no evidence for interaction, this indicates that *I think* is changing in both contexts at the same rate. Following Kroch, I interpret this as evidence of a single abrupt change.

Table 1.2 presents the results of a mixed-effects logistic regression that tests the effects of syntactic position over time on the realization of EPs as *I think*. Given that the distributions of EPs in clause-medial and clause-final positions in Figure 1.2 are roughly identical and there is no a priori reason to assume that either clause-medial or clause-final position is more (or less) grammaticalized, this model treats syntactic position as binary: initial vs. non-initial position.[6]

The model in Table 1.2 includes a main effect of YEAR OF BIRTH with a low *p*-value, suggesting the increase of *I think* across time in the data. The main effect of POSITION also has a low *p*-value: *I think* is disfavored in non-initial position as indicated by the negative coefficient. The coefficient for the interaction of these two main effects is very small and its *p*-value is very high suggesting no evidence for an interaction. The model is visualized in Figure 1.3, which plots the fitted values from the model and binomial regression curves for each level of the POSITION factor.

Although *I think* is shown to favor initial position over non-initial position, the probability of *I think* increases at a constant rate in both contexts. Thus, despite changes in the frequency of *I think*, there is no evidence of gradual grammaticalization (as context expansion) as diagnosed by syntactic position.

1.3.4 Doxastic Strength

Several researchers (e.g., Givón 1989; Thompson and Mulac 1991; Aijmer 1997) have noted that different EPs express different degrees of commitment to belief about the truth of the modified proposition – their doxastic strength.

---

[6] This model excludes all independent EPs and all EPs with intervening material.

Table 1.2 *Mixed-effects logistic regression testing the fixed effects of* YEAR OF BIRTH *(centered, continuous),* POSITION, *and their interaction and a random intercept for* SPEAKER *on the realization of EPs as* I think. *Treatment contrast coding. Coefficients reported in log-odds. Correlations of fixed effects, r<|0.25|*

Observations: 3,354. Overall frequency *I think:* 65.2%. AIC: 3,930					
Fixed effects	coefficient	*p*-value[a]	SE	N	% *I think*
YEAR OF BIRTH (centered)[b]	0.013	0.000	0.003	—	—
POSITION (vs. *initial*)				2,564	68.7
non-initial	−0.698	0.000	0.093	790	52.7
YOB:POSITION (vs. *initial*)				—	—
non-initial	−0.002	0.425	0.003	—	—
Intercept	0.991	0.000	0.104	—	—
Random effects	Variance			Group N	
SPEAKER[c] (intercept)	2.21			127	

Note. [a] I round *p*-values to three digits. 0.000 does not represent true 0 but an extremely small value; [b] Year of Birth *mean*=1950, *SD*=31; [c] mean frequency of *I think* by speaker: 65.1%.

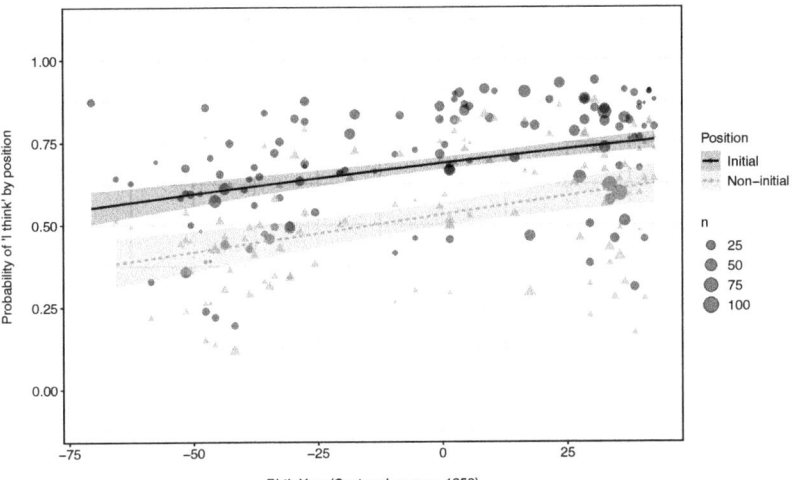

Figure 1.3 Probability of *I think* (vs. all other EPs) by syntactic position over apparent time
Note. Fitted values from the model in Table 1.2. Dot size represents the number of tokens at those coordinates.

These differences have been attributed to the persistence of the lexical meaning of the verbs. Thompson and Mulac (1991: 325) observe that:

I think is a stronger assertion of belief than *I guess*. This is traceable to the difference between *think* and *guess* as verbs: *guess* implies an assertion based on little or no evidence, and hence less commitment to a proposition than *think* does.

Thompson and Mulac (1991: 325) implicate the doxastic strength of EPs as a diagnostic of grammaticalization, arguing that Hopper's (1991: 22) principle of PERSISTENCE predicts that, as EPs grammaticalize, *I think* will remain doxastically stronger than *I guess* and *I suppose* due to the meanings of their lexical verbs.

As far as I am aware, this hypothesis has not been quantitatively tested. The problem is that there is no objective way to directly code a speaker's degree of strength of commitment. In some cases, the analyst might have an intuition but this is bound to be subjective and different analysts might have different interpretations for any given token. As a first attempt at an objective proxy of doxastic strength, I operationalize the grammatical person of the subject of the complement clause of the EP (i.e., the subject of the proposition modified by the EP). My linking hypothesis is that speakers are more likely to express a stronger commitment to propositions about themselves than about others; on average, complement clauses with first-person subjects should co-occur with stronger EPs (*I think* or *I believe* according to Thompson and Mulac 1991), while complement clauses with non-first-person subjects should co-occur with weaker EPs (*I guess* or *I suppose*).

A further distinction can be made between complement clauses with third-person subjects and second-person subjects. Since speakers risk losing face by committing too strongly to a proposition about their interlocutor who is immediately available to deny the truth of that proposition, they may be more likely to use an EP that expresses the weakest commitment to the proposition. Speakers might make stronger commitments to propositions about other people or other things. This theorized cline of commitment is shown in (6).

(6)   First-person subjects > third-person subjects > second-person subjects

The specific hypothesis is that *I think* with its strong commitment will be favored with complement clauses with first-person subjects, as in (7a) while *I guess* and *I suppose* will be favored with complement clauses with third- and second-person subjects, as in (7b) and (7c). Thus, to test the effect of doxastic strength on the realization of EPs, I coded each token for the grammatical person of the subject of the complement clause: first person, second person, and third person.[7]

---

[7] EPs that occurred in sentence fragments were excluded from the analysis, along with any tokens in which the subject was unclear.

(7) a. *I think* I put in a good eight or ten hour day then. (NIA/M/1906)
   b. I never was around and *I guess* HE was glad that I wasn't. (NIA/M/1907)
   c. Well *I suppose* YOU've seen cheese ... maybe you haven't. (EON/M/1904)

Figure 1.4 presents the distribution of the top three EP variants (and all others) by the grammatical person of the subject of the complement clause.

Regardless of the grammatical person of the subject, *I think* is the majority variant across time. The one exception is in EOE where both *I suppose* and *I guess* are more frequently used with second-person subjects. This is in line with the present hypothesis: *I guess* and *I suppose* are weaker EPs and they are more frequent in contexts where speakers risk losing the most face – when they are speaking about their interlocutor. In fact, before *I suppose*'s obsolescence, it seems to have been specialized for second-person complement clause subjects: among tokens with second-person subjects in the EOE, the most frequent EP is *I suppose*.

In TEA, although *I think* increases in frequency, regardless of the grammatical person of the complement clause subject, it is consistently the most frequent with third-person subjects, then first-person subjects, and least frequent with second-person subjects. There is a spike in the frequency of second-person subjects with *I think* for the oldest age group in TEA but the frequency lowers by the next age group. *I guess* is stable for first and third persons. However, while the variant is more frequent with both first- and second-person subjects than with third-person subjects in the older two age groups, it rises in frequency with second-person subjects in the youngest two generations.

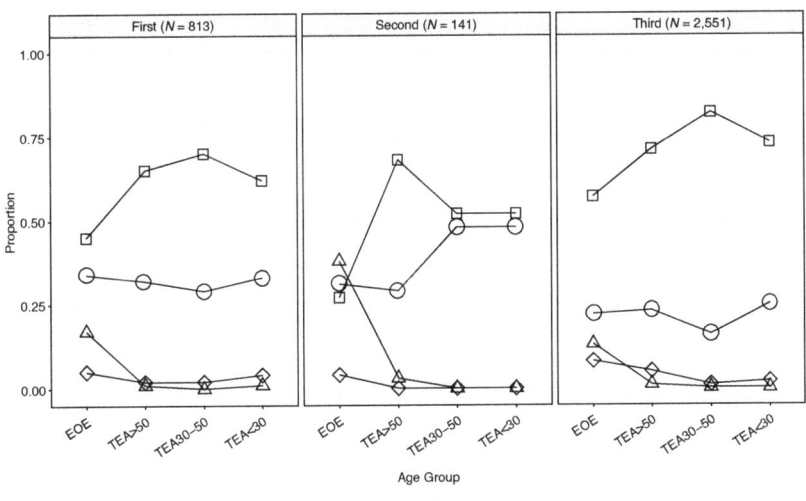

Figure 1.4 Distribution of EPs by subject complement over apparent time

Table 1.3 *Mixed-effects logistic regression testing the fixed effects of* PERIOD, SUBCOMP, *and their interaction and a random intercept for* SPEAKER *on the realization of EPs as* I think. *Treatment contrast coding. Coefficients reported in log-odds. Correlations of fixed effects, r<|0.47|*

Observations: 3018. Overall frequency *I think:* 65.2%. *AIC:* 3,487					
Fixed effects	Coefficient	*p*-value[a]	SE	Token *n*	% *I think*
PERIOD (vs. *EOE*)				814	48.9
TEA	1.180	0.000	0.262	2,836	69.9
SUBCOMP (vs. *first*)				668	57.4
second	−0.547	0.277	0.503	121	51.2
third	0.583	0.002	0.186	2,229	71.0
PERIOD:SUBCOMP (vs. *EOE:first*)				—	—
TEA:second	0.148	0.794	0.564	—	—
TEA:third	−0.249	0.261	0.222	—	—
Intercept	−0.273	0.206	0.216	—	—
Random effects	Variance			Group *n*	
SPEAKER[b] (intercept)	0.78			126	

Note. [a] I round *p*-values to three digits. 0.000 does not represent true 0 but an extremely small value; [b] mean frequency of *I think* by speaker: 65.1%.

To assess the significance of these trends I turn to mixed-effects logistic regression. Different ways of slicing the time dimension were tested to determine what provided the best statistical model. A binary split between time periods (EOE vs. TEA) provided a better model than models that included the four age-group categorization or models that included a continuous predictor of speaker year of birth. The models reported in Tables 1.3 and 1.4 test the persistence of doxastic strength of EP variants in real-time Ontario English.

Table 1.3 presents the best model of the interaction between time period (EOE vs. TEA; EOE as reference) and grammatical person of the complement clause subject (first vs. second vs. third; first as reference) on the realization of *I think* (vs. other EPs).

The positive coefficient and low *p*-value for the main effect of PERIOD indicates that *I think* is more likely in TEA than EOE. The high *p*-value for SUBCOMP(*second*) suggests that *I think* is neither more or less favored with second-person complement clause subjects than first-person complement clause subjects (the reference level). However, the positive coefficient for SUBCOMP(*third*) has a low *p*-value, indicating that third-person complement clause subjects favor *I think* more than first-person complement clause subjects (and by transitivity second-person complement clause subjects). The interactions between PERIOD and SUBCOMP have high *p*-values, which suggest

Table 1.4 *Mixed-effects logistic regression testing the fixed effects of* PERIOD, SUBCOMP, *and their interaction and a random intercept for* SPEAKER *on the realization of EPs as I guess. Treatment contrast coding. Coefficients reported in log-odds. Correlations of fixed effects, r <|0.44|*

Observations: 3018. Overall frequency *I think*: 26.6%. AIC: 3142					
Fixed effects	coefficient	*p*-value[a]	SE	N	% *I think*
PERIOD (VS. *EOE*)				814	26.4
TEA	−0.489	0.086	0.285	2836	26.6
SUBCOMP (VS. *first*)				668	32.6
second	−0.638	0.205	0.504	121	38.8
third	−0.800	0.000	0.209	2229	22.4
PERIOD:SUBCOMP (VS. *EOE:first*)				—	—
TEA:second	1.202	0.034	0.568	—	—
TEA:third	0.496	0.043	0.244	—	—
Intercept	−0.721	0.002	0.236	—	—
Random effects	Variance			Group *N*	
SPEAKER[b] (intercept)	0.96			126	

Note. [a] I round *p*-values to three digits. 0.000 does not represent true 0 but an extremely small value; [b] mean frequency of *I think* by speaker: 25.1%.

that, despite an overall increase in frequency across the twentieth century, there has been no change in the doxastic strength of *I think* (as operationalized here).

Table 1.4 presents the best model of the interaction of time and subject of the complement clause on the realization of *I guess* in the same way as Table 1.3. The overall probability of *I guess* remains steady across the two time periods as indicated by the relatively small main effect of PERIOD. The main effect of SUBCOMP(*second*) has a high *p*-value, suggesting that there is no difference in the probability of *I guess* with first or second-person complement clause subjects (at least in EOE). There appears to be a difference between first- and third-person complement clause subjects such that first persons favor *I guess*, as indicated by the negative coefficient and low *p*-value for SUBCOMP(*third*). Importantly, the interaction coefficients between PERIOD and SUBCOMP have low *p*-values. First, consider the interaction between PERIOD and third-person complement clause subjects. To interpret the interaction, we add together the coefficients of the two main effects and the interaction term (−0.489 + −0.800 + 0.496 = −0.793) and compare this to the main effect for SUBCOMP(*third*) (−0.800). Although the *p*-value is low, the probability of *I guess* with third-person subjects (relative to first-person subjects) exhibits little change across time. The interaction with second-person complement clause subjects suggests a more drastic change. Summing the coefficients of the main effects and the interaction term (−0.489 + −0.638 + 1.202 = 0.075) suggests that relative to (the coefficient for) EOE (−0.638), the probability of *I guess* with second-person complement clause subjects (relative to first-person subjects) has increased such that *I guess* is more favored with second-person subjects (than first-person subjects) in TEA, opposite from the pattern in EOE.

I think, as the EP with the strongest doxastic strength, should be favored with first-person complement clause subjects more so than third or second persons, and *I guess* should be favored with second- and third-person complement clause subjects. However, *I think* is favored in the context that should represent the middle of the scale of doxastic strength. *I guess* is favored by the ends of the scale.

Thus, despite what has been suggested in the literature, these results may indicate that EPs do not nicely fit along a scale of doxastic strength. This would undermine Thompson and Mulac's (1991) claim that EPs exhibit retention or persistence as predicted by grammaticalization theory. However, given the strong intuition that *I think* is indeed stronger than *I guess*, let us explore two other possible explanations for these results. One possibility is that the way I have operationalized grammatical person of the complement clause subject to test doxastic strength might not be accurate. Undoubtedly, there are other factors involved in how strongly a speaker is willing to commit to a proposition other than who or what a speaker is talking about. For example, we have different extents of knowledge about different individuals. However, given the extent of the data, these other factors should balance out and probabilistic trends should emerge regardless. We are left with two facts: (1) different EP variants intuitively express different degrees of commitment and (2) the models demonstrated in the tables in this chapter have captured a real constraint on the realization of EPs (subject of the complement clause). This leads to another possible explanation for these results: the order in (6) is wrong; perhaps first-person complement clause subjects are not the propositions with which speakers will use the doxastically strongest EP. Given our results, perhaps the order should be as in (8).

(8)   Third-person subjects > first-person subjects > second-person subjects

There is evidence from negated EPs that supports this hypothesis. EPs with a negative marker are typically the result of neg-raising, in which the negative marker of the embedded clause is raised to the main clause, as in (9a). Neg-raised sentences are "felt as weaker and more tentative than their otherwise synonymous counterparts with lower-clause negation" as in (9b) (Israel 2004: 704).

(9)   a. *I don't expect* he had too much money to bank as far as that went.
            (EON/F/1906)
        b. *I think* they wouldn't have made a very good jam even. They were too sweet.
            (NIA/F/1916)

Table 1.5 *Cross-tabulation of period and grammatical person of complement clause subject in EOE and TEA, showing the percentage of negated EPs relative to all EPs*

	EOE		TEA	
	% negated	N	% negated	N
Third person	14	72/509	7	151/2042
First person	18	51/285	13	70/528
Second person	22	8/36	9	9/105

If the hypothesis in (8) is correct, there should be a correlation between negated EPs and the grammatical person of the complement clause subjects because both have been implicated as ways in which speakers can weaken their commitment to propositions. This can be tested with a cross-tabulation of negated EPs by complement clause subject types as in Table 1.5.

In EOE, tokens with second-person complement clause subjects occur most frequently with negated EPs, in the middle are first-person complement clause subjects and occurring least frequently with negated EPs are third-person complement clause subjects, suggesting that these are the propositions that speakers mitigate the least. The order proposed in (8) exactly lines up with the frequency of use of negated EPs. In TEA, although first-person complement clause subjects occur more frequently with negated EPs than second-person subjects, it is clear that speakers use more of the "weaker and more tentative" negated EPs with first-person complement clause subjects than third-person subjects.

We now have evidence from the data itself for the order in (8). The explanation may lie with politeness strategies and face-saving. Using weaker EPs with propositions about one's interlocutor might be a politeness strategy that speakers' employ to avoid losing face. If a proposition about one's interlocutor is false, the interlocutor will most certainly know (in contrast to propositions about other people or things, the truth of which the interlocutor is not necessarily expected to know). To minimize the risk of losing face, speakers will mark the weakest commitment to that proposition.

However, Brown and Levinson (1987) observe that "facework involves the maintenance of *every participant's face* for the duration of the social interaction (as far as this is possible)" (Watts 2003: 86, my italics). In addition to maintaining one's own face as a speaker, we are also aiming to reduce any threat to our interlocutor's face. The reason speakers might use an EP that expresses a weaker commitment to propositions about themselves than to propositions about non-participants is the inverse reason for using a weaker EP when talking about an interlocutor. As experts on ourselves, we tend to know the truth about propositions about us. If a speaker states a proposition about themselves that a hearer had hitherto believe to be false, this could threaten the hearer's positive face. In particular, this is more of a face threatening act than stating a proposition about a non-participant in the discourse, since neither speaker nor hearer is the expert. Thus, by only weakly committing to propositions about ourselves (although we are ultimately the experts), we minimize the risk of threatening our interlocutors' face.

Hopper's (1991: 22) principle of PERSISTENCE predicts that some aspects of a grammaticalizing form's previous lexical meaning will persist as the form comes to serve a more functional role. Following our refined interpretation of the cline of complement clause subjects, this hypothesis is confirmed. The verb *think* is a general verb of cognition while *guess* implies estimation. Aspects of these meanings are preserved across time, as *I think* consistently expresses a stronger degree of commitment than *I guess* does. However, this fact alone cannot be used as a diagnostic of the continued, gradual grammaticalization of EPs. Persistence may be predicted to occur during grammaticalization but it is also necessary in cases of non-grammaticalization. That is, if EPs are not grammaticalizing further, we expect persistence of their meanings. Consider the fact that, although *I think* has risen in frequency, the internal conditioning of the variant has remained constant. Thus, the rise in frequency was not because *I think* gradually expanded its functioning to fill the "weak commitment" gap left by *I suppose* (or vice versa). That is, *I think* did not undergo a bleaching of its meaning. The gap left by *I suppose* was primarily filled by the already weaker *I guess*. The increase in frequency of *I think* on the other hand must have been a result of a decrease in frequency of the other low frequency variants in the system (e.g., *I believe*). In sum, there is no evidence from this diagnostic that *I think* or *I guess* has gradually grammaticalized further across the twentieth century.

Returning to Figure 1.1, it is clear that the increase in frequency of *I think* between EOE and TEA is at the expense of all other EPs except for *I guess*, which remains relatively stable. Despite this rise in frequency, there is no substantive evidence for the ongoing gradual grammaticalization of *I think*. Changes in the syntactic position of EPs were used as a diagnostic for further grammaticalization. One hypothesis in the literature is that increased use of EPs in non-initial position indicates further grammaticalization via gradual context expansion (Thompson and Mulac 1991). A series of mixed-effects logistic regressions shows that the rise of *I think* takes place at a constant rate in both initial and non-initial position. The fact that there was no change in the magnitude of this effect across time suggests that there was no gradual grammaticalization of the variant. Second, the complement clause subject was used to operationalize the doxastic strength of EPs. Another series of mixed-effects logistic regressions showed that *I think* is consistently stronger than *I guess*. However, although *I think* rises in frequency, this change was not accompanied by a bleaching of this stronger meaning nor gradual expansion into doxastically weaker contexts.

Before concluding, I must note that I did not track these EPs from their inception. As Brinton (1996) has shown, both *I think* and *I guess* have been used in English for centuries. Thus, although I did not find evidence for the ongoing gradual grammaticalization of EPs, this does not mean that these forms did not grammaticalize at some point in the past. In fact, it is essentially undeniable that EPs did develop from propositional to expressive functioning. Crucially, reflexes of change present in this data suggest that this change was not gradual but abrupt, consistent with the CRE.

1.4 The Development of Pragmatic Markers as Abrupt Reanalysis

If we begin with the contemporary generative assumption that pragmatic markers such as EPs are in a dependency with some functional head above CP as suggested, it is no surprise that the changes discussed conform to the predictions of the CRE. That is, these pragmatic markers, as syntactic objects act like any other syntactic objects through diachrony. Competition between *I think*, *I guess*, and *I suppose*, as competition between minimally different functional heads above CP, is an instantiation of grammar competition.

Further evidence for this comes from an assessment of the predicted outcomes of grammar competition. Kroch (1994: 8) argues that doublet pairs (i.e., variants in grammar competition) will resolve in one of two possible ways:

1. In the absence of further linguistic change, one form eventually disappear[s] through disuse [...],
2. The doublet pair [becomes] stable due to differentiation in meaning and grammatical properties.

The changes that have taken place in the EP system are in line with these possibilities. One form, *I suppose*, appears to be heading to obsolescence (at least in this speech community) while the most frequent two forms (*I think* and *I guess*) remain in stable variation, each filling a probabilistic niche as in Table 1.6.

In Kroch's (1994: 8) model, stability can only result from clear "differentiation in meaning and grammatical properties." However, Wallenberg (2013) and Fruehwald and Wallenberg (2013) have argued that stable *variation* can occur if forms specialize along a continuous dimension. In the case of EPs, *I think* and *I guess* have specialized along the scale of doxastic strength. *I think* has

Table 1.6 *Summary of the probabilistic niches of* I think *and* I guess

	I think	I guess
Syntactic position	Favored in initial position	Favored in non-initial position
Doxastic strength	Stronger commitment	Weaker commitment

specialized at the stronger end of the scale while *I guess* has specialized at the weaker end. This specialization has led to contemporary stable variation. Although favored in different syntactic positions, a speaker's need for a stronger or weaker EP may outweigh this effect; we are left with a variable system.

All told, I have found evidence of the CRE operating, which indicates grammar competition. In addition, the observed obsolescence and specialization of EPs is consistent with cases of such grammar competition. What, then, was the initial, abrupt grammatical change that took place, and what role does grammaticalization play?

1.4.1 The Development of Pragmatic Markers as (Abrupt) Reanalysis

There are many examples of lexical material becoming functional material in linguistic diachrony. How then, do we account for the phenomenon of grammaticalization in a model of language change like Kroch (1989)? Following Roberts and Roussou (2003), these "grammaticalization" phenomena are not a unique kind of language change. Roberts and Roussou (2003: 35) make the strong case that "grammaticalization involves reanalysis of functional categories [...] in such a way that new morphophonological realizations of functional features are created." I end this chapter by making two theory-neutral conjectures about the conditions necessary for the reanalysis of lexical material into pragmatic markers, using EPs as an example.

1.4.1.1 Conjecture 1: Position Matters To become a pragmatic marker, lexical material must be positioned on either periphery of the utterance.[8] Given the hierarchical structure of syntax, these two (linear) positions, under certain conditions, may be parsed by learners as taking scope over the entire utterance. The ambiguity caused by the linearization of hierarchical structure is what leads to reanalysis. In a generative framework, the outer edges of the utterance may contain material above CP that

---

[8] There are pragmatic markers that are limited to utterance medial position, such as German modal particles. The syntax of these features and how they relate to functional material above the CP will not be discussed here but see Bayer and Obenauer (2011) and Wiltschko and Heim (2006).

denote expressive meanings (e.g., Bayer and Obenauer 2011; Wiltschko and Heim 2006).

Assuming that this is the case, the structural reanalysis of EPs might have been along the lines of (10).[9]

(10)
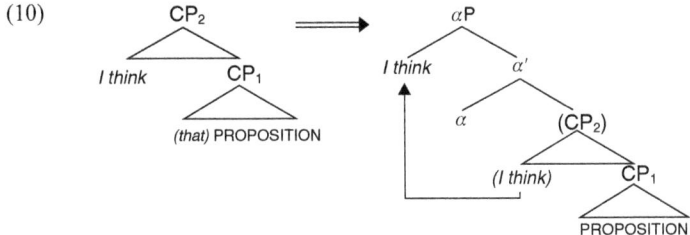

I am agnostic about syntactic details, but the development of EPs proposed here involves the subject and predicate of a CP (a main clause) with scope over another CP (an embedded clause) being reanalyzed as a specifier of a functional head above CP (α). This is similar to what Thompson and Mulac (1991) propose.

Competition between variants of EPs can be interpreted as competition between minimally different α heads above CP (one that relates to *I think*, one that relates to *I guess* and so on). Positional mobility of variants arises via the syntactic movement of material within the CP above αP. This could include movement of the whole CP, resulting in the utterance final position of the EP or some constituent within the CP, resulting in utterance medial position.

1.4.1.2 Conjecture 2: Implicata Matter Only a specific kind of lexical material on the peripheries of utterances are reanalyzable as pragmatic markers: lexical material that already triggers implicatures consistent with the meanings that are conventionalized by functional heads above CP. With respect to the present case, when functioning as the main verb and subject of an utterance, the set of epistemic/doxastic, complement taking, main verbs that co-occur with first-person pronominal subjects trigger the same implicature that EPs express conventionally: weak commitment to what follows. Consider (11).

(11)   A: Where is the cat?
       B: I think that she is hiding under the couch.

---

[9] In this example, I assume the trajectory of change proposed by Thompson and Mulac (1991) but the trajectory observed by Brinton (1996) can be made to be consistent with my conjecture about peripherality.

Speaker A is seeking information about the location of the cat (let's call her "Jam"). She expects a response from speaker B about Jam's location. B does not give a direct response to A's question. Instead, B informs A about one of B's beliefs (that Jam is hiding under the couch). Given Grice's (1975) Maxim of Relevance, A interprets B's response as necessarily relevant to A's question: the implicature is that B must not know for certain the whereabouts of Jam, otherwise B's response would have been "she is hiding under the couch." Thus, main clauses like this already implicate the weak commitment that is conventionalized by EPs.

Taken together, these two conjectures add up to essentially the same trajectory of change that Traugott (1995: 15) suggests for pragmatic markers: "syntax via pragmatic strengthening in discourse > syntax with a different function." The system envisioned here differs from Traugott's in two ways: (1) the change happens through abrupt reanalysis and (2) pragmatic markers are syntactic objects above CP. What remains the same is that both stages belong to syntax proper and reanalysis is driven by the conventionalization of inherently implicated meanings.

1.5 Coming to Consensus

This chapter has argued that the grammaticalization of EPs did not develop gradually. Indeed, a recent development in grammaticalization theory has come to a similar conclusion. Heine (2014: 1205–1206), following Kaltenböck et al. (2011), argues that the development of pragmatic markers is not the result of grammaticalization but rather a spontaneous process of "cooptation, which has the effect that information units such as clauses, phrases, or words are taken from the domain of sentence grammar and deployed for the purposes of discourse organization." The proposal is situated within a theory of language that includes a Discourse Grammar composed of a Sentence Grammar and Thetical Grammar: the development of pragmatic markers involves the cooptation by Thetical Grammar of Sentence Grammar elements during discourse.

Evidence for instantaneous cooptation come from spontaneously created thetical material. Heine (2014) suggests that all of the options in (12), while functioning as theticals, are an open class (i.e., not formulaic) composed of elements from Sentence Grammar.

(12) This may {*it need hardly be said/and this is not really surprising/would you believe it/if you please forgive me saying that/* ...} lead to compromise over the patient's best medical treatments to promote personal and commercial interests. (Heine 2014: 1221)

Elements of Sentence Grammar that are frequently coopted by Thetical Grammar "may subsequently develop from an instantaneous [i.e., spontaneous] to formulaic thetical" via constructionalization (Heine 2014: 1223). While theoretical details differ, this proposal is in line with what I have proposed: lexical material within a CP (Sentence Grammar) that expresses particular implicatures (coopted instantaneous thetical) has been reanalyzed (constructionalization) as pragmatic markers (formulaic theticals) that are located above CP (Thetical Grammar). While Heine (2014) and Kaltenböck et al. (2011) recognize that some part of the development of pragmatic markers is abrupt, they maintain that the constructionalization process is gradual. Recalling Adger's (2007) distinction between grammar and usage, this may be a difference in theoretical terminology to the extent that Kaltenböck et al.'s (2011) cooptation may be a process of the Grammar and constructionalization a part of Usage. In both cases, we have Traugott's (1995: 15) "syntax via pragmatic strengthening in discourse > syntax with a different function." Despite the terminological differences, this concurrence of two distinct theoretical approaches to language is worth celebrating.

2 Evaluation of Pragmatic Markers
The Case of *You Know*

Erik Schleef and Bradley Mackay

2.1 Introduction

The study of language attitudes has a long tradition, with its origins in questions relating to the sociology of language(s): attitudes toward entire languages or dialects have been studied in an attempt to uncover potential bias and discrimination toward them. This strand of research has identified two core dimensions that seem to give the evaluation of standard and nonstandard varieties direction: prestige and solidarity. Standard varieties are often rated high on prestige features, while nonstandard varieties are often rated high on solidarity features (e.g., Lambert et al. 1960; Giles et al. 1974; Trudgill and Giles 1978; Gallois et al. 1984; Preston 2002; Clark and Schleef 2010). In addition to the two core dimensions of prestige and solidarity, some studies reviewed by Zahn and Hopper (1985) uncovered evidence of a third dimension relating to dynamism and involving features such as confidence and self-assurance. Items within this category relate to "raters' concern for speakers' social power, activity level, and the self-representational aspects of speech" (Zahn and Hopper 1985: 119). Findings like these are usually based on speaker evaluation studies, in which participants listen to a number of recordings of different voices and are asked to rate them on several evaluative scales. More recent research has focused on the study of individual phonological, morphological, or syntactic features, for example on the evaluation of variants of *(ing)*, rather than investigating entire varieties (Campbell-Kibler 2007). To an extent, these three dimensions are also reflected in the evaluation of individual linguistic features; yet at the same time, this latter line of research has stressed the context-dependency and dynamic nature of evaluation (Campbell-Kibler 2008; Schleef 2019; Schleef 2020). This study compares the evaluation of speech with the pragmatic marker *you know* in British English to speech without any pragmatic markers, in order to find out how these three dimensions relate to this individual variable feature in an indirect attitude study. The comparison is based on a set of perception surveys in which participants listened to manipulated audio stimuli and rated them on a series of scales.

Zahn and Hopper (1985) formed a particular interest in studies that evaluated linguistic diversity, such as nonstandardness or ethnicity. Although they speculate that their three-factor model of speech evaluation may be sufficiently general to be useful in other speech evaluation tasks, these methods have not been widely applied to discourse and conversational features. There are various reasons for this. It is harder to design audio stimuli for these, which is why this line of research often resorts to written stimuli, for instance Buchstaller (2006) and Davydova et al. (2017) for *be like* and Beeching (2016) for *you know* and other pragmatic markers. Second, not all variable discourse and conversational features are suitably described as standard versus nonstandard variation. *You know* is a case in point: the use of *you know* may make speech appear informal but not nonstandard. *You know* is perfectly standard English. This makes *you know* different from vernacular discourse feature *like*, for example, for which sensitivity to the dimensions of prestige, solidarity, and dynamism has been shown (Dailey-O'Cain 2000; Buchstaller 2006).

It has been pointed out that politicians such as Barack Obama and Tony Blair seem to use *you know* quite frequently in political discourse. Beeching (2016: 116) argues that its use among intimates and in informal speech gives it the capacity to index an informal and relaxed persona, one that is in touch with ordinary voters and shares their views. Thus, at the conversational level, *you know* appears to bring something positive to the conversation that is suggestive of social attributes associated with solidarity. However, *you know* also appears to be associated with moderate degrees of uneducatedness among older respondents (Beeching 2016: 114–115), which is suggestive of an association with the classic prestige domain. Nonetheless, based on a short, written survey that asked respondents directly to compare the same sentence with and without a *you know* token, Beeching concludes that utterance-final *you know* is not particularly salient nor sociolinguistically stigmatized overall. Of course, ultimately the evaluation of *you know* hinges on what everyday speaker-listeners think about the work it does. It is certainly possible that a speech with *you know* tokens is heard as less standard. Although from a linguistic perspective *you know* is not normally considered a nonstandard feature, survey participants may disagree. If this were the case, we would expect *you know* to be sensitive to social attributes associated with less prestige.

While some results on the evaluation of *you know* suggest that it may well fit in with findings made for standard versus nonstandard linguistic features, this study tests this by exploring the evaluation of *you know* in audio-matched guises. Specifically, the study aims to find out how the three dimensions of prestige, solidarity, and dynamism relate to this individual variable feature in an indirect attitude study when listeners' attention is not drawn to the feature of interest. It is clear that *you know* is evaluated. What remains unclear is to what extent evaluative dimensions that relate to non-standardness and ethnicity also apply to the use of *you know*. This is important because *you know* is not typically discussed under the heading of nonstandard socially or regionally variable speech. In addition, many pragmatic markers are an obvious processing outcome. They occur at important processing junctures and, as a consequence, have found some mention in the psycholinguistic literature (Warren 2013: 15, 77) as they can provide insights into the dynamics of speech production, specifically about how speakers construct utterances and the choices they make as they talk. Thus, *you know* is somewhat different from features that are associated with nonstandardness, and we might not expect Zahn and Hopper's (1985) three-factor model to apply here.

Thus, the link of *you know* to speech processing and its nature regarding standardness opens up new questions in attitude research. These are questions that are of an empirical rather than a theoretical nature. This chapter does not attempt to contribute to a specific theory of perception but to test empirically where the limits of the classic prestige, solidarity, and dynamism model lie. This is investigated by conducting a series of matched guise tests with manipulated voices differing in the presence or absence of *you know*. Specifically, we aim to find answers to the following questions:

- What positive social attributes does *you know* bring to the conversation?
- Is the use of *you know* associated with particular social groups?
- Is the use of *you know* stigmatized?
- Does the evaluation of *you know* vary by age, social class, or hearer sex?
- Finally, are Zahn and Hopper's (1985) three evaluative dimensions a good fit for the pragmatic marker *you know*?

Before the experimental methods are outlined in detail, it is instructive to review what we already know about the evaluation of this feature.

2.2   *You Know*: Function and Evaluation

In order to explore the evaluation of *you know* experimentally, it is crucial to consider (1) how *you know* is used as well as where it occurs and (2) what we already know about the evaluation of *you know*. These two issues are discussed in turn.

You know has received academic attention since the inception of the field of discourse-pragmatic variation (e.g., Östman 1981; Schourup 1983; Schiffrin 1987). While the focus of this research was placed on the forms and functions of *you know*, many studies have since also explored its sociolinguistic (Holmes 1986) and regional distribution (Kallen 2005) as well as the use by non-native and native speakers (Müller 2005; Fung and Carter 2007; Hellermann and Vergun 2007; Diskin-Holdaway, Chapter 9, this volume).

Various terms have been used to refer to the large variety of pragmatic functions that *you know* can serve (see, e.g., Beeching 2016: 98–106; Diskin-Holdaway, Chapter 9). They include textual as well as interpersonal functions. Holmes (1986: 7–12) provides a useful list of functions of *you know*, which she organizes along a scale of speaker-certainty "concerning a variety of aspects of the situation, including the linguistic expression of the message and the speaker's relationship to the addressee." Three functions fall on the certainty side of her scale: (1) expressing mutual knowledge, (2) emphasizing, intensifying, or boosting the strength of a speech act, and (3) the attributive function of *you know*, which indicates the certainty of a speaker that the addressee knows what is being referred to. On the uncertainty side of her scale, she lists (4) the appealing function of *you know*, which may be appeals for reassurance, agreement, or similar speech acts. *You know* is also used to (5) flag linguistic imprecision and appeal for tolerance while searching for a suitable word or phrase, when introducing qualifying information, or for indicating false starts: "The money seems to be going for basics rather than for things like / you know extra equipment" (Holmes 1986: 11). Other researchers have provided similar lists, most of which are highly similar to Holmes'. For example, most of Holmes' (1986) functions are also covered by Beeching (2016: 99–103) and Diskin-Holdaway (Chapter 9). Beeching adds an attention-getting function, which does not clearly fall into any of Holmes' categories.

These functions are often associated with specific positions in the speech stream. *You know* can occur in initial, medial, and final position (Crystal and Davy 1975: 92–95; Holmes 1986: 8–11), summarized as:
- The function of expressing conjoint knowledge tends to precede the proposition.
- When signaling linguistic imprecision, *you know* occurs clause-internally.
- The functions of emphasis tend to occur in final position, although they can also occasionally precede the proposition or occur medially.
- The attributive and appealing functions of *you know* are normally utterance-final.

Given that the linguistic imprecision function provides the largest number of insertion options into the speech stream, this is the function of *you know* that may be most suitable for a matched guise study. It is also the function that could be most naturally inserted into the speech stream if it is the goal to insert more than one token into audio guises as the medial position is the most frequent position in which *you know* occurs (Beeching 2016: 106). However, an important caveat must be made at this point: pragmatic particles are always multifunctional. While in any one context one function may certainly dominate, *you know* may serve related functions at the same time.

Sociolinguistic studies of *you know* have noted some social characteristics of typical *you know* users but the pragmatic marker has a rather diffuse social component when comparing its use across different varieties. Beeching's (2016) study is particularly relevant here as it is one of the most recent studies on British English. She notes that *you know* is used less by professional classes than by lower middle classes. Women prefer it slightly over men in initial and medial position, and speakers over the age of sixty use it more frequently than other age groups. In other regions, these distributions may differ slightly. Investigating New Zealand English, Stubbe and Holmes (1995) found no gender differences in the middle classes, while gender appeared to matter in the working classes, with young, male working-class speakers using *you know* more than their female counterparts. In his Scottish data, Macaulay (2002) found women to use *you know* more than men. Since social meanings are often derived from the social characteristics of their users (Eckert 2012: 94), we might, in the British English context, expect *you know* to be associated with lower middle-class, female, and older speakers.

As previously suggested, *you know* is reported to be subject to evaluation. Beeching's (2016) short, text-based attitude study is particularly enlightening. It probes the evaluation of *you know* in utterance-final position on four scales: politeness, directness, educatedness, and friendliness. The survey is somewhat problematic as respondents were asked to compare speaker A, who does not use the specific pragmatic marker in question, to speaker B, who does. Unfortunately, ratings were only elicited for speaker B, which makes it difficult to compare responses across participants as we do not know how they each rated speaker A, the neutral guise. The study suggests that the inclusion of *you know* in written guises makes no difference to how polite or friendly an utterance sounds, and it makes utterances appear only slightly more indirect and uneducated. In fact, the means for directness and educatedness do not differ between the two guises, only the modes do. Compared to the large amount of research on the evaluation of *like* in its various functions, relatively little is known about that of *you know*, which makes it a perfect candidate for the exploration of the evaluation of one of its functions in more detail.

We have shown in this section that *you know* in its function of indexing linguistic imprecision and the medial syntactic slot are particularly suited for an audio-matched guise study of *you know*. It has also become clear that *you know* is subject to evaluation and that this evaluation may be mediated by demographic factors and possibly even personality traits of the evaluators. The next section describes how these deliberations have been put into practice when designing the experiment and survey.

2.3 Methods

2.3.1 Creating Guises

In an initial step, guises were created for an experimental online perception study testing the evaluation of the linguistic imprecision *you know*. The guises were based on three short interview sections extracted from the British National Corpus, each of which contained *you know* and which comprised circa seventy words. We selected guises that are similar in that they report the actions of others, yet the actual subject matter differs (see the chapter appendix). The topic of an excerpt can of course influence evaluation, which is why we tested for interaction effects between topic and *you know* occurrence in our statistical analysis. Apart from length and subject matter, excerpt selection was otherwise arbitrary. The excerpts were modified somewhat in structure and content to make them comparable to each other; for example, other pragmatic markers and pauses were removed and exactly three *you know* tokens were included in each text excerpt.

In a second step, the guises were each reenacted by two mid-twenties females from Greater Manchester: Bella, who spoke with a middle-class northern accent, and Dana, who spoke with a local Manchester accent. Bella spoke with a clear voice at a pitch that ranged from 74 to 334 Hz and a pitch mean of 199 Hz. Dana's voice, too, was clear but slightly nasal in places. With a mean pitch of 197 Hz, her pitch is comparable to that of Bella, although it was somewhat less variable, ranging from a minimum of 76 Hz to a maximum of 289 Hz. They each reenacted these guises in a version without *you knows* and, to get an idea of what these texts would sound like with *you know*, a version with three *you know* tokens in the three locations marked in the reenactment script (see the chapter appendix). The pragmatic markers were inserted within clauses before adjectival phrases (APs), noun phrases (NPs), and a prepositional phrase (PP) in one case. Recordings were conducted in a studio at the University of Manchester. Speakers wore head-mounted microphones.

As this is an experimental study, many factors must be controlled in order to pin down exactly which variable factors result in different listener reactions. While several variable phenomena are tested in the research (variable, topic, hearer characteristics), other factors had to remain stable, as exploring additional factors would have resulted in exponential increases in the number of guises. Specifically, the following factors were not varied: the task, the number of pragmatic markers in the guises, the sex of the speakers.

Only two females were recorded, as the inclusion of one or two males would not have been sufficient to make generalizations if sex-based differences had been found. While negative results would not have been problematic in this

Table 2.1 *Overview of guises*

	Topic	"Neutral"	*You know*
Dana	Tough Company	1	1
	Sick Sam	1	1
	Upset Alex	1	1
Bella	Tough Company	1	1
	Sick Sam	1	1
	Upset Alex	1	1

respect, positive results would have made it difficult to separate speaker sex from voice characteristics or accent. The reason why females were selected was simply due to speaker availability.

To ensure extracts differ only in the (non)occurrence of *you know*, the guises without *you know* were used as stimuli matrices and three *you know* tokens were inserted into these in Praat (Boersma and Weenink 2014). This resulted in two versions of each of the three excerpts per speaker for a total of twelve guises, each pair of which differs only in the (non)occurrence of the *you know* tokens (see Table 2.1). Everything else in each pair was identical. Stimuli were tested for naturalness in focus groups: participants were unable to tell which of the guises they heard had been manipulated.

When deciding how many *you know* tokens to insert into the stimuli, we initially considered a frequency of one, two, three, four, or five. We were concerned that only one or two tokens of *you know* may easily get missed by listeners in our audio stimuli, which left us with making a decision between three, four, or five tokens. Four or five tokens might have been heard as an overuse of *you know* in the excerpts of, on average, 23 seconds, which is why we selected to include three tokens into every excerpt. We also consulted further literature on the distribution of pauses and disfluent phenomena such as false starts and repairs to help us in making this decision.

Bortfeld et al.'s (2001: 134) measures of disfluency rates in conversations recorded at Stanford University provided some guidance as to how many tokens to insert into the guises. They provide total rates of disfluencies for various social groups and found these to range between 5.24 and 7.36 per 100 words for various different groups. Since these included repeats and restarts, we considered 5 token insertions in 100 words to be our upper limit. The text stimuli had a mean word length of 76, which meant that we would not want to include more than 3.75 tokens in each excerpt, so three were inserted into each stimulus.

2.3.2 Survey Design

Eight online surveys were generated using SurveyGizmo (2015) with the goal of eliciting information on the evaluation of the stimuli pairs. Six doublets (three from each speaker) were distributed across these eight surveys to keep the length manageable. These surveys also included stimuli for several other variables, which are not part of the current study and which serve as distractors for the neutral and *you know* tokens considered here. These distractor guises did not include any *you know* tokens. Table 2.2 presents the stimuli distribution across these subsurveys. Those considered in this chapter are marked in bold.

The guises were distributed across these surveys in such a way that topics were never repeated, each participant heard each Bella and Dana at least once, and the order of guises within each survey was randomized each time a new participant entered a new survey (to counteract order effects in the results). Thus, every participant heard only one guise of a paired set. This between-subjects design is particularly suited to experimental setups like that of the current study, where the same hearer repeats the experiment in that they hear more than one guise. Conversely, a within-subjects design would have created undesirable practice and demand effects, sensitization, and carryover (Greenwald 1976: 314) under such circumstances. The between-subjects design also reduces survey time and, crucially, circumvents the problem of the listener recognizing the speaker and the feature of investigation when hearing a stimulus twice with only slight modifications. It is this last point that made it impossible to use a within-subjects design for the current study, as we were interested in how speakers evaluate *you know* when their attention is not drawn to the feature of interest – very much in contrast to the more direct reading approach used by Beeching (2016: 114–115).

Each survey contained a welcome page with an audio test and a short training set, which did not take more than a minute of the participants' time. At the very end, the survey included questions about the respondents, such as self-reported

Table 2.2 *Guise distribution across eight subsurveys*

Survey/Topic	S 1	S 2	S 3	S 4	S 5	S 6	S 7	S 8
Tough Company	**Bella** **Neutral**	Bella Other	Bella Other	**Bella** **yk**	**Dana** **Neutral**	Dana Other	**Dana** **yk**	Dana Other
Sick Sam	Dana Other	**Dana** **Neutral**	**Dana** **yk**	Dana Other	Bella Other	**Bella** **yk**	Bella Other	**Bella** **neutral**
Upset Alex	**Bella** **yk**	Bella Other	Bella Other	**Bella** **Neutral**	**Dana** **yk**	Dana Other	**Dana** **neutral**	Dana Other

sex, age, and social class. After seeing an example sentence, respondents were asked whether they use *you know* themselves; they had to select among three options: never, sometimes, often. The survey was produced by us and presented to participants following usual guidelines on questionnaire design and administration (e.g., Schleef 2013; Meyerhoff et al. 2015). The three pages in between the welcome page and the final page were dedicated to one guise each, consisting of eight questions that each related to one of the three guises. The questions are based on social attributes that were generated based on previous research (e.g., Zahn and Hopper 1985; Campbell-Kibler 2007) and focus group comments. We made sure attributes would be included that may be associated with prestige (e.g., articulate), solidarity (e.g., friendly), and dynamism (e.g., outgoing). Considering the conversational functions of *you know*, we also included attributes that relate to clear and fluent speech as well as conversational skills. A total of twenty-nine scales were included, as shown in Table 2.3.

We limited the number of scales for inclusion to twenty-nine, as long surveys tend to reduce response rate and data accuracy. To prevent item order affecting the results, the social attributes were randomized in each individual survey by means of a procedure within SurveyGizmo. A new item order was created for each individual participant accessing a page. After hearing each stimulus, listeners were invited to rate it on these attributes, provided in the form of

Table 2.3 *Twenty-nine scales presented to participants in the survey*

articulate —— inarticulate		intelligent —— thick	
assertive —— not assertive		involving listener —— not involving listener	
attractive —— unattractive		laidback —— uptight	
authoritative —— not authoritative		outgoing/ sociable —— shy	
casual —— formal		masculine —— feminine	
certain —— uncertain		perceived age in 11 categories	
clear —— unclear		polite —— impolite	
common —— posh		precise —— imprecise	
confident —— self-conscious		professional —— unprofessional	
educated —— uneducated		reliable —— unreliable	
experienced/ knowledgeable —— inexperienced/ not knowledgeable		supportive/ caring —— not supportive/ not caring	
friendly —— unfriendly		trendy —— untrendy	
genuine —— pretentious		trustworthy —— not trustworthy	
hardworking —— lazy		working class —— upper class	
hesitant —— fluent			

seven-point semantic differential scales or sliders. Listeners were asked to indicate the degree to which these items applied to the voice they heard. The listeners were instructed to listen to the stimuli on their computers, but they were not instructed to use headphones. They could listen to each stimulus twice, once at the beginning and once in the middle of the survey.

Access to one of the surveys was randomized to balance uptake. To participate in the survey, respondents were required to have lived in Greater Manchester for at least ten years. Consequently, this study is testing how evaluations may vary if respondents hear guises in a variety that they hear on a regular basis. Respondents were recruited using two methods: flyers and emails were sent to schools and universities for distribution to pupils and students; and the survey was advertised on a social networking site. Once a respondent completed the survey, they were sent a thank you email asking them to pass on the survey to their family and friends.

2.3.3 Data Analysis

A total of 436 respondents accessed the surveys, which resulted in 1,308 responses. These were extracted into a spreadsheet after data collection was complete. The database was then inspected for anomalies, as a result of which 659 responses were removed. The vast majority of these ($N=561$) had to be removed because many participants did not complete the survey. Of the 659 responses, 98 were removed because respondents had accessed the survey from a computer with a non-UK IP address, because they claimed not to speak English natively, or because they took less than 5 minutes and 30 seconds to complete the survey (5.5 minutes was considered the minimum time to complete the survey).

This left a total of 649 responses for analysis: 310 responses from males and 339 from females. Class background was based on self-reported evaluation on a slider, which participants could move on a scale that ranged from a label that read *working class* on the left to one that read *upper class* on the right, with *middle class* inserted at midpoint. Of these, 134 responses came from people who considered themselves to belong on the upper-class side of the scale, 273 on the working-class side and 242 who placed themselves between these two extremes. The majority of respondents were between 20 and 45 years of age.

Respondent ratings were subjected to statistical testing using R (R Core Team 2013). A factor analysis using the principal axis factoring (PAF) extraction method with a scree test criterion for factor extraction was conducted on the ratings of the social attributes. A factor analysis is a technique that uncovers whether response patterns on a number of scales can be explained by a smaller number of underlying factors (Streiner 1994:

135). Evaluations for each scale or group of scales (=factors) were then subjected to statistical testing using regressions in R. We set a fairly conservative *p*-value of 0.025 at which to reject the null hypothesis. This was to counteract the increased probability of a type I error due to individual scales accessing the same target. Intercepts for respondent and speaker were entered as a random effect. The ratings for social attributes were treated as the response variable with the following predictors:
- Feature in the stimulus: *you know*, no *you know*
- Respondent sex: male, female
- Respondent class: working (WC), middle (MC), upper middle (UMC)
- Respondent age: continuous
- Topic: Tough Company, Sick Sam, Upset Alex
- *You know* use: user, nonuser

We checked for main effects and interactions between stimulus feature and all other predictors.

2.4 Results

The data was tested for multivariate normality by means of a Royston test for multivariate normality through the MvnTest package (Pya et al. 2016) in R (R Core Team 2013). As the data was found not to have a normal multivariate distribution, the maximum likelihood method was not deemed to be an appropriate means of conducting the factor analysis. This was instead achieved by PAF with Kaiser normalization prior to a varimax rotation, in line with the recommendations made in Costello and Osborne (2005) and Osborne et al. (2008). The PAF extraction returns values that indicate how strongly each scale loads onto a given factor. Following Zahn and Hopper (1985: 117), a scale was considered as loading to a factor if it had a primary loading of 0.5 with no secondary loading of above 0.3 on another factor. Only factors containing three or more scales were considered viable. The scales that met these criteria were then conflated for further statistical analyses. In order to assess the appropriate number of factors to include, a scree plot was run in R through the Psych package (Revelle 2018). Although initial scree test plotting suggested there were four possible factors within the dataset, upon further inspection, the fourth factor did not meet the selection criteria as there was no primary loading above 0.5 for any of the scales.

From the twenty-nine scales, three factors were established, which we named Status, Solidarity, and Determination. The conflated Status factor contains nine scales. It relates to the listeners' perception of the speakers' social status and includes *articulate, intelligent, class, formal, feminine, professional, posh, educated,* and *clarity*. The second conflated factor, Solidarity, indicates the degree to which speakers were judged as amiable or generally likeable and includes the factors *genuine, trustworthy, friendly,* and *supportive.* The final factor, Determination, includes scales that relate to more power-based aspects of a personality: *confident, assertive,* and *certain.*[1]

These three factors were submitted to mixed-effects linear regression models in R, using the lmerTest package (Kuznetsova et al. 2017). The Status factor failed to converge, however, so this factor was instead submitted to a linear regression model without the random effects of speaker and respondent. Results from the models are presented in Table 2.4. Results indicate that the use of *you know* did not affect listeners' judgments of the speakers on either the Status or Solidarity factor. Guises with *you know*, however, were rated significantly lower on the Determination factor. Although there were no significant interactions between the use of *you know* and other predictors, there were a few main effects for topic and respondent class in the Status and Solidarity factors, but these are not relevant to the current analysis.

As *you know* was not found to affect listener responses to the conflated factors Status or Solidarity, all remaining twenty-six factors were submitted to individual mixed-effects ordinal regression models, which were built in R using the ordinal package (Christensen 2019). Ordinal regression models work much in the same way as linear mixed-effects regression models with fixed and random effects, and, as the name suggests, they are suited for hierarchical ordinal data. Models were built through the same process with fixed effects added only if they improved the model fit. *You know* was found to have a statistically significant effect on the rating of five of the twenty-six scales, as shown in Table 2.5. In addition to *you know* guises appearing less determined, guises with *you know* were also rated as less experienced, less trustworthy, less precise, less formal, and less fluent than guises without *you know*.

Of these five scales, *trustworthy* was originally assigned to the Solidarity factor, so there is a minor reflex of this dimension, although *trustworthy* does not pattern in the expected direction. The results are summarized in Figure 2.1. The only model that was found to have a significant interaction between *you know* guises and other predictors was in listener responses to *experienced*, where there was a significant interaction with class. While neutral and *you know* guises were judged fairly evenly between MC and UMC respondents, WC respondents judged the *you know* guises less favorably on the *experienced* scale.

---

[1] When we first ran the PAF model, we did not normalize the data. While the resulting factors were largely the same, the Status factor included only seven scales (without *formal* and *professional*) and the Determination factor also included *authoritative*. The *you know* guise did not affect listener judgments on any of the three original conflated factors. Following a comment during the review process, we went back to the analysis and reran the PAF model on normalized data, using the Kaiser normalization method. This changed results slightly. As analyses of this nature are by default submitted to Kaiser normalization in both SPSS (Statistical Package for the Social Sciences) and SAS (Statistical Analysis System) (Egbert and Staples 2019: 134), this brings our analysis in line with comparable studies conducted in these formats.

Table 2.4 *Best models for the three factors. Reference levels are neutral guise, Bella, Sick Sam topic, female respondent, middle class, and* you know *user*

	Estimate	SE	*t*-value	*p*-value
STATUS				
(INTERCEPT)	3.98	0.14	27.64	< 0.01*
YOU KNOW GUISE	−0.12	0.10	−1.20	0.23
TOPIC (TOUGH COMPANY)	0.30	0.12	2.40	0.02*
TOPIC (UPSET ALEX)	−0.11	0.12	−0.92	0.36
RESPONDENT SEX (MALE)	−0.06	0.10	−0.61	0.54
RESPONDENT CLASS (UMC)	0.75	0.21	3.65	< 0.01*
RESPONDENT CLASS (WC)	−0.40	0.12	−3.46	< 0.01*
RESPONDENT USES YOU KNOW	0.06	0.12	0.47	0.64
SOLIDARITY				
(INTERCEPT)	4.52	0.13	35.54	< 0.01*
YOU KNOW GUISE	0.06	0.08	0.69	0.49
TOPIC (TOUGH COMPANY)	0.02	0.11	0.21	0.84
TOPIC (UPSET ALEX)	−0.59	0.11	−5.21	< 0.01*
RESPONDENT SEX (MALE)	−0.01	0.10	−0.06	0.95
RESPONDENT CLASS (UMC)	0.18	0.11	1.63	0.10
RESPONDENT CLASS (WC)	0.76	0.21	3.55	< 0.01*
RESPONDENT USES YOU KNOW	−0.03	0.12	−0.23	0.82
DETERMINATION				
(INTERCEPT)	4.89	0.17	28.24	< 0.01*
YOU KNOW GUISE	−0.25	0.09	−2.86	< 0.01*
TOPIC (TOUGH COMPANY)	−0.12	0.12	−0.99	0.32
TOPIC (UPSET ALEX)	−0.04	0.12	−0.36	0.72
RESPONDENT SEX (MALE)	−0.20	0.10	−1.96	0.05
RESPONDENT CLASS (UMC)	0.32	0.21	1.57	0.12
RESPONDENT CLASS (WC)	−0.09	0.12	−0.73	0.46
RESPONDENT USES YOU KNOW	0.09	0.12	0.73	0.47

Note. UMC, upper middle class; WC, working class.

2.5 Discussion

This section returns to the characteristics of *you know* described in the Introduction to the chapter, and it discusses results in relation to the questions posed therein, namely how the three evaluative dimensions of prestige, solidarity, and dynamism relate to the pragmatic marker *you know*, what it is that *you know* brings to the conversation in terms of social meanings – including association with social groups – and whether the evaluation of *you know* varies by hearer age, social class, or sex. We explain our findings by utilizing Preston's

Table 2.5 *Results from the mixed-effects ordinal regression models for scales on which the ratings of* you know *and neutral guises were judged to be statistically different. References levels are neutral guise, Sick Sam topic, female respondent, middle class, and* you know *user*

	Estimate	SE	*p*-value
Experienced			
YOU KNOW GUISE	−1.25	0.40	< 0.01*
RESPONDENT CLASS (UMC)	1.43	0.54	< 0.01*
TOPIC (TOUGH COMPANY)	0.83	0.28	< 0.01*
RESPONDENT AGE	0.12	0.04	< 0.02*
YOU KNOW GUISE: CLASS	0.78	0.34	0.024*
Formal			
YOU KNOW GUISE	−0.35	0.14	< 0.02*
RESPONDENT CLASS (UMC)	0.74	0.37	< 0.01*
Trustworthy			
YOU KNOW GUISE	−0.07	0.01	< 0.01*
RESPONDENT CLASS (UMC)	0.94	0.30	< 0.01*
RESPONDENT AGE	0.10	0.01	< 0.01*
RESPONDENT SEX (MALE)	−0.13	0.17	< 0.01*
RESPONDENT USES YOU KNOW	0.30	0.01	< 0.01*
Precise			
YOU KNOW GUISE	−0.42	0.15	< 0.01*
RESPONDENT AGE	0.16	0.05	< 0.01*
Fluent			
YOU KNOW GUISE	−0.53	0.15	< 0.02*

Note. UMC, upper middle class.

(2010, 2011) processual model of speech evaluation and argue that results suggest that the social salience of the pragmatic marker *you know* is very low.

2.5.1 The Evaluation of You Know Is Multidimensional

First, this study confirms that the evaluation of the specific function of *you know* is multidimensional. *You know* is associated with a small set of different social meanings, ranging from *informal* to *less trustworthy* and *uncertain* (a scale within the Determination factor), which may get activated in different contexts. In other words, evaluation is not limited to just one evaluative domain. This is important because models of sociolinguistic processing have been developed

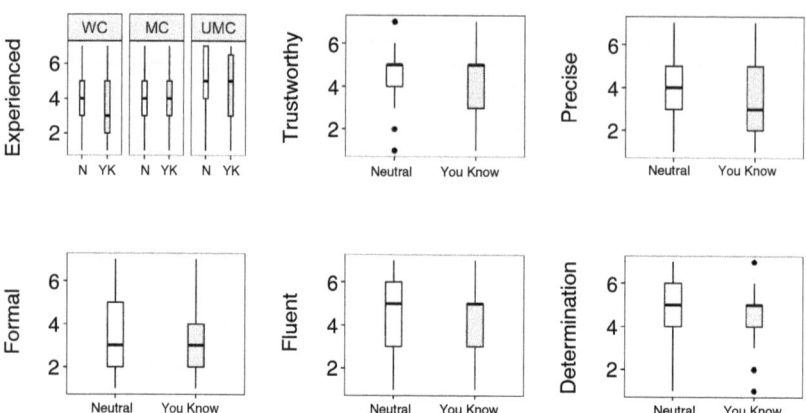

Figure 2.1 Significant scales and factors

that theorize how variable features are processed and monitored. One such theoretical concept is the sociolinguistic monitor (Labov et al. 2011; Levon and Fox 2014; Wagner and Hesson 2014), which focuses exclusively on the prestige domain. It is hypothesized to be a cognitive mechanism that tracks the speech signal for socially meaningful cues of variable features and monitors the frequency of these language forms. Whether it also applies to *you know* is an empirical question. Frequency-based methods used to test how *you know* is tracked, stored, and processed in time have not been used here. Testing how *you know* relates to this concept is a useful area of future research. However, the fact that *you know* is evaluated multidimensionally and that results in the prestige factor were not significant points to a potential shortcoming of this unidimensional concept. To produce contextually appropriate speech, a sociolinguistic monitor must certainly also monitor speech for formality and perceived social attractiveness, which are relevant social attributes for *you know*.

2.5.2 The Social Salience of You Know *Is Very Low*

Second, negative results are taken into account. Of course, we must exercise caution when interpreting null results and when trying to make generalizations. Nonetheless, we believe some tentative generalizations are certainly possible that speak to the questions we posed in our Introduction. None of the classic evaluative dimensions – status/prestige, solidarity/social attractiveness – yielded significant results. This is reminiscent of results from Beeching's (2016: 114–115) direct, within-subject, short written survey on utterance-final *you know*, which she characterized as not particularly salient nor sociolinguistically stigmatized.

In the current study, only some minor reflexes of the factor of Solidarity in the scale *trustworthy* and evidence of the factor of Determination (closely related to that of Dynamism discussed in other studies) could be uncovered. Since the studies that found Status, Solidarity, and Dynamism to be relevant focus on a comparison of standard with nonstandard or ethnically marked speech, this finding is not completely surprising. We have argued that *you know* is not a nonstandard feature, yet the prestige dimension does matter for similar features such as unfilled pauses (Schleef 2019), so one may have expected a similar pattern for *you know*. Results question the usefulness of Zahn and Hopper's (1985) three-factor model of speech evaluation for certain pragmatic markers. Of course, the data is patterned along their three dimensions, which suggests that raters generally seem to structure rating processes along these lines. They did this for the neutral and *you know* guises in similar ways.

This study has also shown that the social characteristics of listeners, such as their age, sex, and whether or not they use *you know*, do not influence the evaluation of *you know*, with one exception: working-class individuals rate the *you know* guises as less experienced than the other participants. This study has further shown that *you know* is not associated with specific social groups. Although several sociolinguistic studies have indicated that some social groups use *you know* differently, these usage differences have not led to an enregisterment process of these social groups with *you know*. We have argued here that the pragmatic marker has a rather diffuse social component when comparing its use across different varieties, which may explain this finding.

The negative results of this study suggest that the social salience of *you know* is rather low. Levon and Fox (2014) define social salience as "the relative ability of a linguistic variant to evoke social meaning." The ability of *you know* to do this – at least in the contexts and function investigated – is not very pronounced, particularly when compared with results of studies on *like* (e.g., Dailey-O'Cain 2000; Buchstaller 2006; Hesson and Shellgreen 2015; Davydova et al. 2017). This, we believe, allows us to make a tentative generalization about pragmatic markers that do not pattern along a standard/nonstandard dimension, such as *you know*. Such pragmatic markers do have social meanings but if their social salience is low, their social meanings are unlikely to give rise to the classic prestige, solidarity, and dynamism dimensions. We do not want to exclude the possibility that informal standard features cannot do this. As the case of unfilled pauses suggests, they can. We argue that they can only do this under certain conditions, one of which is that their social salience is not low.

2.5.3 Social Meanings of You Know

So, what is it that *you know* brings to the conversation? Compared to guises without pragmatic markers, guises with *you know* are heard as less formal, less trustworthy, less precise, less determined, less experienced, and less professional. Where are these evaluations coming from? Preston (2010, 2011) has developed a processual model of language regard that aims to describe where and why variability in evaluation may emerge. In a first step, listeners must become aware of a form ("noticing"), otherwise they cannot react to it. This is the case in the current study. *You know* tokens are noticed, otherwise no significant results would have emerged. In a second step, the noticed form is "classified" according to social, contextual, or linguistic criteria; for example, listeners may classify speech as Yorkshire English, casual, or Cockney. Once speech has been classified, it is "imbued" with evaluative information. This information is drawn from the listener's stored cognitive representations of the classification (and may thus vary between individuals or groups of individuals): a Yorkshire accent may be associated with friendliness and similar attitudes. In a final step, there is a reaction.

It is the classification process that concerns us here. Excerpts with or without *you know* are classified as specific instances of speech and then imbued with evaluative information. The categories into which excerpts with or without *you know* are classified will, for instance, for Dana, include characteristics such as casual, urban Manchester dialect no matter whether or not listeners hear *you know*. Guises with *you know* are classified slightly differently from those without *you know* tokens. For speaker Dana, for example, this may include characteristics such as casual, very informal, urban Manchester dialect produced by a person who appears to not be completely sure of what she is saying and doing. This results in evaluative information and gives rise to the social meanings of informality, lack of precision, determination, experience, and professionalism; and, presumably as an ideological extension of the lack of determination and experience, the person is heard as less trustworthy.

The social meanings of this sentence-internal function of *you know* are, thus, in stark contrast to Beeching's (2016: 115–116) discussion of the use of *you know* by Barack Obama and Tony Blair to index an informal and relaxed persona, one that is in touch with ordinary voters and shares their views. The social meanings uncovered for the sentence-internal function of *you know* are certainly not social meanings that politicians would want to evoke. This would also suggest that other functions of *you know* may express different meanings.

2.5.4 Limitations and Future Research

The meanings of the linguistic imprecision function of *you know* are not particularly variable. For example, we would expect interaction effects with the topic to surface, but this was not the case, which might suggest that these meanings are relatively stable across topics and social groups. This would have to be confirmed empirically: although three different topics were used in this study, they were similar in that they report somewhat negative actions, which may have influenced evaluation.

There are a few further limitations that we would like to discuss, as these point us toward directions for future research. Recent research has revealed that the evaluation of linguistic features may depend on a variety of factors, including speaker and hearer characteristics (e.g., Hay et al. 2006), listeners' prior experiences, and various contextual conditions, including eliciting conditions (Hay et al. 2010) and topic (e.g., Campbell-Kibler 2009). This is important as variation in any of these factors may alter results to a certain degree. In particular, the evaluation of *you know* in an experimental setting may differ from evaluation in an actual conversation. While topic and the hearer characteristics investigated do not appear to influence evaluation, future research must determine to what extent the factors held constant in the current study alter the evaluation of *you know*.

Specifically, the two guises both featured female speakers. The need to keep the survey short and to the point while varying topic and class meant that speaker sex could not be varied, although it could in principle moderate the evaluation of *you know*. Additionally, only one *you know* function was investigated. Comparing the evaluation of different functions in different syntactic slots is paramount as the results of the current study appear at odds with the advice that politicians seem to receive regarding the conversational effects of *you know*. Furthermore, considering the low social salience of *you know*, it may be worth exploring a variety of other methods to tap into the evaluation of this pragmatic marker. We selected an indirect between-subject approach as we were interested in the evaluation of *you know* when attention is not drawn to the feature under investigation. Finally, only one token frequency (three *you knows*) was tested. Variations of these may certainly alter evaluation and this represents an additional important area for future research.

2.6   Conclusion

Results of the current study suggest that *you know* in the function of flagging linguistic imprecision is not involved in beliefs relating to prestige and solidarity to any large extent, which suggests that its evaluation does not get direction from standard language ideology (Lippi-Green 2012: 67), the "bias toward an abstracted, idealized homogeneous language." Its social meanings arise primarily out of its immediate pragmatic contexts, namely its use in interactional discourse when addressing another person (see Eiswirth, Chapter 8, this volume), and, as a consequence of this, its more frequent occurrence in informal speech. Similarly, the immediate pragmatic context of linguistic imprecision *you know* results in associations with a lack of precision, determination, and professionalism and, as a consequence, a second order indexicality to a lack of trustworthiness arises.

The low social salience of *you know* constrains any further evaluative dimensions that may emerge, and we argue that this is an essential difference between linguistic features that pattern primarily along a standard–nonstandard continuum and pragmatic markers, such as *you know*. Many features of the former category are much more likely to be pulled into the ideological haze of standard language ideology, which may result in major significant results in the prestige, solidarity, and dynamism dimensions; in experimental settings, those may even occur for such features when their social salience is not particularly high. The same argument cannot be made for pragmatic markers with low social salience. Here, social meanings arise from their most immediate pragmatic and interactional contexts of use.

Appendix

1. Stimuli texts

You know tokens were inserted in the spots marked with an **X**.

I'm feeling so sorry for Sam and compensation for the medical bills has been dragging out for **X** so long. At first I thought, what's the matter with you but, Sam's IQ has **X** gone right down. Sam can't concentrate on things, just can't **X** do much anymore. And, has to have tests every now and again. The money will come eventually, but, it's just when, but isn't it an awful thing?

Alex was upset I won't even tell who we're not getting along with. Coz you never know. They use it **X** against you some time. And I told Alex quite clearly. I was quite blunt but it had to **X** be said. You've got to be really stupid to tell anyone anything in this place and Alex said yeah but I'm not like that. I'm new. But I wasn't **X** convinced. And I said yeah but you're gonna get that way.

Some tough decisions had to be made. It was up with **X** the company or down with the company. And I think certainly some colleagues sort of saw it as an infringement on **X** their future. Some colleagues were gonna see a drop in **X** their standard of living. I think people were getting a bit upset that a new face had come in, and all of a sudden changes were being made.

2. Excerpts from Survey

Note that scales were randomized for each individual participant and that the layout, font, and so on differed somewhat as this was automatically adjusted in SurveyGizmo for different computers and internet platforms. After a welcome page with an audio test and a short training set, respondents would evaluate three voices on three different pages. An example for such a page is given below.

Evaluation of Pragmatic Markers 59

Voice 1

Listen to the Recording.

1. From what you've heard, this person gives the impression of being:

	+3	+2	+1	0	−1	−2	−3	
trustworthy	O	O	O	O	O	O	O	not trustworthy
formal	O	O	O	O	O	O	O	casual
assertive	O	O	O	O	O	O	O	not assertive
trendy	O	O	O	O	O	O	O	untrendy
	+3	+2	+1	0	−1	−2	−3	
confident	O	O	O	O	O	O	O	self-conscious
hardworking	O	O	O	O	O	O	O	lazy
polite	O	O	O	O	O	O	O	impolite

2. How would you describe this person's social background? Move the slider on the working class to upper class scale below.

   working class   middle class   upper class

3. How old do you think this person is?
   O 10–14   O 15–19   O 20–24   O 25–29   O 30–34   O 35–39
   O 40–44   O 45–49
   O 50s   O 60s   O Above 70

4. Still focusing on the voice – feel free to listen to it again – this person gives the impression of being:

	+3	+2	+1	0	−1	−2	−3	
reliable	O	O	O	O	O	O	O	unreliable
genuine	O	O	O	O	O	O	O	pretentious
attractive	O	O	O	O	O	O	O	unattractive
outgoing/sociable	O	O	O	O	O	O	O	shy
	+3	+2	+1	0	−1	−2	−3	
friendly	O	O	O	O	O	O	O	unfriendly
articulate	O	O	O	O	O	O	O	inarticulate
intelligent	O	O	O	O	O	O	O	thick

5. On a scale from feminine to not very feminine, where would you place this voice?

   not very feminine   very feminine

6. With a full 7 stars meaning they did an excellent job and fewer stars meaning they did less well, how many stars would you give this speaker for . . .
   being precise

   ☆☆☆☆☆☆☆
   involving the person they are talking to

   ☆☆☆☆☆☆☆

appearing experienced and knowledgeable

☆☆☆☆☆☆☆

being supportive, caring

☆☆☆☆☆☆☆

7. Finally, this person also gives the impression of being:

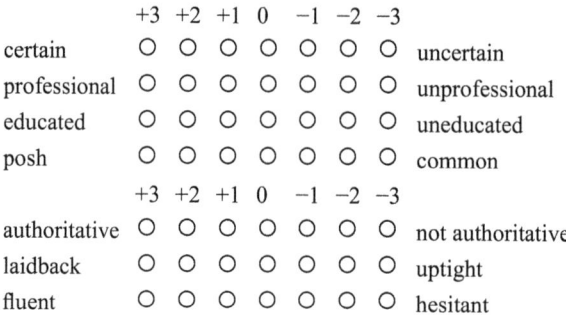

8. How would you rate the clarity of speech of this person?
completely unclear   very clear

Final Questions. The same items were repeated for the second and third voice. Item order was randomized. At the very end of the survey the following questions were asked:

How old are you?

Are you [options given]: female / male

On a scale from working class to upper class, where would you place yourself? [options given: scale ranging from 1 to 50]

What is your current employment status? [options given: not currently active on the job market / permanent job and happy there / permanent job but looking to change / student / temporary job / unemployed and looking]

You may have heard one of the voices using *you know* in a sentence such as "we were organizing meetings to tell people about you know the changes." Do you ever use *you know* like this yourself? [options given: never, often, sometimes]

Where did you grow up? (You may put several locales, e.g., London, Preston, York)

Where do you live now?

For how many years have you lived there?

What is/are your native language(s)?

3 Quotative Variation and Change in French with Additional Insights from Brazilian Portuguese and Italian

Stephen Levey, Laura Kastronic, Salvio Digesto, and Mélissa Chiasson

3.1 Introduction

Research on the quotative systems of other languages has made less cumulative progress in addressing the central question of linguistic change that has heavily preoccupied investigators of the English quotative system (see, e.g., Tagliamonte and D'Arcy 2007; Buchstaller 2014). A fundamental issue concerns the extent to which other languages are the loci of innovative phenomena mirroring the vertiginous rise and cross-varietal spread of *be like* in English. Inspection of the literature certainly reveals no shortage of claims endorsing a *parallel* scenario in various typologically related and unrelated languages (Foolen 2008: 117; Buchstaller and Van Alphen 2012: xii; Buchstaller 2014: 19). With a few notable exceptions (e.g., Palacios Martínez 2014; Cheshire and Secova 2018), however, empirically accountable demonstrations of change in the variable expression of quotatives in languages other than English remain the exception to the rule. Instead, change has often been intuited from isolated, anecdotal, or casually observed examples (e.g., Foolen 2008), without situating the features in question within the larger variable systems of which they are part, or confirming whether they have assumed a socially regular distribution in a speech community.

In this chapter, we argue that the framework of variationist sociolinguistics can refine our understanding of cross-linguistic trends in the quotative system by capitalizing on the inherent variability found in naturally occurring speech. We suggest that the conditioning of this variability, viewed in apparent- and (where available) real-time perspective, can be used to determine *what* has changed in the quotative system or even if there *has been* change.

Our primary research focus is on French (Quebec, Acadian, and European varieties), drawing on additional insights from Brazilian Portuguese and Italian. Our cross-linguistic perspective enables us to identify any prevailing typological tendencies that may motivate shared or similar developments across different varieties. Another issue that we confront is whether any shared candidates for change detected in two (or more) varieties can be reasonably qualified as *parallel developments* (Buchstaller 2014: 19).

In the following sections, we first review the evidence for change in targeted Romance varieties. We subsequently describe the corpora on which our investigation is based before characterizing our theoretical framework and key methodological procedures. After presenting the major findings associated with each of our comparison varieties, we examine the contribution of the results to elucidating our major research objectives.

3.2 Variation and Change in the Quotative System of Romance Varieties

Inspection of spontaneous speech data from French, Brazilian Portuguese, and Italian confirms the presence of a broad range of "non-canonical" quotative constructions in those languages, as shown in (1) through (12):

(1) *parce que dans le fond il **était comme**, "Pff fais qu'est-ce que tu veux"* (AF2013/P0 CL/30:33)[1]
because in the end he was like, "Pff do what you want"

(2) *elle **est comme**, "C'est bien, cest bien, mais c'est pas exactement comme qu'est-ce qu'on cherche, comme merci"* (QF2014/JS/14:43)
she's like, "It's fine, it's fine, but it's not exactly like what we're looking for, like thanks"

(3) *eu não fico me preocupando muito **como**, "Ah será que eu vou voltar pra casa?"* (SP2010/RS/35:30)
I'm not worrying too much like, "Oh will I ever go home?"

(4) *moi, j'**étais là**, "Essaie! Tu diras non après!"* (QF2014/ML/00:44)
I was there, "Try! You'll say no afterwards!"

(5) (...) *a Presidente fala e não acontece quando acontece alguma coisa acontece muito devagar num tempo muito que **é tipo**, "Estou esperando isso há muito tempo e não vem a resposta"* (SP2010/DA/34:35)

---

[1] All examples are reproduced verbatim from the original audio recordings. Codes in parentheses refer to the corpora (AF2013=Acadian French 2013; QF2014=Quebec French 2014; AF2019=Acadian French 2019; QF2019=Quebec French 2019; CFPP=European French; SP2010=Brazilian Portuguese; C-ORAL-ROM=Italian) as well as the speaker identifier, and the line number/timestamp in the corpus indicating the location of a specific token. All translations are our own. We express our gratitude to Ronald B. Mendes for access to the SP2010 corpus. We are grateful to Robert Prazeres, Jeanne Brown, Alice Marsh, Priscilla Hubert Breton, Sarah Lefebvre, and Ariane Dei Tos Cardenuto for extracting and coding data on which this research is based. We also acknowledge the generous financial support of the Social Sciences and Humanities Research Council of Canada, which contributed to parts of the research targeting Quebec French.

(...) the President speaks and nothing happens when something happens it happens very slowly it's like, "I've been waiting for this for a long time and the answer does not come."

(6) ... ça a un côté frimeur un peu **genre**, *"Voilà j'suis"* (CFPP/KT/4612)
... it's got a flashy side a bit like, "Here I am"

(7) *la Sandra a un certo punto ha cominciato a fare dei discorsi **del genere**, "Mah io per m ... io non avevo nessun problema se venivate anche voi"* (C-ORAL-ROM/029/72)
at a certain point Sandra began to say things like, "But I, as for m ... I had no problem if you were coming too"

(8) *gli **feci**, "T'ho a compra' un giochino?"* (C-ORAL-ROM/206/66)
I said (lit. "did") to him, "I have to buy you a little game?"

(9) *il **fait**, "Ouais non euh c'est pas de ta faute il est comme ça et tout et tout"* (CFPP/YZ/4102)
he says (lit. 'does'), "Yeah no uh it's not your fault he's like that and everything"

(10) *ela fazia **assim**, "Vocês não precisa de fazer a lição não ... só vai fazer a prova só presta atenção aí"* (SP2010/NF/22:20)
she said (lit. 'did') like this, "You don't need to do the lesson ... just do the test just pay attention to that"

(11) *eu brinco com ele, **ele**, "Não! você não sabe?"* (SP2010/RO/51:21)
I tease him, he (says), "No! you don't know?"

(12) *e **il lupo**, "Chi è? Ehm chi è?"* (C-ORAL-ROM/087/27)
and the wolf (says), "Who is it? Ehm who is it?"

In contrast with canonical constructions used to report speech (or thought), traditionally construed as comprising a verbal predicate encoding a speech event and a nominal referring to the speaker (Güldemann 2008: 3), non-canonical quotatives encompass a broad range of constructions based on semantically non-reportative lexico-grammatical material (Buchstaller and Van Alphen 2012: xii). This material is by no means limited to verbs. Cross-linguistically, it also includes the use of non-verbal elements such as particles, clitics, or affixes in a quotative function (Güldemann 2008: 56, 123). Moreover, there may be no overt linguistic material introducing a quoted extract, which can be signaled in speech by alternative means such as the manipulation of suprasegmental properties of intonation, phonation type, and timbre (Güldemann 2008: 40), an option that we refer to as the zero variant.

One putatively new construction concerns *être comme*, illustrated in (1) and (2), found in Acadian and Quebec French respectively, as well as its cognate *como* in Brazilian Portuguese, illustrated in (3). These so-called similative quotatives (Güldemann 2008: 318), superficially resembling the English (*be*) *like* construction, are reported to have structural analogues in a number of languages (see, e.g., Heine and Kuteva 2002: 274).

Another source for quotative constructions involves the recruitment of deictic lexemes (Güldemann 2008: 187, 361; Buchstaller 2014: 22, 89), as in (4), where the deictic marker *là* 'there' introduces a reported speech event, exemplifying a construction type that has congeners in numerous languages (see, e.g., Güldemann 2008: 364; Buchstaller 2014: 16).

Other non-canonical quotative constructions involve the use of type or taxonomic nouns designating categories or (sub-)kinds (Mihatsch 2018: 154), as in *tipo* in (5) in Brazilian Portuguese, and *genre/genere* in (6) and (7), found in European French and Italian respectively, all translatable as 'type/kind/sort' (see Bittencourt 1999; Fleischman and Yaguello 2004).

Generic performance or action verbs, such as Italian *fare*, French *faire*, and (Brazilian) Portuguese *fazer* 'to do', illustrated in (8), (9), and (10) respectively, also found in Spanish (Cameron 1998), bear further testimony to the range of quotative source constructions documented cross-linguistically.

Examples (11) and (12), from Brazilian Portuguese and Italian, illustrate an additional option, also attested in Spanish (Cameron 1998; Palacios Martínez 2014), comprising a free-standing nominal, usually a pronoun, or (more rarely) a full lexical noun phrase indexing the speaker.

To what extent do the non-canonical quotative constructions we have exemplified count as bona fide products of recent linguistic change? We first note that although reports of innovative quotative constructions in French have multiplied (e.g., Fleischman and Yaguello 2004; Levey et al. 2013; Blondeau and Moreno 2018; Cheshire and Secova 2018), in contrast with much sparser information on quotative innovation in (Brazilian) Portuguese and Italian, none of the candidates for change detected in those languages strictly qualifies as an *ex nihilo* creation (Foolen 2008: 117). Rather, so-called "new" quotatives draw heavily on the assembly of preexisting elements whose semantic and pragmatic versatility is believed to enhance their incorporation into new routinized constructions encoding a quotative function. For example, French *comme* 'like/as', and its analogues in other Romance languages (e.g., Spanish and Portuguese *como*), has multiple uses, operating as a coordinating conjunction, a comparator, and an approximative marker (Mihatsch 2009: 69). Similarly, type or taxonomic nouns such as Portuguese *tipo* and French *genre* have been documented as markers of imprecision, ad hoc categorization, exemplification, and comparison (see e.g., Bittencourt 1999; Cheshire and Secova 2018; Mihatsch 2018). Cheshire and Secova (2018: 209) argue that when key lexical items become syntactically multifunctional and reach a "critical frequency threshold," these developments conspire in paving the way to the emergence of "new" quotative constructions.

together, these two varieties of Acadian French afford an unprecedented opportunity to contrast quotative variation and change in rural and urban locations. To the extent that change is instantiated in either variety, we expect it to be more advanced in the mainstream (and more recently sampled) urban setting of Moncton.

Enhancing our comparative focus, two additional corpora representing Quebec French, as spoken in the highly bilingual Canadian national capital (Ottawa-Gatineau) region, allow us to track patterns of quotative variation and change between 2014 and 2019. These corpora were compiled within a similar time frame to those representing Acadian French, enabling us to contrast the quotative system in two major varieties of Canadian French.

We also include a transatlantic variety of European French, based on recordings comprising the publicly available *Corpus de Français Parlé Parisien des années 2000* (CFPP) (Branca-Rosoff et al. 2012). These data were collected between 2005 and 2012 in Paris, the largest urban center in France. Because the CFPP includes a number of recordings made several years before those in the Canadian French datasets, we use it to draw cautious comparisons with the quotative system in Canadian varieties.

Extending the investigation beyond French, we examine Brazilian Portuguese, as spoken in São Paulo, the largest lusophone city in the world, with a population of some 11 million people. We draw on sixty sociolinguistic interviews from the SP2010 corpus (Mendes 2013), constituted between 2009 and 2013 and stratified by age, sex, and level of education. In selecting São Paulo, our working hypothesis is that its status as a diverse global city of considerable socioeconomic and political importance meets all the extralinguistic criteria considered to be particularly favorable to linguistic change.

Our Italian data are based on recordings of natural speech in the Italian portion of the *C-ORAL-ROM Integrated Reference Corpus for Spoken Romance Languages* (Cresti and Moneglia 2005). In terms of state-of-the art sociolinguistic sampling methodologies, this dataset has several drawbacks. Certain geographical regions are disproportionately represented, with roughly half the speakers originating in Florence and surrounding areas (Digesto 2019: 44). The recordings are also the oldest of all our sources, dating back to the early 2000s, and comprise relatively small amounts of speech recorded from a large number of different individuals. Despite these evident limitations, we retain it as a "gateway" to the investigation of the Italian quotative system, which has previously received little, if any, systematic quantitative treatment.

3.4 Theoretical Framework

This study is informed by the recognition that variability is an intrinsic property of everyday speech and that it is governed by multiple social and linguistic constraints (Labov 1972b). The nature of the structured system underlying the alternation of competing variants within a particular variable context can be inferred from variant distributions and conditioning (Poplack and Tagliamonte 2001: 6). Once this system has been quantitatively modeled, the resultant information can then be systematically compared across different varieties, with a view to establishing the extent to which comparison varieties share the same underlying "grammar," as gauged from the fine-grained conditioning of variant choice. We draw most heavily on this theoretical framework in our investigation of French, where access to different geographical varieties, coupled with robust variation in the use of innovative features, lend themselves particularly well to detailed comparative analysis.

3.5 Method

3.5.1 Circumscribing the Variable Context

We limit the variable context to all strategies (including the zero variant) used to introduce reported speech, sounds, or representations of cognitive acts or states associated with reported thought/attitude (Güldemann 2008: 7). We excluded contexts where a quotative introduced indirect speech/thought (e.g., *I said/thought that she was coming*), written extracts (e.g., computer-mediated communication, text messages), and performed gestures, which can't be reliably reconstructed from audio data alone.

3.5.2 Coding Protocol

In terms of extra-linguistic parameters, we consider speaker age, sex, and, where available, level of education. Capitalizing on investigations of variation and change in the English and French quotative systems (e.g., Tagliamonte and D'Arcy 2007; Levey et al. 2013), we operationalize a series of linguistic constraints reported to constrain variant selection.

A first major constraint reported to have consistent effects on the selection of "new" quotatives is grammatical person, with English *be like* and Canadian French *être comme* both exhibiting a significant association with first-person contexts (Tagliamonte and D'Arcy 2004: 509; 2007: 203; Levey et al., 2013: 242). Accordingly, we coded each finite quotative verb for grammatical person and number, targeting the key distinction between first- and third-person contexts.

A second major constraint concerns the content of the quote. *Be like* and *être comme* are said to favor internal dialogue or reported thought, at least in earlier stages of their development (e.g., Tagliamonte and D'Arcy 2004: 503; Levey et al. 2013: 242). In the present study, we differentiated contexts such as (13), where the quotative verb reports internal dialogue, from (14), where the quotative verb introduces externally realized speech.

(13) *J'ai eu cherché mon relevé de notes, pis j'étais surpris. J'**étais comme**, "C'est pas des belles notes ça, des notes de marde."* (AF2013/RJ/40:20)
I had collected my grade transcript, and I was surprised. I was like, "Those aren't good marks [those are] crap marks."

(14) *... j'adoptais l'accent quand je leur parlais, pis là mes amis **étaient comme**, "T'es-tu raciste?"* (QF2019/JGV/30:07)
I put on the accent when I spoke to them, and my friends were like, "Are you racist?"

Yet another factor considered to affect the selection of "new" quotatives is mimesis (Güldemann 2008: 373). We associate mimesis with the use of sound symbolism and the modulation of supra-segmental features (e.g., loudness, stress, pitch) to construct dramatized dialogue or stylized renditions of human verbal behavior. We distinguished contexts such as (15), containing mimetic content, as indicated by the presence of non-lexicalized sound in this instance, from contexts such as (16) containing no evidence of mimesis.

(15) *batte i piedi e **fa**, "Tun tun tun"* (C-ORAL ROM/046/207)
stamps his feet and goes (lit. 'does'), "Tun, tun, tun"

(16) *allora io **ho fatto**, "Senti Antonio io ho imparato una cosa"* (C-ORAL ROM/225/075)
then I said (lit. 'have done'), "Listen Antonio I have learned one thing"

The final conditioning factor that we investigate is temporal reference, a constraint reported in related research to exhibit locally idiosyncratic effects (Buchstaller and D'Arcy 2009: 308). We distinguished preterite forms (found in spoken Brazilian Portuguese and Italian but not spoken French) from present perfect and imperfect forms. We further differentiated non-past tense morphology with present temporal reference, traditionally referred to as "the present," as in (17), from non-past tense morphology with past temporal reference, otherwise referred to as the conversational historical present, as in (18).

(17) *Donc il y a plein de monde qui crie ton nom, pis t'**es comme**, "Pourquoi? Comment ça qu'ils connaissent mon nom?"* (QF2014/VL/28:44)
So there's lots of people shouting your name, and you're like, "Why? How come they know my name?"

(18) so là je drive sur le bike trail pis je **suis comme**, *"Qu'est-ce que je fais s'il commence à chaser après moi right now?"* (AF2019/10/01:42)
so I'm riding along the bike trail and I'm like, "What do I do if he starts chasing after me right now?"

3.6 Results

3.6.1 Variant Distributions in French

We first compare quotative variation and change across three varieties of French, drawing on our earliest data (2005–2014).

With an overall rate of 42 percent, a first important finding is that quotative *être comme* dominates the quotative system of younger speakers of urban Quebec French, as spoken in the national capital region. By contrast, *être comme* is only used to a limited extent by older speakers of this variety, whose system largely comprises *dire* and *zero*. *Être comme*, entirely restricted to younger speakers, occurs in rural Acadian French, too, but at a much lower rate (13 percent) in comparison with urban Quebec French, a finding that we attribute to the sociolinguistic peripherality of the rural communities where the Acadian data were recorded.

We also observe that the *c'est comme* quotative variant, formally similar to *être comme* but functionally differentiated from the latter insofar as it is almost always used to enquote reported thoughts, feelings, and attitudes, is instantiated in both Quebec and Acadian French but its scant occurrence limits it to a marginal role in the quotative system.[2]

A first important conclusion that we draw from these distributions is that *être comme* qualifies as a supra-regional change that is attested outside areas characterized by high levels of English–French bilingualism, as confirmed by its presence in an insular variety of Acadian French spoken in an overwhelmingly French-dominant area. Real-time evidence drawn from the *Récits du français québécois d'autrefois*, a compendium of recordings from Canadian francophones born between 1846 and 1895, and the *Ottawa-Hull Corpus*,[3] based on sociolinguistic interviews with francophones conducted in Ottawa in the early 1980s, confirms that *être comme* is not found in either of these diachronic benchmarks (see Levey et al. 2013), further corroborating its status as a recent change.

---

[2] *C'est comme* and *discourse comme*, both low-level variants in our data, are treated separately from *être comme*.

[3] We thank Shana Poplack for access to these corpora, both archived in the *Sociolinguistics Laboratory*, University of Ottawa.

Table 3.2 *Variant distribution by age in three varieties of French*

	Quebec French 2014				Acadian French 2013				European French 2005–2012			
	Younger (18–38)		Older (43–62)		Younger (19–40)		Older (50–80)		Younger (15–37)		Older (43–85)	
Variant	N	%	N	%	N	%	N	%	N	%	N	%
être comme	238	42%	5	3%	46	13%	0	0%	0	0%	0	0%
dire	179	31%	111	55%	206	58%	368	69%	262	55%	220	73%
zero	53	9%	48	24%	58	16%	113	21%	47	10%	32	11%
c'est comme	14	2%	6	3%	4	1%	2	0%	0	0%	0	0%
être	10	2%	2	1%	3	1%	4	1%	18	4%	3	1%
se dire	12	2%	14	7%	17	5%	17	3%	64	13%	29	10%
faire	9	2%	1	1%	0	0%	2	0%	57	12%	3	1%
genre	6	1%	0	0%	0	0%	0	0%	7	1.5%	0	0%
être là	6	1%	0	0%	0	0%	0	0%	3	1%	0	0%
other	47	8%	14	7%	23	6%	30	6%	19	4%	14	5%
Totals	574		201		357		536		477		301	

Turning to European French, we find no examples of *être comme* or *c'est comme* in that variety. This would initially seem to confirm that both variants are homegrown Canadian innovations, possibly calqued on *be like* as a result of intense and sustained contact with English. Though long-term contact with English is habitually invoked to account for "exceptional" usage facts in Canadian French (Levey et al. 2013), we cannot rule out the alternate possibility of an independent internal motivation for change. In this regard, it is instructive to note that non-canonical variants such as *faire comme ça* as well as *être comme ça* (grouped with OTHER in Table 3.2), though rare, are found in the European corpus. Cheshire and Secova (2018: 212) likewise report that *être comme ça* occurs to a limited extent (N=13) in their corpus of Multicultural Paris French,[4] a variety they consider to be less susceptible to contact-induced grammatical change triggered by English. These findings, together with the existence of "similative" quotatives in a range of languages, reinforce our belief that contact with English need not be a *sine qua non* for the emergence of *être comme* in Canadian French (see further Levey et al. 2013).

What about the presence of other non-canonical quotatives in the three comparison varieties? Both *genre* and *être là* have been identified as possible ongoing changes in Multicultural Paris French (Cheshire and Secova 2018). However, in a dataset based on more than 1,000 tokens gathered from speakers

---

[4] This research is based on 60 young speakers aged 12–19 recorded in Paris between 2010 and 2014 (Cheshire and Secova 2018:210).

born between 1995 and 2001, neither variant was found to exceed 3 percent of the variable context (Cheshire and Secova 2018: 212). Table 3.2 shows that in the CFPP the combined frequency of *genre* and *être là*, both absent from the older speaker cohort, accounts for a mere 2.5 percent of quotative constructions produced by younger speakers, in line with low rates reported by Cheshire and Secova (2018).

There are no traces of *genre* or *être là* in the Acadian French data, but both are occasionally employed by younger speakers of Quebec French (grouped with OTHER in Table 3.2). Of the six tokens of *être là*, five are used by young females to introduce mimetic discourse, as in (19), where *être là* introduces an affectively charged response in a narrative recount (see also Cheshire and Secova 2018):

(19) *J'étais là*, *"Ben fais pas ça, là."* (QF2014/SK/19:46)
 I was there, "Well don't do *that*"

Genre, by contrast, is mostly confined to the collocation *c'est genre* 'it's like', used to introduce hypothetical speech or foreground generalized thoughts and attitudes unattributed to a particular speaker.

Clearly, neither *genre* nor *être là* in Quebec French competes to any appreciable extent with their much more quantitatively robust covariant, *être comme*, perhaps indicating that the former are more recent and less well-established options in the quotative system. Somewhat damaging to this interpretation, however, are scattered attestations of *être là* in the 1984 Montreal French corpus (Blondeau and Moreno 2018: 49), suggesting that this variant has existed in Quebec French as a low-level option for quite some time, possibly predating the rise of *être comme*.

Among other candidates for change in the French quotative system, *faire* stands out in the CFPP by virtue of its comparatively higher rate of use by younger (male) speakers, who mainly deploy it in first-person narratives and in contexts where it encodes mimetic content. Though perceived as a colloquial variant in the modern spoken language, it has a lengthy history as a quotative extending back to medieval French (Marnette 2005: 211), demonstrating that it is by no means a recent addition to the system. The proportionally greater use of *faire* by younger speakers in the CFPP, together with its prevalence in Cheshire and Secova's (2018: 212) corpus of Multicultural Paris French, where it accounts for nearly 30 percent of the variable context, suggests that it may instead be experiencing a revival as a "renewed" or "recycled" variant in the discourse of younger speakers in Paris (Cheshire and Secova 2018: 213). This interpretation, if correct for European French, proves far less compelling in the case of Canadian French, where *faire* remains a marginal contender (see also Levey et al. 2013: 238, table 10), albeit one that exhibits the same functional

Table 3.3 *Variant distribution by age in Quebec and Acadian French*

	QUEBEC FRENCH 2019				ACADIAN FRENCH 2019			
	YOUNGER (19–30)		OLDER (51–65)		YOUNGER (18–36)		OLDER (51–77)	
VARIANT	N	%	N	%	N	%	N	%
être comme	260	52	6	5	181	56	1	1
dire	66	13	73	58	66	20	118	76
c'est comme	40	8	1	1	15	5	1	1
discourse comme	40	8	4	3	8	2.5	1	1
zero	30	6	28	22	18	5.5	24	15
faire	7	1	1	1	0	0	2	1
penser	1	0.2	0	0	7	2	1	1
other	59	12	14	11	30	9	8	5
TOTAL	503		127		325		156	

association with mimetic content (e.g., sound symbolism, etc.) as its European counterpart.

We next turn to the most recent datasets representing Quebec and Acadian French respectively. Table 3.3 provides a breakdown of variant distributions by age in each variety.

Situating these data vis-à-vis those depicted in Table 3.2, we see that there has been a modest rate increase in the use of *être comme* in Quebec French, with this variant now accounting for more than half (52 percent) of the variable context. Likewise, in the urban Acadian French data from the Greater Moncton region, *être comme* makes up 56 percent of the variable context, on a quantitative par with urban Quebec French, provisionally suggesting that this change is infiltrating both urban varieties at roughly equivalent rates. As in the data from rural northeast New Brunswick, *être là* and *genre* are absent from the Moncton corpus. By contrast, in keeping with what was found in the 2014 corpus of Quebec French, both *être là* and *genre* (grouped with OTHER in Table 3.3) persist at low levels in Quebec French in 2019. Insofar as *être là* and *genre* are implicated in any ongoing linguistic change in Canadian varieties, the weight of the quantitative evidence suggests that they currently play a very minor role in the Quebec French quotative system and have made no inroads, as far as we can tell, into Acadian French.

3.6.2 *Transcending Frequency Data: Comparing Variable Grammars*

Thus far, we have determined that the most clear-cut evidence of quotative innovation emerges in relation to *être comme* in Canadian French. The next step is to ascertain whether *être comme* is the product of identical or divergent underlying grammatical processes in Quebec and Acadian French. In other words, is *être comme* adopted wholesale into different regional varieties, or does it exhibit evidence of locally specific constraints as it is adapted to community-based norms? To address this question, we draw on multivariate analysis using Goldvarb X (Sankoff et al. 2005), focusing initially on younger speakers recorded between 2013 and 2014 before considering data from 2019.

In the ensuing tables of results, numbers are to be interpreted as follows. The *corrected mean* is an overall measure of the frequency of *être comme* in each variety. The *range* provides a measure of the magnitude, or strength, of effects selected as significant. Factor weights (FW) indicate the probabilistic contribution of each factor listed in the left-hand side of the table to the selection of *être comme*. Factor weights vary between 0 and 1. The higher the factor weight, the greater the probability that *être comme* will be favored in the relevant contexts; conversely, the lower the factor weight, the greater the likelihood that *être comme* is disfavored in these contexts. The constraint hierarchy, or patterning of favoring and disfavoring effects, is our key heuristic for comparing variable grammars across varieties (see Poplack and Tagliamonte 2001: 94).

Table 3.4 depicts the results of two independent multivariate analyses of the contribution of speaker sex and linguistic factors to the selection of *être comme* in Quebec and Acadian French respectively. At first glance, asymmetries in the direction of effect for speaker sex would seem to point to a key distinction in the social conditioning of *être comme*, correlated with females in Acadian French but showing a slight, though nonsignificant, association with males in Quebec French. On closer inspection, the effect in Quebec French turns out to be somewhat spurious and is likely attributable to one male speaker's highly disproportionate use of *être comme* relative to other males in his cohort. When this male outlier is removed and the analysis is repeated (not shown), speaker sex makes a significant contribution to variant choice and the direction of effect, this time showing a female lead, and mirrors Acadian French, pointing to a familiar sex-differentiated pattern reported for other "new" quotatives (see e.g., Tagliamonte and D'Arcy 2007).

Turning to the contribution of linguistic factors to the selection of *être comme*, most are significant determinants of variant choice in both varieties. Clearly, however, the grammatical conditioning of variant choice is by no means identical in the comparison varieties, as gauged from the magnitude and direction of individual effects. An important distinction resides in the content of the quote. This is not selected as significant in Quebec French (as indicated by []), with probability values for internal dialogue and reported speech both gravitating toward the median ($FW=0.50$). In Acadian French,

Table 3.4 *Two independent multivariate analyses of social and linguistic factors contributing to the selection of* être comme *in Quebec French and Acadian French (younger speakers only)*

	QUEBEC FRENCH 2014			ACADIAN FRENCH 2013		
Total *N*	574			357		
Corrected Mean	0.562			0.111		
SOCIAL	FW	%	N	FW	%	N
Speaker sex						
Male	[0.55]	46	171	0.35	7	115
Female	[0.48]	40	403	0.57	16	242
Range				22		
LINGUISTIC						
Tense						
Conv. Historical Present	0.57	64	215	0.18	3	99
Imperfect	0.49	58	96	0.91	58	66
Present	0.35	40	93	0.49	12	42
Range	22			73		
Grammatical Person						
First	0.63	62	185	0.62	25	140
Third	0.41	41	264	0.37	8	131
Range	22			25		
Mimesis						
Mimetic	0.60	48	282	0.72	23	108
Non-mimetic	0.40	35	288	0.40	8	249
Range	20			32		
Content of Quote						
Internal dialogue	[0.50]	40	97	0.82	46	44
Reported speech	[0.50]	41	438	0.45	8	308
Range				37		

Note. In this and other tables showing results derived from multivariate analysis, different factor-group configurations may result in the total *N* for individual factor groups not being equivalent to the total number of tokens factored into the relevant analysis (e.g., for grammatical person, second-person tokens are excluded).

though, it is the second-ranked linguistic constraint (*range*=37) after tense (*range*=73). This factor group additionally shows evidence of functional differentiation in Acadian French, with *être comme* entertaining a strong association with internal dialogue.

Though grammatical person and mimesis share the same direction of effect in both comparison varieties, the patterning of temporal reference is different. *Être comme* is positively associated with the conversational historical present in Quebec French, but it is disfavored with the (nonhistorical) present. In contrast with Quebec French, where the imperfect has a relatively neutral effect on the selection of *être comme* (*FW* = 0.49), in Acadian French it is highly correlated with this variant. *Être comme* has no definitive association with the (nonhistorical) present in Acadian French, but it is strongly dispreferred with the conversational historical present. We interpret these findings as important indications of the operation of locally specific constraints on *être comme*. We attribute cross-varietal differences in the patterning of *être comme*, at least in part, to the sociodemographic makeup of the respective communities contrasted in Table 3.4. In the National Capital Region, situated in the urban mainstream, *être comme* appears to have advanced further along the pathway of change, as indicated by its higher overall rate of use and the attenuated effect of certain linguistic constraints (i.e., content of the quote) on its selection. By contrast, in the relatively insular variety of French spoken in northeast New Brunswick, *être comme* is positioned less far along the cline of change, as evidenced by its lower rate of occurrence compared with Quebec French, as well as the preservation of relatively robust linguistic constraints on its selection.

Table 3.5 replicates the multivariate analysis in Table 3.4, this time drawing on the more recent 2019 data from Quebec and Acadian French. In both varieties, the results for speaker sex remain consistent with a female lead in change, although the respective magnitude of this effect differs across comparison varieties. With a range of 31, speaker sex is the strongest predictor of variant choice in Quebec French, but it exerts a lesser effect in Acadian French relative to the respective strength of linguistic predictors in that variety.

Turning to the linguistic conditioning, the ranking of significant effects, as assessed by their respective magnitude, is different in each variety. For example, the strength of content of the quote in Quebec French is more modest (see also Table 3.4 where this effect is neutralized) compared with its parallel effect in Acadian French, where content of the quote is the second-ranked linguistic constraint (*range* = 21) after tense (*range* = 36), the overriding predictor of variant choice in that variety. Notwithstanding these differences, inspection of the constraint hierarchies reveals a number of intervarietal parallelisms, most notably in the absence of any effect associated with mimesis. We attribute this finding to the paradigmatic expansion of *être comme*, concomitant with the weakening of its archetypal mimetic functions, as it progressively infiltrates the quotative system en route to achieving the status of default variant in both urban comparison varieties (see Güldemann 2008: 179). In the case of temporal reference, there are, once again, hints of structural distinctions between varieties. In Table 3.5, we see that *être comme* is very positively correlated with the imperfect in Acadian French, as in its rural New Brunswick counterpart, and has a relatively neutral association with the conversational historical present but shows a strong aversion to the (nonhistorical) present. In Quebec French, on the other hand, both the imperfect and the conversational historical present are modestly correlated with *être comme*. These results

Table 3.5 *Two independent multivariate analyses of factors contributing to the selection of* être comme *in Quebec French and Acadian French (younger speakers only)*

	QUEBEC FRENCH 2019			ACADIAN FRENCH 2019		
Total *N*	503			325		
Corrected Mean	0.519			0.557		
SOCIAL	FW	%	N	FW	%	N
Speaker sex						
Female	0.66	68	243	0.57	62	154
Male	0.35	37	260	0.44	50	171
Range	*31*			*13*		
LINGUISTIC						
Grammatical Person						
First	0.59	79	191	0.59	72	131
Third	0.39	58	149	0.41	57	123
Range	*20*			*18*		
Tense						
Imperfect	0.57	76	128	0.63	84	135
Conv. Historical Present	0.55	73	89	0.49	75	32
Present	0.41	58	156	0.27	54	71
Range	*16*			*36*		
Content of Quote						
Internal dialogue	0.59	63	160	0.65	75	88
Reported speech	0.45	47	305	0.44	49	226
Range	*14*			*21*		
Mimesis						
Mimetic	[0.53]	55	258	[0.50]	56	286
Non-Mimetic	[0.47]	49	245	[0.48]	54	39

accord with our earlier observations that temporal reference is a diagnostic of locally specific effects across varieties (see Buchstaller and D'Arcy 2009: 308).

In sum, fined-grained statistical comparisons have enabled us to uncover a number of shared structural correspondences in the patterning of *être comme* in geographically discontinuous varieties. At the same time, this comparative exercise revealed subtle evidence of underlying structural divergence in the linguistic conditioning of *être comme*, highlighting the risks of inferring *parallel* trajectories of change across varieties without contextualizing this innovation in relation to the localized linguistic systems hosting it.

3.7 Additional Insights from Brazilian Portuguese and Italian

Any assessment of whether the emergence of "new" quotatives can be accurately described as a robust cross-linguistic tendency (Buchstaller 2014: 4) must necessarily consider evidence from languages other than French (or English). In this regard, the size and representativeness of the Brazilian Portuguese corpus are particularly valuable to our comparative exercise. Table 3.6 provides a breakdown of variant distributions according to multiple age groups, furnishing a detailed apparent-time perspective on the Brazilian Portuguese (São Paulo) quotative system.

Contrary to any expectation of vigorous change, we find that the long-established variants, *falar* 'to speak' and *zero* are unrivaled in the system, accounting for at least 80 percent of the variable context in the case of speakers aged 30 and above. No other variant accounts for more than 10 percent of quotative use in any age cohort. *Falar* and *zero* are also well represented in the youngest (18–29) cohort of speakers, although here we observe what Buchstaller (2014: 183) refers to as "increased systemic entropy" relative to the other age groups. This is evidenced, for example, by younger speakers' proportionally greater recourse to miscellaneous (other) variants, accounting for 11 percent of the variable context. Among these assorted variants, we find semantically specific verbs such as *comentar* 'comment', *gritar* 'shout out', and so on; sporadic use of the polysemous verb *ficar* ('stay', 'be', 'become'), used alone or in combination with the deictic adverb *assim* 'like this', as well as scattered instances of *como*, as illustrated in example (3). Of particular note in the youngest group are restricted instances of *tipo*, found only once in the adjacent 30–39 cohort and absent from all other age groups. Attested in a quotative function in Brazilian Portuguese for a number of decades (see, e.g., Bittencourt 1999: 43), this variant accounts for just 3 percent of quotatives produced by the 18–29 age group. Its sparseness in the data reveals little evidence of functional specialization, nor does it correlate sufficiently with any other extra-linguistic parameter (e.g., speaker sex or education) to be particularly informative. To the extent that *tipo* can be considered a newcomer to the quotative paradigm, its profile is that of a relatively incipient change, judging from the apparent-time information available to us. No other variant in Table 3.6 exhibits a monotonic age distribution consistent with ongoing change. Although *assim* has been implicated in the emergence of "new" quotatives in Brazilian Portuguese (see, e.g., Foolen 2008; Castelano and Ladeira 2010), Table 3.6 shows that in its most productive use, combined with *falar*, it is just as likely to be uttered by older speakers as younger ones.

We conclude, then, that the Brazilian quotative data attest to a highly variable, yet relatively stable system, rather than one characterized by extensive innovation and reorganization.

Relative stability is also a hallmark of the Italian quotative system, as inferred from Table 3.7 depicting variant distributions in the four age groups associated with the Italian speech-based portion of the C-ORAL-ROM corpus.

Table 3.6 *Variant distributions in Brazilian Portuguese by age*

	18–29		30–39		40–49		50–59		60+	
VARIANT	N	%	N	%	N	%	N	%	N	%
falar	90	38%	158	55%	111	61%	71	51%	248	54%
zero	79	33%	76	26%	38	21%	46	33%	121	26%
falar assim	18	8%	20	7%	19	10%	11	8%	35	8%
speaker-centered	10	4%	14	5%	4	2%	3	2%	15	3%
tipo	8	3%	1	0%	0	0%	0	0%	0	0%
assim	2	1%	1	0%	2	1%	1	1%	3	0%
dizer	2	1%	1	0%	1	1%	0	0%	10	2%
other	27	11%	17	6%	7	4%	6	4%	31	7%
TOTALS	236		288		182		138		463	

Table 3.7 *Variant distributions in Italian by age*

	18–25		25–39		40–50		60+	
VARIANT	N	%	N	%	N	%	N	%
dire	32	63%	130	65%	173	68%	106	65%
zero	12	24%	37	18%	57	22%	46	28%
fare	5	10%	14	7%	13	5%	10	6%
speaker-centered	1	2%	11	5%	5	2%	0	0%
other	1	2%	9	4%	8	3%	2	1%
TOTALS	51		201		256		164	

Though the token count is low in the 18–25 age group, meriting cautious interpretation of these data, the proportionally dominant variants in this age division and all others are *dire* 'say' and *zero*. *Fare* 'do', the next most frequent variant across the board, albeit a decidedly minority form in the system as a whole, has been identified as a possible innovation in spoken Italian (Guardamagna 2010: 66). Although it is marginally more common in the younger age cohorts shown in Table 3.7, especially in the 18–25 age range, the data are too limited to substantiate any inference of change in progress. Nor does this variant exhibit meaningful correlations with any other extra-linguistic concomitant of change such as speaker sex, where rates (not shown) are evenly partitioned across males and females. Moreover, as in the case of French *faire*, the use of *fare* in a quotative function is documented in older varieties of Italian, particularly as an introducer of non-propositional content (Guaradamagna 2010: 68), essentially invalidating it as a newcomer to the Italian quotative system. Insofar as *fare* is engaged in change, this would seem to involve its extension beyond prototypical mimetic contexts, where it introduces gestures, ideophones, and non-linguistic sound, as in example (15), to reporting externally realized speech (see Guardamagna 2010), as in example (16). Inspection of variant use according to content of the quote (not shown) reveals that, as per earlier descriptions, its niche function resides in its capacity to introduce non-lexicalized sounds (i.e., expressive content), whereas it accounts for only a limited proportion of the contexts associated with externally realized speech, much more likely to be introduced by *dire* or *zero*.

To summarize, the volatility that researchers have detected in the quotative system of multiple languages, most visible in our results for Canadian French, finds little support in either the Brazilian Portuguese or the Italian corpora we examined.

3.8 Discussion and Conclusion

What have we learned from this comparative enterprise? Using an empirically accountable framework, we first discovered that the lexico-grammatical apparatus used to express quotation in the varieties we targeted is by no means limited to generic speech verbs and includes an array of non-canonical constructions derived from multiple (non-speech-based) sources. The fact that in several varieties the same source domains (e.g., markers of similarity and manner, generic action verbs, etc.; see Güldemann 2008: 372) give rise to similar constructions, though occurring at very disproportionate rates in the varieties concerned (compare *être comme* in Canadian French with *être comme ça* in Paris French), raises the possibility of *drift*, or parallel autonomous development, as an explanatory factor accounting for structural similarities found in geographically very distant varieties (e.g., European vs. Canadian French). This does not necessarily preclude the possibility that an innovation found in geographically discontinuous varieties may be the product of diffusion rather than independent parallel development. Our analyses of *être comme* in Quebec and Acadian French, however, sound a cautionary note that the "same" innovation does not migrate "wholesale" to different varieties but is sensitive to idiosyncratic linguistic constraints imposed by locally situated variable systems (see Buchstaller and D'Arcy 2009).

At the core of our investigation lies the contentious issue of parallel cross-linguistic change in the quotative system. Table 3.8 summarizes our major quantitative findings in relation to this question (omitting Italian on account of the paucity of relevant data indicating linguistic change).

Table 3.8 is based on a modified four-stage taxonomy of change proposed by Nevalainen and Raumolin-Brunberg (2003: 55), correlating with the different stages depicted in (idealized) S-shaped representations of linguistic change. We stress that our own addition of the embryonic category to this taxonomy is simply intended as a heuristic to tentatively capture – rather than firmly endorse – *possible* changes at a very nascent stage of development.

Table 3.8 *Summary of major findings in relation to the rate of change exhibited by quotative innovations in French and Brazilian Portuguese*

CORPUS/ VARIANT	EMBRYONIC (Below 5%)	INCIPIENT (5%–15%)	NEW & VIGOROUS (15%–35%)	MID-RANGE (36%–65%)
(Quebec French 2014, 2019) *être comme*				✔
(Acadian French 2013) *être comme*		✔		
(Acadian French 2019) *être comme*				✔
(Eur. French CFPP 2005–2012) *être là/genre*	✔			
(Quebec French 2014, 2019) *être là/genre*	✔			
(Braz. Portuguese SP 2010) *tipo*	✔			

The central finding to emerge from this comparison is that *être comme* in urban varieties of Quebec and Acadian French qualifies as the only mid-range change that we detected, resulting in the relegation of long-standing covariants such as *dire* 'say' to a less central role in the quotative system. As far as we can ascertain, a similar change is unfolding in rural Acadian French, albeit one that remains relatively incipient according to the metrics operationalized in Table 3.8.

Aside from *être comme*, every other candidate for change is classified as "embryonic" based on their quantitative correlates, a result that is somewhat difficult to reconcile with the thesis that *simultaneous parallel developments* are purportedly affecting the quotative systems of multiple languages. With the exception of *être comme* in Canadian French, why should our quantitatively informed findings for other candidates for change diverge from the received wisdom that the quotative system is the locus of "fervent productivity" (Buchstaller 2014: 12)? We cannot rule out that the quality of our data has somehow impeded our detection of innovation, although our sources were exhaustively searched for relevant signs of change. Nor would we claim that our investigation, limited as it is to specific geographical varieties, can do full justice to other varieties of French, (Brazilian) Portuguese, or Italian, where quotative change may be aggressively unfolding – an issue that would benefit from further empirical investigation. Though our findings do not provide sufficient cause to retract claims of cross-linguistic change in the quotative system, we submit that empirically accountable studies of the type pursued in this chapter are indispensable to analysts seeking to bridge the gap between their *intuitions* about linguistic change and the actual *existence and distribution* of change found in authentic community-based speech data (see Poplack and Torres Cacoullos 2015: 287).

4 Cross-Linguistic Variation in Spoken Discourse Markers
Distribution, Functions, and Domains

Liesbeth Degand, Zoé Broisson, Ludivine Crible, and Karolina Grzech

4.1 Introduction

According to Du Bois (1985: 363), "Grammars code best what speakers do most." What speakers do a lot is use discourse markers (DMs). In spontaneous conversation, speakers use approximately one DM every twelve words in French and one DM every eighteen words in English (Crible 2018). Yet, despite an impressive quantity of work starting in the early 1980s, the linguistic description of DMs remains scattered, first and foremost because it is a very heterogeneous linguistic category, fulfilling many different functions in discourse (for recent overviews, see Maschler and Schiffrin 2015; Blühdorn et al. 2017). This has led to a multitude of case studies on particular DMs in a diversity of languages but much less to a categorical description of DMs as a linguistic class (some exceptions are Fraser 1999; Fischer 2014; Crible 2018). To gain deeper insight into this complex linguistic category, we believe more systematic cross-linguistic work is needed based on authentic data. Indeed, corpora reflect best how we use language in different situational settings, and corpora of spontaneous speech are probably the most accurate outcome of the cognitive processes underlying language production. Thus, looking at *how* we use DMs is a crucial step in finding out *why* we use them. This is where discourse annotation comes into play as a method to enrich corpus data with linguistic and extra-linguistic information in order to uncover patterns of language use. While some of these patterns are language-specific, others are shared cross-linguistically, thus informing of inherent linguistic properties. In this chapter, we present a functional annotation scheme of DMs (Crible and Degand 2019a) on the basis of which we analyze the variation in use and functions of a broad bottom-up selection of DMs across four languages from different typological families, namely French and Spanish (Romance), English (Germanic), and Polish (Slavic). Results indicate that the multilingual annotation scheme may be applied validly to the four different languages. This makes it possible to uncover both similarities and divergences in the functional and semantic distribution of DMs.

4.2 Annotating DMs in Spoken Languages

Discourse annotation consists in enriching corpus data with information regarding phenomena beyond the clause. Thus, depending on the research question, the need to locate and extract the relevant data before analyzing and interpreting it may arise. Examples of discourse phenomena for which annotation schemes have been developed include information structure (e.g., Calhoun et al. 2005), argument structure (Marcus et al. 1993, Palmer et al. 2005), speech acts (Kirk 2016), reference (e.g., Garside 1993; Stede 2016), fluency and disfluency cues (e.g., Shriberg 1994; Crible et al. 2019), but the most prolific work is in the annotation of discourse relations and their markers. Many different taxonomies exist, operationalized in as many discourse annotation schemes, mainly for written (Carlson et al. 2001; Prasad et al. 2008; Afantenos et al. 2012; Scholman et al. 2016) but also for spoken data (Tonelli et al. 2010; Crible and Degand 2019a). Reliable DM annotation is a highly challenging task (Spooren and Degand 2010; Stede and Pelszus 2012; Halbe 2013; Taboada and Das 2013; Crible and Degand 2019b). This difficulty is linked both to the inherent complexity of discourse annotation and to the linguistic phenomenon under scrutiny, here the discourse marker category itself.

Ideally, discourse annotation schemes should meet four different objectives in order to be of benefit for linguistic analysis. They should be (1) fine-grained; (2) reliable; (3) theoretically sound; and (4) cognitively realistic. In other words, the ideal discourse annotation scheme provides information that is precise and fine-grained enough to allow for detailed linguistic analyses. It is also designed in view of maximal reliability warranting replicable and unbiased results and allowing objective comparison when the model is applied to different types of data (different languages, different registers), thus promoting reusability. Basing the annotation scheme on theoretically sound foundations has the advantage of bringing empirical evidence to theoretical findings, thus strengthening our linguistic models and theories. Finally, in order to bridge the gap between corpus-based work and psycholinguistic research on language processing, a cognitively realistic annotation scheme will favor fruitful multidisciplinary and multi-method studies. The aim is thus to find the balance between methodological elegance and cognitive soundness (see Schmid 2012: 4–5).

Discourse annotation, and specifically DM annotation, also faces the specific challenges of working with spoken language. While written DM annotation, usually referred to as (discourse) connective annotation (e.g., Prasad et al. 2008), is generally restricted to the annotation of lexical cues marking discourse relations, spoken DM annotation involves a wider class, both in terms of (syntactic) forms (conjunctions, adverbs, prepositional phrases, verbal phrases, interjections, and more) and their spectrum of functions, such as topic-related functions, interpersonal functions, or speaker-oriented functions, reflecting the speaker's difficulty in the production process. In general, the functional spectrum of DMs is larger in spoken language and there is more often simultaneous multifunctionality (Crible and Cuenca 2017). Speech is also characterized by contextual and co-textual features complicating the annotator's task. Among these, there are interruptions, missing context, inaudible context, bleached meaning, and more ambiguity in general. Yet, since spoken language is not inherently different from written language (or vice versa), we believe it is important that any annotation model of spoken language be comparable with models for written data.

4.3 A Two-Dimensional Account of Discourse Markers

The model we use in this study was originally developed for spoken French and then extended to English. An up-to-date presentation is given in Crible and Degand (2019a, 2019b).[1] Here, we focus on the model's main characteristics.

First, the annotation model follows a marker-based approach. In other words, the focus of the annotation process is on the linguistic expressions that function as DMs, not the relations underlying them. Such a functional description defines DMs as a grammatically heterogeneous, syntactically optional, polyfunctional type of pragmatic marker. Their specificity is to function on a meta-discursive level as procedural cues to constrain the interpretation of the host unit in a co-built representation of ongoing discourse. They do so by either signaling a discourse relation between the host unit and its context, making the structural sequencing of discourse segments explicit, expressing the speaker's meta-comment on their phrasing, or contributing to the speaker–hearer relationship (Crible 2018: 62).

As such, the annotation model is meant to cover the whole category of DMs, accounting for its full functional spectrum. This makes it suitable for categorical studies, which investigate the behavior of DMs as a linguistic category, but less so for case studies, which tease apart all the subtle meaning differences of a specific DM. Identification of DMs in the data is determined by a number of core features, namely syntactic optionality, procedural meaning, invariability, and discourse-level scope (see, e.g., Crible 2018).

---

[1] The present study used a slightly different version of the scheme as it was in its development phase.

To account for the functional spectrum of DMs, the model proposes two independent dimensions of analysis. On the one hand, DMs are coded according to the discourse domain in which they work, corresponding to the speaker's communicative intention. The question at stake is: What aspect of discourse is the marker targeting? Is it relating events in the world (ideational domain), linking mental states or attitudes (rhetorical domain), structuring the discourse (sequential domain), or managing speaker–hearer interaction (interpersonal domain)? Independently from the domain annotation, DMs are attributed a discourse function corresponding to the specific contribution of the marker to the given context (one of fifteen functions among which [consequence], [addition], [temporal], [specification], [contrast], ...). Examples (1) through (4) illustrate how the DM *donc* 'so' can be used to express the function [consequence] in the four domains.

(1) *euh Dreyfus donc euh a valu on va dire à Zola euh de s/ d'émigrer en en Angleterre pourquoi parce qu'on on lui a reproché son intervention peut-être un peu trop radicale euh et **donc** Zola euh Zola va devoir partir euh parce que peut-être a-t-il été trop franc*
uh Dreyfus caused let's say Zola uh to emigrate in England why because he was criticized for his intervention maybe a little too radical uh and **donc** 'so' Zola uh Zola will have to leave uh because maybe he was too frank [ideational domain] (LOCAS-F, conv-f_2)

(2) *c'est pas évident quand euh on n'a que le _ que le CESS _ **donc** euh je me dis que peut-être euh à la recherche d'une euh d'une formation*
'it's not easy when uh you only you only went to high school **donc** 'so' uh I think that maybe uh looking for some training [rhetorical domain] (LOCAS-F, conv-f_1)

(3) *et donc voilà **donc** euh _ suite à ça ben j'avais con/ j'ai continué les cours et puis euh*
and so that's it **donc** 'so' uh after this well I took the classes again and then uh [sequential domain] (LOCAS-F, conv-f_1)

(4) *<speaker1> euh enfin je n- ça ne me convenait pas **donc** euh <speaker2> et qu'est-ce qui s'est passé?*
<speaker1> uh well I it didn't work for me donc 'so' uh <speaker2> and what happened? [interpersonal domain] (LOCAS-F, conv-f_1)

In (1), the fact that Zola moved to England is the direct, factual consequence of his involvement in Dreyfus's case. In (2) the speaker concludes that she should look for training on the basis of a fact (she does not have a superior degree), and this conclusion uses evaluative language ("maybe," "I think") and hesitation markers ("uh"), which testifies of its epistemic, rhetorical nature. In (3), *donc* is used in the context of hesitations and helps the speaker restart after a short interruption, taking up her previous narrative. In (4), the consequence is left open, to be reconstructed by the other speaker, as signaled by the turn-final position and the suspensive intonation.

This model combines the strengths of attested semantically driven taxonomies (see Prasad et al. 2014) with the flexibility of domain or discourse-level oriented approaches (Schiffrin 1987; Sweetser 1990). It allows a simultaneous account in terms of polyfunctionality (i.e., the fact that a marker can be used in different domains) and polysemy (i.e., the fact that a marker can express different senses), two aspects that are intrinsically bound to the use of DMs in context. This aligns with Schiffrin's (1987: 325) seminal observation that

[i]t is because discourse is multiply structured, and its various components integrated with each other, that multiple relations hold between utterances – not because markers themselves realize a different function (one devoted to ideas, one to action, and so on) with each occasion of use. (Schiffrin 1987: 325)

Theoretically, every domain-function combination is possible, yet systematic corpus analysis should make out which combinations are attested across languages and registers.

4.4 French, Spanish, English, and Polish Discourse in Contrast

The taxonomy with two independent levels of analysis was applied to spoken unplanned dialogues in four languages from three typologically distinct families: French and Spanish (Romance), English (Germanic), and Polish (Slavic). For each language, we annotated a comparable dataset of approximately 30 minutes of conversational speech, amounting to 5,000–6,000 words. Data for English was extracted from the British component of the International Corpus of English (ICE-GB) (Nelson et al. 2002). For French, we used the Louvain Corpus of Annotated Speech–French (LoCAS-F) (Degand et al. 2014), with recordings from France and Belgium. Spanish (Peninsular) data came from the spoken component of the Backbone corpus (Kohn 2012) and the Polish data from the spoken corpus from the Polish CLARIN infrastructure (Pęzik 2015). Annotators used sound-aligned transcripts and the sound was available during annotation. Both French and Polish were double-blind annotated, while the English and Spanish data were analyzed by only one annotator.

The first step in the coding process consists in identifying the DMs in the four datasets following the criteria mentioned in Section 4.3: syntactic optionality, procedural meaning, invariability, and discourse-level scope. This step resulted in the identification of 286 DMs in English (30 types), 442 DMs in French (35 types), 690 DMs in Spanish (71 types), and 847 DMs in Polish (79 types). All segments containing a DM were extracted with context and were assigned one domain and one function, making use of an operationalized coding scheme.

Table 4.1 *Taxonomy of domains and functions (Crible and Degand 2019b)*

ideational	rhetorical	sequential	interpersonal
[addition] [alternative]	[cause] [concession]	[condition] [consequence]	[contrast] [punctuation]
	[specification]	[temporal] [topic]	

For this study, the taxonomy used is presented in Table 4.1, based on Crible and Degand (2019b). In view of the results of the present contrastive analysis, it was slightly revised in later work (Crible and Degand 2019a).

A total of 442 DMs were consensually identified by 2 annotators in the French dataset. After the first annotation training phase, agreement on domains was 71 percent (314/442) and 78 percent (343/443) for functions. Thus, it appears that functions are easier to code, since they are closer to the DMs' core meaning. After discussion of all disagreements, a revised operational coding scheme was established that led to an improved agreement of 84 percent for the domains and 83 percent for the functions. This coding scheme was used for the four languages under scrutiny.

4.4.1 French Discourse Markers in Spontaneous Interaction

Table 4.2 illustrates that DM use is unevenly distributed over domains and functions in the French dataset, with 50 percent of the DMs being used in the sequential domain, followed by the rhetorical domain (30.5 percent) and the ideational (9.9 percent) and interpersonal (9.5 percent) domains at some fair distance. The imbalance is also present in the frequency of functions fulfilled by the DMs. All functions appear to be distributed unevenly over the four domains, and most of them have a privileged domain in which they come to expression (highlighted in Table 4.2). Strikingly, the function [condition] was not used in this subcorpus of spontaneous face-to-face interaction, while the functions [contrast] and [topic] are hardly used and occur only in the ideational and sequential domains, respectively.

A further imbalance in the data comes from the highly diverging frequencies with which the different functions are expressed by means of DMs. In French spontaneous interaction, the most frequent DM function is [punctuation] amounting to 26 percent of the DM uses. In other words, in a quarter of the cases speakers use DMs in a semantically vaguely defined way as "discourse punctuators," corresponding to a kind of typographical comma, as illustrated with the use of *hein* 'right' in example (5).

Table 4.2 *Distribution of DMs across domains and functions in the French dataset (dominant functions are highlighted)*

Function	Domain				Total
	Ideational	Rhetorical	Sequential	Interpersonal	
punctuation	0	3	**78**	33	114
addition	8	10	**65**	0	83
concession	1	**51**	22	7	81
consequence	6	**31**	12	1	50
alternative	3	11	**21**	0	35
specification	0	13	12	0	25
temporal	**22**	0	2	0	24
cause	0	**16**	0	1	17
topic	0	0	**9**	0	9
contrast	4	0	0	0	4
condition	0	0	0	0	0
Total	44	135	221	42	442

(5) *j'avais déjà hésité **hein** donc entre euh enfin entre institutrice primaire ou euh GRH* (LOCAS-F, conv-f_1)
I had already hesitated hein ('right') donc ('well') over uhm enfin ('like') over primary school teacher and uhm HR

Further qualitative analysis of the data shows that the expression of the function [punctuation] actually comes on the account of four (nearly) monosemous DMs, adding up together to 84 percent of the DM spectrum for this function, namely the already mentioned *hein* (17/17), *quoi* (17/17), *bon* (36/36), and *ben* (26/28) (see Table 4.3). In other words, French seems to have developed specific semantically vague DMs that are used to punctuate speakers' discourse, thus indicating their will to hold the floor, weakly structuring their discourse while planning. Comparison with the other languages will make clear whether this is a specific idiosyncratic French phenomenon or whether it might be specific to the register under analysis.

Table 4.3 displays the DM types used to express the different DM functions in the taxonomy. The most frequent DM types per function are highlighted in bold, and DMs expressing more than one function are underlined. It clearly appears that there is no one-to-one mapping between DM types and the functions they express, even if most markers seem to be more dedicated to expressing one function depending on the core meaning they express. Thus, *et* 'and' is a typical additional marker, *mais* 'but' a typical concessive marker, and *donc* 'so' is most often used to express consequence. This by no means makes these markers monosemous, however. Notwithstanding the fairly limited

Table 4.3 *Distribution of DM types over discourse functions in the French dataset*

Function	DM types
punctuation	**bon**, **ben**, **quoi**, **hein**, voilà, beh, eh ben, tu vois, <u>alors</u>, eh bien, là, allez
addition	**et**, **puis**, <u>alors</u>, en plus, <u>même</u>
concession	**mais**, <u>en fait</u>, pourtant, bien que, quoique, <u>même</u>, en même temps, quand même, encore que, après, maintenant
consequence	**donc**, <u>alors</u>, <u>enfin</u>
alternative	**enfin**, ou, <u>alors</u>
temporal	**puis**, <u>et</u>, <u>alors</u>
cause	**parce que**
specification	<u>enfin</u>, <u>mais</u>, <u>en fait</u>, <u>donc</u>, <u>ben</u>, <u>alors</u>
topic	<u>et</u>, <u>alors</u>, <u>donc</u>, <u>puis</u>
contrast	<u>mais</u>

dataset, it is noteworthy to observe that only three functions ([punctuation], [concession], [cause]) attract mainly specific (monosemous) DM types, while the other functions are expressed mainly by means of polysemous DM types (underlined in Table 4.3).

Taking into account DM types with a raw frequency of ten and more (covering 90.7 percent of the tokens), Figure 4.1 suggests that high frequency goes hand in hand with high polyfunctionality (use in more than one discourse domain), with

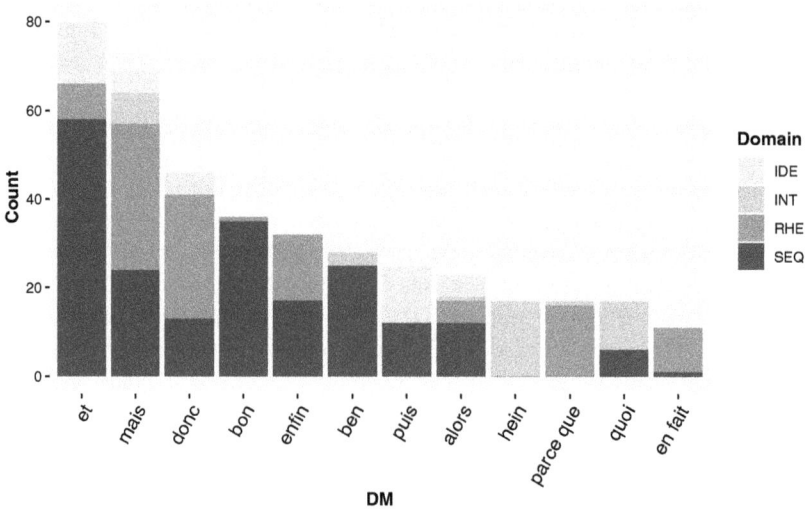

Figure 4.1 Frequency and polyfunctionality of DM use in the French dataset

the exception of the interpersonal DM *hein* 'right.' Whether this correlation holds cross-linguistically needs to be confirmed in the remainder of this study.

4.4.2 Spanish Discourse Markers in Spontaneous Interaction

The second Romance language under investigation in this study is Spanish. As can be observed in Table 4.4, DM tokens are also unevenly distributed across both domains and functions in this sample. Similarly to French, the sequential domain is the most represented, with 39.1 percent of the tokens. Conversely, however, the interpersonal domain is more frequent and ranks second, with 30.6 percent of all tokens, followed by rhetorical (19.8 percent) and ideational DMs (10.4 percent). The interpersonal domain thus appears to play a more prominent role in Spanish, which suggests that DMs in conversational Spanish may be more diversified than in French and are often used as a means to manage the interactivity of an exchange besides structuring it.

Zooming in, functions also appear to be unevenly distributed, and this both generally in the sample and across the four domains. Seven functions show a preference for one domain over the others (highlighted in Table 4.4). Once again, [punctuation] is found to be the most frequent function, representing approximately a third of the total number of identified DMs (34 percent). More than half of its instances are associated with the interpersonal domain, as illustrated in example (6).

Table 4.4 *Distribution of DMs across domains and functions in the Spanish dataset*

Function	Domain				Total
	Ideational	Rhetorical	Sequential	Interpersonal	
Punctuation	0	0	87	**148**	235
Addition	12	14	**66**	19	111
Specification	7	**48**	23	21	99
Consequence	10	**23**	9	8	50
Topic	0	1	**47**	0	48
Concession	6	**24**	5	4	39
Temporal	6	10	9	4	29
Contrast	**14**	5	6	3	28
Cause	6	10	4	4	24
Alternative	8	0	10	0	18
Condition	3	2	4	0	9
Total	72	137	270	211	690

(6) No, **hombre**, después de la carrera supongo que tendré que hacer la oposición (Backbone bb_es021)
No, **hombre** ('man'), after my degree I suppose I'll have to do teacher training

The most frequent functions of Spanish DMs are the same as in the French data (i.e., [addition], [concession], and [consequence]). In the Spanish sample, [specification] DMs are better represented and seem to be particularly typical of the rhetorical domain, such as in example (7).

(7) ... la oportunidad de viajar, de conocer otros investigadores, otros sitios, **es decir**, otras experiencias, ¿no? (Backbone bb_es012)
... the opportunity to travel, to meet other researchers, to discover new places, **in other words** new experiences, right?

When examining frequent discourse functions in the Spanish data, [punctuation] and [specification] stand out as functions that come in many different DM types, as reported in Table 4.5. While *pues*, *no*, and *bueno* are not restricted to [punctuation], *por ejemplo* and *es decir* are typical as well as exclusive representatives of [specification]. Here, the case of [punctuation] is particularly interesting, as DMs labeled with this function tend to be monosemous in French (and in English, as will be described in Section 4.4.3). Functions that express basic discourse relations such as [addition] and [consequence] are mainly

Table 4.5 *Distribution of DM types over discourse functions in the Spanish dataset*

Function	DM types
Punctuation	***pues***, ***no***, ***bueno***, *la verdad*, *muy bien*, *claro*, *y*, <u>*en fin*</u>, *ya*, *y demás*, *bien*, *hombre*, <u>*no sé*</u>, *nada*, <u>*o*</u>, <u>*ahora*</u>, *a lo mejor*, *a ver*, *de acuerdo*, <u>*entonces*</u>, *perfecto*, <u>*pero*</u>, *por cierto*, *por lo menos*, *por supuesto*, <u>*sí*</u>, <u>*sobre todo*</u>, *vale*, *vamos*
Addition	*y*, *también*, *además*, *de hecho*, *pues*, *bueno*, *en verdad*, *la verdad*, <u>*luego*</u>, *pero después*, <u>*sobre todo*</u>, *tampoco*
Specification	***por ejemplo***, ***es decir***, *y*, <u>*la verdad*</u>, *a lo mejor*, *o sea*, *pues*, *a ver*, *así*, <u>*no*</u>, <u>*o*</u>, <u>*sí*</u>, *a mí*, *a nivel*, *bueno*, <u>*en fin*</u>, *más bien*, <u>*no sé*</u>, *quizá*, <u>*sobre todo*</u>
Consequence	<u>*entonces*</u>, *y*, <u>*pues*</u>, *así*, *para luego*, *a mí*, *de hecho*, *por consiguiente*, *por eso*, *por lo tanto*
Topic	*y*, <u>*pero*</u>, <u>*ahora*</u>, *por otro lado*, *pero luego*
Concession	***pero***, *aunque*, *aún*, *ahí*, <u>*entonces*</u>, *no*, <u>*sino*</u>, *y*
Temporal	*y*, ***ahora (mismo)***, *a la hora*, *hoy en día*, <u>*luego*</u>, *siempre*, *cada vez*, *de momento*, *en principio*, <u>*entonces*</u>, *hoy*, *mañana*, *pronto*, *una vez que*
Contrast	*pero*, *y*, *sin embargo*, <u>*sino*</u>
Cause	*porque*, *ya que*, *por lo que*, <u>*luego*</u>
Alternative	<u>*o*</u>, *o bien*
Conditional	*si*

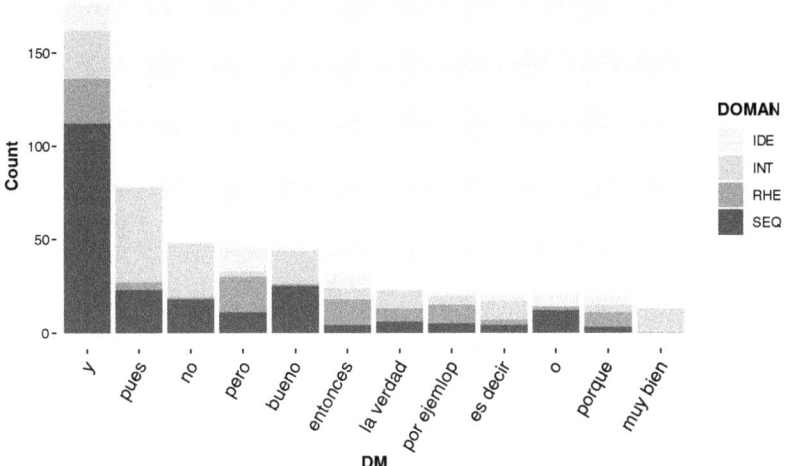

Figure 4.2 Frequency and polyfunctionality of DM use in the Spanish dataset

expressed by one DM type. Generally, the trends uncovered in the use of Spanish DMs coincide with those found for French and further suggest that there is no one-to-one mapping between DM types and functions.

We next focus on the twelve DM types with a raw frequency of ten or more ($N=543$, 78.7 percent). Figure 4.2 displays signs of a positive relationship between frequency and polyfunctionality (across domains), similar to the French data. In terms of polysemy, however, most Spanish DMs express one main function only, with the notable exception of the DM *y* 'and', which occurs in all four domains and across a total of eight functions. At the other end of the spectrum, *muy bien* is only found as the combination of the interpersonal domain and the [punctuation] function.

Overall, this first analysis of Spanish data using Crible and Degand's (2019b) taxonomy reveals that much like in French, Spanish markers produced in spontaneous settings operate in both relational and interactive aspects of discourse. The latter include the more speech-specific domains and functions of the taxonomy, such as the sequential and interpersonal domains and the [punctuation] function all widely represented in the data, while the former correspond to the rhetorical domain and functions such as [addition], [consequence], and [concession]. While these results highlight similarities with French when it comes to the distribution of domains and functions, several differences between the two languages are also brought to light, particularly regarding the overall degree of polysemy of their respective frequent marker types.

Table 4.6 *Distribution of DMs across domains and functions in the English dataset*

Function	Domain				Total
	Ideational	Rhetorical	Sequential	Interpersonal	
Punctuation	0	0	39	48	87
Addition	20	2	48	0	70
Concession	0	32	10	0	42
Specification	0	18	15	0	33
Consequence	1	11	3	0	15
Contrast	7	1	3	0	11
Cause	0	11	0	0	11
Alternative	3	4	0	0	7
Condition	0	4	0	0	4
Topic	0	0	4	0	4
Temporal	0	0	2	0	2
Total	31	83	124	48	286

4.4.3 English Discourse Markers in Spontaneous Interaction

The English data shows the same imbalance as observed in the two Romance languages and a similar preference for the sequential domain, which takes up 43.36 percent of all DMs, as can be seen in Table 4.6.

The ranking of domains is closer to Spanish than to French, with a higher proportion of interpersonal uses of DMs, mainly expressed by the highly frequent *you know*. Almost all functions can be expressed in the rhetorical and/or sequential domains, whereas the interpersonal domain is restricted to the [punctuation] function, and the ideational domain mainly consists of [addition] and [contrast] uses. As in French and Spanish, some DM functions show one prevalent domain, but the distribution of domain–function combinations seems more balanced than in Romance languages, with smaller differences between domains for [addition], [punctuation], and [specification]. Similar to the French data, the most frequent function in this English sample is [punctuation], as in example (8).

(8) you can't actually rely on what he's going to have always (0.473) **you know** you think oh I'll uh **you know** I've got people coming I'll get some salmon (ICE-GB S1A-010)

Again, most DMs expressing the function of [punctuation] are monosemous, with the exception of *well*, which also shows some uses of [specification] (five cases) and [alternative] (one case). Like French, but unlike Spanish,

Table 4.7 *Distribution of DM types over discourse functions in the English dataset*

Function	DM types
punctuation	**_well_**, **_you know_**, *you see, look, yeah*
addition	**_and_**, *plus*
concession	**_but_**, *although*, _actually_, *though, even if*
specification	**_I mean_**, _well_, _actually_, *sort of,* _so_, *like, for instance, as it were, kind of, in fact*
consequence	**_so_**, *then*
contrast	**_but_**, **_and_**
cause	**_because_**, *insofar as*
alternative	*or*, **_well_**, **_I mean_**
topic	**_and_**, *now, anyway*
condition	*if*
temporal	*secondly, first of all*

[punctuation] tends to be expressed by semantically specialized DMs in English. The other frequent functions are quite similar to the other languages in their nature and ranking, as can be seen in Table 4.7.

Seven DMs, with ten occurrences or more, account for 58.5 percent of the data and their domain distribution is represented in Figure 4.3. In English, too, high frequency tends to be associated with high polyfunctionality (several domains) and high polysemy (several functions), with the exceptions of *you know* (exclusively interpersonal punctuation uses) and *because* (exclusively rhetorical causal uses). All other DMs in this subset express at least two domains and two functions, although there is always one dominant value. The most polyfunctional DM is *and* with three other values besides [addition]. All in all, while there is no one-to-one mapping between DMs and their functions, and DM polyfunctionality has been confirmed in this dataset, we can observe that the most frequent DM types in English are mainly used to express basic discourse relations as well as more speech-specific functions related to the management of the discourse flow and interaction.

4.4.4 Polish Discourse Markers in Spontaneous Interaction

In the Polish dataset, like in French, Spanish, and English, DMs are most often used sequentially (36.2 percent), as shown in Table 4.8. Second in line is the interpersonal domain (25.5 percent), while the ideational and rhetorical domains both take up around 19 percent of the DM use. As compared to the other languages in our dataset, the interpersonal domain is strongly represented. We do not believe that this higher frequency follows from an artifact of the data, as we were careful to work with comparable samples in the four

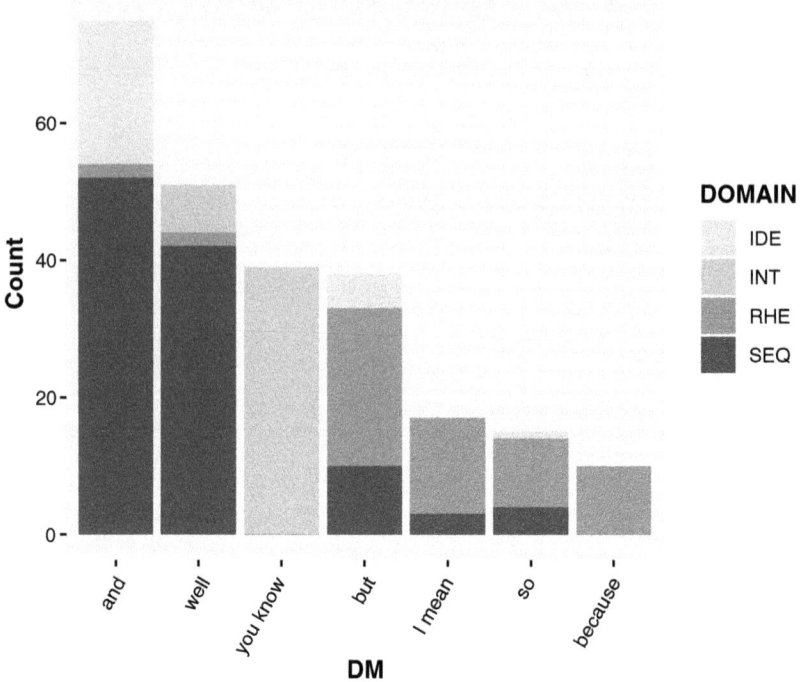

Figure 4.3 Frequency and polyfunctionality of DM use in the English dataset

languages, that is, informal, private, face-to-face conversations between two or more acquainted speech partners. Moreover, we do not think that corpus size is the main reason for this discrepancy either, since the analysis of larger datasets in English and French (Crible 2018) shows a similar weaker presence of the interpersonal domain. Possible explanations will be developed in Section 4.5.

Similar to English, only a few functions show one prevalent domain, while several others are frequent in two domains. The function of [punctuation] was the most frequent, with a large number of tokens in both the sequential and the interpersonal domains. Patterns of domain-function combinations are generally similar to the other languages in the study. All four domains of the taxonomy see the expression of a variety of functions in the Polish data. None of the domains can be said to be homogeneous with respect to the discourse functions of the DMs they cover.

Table 4.9 shows the distribution of DM types across the different functions, ordered according to their decreasing frequency in the sample. Each function is expressed through a heterogeneous set of DMs. The rich inventory of DM types

Table 4.8 *Distribution of DMs across domains and functions in the Polish dataset*

Function	Domain				Total
	Ideational	Rhetorical	Sequential	Interpersonal	
punctuation	3	3	153	144	303
addition	35	15	70	19	139
specification	18	37	35	12	102
topic	2	3	31	33	69
temporal	55	7	1	0	63
adversative*	13	32	4	8	57
cause	10	38	7	0	55
alternative	10	11	2	0	23
condition	11	10	1	0	22
consequence	3	8	3	0	14
Total	160	164	307	216	847

* [Concession] and [contrast] were merged into the [adversative] function after consideration of systematic disagreements between annotators.

within each function sets Polish apart from English and French and is more in line with the Spanish data. This may be due to the larger number of DM types attested in the analyzed sample (English: 30, French: 35, Spanish: 71, Polish: 79) and the larger number of tokens (English: 286, French: 442, Spanish: 690, Polish: 847), but this explanation is not convincing in comparison to the Spanish data.

Figure 4.4 shows how the Polish DM types, listed in Table 4.9, are distributed across the four discourse domains.

The marker type that stands out as the most frequent in the data is *wiesz* 'you know' (cf. Diskin-Holdaway, Chapter 9, this volume). It occurs 169 times, which constitutes almost 20 percent of all the DM tokens in the dataset. The occurrences of *wiesz* are distributed between the sequential (*N*=81) and the interpersonal (*N*=88) domain. Interestingly, the composite *wiesz co* 'you know what' patterns differently from *wiesz*. Rather than being polyfunctional, this marker is only attested in the interpersonal domain. On the other hand, while for *wiesz* the dominant function is [punctuation], attributed to 156 out of 169 tokens of the DM in the sample, *wiesz co* is more polysemous (several functions).

Polysemy is by no means unique to *wiesz co*. In the analyzed dataset, only two of the seventeen frequent DM types are monosemous, namely *potem* 'then'/'after', *no nie* (roughly translatable as 'you know', but literally meaning 'well no'). Apart from being a strictly [temporal] DM, *potem* is also only

Table 4.9 *Distribution of DM types over discourse functions in the Polish dataset*

Function	DM Types
punctuation	**wiesz**, *no*, *no nie*, *nie*, *słuchaj*, *tak*, *to*, *no to*, *wiesz co*, *a*, *po prostu*, *prawda*, *w ogóle*, *znaczy*
addition	*i*, *no*, *a*, *słuchaj*, *jeszcze*, *no to*, *bo*, *poza tym*, *aż*, *to*, *tylko*, *wiesz*, *wiesz co*, *z resztą*, *ale*, *e*, *gdzie*, *i w ogóle*, *nie dosyć że* ... *to jeszcze*, *no słuchaj*, *po prostu*, *tak*, *w każdym razie*, *w ogóle*, *że*
specification	**no**, *to*, *w ogóle*, *na przykład*, *to znaczy*, *wiesz*, *po prostu*, *znaczy*, *ale*, *bo*, *i*, *jeszcze*, *no to*, *wiesz co*, *a*, *i tak dalej*, *tylko*, *ale to*, *byle by*, *czekaj*, *jak*, *nawet*, *oczywiście*, *patrz*, *poza tym*, *przecież*, *tak*, *tak że*, *tak że wiesz*, *w końcu*, *więc*, *właściwie*, *z resztą*
topic	**słuchaj**, *a*, **no**, **wiesz co**, *wiesz*, *to*, *ale*, *bo*, *i wiesz*, *na przykład*, *naprawdę*, *no i*, *no i tak*, *no słuchaj*, *no to*, *no to słuchaj*, *no wiesz*, *o*, *patrz*, *tak*, *tak że*, *w ogóle*
temporal	**jak**, **potem**, **jak ... to ...**, *wtedy*, *najpierw*, *jak ... no to ...*, *kiedy*, *teraz*, *a*, *co*, *co ... to ...*, *jak tylko*, *po*, *po czym*, *to*
adversative	**ale**, *a*, *przecież*, *tylko*, *a tam*, *bo*, *e*, *gdzie tam*, *nie*, *nie no*, *no*, *słuchaj*, *tylko że*, *wprawdzie*, *z tym że*, *żeby*
cause	**bo**, *dlatego że*, *to*, *żeby*, *jak ... to ...*, *ponieważ*, *więc*
alternative	*a*, *ale*, *znaczy*, *bo*, *albo*, *chyba że*, *czy*, *natomiast*, *teraz*
condition	**jak ... to ...**, **jak**, *jakby*, *to*, *a*, *chyba że*, *jak*, *jeżeli*, *tak*
consequence	*to*, *żeby*, *no to*, *tak że*, *jak ... to ...*, *no*

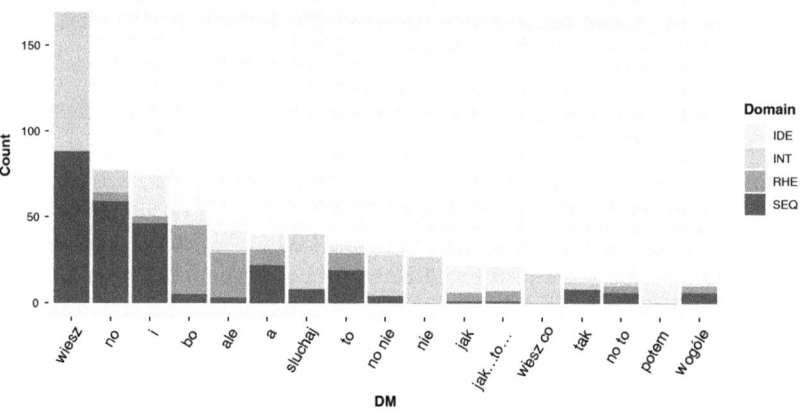

Figure 4.4 Frequency and polyfunctionality of DM use in the Polish dataset

attested in the ideational domain. Thus, it is the only DM type in the data that is not only monofunctional but also monosemous. The only other marker in the dataset that is nearly monofunctional and monosemous is *nie* 'no' (homophonous with the Polish negative particle). All its twenty-seven tokens occur in the interpersonal domain. Out of these, twenty-six serve the function of [punctuation] and only one serves the [adversative] function.

Comparing the polyfunctionality of the Polish DMs with that of the other languages, the strikingly high number of (frequent) DM types used interpersonally stands out. Polish counts no less than nine DM types in the interpersonal domain, while French counts six, English only two. These are all outnumbered by Spanish with eleven DM types, which are, however, used less frequently token-wise.

4.5 Measuring the Crosslinguistic Distribution of DMs across Domains and Functions

It is now time to investigate to what extent the two-dimensional annotation model makes it possible to uncover (sometimes hidden) similarities and divergences between the four languages under study. Figure 4.5 visualizes the DM domain distribution across French, Spanish, English, and Polish. In general terms, speakers across the four languages use DMs in similar ways. The most frequent domain of use is the sequential one. Thus, in spontaneous spoken face-to-face interaction, speakers use DMs in the first place to structure and organize their discourse. In the second place, DMs serve to express the speakers' rhetorical attitude and stance toward the message they are conveying. Third, speakers use DMs to maintain and manage the speaker–hearer relation during

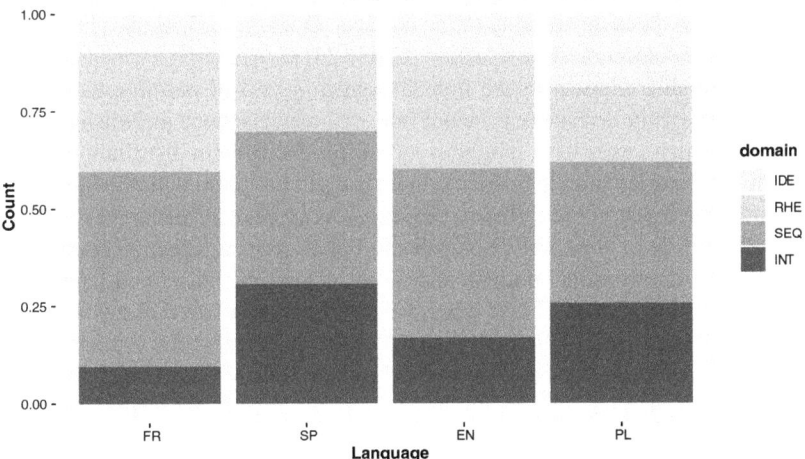

Figure 4.5 Cross-linguistic domain distribution of discourse markers

the interaction. These three general uses of DMs are all metalinguistic in nature and form the bulk of speakers' choices to make use of a DM. The least frequent use across the four languages is the ideational domain, that is, to relate discourse segments semantically and in terms of content.

Zooming in, this distribution appears to be cross-linguistically diverging in a statistically significant way (χ^2=126.1, df=9, p<0.001). More precisely, an examination of the standardized residuals shows that, compared to the other languages, French stands out with its low rate of interpersonal DMs and, conversely, high frequency of rhetorical and sequential DMs. By contrast, Spanish shows a significantly higher frequency of interpersonal DMs. Polish DMs show a particularly large proportion of ideational uses and a lower proportion of rhetorical uses. The English data does not strongly differ from the other languages. DM domains reflect the speaker's communicative intentions. Given that all samples in the study correspond to very similar communicative contexts, such discrepancies in the results were not expected. Several explanations come to mind.

The first explanation is methodological. The annotation of the four languages was performed independently from one another. In other words, even if the annotation procedure was the same in the four languages, it is possible that they were not applied in exactly the same way throughout the four datasets. What is at stake here is the reliability of subtle contextual interpretations, which have been shown to be fragile when it comes to distinguishing between the sequential and the rhetorical domains as well as between the ideational and the rhetorical domains (Spooren and Degand 2010; Crible and Degand 2019b). These are precisely the domains where French and Polish show a discrepant distribution pattern. The second explanation is also methodological in nature and concerns the comparability of the datasets. Domains of DM use are tightly bound to the communicative situation (Crible 2018). Although we have tried to use comparable datasets in the four languages, it is still possible that these situations slightly diverge (e.g., more informal conversations in Polish than in French), which might have (slightly) influenced the domain distribution.

The third explanation is linguistic in nature and has to do with the linguistic potential available in the different languages to express the different domains by means of DMs. Strikingly, Spanish and Polish show a higher proportion of DMs in the interpersonal domain and, at the same time, these two languages also have a higher stock of DM types that are (frequently) used in this domain, viz. eleven and nine, respectively. We therefore suggest that the availability of DMs that are (more) typical of a specific domain influence how likely a given speaker is to use that domain. Put more simply, if a given language has more interpersonal DMs to offer, speakers will use this domain more. Examining the discrepancies observed between French and Polish, the same line of reasoning holds for the ideational domain, where thirteen different DM types are used ideationally in Polish *versus* five DM types in French. For the rhetorical domain, however, such a relation is not found, since the two languages show a similar number of frequent DM types used in this domain (ten for Polish, eight for French). We should keep in mind here, however, that the total number of DM tokens analyzed in the two languages is very different (442 for French, 847 in Polish), making the comparison skewed because of the frequency impact. Notwithstanding this difference in the data, we would like to suggest that investigating the relation between the linguistic DM potential of a language and their domains of use is a promising avenue for further research.

As regards the expression of DM functions across the four discourse domains, we also observe a number of cross-linguistic similarities and differences. Recall that the two-dimensional annotation scheme foresees that, in principle, all DM functions can combine with all four DM domains. In the present study, we coded our data making use of eleven functions. Table 4.10 displays the domain–function mappings across the four languages studied. The domain–function mappings that are realized in all four languages are marked by the check symbol (✓), when the mapping is attested in all languages but one, the missing language is indicated preceded by the negation symbol (≠), when only one or two languages attest the domain–function mapping, these languages are mentioned.

Table 4.10 shows only two empty cells, viz. interpersonal [alternative] and interpersonal [condition], which were not expressed by a DM in any of the four languages. This is not to say that alternative or conditional DMs are never used

Table 4.10 *Cross-linguistic distribution of DM functions across discourse domains*

Function	Domain			
	Ideational	Rhetorical	Sequential	Interpersonal
Addition	✓	✓	✓	SP/PO
Alternative	✓	≠SP	≠EN	∅
Cause	SP/PO	✓	SP/PO	FR/SP
Concession*	≠EN	✓	✓	≠EN
Condition	SP/PO	≠FR	SP/PO	∅
Consequence	✓	✓	✓	FR/SP
Contrast*	✓	SP/EN	SP/EN	SP
Punctuation	PO	FR/PO	✓	✓
Specification	SP/PO	✓	✓	SP/PO
Temporal	≠EN	SP/PO	≠FR	SP
Topic	PO	SP/PO	✓	PO

* The function [adversative] that was used for the Polish data was recategorized here as Concession.

interpersonally in these languages, but in any case, this use would be very rare. In contrast, no fewer than sixteen cells in Table 4.10 are realized for all four languages, and an additional six cells are filled for three languages (the cells mention the language that does not attest the mapping). Thus, across the four languages, most discourse domains are compatible with several functions. In particular, the sequential domain is compatible with nearly all functions in the taxonomy across languages, whereas the interpersonal domain is the most restricted, since only two combinations are present in three or more languages, namely [punctuation] and [concession]. Cross-linguistically, it is noteworthy to observe that Spanish and Polish DMs very often express the same domain–function mappings.

Taking functions as a starting point, the two-dimensional approach also makes it possible to distinguish those functional meanings that are more tied to a specific domain and the ones that are more polyfunctional. Thus, the functions [addition], [alternative], [concession], and [consequence] are cross-linguistically realized in three of the four domains for three languages or more. Cross-linguistically, none of the functions is linked to a single domain, thus confirming the strength of the two-dimensional framework to describe the meaning and functions of DMs across languages. Of course, languages diverge in the means they provide to express these meanings and functions, balancing between functionally and semantically underdetermined DMs (DMs used in several domains and with several functions) and functionally and semantically very specific DMs (DMs used in a single domain and/or with a single function).

The results in Section 4.4 showed that the two-dimensional framework makes it possible to uncover detailed tendencies in the use of specific DMs. We believe that applying the method cross-linguistically opens up interesting perspectives in terms of DM equivalence across languages, a domain that has proven to be notoriously complex (Mortier and Degand 2009; Dupont and Zufferey 2017) as semantic meanings and contextual use do not always align across languages.

4.6 Conclusions

This contrastive study tested the validity of a two-dimensional annotation scheme for the domains and functions of discourse markers across four spoken languages with a different typological genus, namely English (Germanic), Polish (Slavic), French, and Spanish (Romance). The analysis shows that the model can be applied to all four languages in the sample and accurately depicts the polyfunctional behavior of discourse markers as well as allows for fine-grained observations of polysemy (several functions) and polyfunctionality (several domains). Of all the theoretically possible combinations of domains and functions, only two were not attested in any language. Our comparative findings reveal that discourse markers are primarily used to structure minor and major boundaries in the discourse flow in all languages (i.e., sequential domain) and least frequently used to relate objective facts (i.e., ideational domain). Discourse markers in all languages further share the ability to express multiple functions and domains in different contexts. The most striking difference in our dataset is the particularly high frequency of interpersonal uses of discourse markers in Spanish and Polish, which can be explained by their large number of DM types with an interpersonal core (in addition to potential methodological differences). Therefore, this study has shown that typological family cannot always account for similarities and differences in discourse-level phenomena.

This study and the annotation scheme it applies illustrate the importance of research on spoken language. The most prominent results stemming from our study concern functions of discourse markers that are specific to interactive settings (interpersonal and, to a lesser extent, sequential uses) and therefore cannot be observed in written texts. Annotation studies in written corpora are usually larger in scope and particularly useful for computational applications. However, only spoken corpora can accurately access the intricate processes of language use in interaction and how discourse is used to achieve goals and maintain interpersonal relationships. Such an endeavor is limited by the smaller size and general low availability of spoken/audio data, but the present chapter vouches for the feasibility and relevance of this line of research. This type of study also opens up cross-linguistic and cross-cultural perspectives in the prominent fields of interactional linguistics (e.g., Couper-Kuhlen and Selting 2018). Complementary approaches to DMs, combining insights from conversation analysis (e.g., Bolden 2009) and sociolinguistics (e.g., Tagliamonte 2005), would also further enrich our understanding of *how* and *why* speakers use DMs.

Further avenues of research include a detailed examination of individual differences in order to measure to what extent the observed cross-linguistic differences are idiosyncratic, as recent research has shown that individuals exhibit preferences that can relate to many variables of their background (e.g., Zufferey and Gygax 2020). This potential variation can also be checked by adding more data (more speakers) to the sample. Within the languages under scrutiny, comparison with written corpora is another promising and much wanted avenue, as speech-writing comparisons remain rare in the field (Fox Tree 2015; Kunz and Lapshinova-Koltunski 2015).

Part II

Innovative Variables in English

5 An Emerging Pragmatic Marker
Sentence-Final *Is All*

Daniela Kolbe-Hanna and Laurel J. Brinton

5.1 Introduction

Sentence-final *is all*, which has so far received little attention in the linguistic literature, may be understood as functioning as a pragmatic marker. When appended to a statement, as in the examples in (1), it often expresses the speaker's desires for the recipient not to infer more than has been said. Sentence-final past tense *was all* also occurs (1d).

(1) a. "You're not seriously sick, are you?" "No. I'm just pregnant, **is all**." (1999 *PayItForward*; The Corpus of Contemporary American English [COCA])
  b. "Well, actually it's been hurting a little more lately. It's probably nothing," I say, gaily. "Maybe a little touch of inflammatory breast cancer, **is all**." (2001 *Commentary*; COCA)
  c. Amanda: Hey. What's wrong? Jake: Sometimes it just hits me **is all**. Amanda: What does? Jake: How much I love you (2011 AMC; *Corpus of American Soap Operas* [SOAP])
  d. If he had a girlfriend, that's fine. I just wanted to know, **was all**. (2013 CNN: *Nancy Grace*; COCA)

Here, we define a pragmatic marker as an extra-sentential form occurring preferentially at the clause boundary that has procedural rather than propositional meaning. It serves a range of "pragmatic" (textual, metatextual, (inter-)subjective) functions. Pragmatic markers are generally of high frequency in colloquial and oral discourse (see Brinton 2017: 2–11; cf. Denis, Chapter 1, and Blondeau, Mougeon, and Tremblay, Chapter 11, this volume). In this chapter, drawing on data from a wide array of corpora, we describe the occurrence and use of sentence-final *is all* and provide evidence for its origin in postposed (*and/but*) *that/this is all*. Following a brief review of the existing scholarship on sentence-final *is all* (Section 5.1.1), this chapter consists of two main parts. The first part presents and analyzes the synchronic data on *is all* and covers its pragmatic function and distribution (dialect, genre) (Section 5.2). The second part consists of the presentation and analysis of the diachronic data, including the earliest instances and the form's syntactic source (Section 5.3). Section 5.4 postulates the development of *is all*, and Section 5.5 concludes the chapter.

5.1.1 Literature on Is All

The *Oxford English Dictionary* (OED) includes an entry for sentence-final *is/ was all* (s.v. *be*, v., P2h), noting that it is a US or Canadian colloquialism deriving from "that is [or was] all" or "that's all." The earliest entries are given in (2):

(2) a. Expensive? Naaw. Three hundred, **is all**. (1939 J. Fante, *Wait until Spring, Bandini* vi.134)
     b. She was just cleaning her bureau, **was all**. (1982 A. Tyler, *Dinner at Homesick Restaurant* i.20)

Apart from the OED entry, there have been sporadic observations concerning sentence-final *is all* in the literature. In an early reference, Mencken ([1948] 1952: 148, 160, 175, 201–202, 230, 233; quoted in Shibasaki 2019: 227–228) cites the example *It's in a bad neighborhood, is all* (1939, Iowa), which Mencken erroneously compares to the "analogous" use of *all* from German *alle* "exhausted, finished" as in *The butter is all* (see *The Dictionary of American Regional English* [DARE], s.v. *all*, adj.). Follett (1998/1966: s.v. *all*) points to sentence-final *is all* as a colloquialism resulting from ellipsis, as in *He has his facts wrong is all* ~~that's the matter with him~~, while Burchfield (1996: s.v. *is*, 8) describes its function as "often reinforcing the regret or sadness of the statement just made," giving examples from standard American fictional sources. Delin (1992) postulates that sentence-final *is all*, which she considers American, is one step in the derivation of the form *alls*, as in *alls you need to do is* x.[1] Crystal (2017: 171–172) notes the growing use of *is all* in colloquial discourse in the twentieth century, seeing it as an elliptical form of *that is/was all*. For him, it expresses a range of attitudes and serves interpersonal functions, "always with summarizing force" ('that is all that is to be said').

The most extensive discussions of *is all* are provided by three Japanese scholars. Both Ando (2005: 28–29) and Fujii (2006: 220–222) find literary examples in American writers, such as *My hands are sore is all* (Hemingway) or *I just gotta shave, is all* (Salinger) and point to related forms with sentence-final *what* (*what I mean/I think of it, that's what I mean*, etc.).[2] Ando argues for

---

[1] On *alls*, see, for example, Putnam and van Koppen (2011) and Yale Grammatical Diversity Project (n.d.), "The *alls* construction."
[2] We are grateful to Keisuke Sanada and Tomoharu Hirota for translations of Ando and Fujii.

"apo koinou," or a blend of both constructions. Furthermore, he sees the main clause as serving as a bare (*that*-less) subject of *is all* and analyzable as a "quotation substantive (without quotation marks)." Fujii (2006: 220–222) argues more simply that sentence-final *is all* derives from *that is all* by omission of *that*. Shibasaki (2019: 239–240) considers sentence-final *is all* a case of "anacoluthon," or lack of grammatical sequence; it results from an amalgam of two paratactic sentences, the second being of the form *And that's all* [relative clause], which gradually reduces to *is all* and is integrated into the preceding sentence. Like Ando, he also suggests that *is all* functions as a predicate, with the preceding clause as clausal subject (Shibasaki 2019: 230). While these accounts of the use and development of *is all* are suggestive, we aim to verify the accounts using corpus data from a wide range of contemporary and historical English data.

5.2 Synchronic Study

This section presents a study of the use and pragmatic function of sentence-final *is all* in present-day English. We are not concerned with predicative uses of *is all*, for instance *Love is all* or *God is all* as in (3) where *all* means "everything" or "the sum total of a person's needs or desires; the entirety of what matters" (s.v. *all*, adj., pron., and n., adv., and conj., B2c, OED).

(3) a. ... your hands out in front of you. Balance **is all**. (2008 *SouthernRev*; COCA)

b. Use it wisely, never forgetting that we are nothing, while He **is all**. (1992 *MalcolmX*; COCA)

5.2.1 Data and Methods

For the purpose of this study, we draw on data from corpora of British English (BrE) and American English (AmE) as set out in Table 5.1.

COCA and BNC were chosen because they are the largest reference corpora of AmE and BrE readily available covering a variety of genres, most importantly spoken and fictional language (containing actual speech and represented speech, respectively) but also academic texts and excerpts from newspapers and magazines. SOAP, TV, and Movies contain examples of scripted colloquial speech from both dialects. Switchboard contains the recordings of actual phone conversations in AmE and is a relatively small corpus.

To analyze the current use of *is all*, we initially conducted a pilot search of *is all* in COCA. Since *is all* is highly frequent here (more than 19,000 instances) and occurs in a large variety of constructions, we restricted the search to sentence-final position by including a period after *all* in the search string "is all ." (the space between *all* and "." is required by the search tool). The initial findings show that *is*

Table 5.1 *Synchronic corpora used in this study*

	No. of words	Time period
American data		
The Corpus of Contemporary American English (COCA)	560 million	1990–2017
Corpus of American Soap Operas (SOAP)	100 million	2001–2012
The Switchboard-1 Telephone Speech Corpus (Switchboard)	3 million	1990–1991
British and American data		
The TV Corpus (TV)	200 million	1950–2018
The Movie Corpus (Movies)	325 million	1930–2018
British data		
British National Corpus (BNC)	100 million	1990s

Note. The research for this chapter was completed before the March 2020 update of COCA, which expanded the size of the corpus to 1 billion words, covering eight genres.

all is often set off from the preceding part of the sentence by a comma and/or preceded by *that*, sometimes forming the complete sentence *That is all*. Following up on these results, we searched for variations of *is all* in sentence-final position, such as *was all* or *been all*, which we refer to collectively with *is all* as *BE all*. Since *that is all* appeared to be used like *is all*, we also extracted instances of *that BE all* as an independent sentence or in sentence-final position via the search string "that is all ."[3]

All instances of sentence-final *(that) BE all* were annotated manually. These annotations were at first impressionistic, in order to tease apart lexical and non-lexical uses. For example, a potential complementation of *is all* such as [I did] – as in *I took notice of him. That is all* (2014 *QueensDwarfNovel*; COCA) or *I just lost track of time is all* (1990 *CrazyLadies*; COCA) – identified a lexical use. Punctuation or the use or non-use of a demonstrative pronoun (*that*, *this*) before *BE all* also allowed us to identify lexical uses such as *Jesus is all* (2015 *ChristToday*; COCA) (see also example (3)). The pragmatic function(s) of the non-lexical uses were determined by close inspection of the examples. Pragmatically, sentence-final *is all* often conveys the speaker's desire that the recipient should not infer anything else but what has been said, and *That is all* in particular is often used to close a conversation or a topic. However, these pragmatic functions are intertwined and occur in various subtle differences. In

---

[3] Since we allowed for variation in the verb form and preceding context, we restricted the final punctuation mark to a period and did not include instances of *BE all* followed by exclamation marks, commas, question marks, or semicolons. These add up to around 1,000 instances of *BE all* and 100 instances of *is all* in COCA. When followed by a comma, *BE all* is mostly used as a quotative (*And I was all, "Sorry, pal ... "* (2012 *Robot Chicken*; COCA). The potential differentiation of the functions of sentence-final *BE all* before different punctuation marks deserves a study of its own and is beyond the scope of this chapter.

order to do justice to these differences and ambiguous uses in the data, we refrain from defining any fine-grained and exclusive pragmatic categories, as explained in Section 5.2.2.2.

5.2.2 Results

The search results display hardly any use of sentence-final *is all* in the BNC (<0.1 occurrences per million words (pmw)) with the pragmatic function described in Section 5.2.1, but a notable frequency in COCA and SOAP (>1 occurrence pmw, see Section 5.2.2.1). In 1,002 instances of sentence-final *BE all* in the BNC, we found only 8 instances of sentence-final *is all* with pragmatic function.

Table 5.2 presents an overview of the distribution across linguistic forms in COCA and SOAP. Sentence-final *BE all* occurs in eight types, five of which are sometimes preceded by *that*. The two instances of *that are all* from SOAP, presented in (4), perhaps illustrate the function of asking the recipient not to infer anything that has not been said, but more likely seem to be aborted sentences or errors in the transcript:

(4) a. Sarah: You're gonna send me back to my father. Jessica: No, I just want to talk to you **that are all**. Sarah: Well, I'm not going to go. (2003 AWT; SOAP)
b. Ethan: What makes you say that? Theresa: I know you, **that are all**. I know that you'd never let anything get in the way of you being true to your feelings (2002 PASS; SOAP)

All remaining constructions, *be all*, *been all*, *'re all*, *are all*, and *were all*, often following *that* AUX (HAVE / MODAL), either occur in predicative use (e.g., *And that had been all*. 1992 *DragonToken*; COCA) or are not in sentence-final position (e.g., *they're ALL. ADDRESSED. TO. HER.* 1996 *Neither Rain nor Sleet*; COCA) and hence are not germane to this study. For this reason, we restrict the following discussion to *(that) 's/is/was all*. Non-relevant structures are shaded in Table 5.2.

As Table 5.2 shows, nearly all tokens of *'s all* are actually tokens of *that's all* (99 percent, other forms include *it's all* or *is all*). However, in the non-contracted types *(that) is/was all*, the proportion of tokens introduced by *that* decreases from 90 percent of *was all* tokens to around a quarter of tokens of *is all*. Only *is all* and *(that)'s all* occur more than once per 1 million words and both are distinctly more frequent in the SOAP corpus than in COCA.

The meaning of sentence-final *(,) is all* can be described as 'that is all that needs to be said,' as in the examples in (5). The resulting pragmatic functions express the speaker's wish either to close the topic or for the recipient not to infer anything more or else than has been said, or both. These functions are

Table 5.2 Sentence-final (that) BE all in COCA and SOAP (search string: "_vb* all .")

Type	COCA		CORPUS	SOAP	
	N	pmw		N	pmw
's all	2,625	5.25		8,991	89.91
that's all	2,599 (98.7%)	5.18		8,985 (99.9%)	89.85
is all	577	1.15		227	2.27
that is all	121 (21%)			72 (32%)	0.72
was all	488	0.24		24	0.24
that was all	438 (89%)			22 (92%)	0.22
be all	39	0.97		71	0.71
that MODAL be all	28 (71.8%)			70 (98.6%)	
been all	4	0.02		0	0
that would have/had been	3 (75%)				
're all	10	0.87		0	0
?that 're all	0				
are all	4	0.01		3	0.03
that are all	0			2	
were all	4	0.08		0	0
that were all	2				
Total BE all	3,751	6.7		9,316	93.16
Total that BE all	3,191	5.7		9,151	91.51

Note. Search strings cited in this chapter are based on the CLAWS tagset used in these corpora: http://ucrel.lancs.ac.uk/claws7tags.html.

closely connected to each other – by expressing that all that needs to be said has been said, the speaker invites the hearer not to infer anything else and signals his or her intention to close the topic. It is often only a matter of degree to which each interpretation is more salient.

(5)   a.   ... for your information, he is not my boyfriend. we're partners, **is all**. Partners! (2000 *Analog*; COCA)
         b.   Yeah. I'm a little edgy. I haven't slept much **is all**. (2001 *Port Charlies*; SOAP)
         c.   LULA You been drinkin, huh? SAILOR Few beers **is all**. (1990 *WildatHeart*; COCA)

In some instances of sentence-final *is all*, as illustrated in (6), speakers spell out this pragmatic inference. In (6a), *is all* precedes an explanation as to why the speaker is undecided, while in (6b–f) the explanation precedes the sentence containing *is all*. Each of these preceding sentences contains a negation with scope over the unwanted inference.

(6)   a.   Look, I'm just saying I'm undecided, **is all**. I'm open to the idea, but I want to be convinced, (2015 NPR: *Fresh Air*; COCA)
         b.   I don't doubt that. I just wish I'd known sooner, **is all**. (2007 *Analog*; COCA)
         c.   BOB I'm not cranky. I've been through this before, **is all**. (2007 *JesseJames*; COCA)
         d.   And in this case I have no idea. I have suspicions **is all**. (2001 *ABC_GMA*; COCA)
         e.   It isn't ruined, miss. It needs to be repaired **is all**. (1997 *MemiorGeisha* [sic]; COCA)
         f.   I wasn't prying. I just wanted to be pretty, **was all**. (2001 *Atlantic*; COCA)

To summarize the findings so far, sentence-final *BE all* often serves a pragmatic function, asking the hearer not to infer more than was said. It predominantly occurs in American English and, in our data, is restricted to the sequences *(that) is all*, *(that) was all*, and *that's all*.

5.2.2.1 Sentence-Final Is/Was All

This section focuses on the use and functions of sentence-final *is all* and *was all*; the forms introduced by *that* will be discussed in Section 5.2.2.2. Table 5.3 details the proportions of the pragmatic use of sentence-final *is/was all* in COCA and SOAP.

Was all is used like *is all* when the utterance from which nothing else is to be inferred is clearly past, as in examples (1d), (2b), or (6f) and marked by the use of past perfect in example (7).

(7)   He hadn't thought he'd heard rightly, **was all**. (2017 *Analog*; COCA)

Table 5.3 *Sentence-final* is/was all *in COCA and SOAP (search string "vb* all ."; PM=pragmatic marker)*

Type	COCA N	COCA PM	SOAP N	SOAP PM
is all	577	400 (70%)	227	174 (66%)
was all	488	33 (7%)	24	1 (4%)

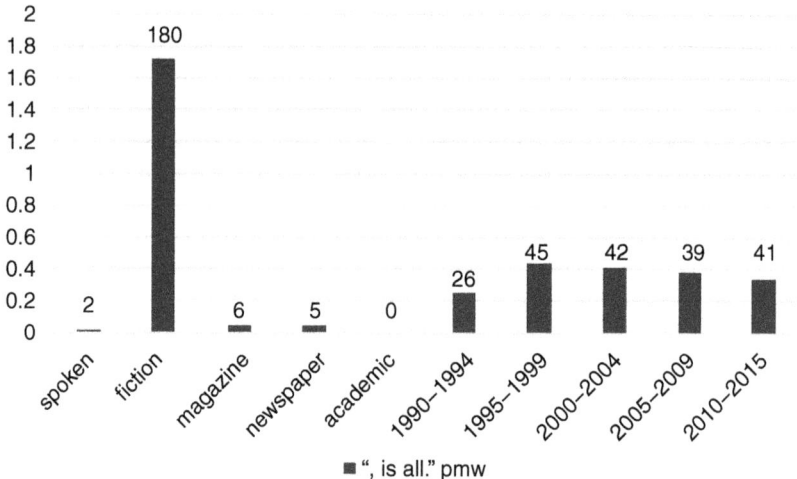

Figure 5.1 Distribution of ", is all ." in COCA per million words (pmw) across text types and time periods
The numbers above the bars show the absolute frequencies.

After a comma, *is all* or *was all* always functions as a pragmatic marker in the data. To conduct automated quantitative analyses in COCA and SOAP online, we therefore used the search string(s) ", is/was all ."

Sentence-final ", is all ," occurs 394 times in COCA and 148 times in SOAP, viz. 0.7 times per 1 million words in COCA and 1.48 times per 1 million words in SOAP. The fact that SOAP consists of colloquial scripted language, but COCA also includes academic language, as well as data from newspapers and magazines, suggests that *is all* is preferred in colloquial language. Figure 5.1 illustrates that *is all* is more frequent in fictional than in spoken language in COCA (see also Shibasaki 2019: 236). The examples of *is all* in the fiction section of COCA (COCA:FIC) are exclusively found in represented speech, thus accounting for the similar rates of frequency of *is all* in COCA:FIC (1.74 pmw) and in SOAP

(1.48 pmw). The spoken language represented in COCA consists of unscripted broadcast conversation. Its public nature may lead speakers to use a speech style that is less colloquial and more monitored than in private conversations (see Koch and Österreicher 1985).

A search for *is all* in the Switchboard corpus of spoken AmE did not elicit any instances of the pragmatic marker sentence-final *is all*. This corpus is distinctly smaller than the other two corpora (3 million words) but with the same rate of occurrence as in COCA or SOAP, *is all* should occur two or three times. Its absence in the Switchboard corpus replicates its low frequency in the spoken data in COCA. However, although the conversations in the Switchboard corpus are spontaneous and not conducted to be public, the speakers did not know each other before talking to each other. In more intimate conversations between speakers familiar with each other, sentence-final *is all* would perhaps be as frequent as in the fictional data in COCA and SOAP, but we have no corpus evidence to support this hypothesis.

The data also show a frequent co-occurrence of sentence-final *is all* with *just* (see, e.g., (1a), (1c), (1d), (2b), (6a), (6b), and (6f)), as laid out in Table 5.4. *Just* occurs in the same sentence that ends in *is all* or in the previous sentence in nearly 50 percent of the cases from COCA and in more than three-quarters of the examples from SOAP. The frequencies of the co-occurrence in the American sections of the TV and Movies corpora data lie between the percentages in COCA and SOAP.[4]

In the context of *is all*, the restrictive attitude diminisher *just* (Quirk et al. 1985: 597–598, 604) adds to the function of expressing a delimitation of what is to be understood (see (8a)). Biber et al. (1999: 781, 799) observe that *just* "often seems to have qualities of both restricting the action and lessening the intensity" and "of softening what is being said [...] particularly when people are

Table 5.4 *Co-occurrence of sentence-final* is all *with* just

Corpora	N	just ... is all
COCA	395	181 (46%)
SOAP	148	115 (78%)
MOVIE:US/CA	709	442 (62%)
TV:US	965	616 (64%)
Total	2,217	1,354 (61%)

[4] Since TV and Movies consist of the genre in which the pragmatic marker *is all* is most frequent, we used these data to corroborate our findings.

justifying their or others' actions." While expressions like *only* or *a little* (e.g., (1b), (5b), (8b)) fulfill similar functions as *just*, *just* stands out with more than 100 examples in each corpus.

(8)   a.   John: Did Natalie call in sick or something? # Gloria: No, she's fine. We **just** switched shifts, **is all** (2007 AWT; SOAP)
          b.   [choking] You good, Finn? You're strangling me **a little**, **is all**. (2010, *Adventure Time*; TV)

The pragmatic function of sentence-final *BE all* is largely restricted to the form *is all* and mostly documented in fictional data in our database. It is often accompanied by the adverbial *just*, softening an implied directive to the hearer not to infer more than what has been said. Section 5.2.2.2 compares the use of sentence-final *that BE all* to that of sentence-final *BE all*.

5.2.2.2 Sentence-final that is/was all As outlined in section 5.2.2 and shown in Table 5.2, sentence-final *that BE all* is a frequent variant of sentence-final *BE all*, and sentence-final *that's all* accounts for virtually all instances of sentence-final *'s all*. Figure 5.2 shows that the distribution of *that BE all* is similar to that of sentence-final *is all* (see Figure 5.1); it is mostly restricted to the fiction section of COCA. With nearly 20 tokens pmw, the frequency of *that BE all* is also markedly higher than that of *is all*.

Figure 5.2 also shows some decrease in the use of *that BE all* from the 1990s until today, but this is not paralleled by a clear increase of the frequency in the use of sentence-final *is all* (see Figure 5.1), as one might expect if *is all* derives from *that is all* (see Section 5.3.3). In the remaining corpora, a slight increase in the last decade in SOAP and in the US/CA section of the TV corpus from the 1950s to the 2000s counterbalances the decline of the frequency of *is all* in COCA, as well as in the US/CA section of the Movies corpus from the 1990s to this decade.

While sentence-final *is all* is overall used either lexically or with the pragmatic meaning 'do not infer more than I have just said,' there is a wider range of the functions of *that BE all*. Some of the more clearly separable instances are illustrated in (9) with our paraphrases of the meaning or function included after the examples. We believe that from (9a) to (9f) these examples represent a cline from more literal to more pragmatic uses. This cline could be summarized in the following way: closing a list > closing a topic > closing the account > ending the conversation > dismissal > refuting an unwanted inference.

Example (9a) contains a literal function of *that is all* referring to all items in an array. In (9b) *that is all* can be rephrased literally but also has the pragmatic effect of closing a topic. There is nothing that could or should be inferred, but the speaker quite explicitly states what she does and does not want to do. In (9c), *that's all* refers to the entirety of the story the speaker remembers and

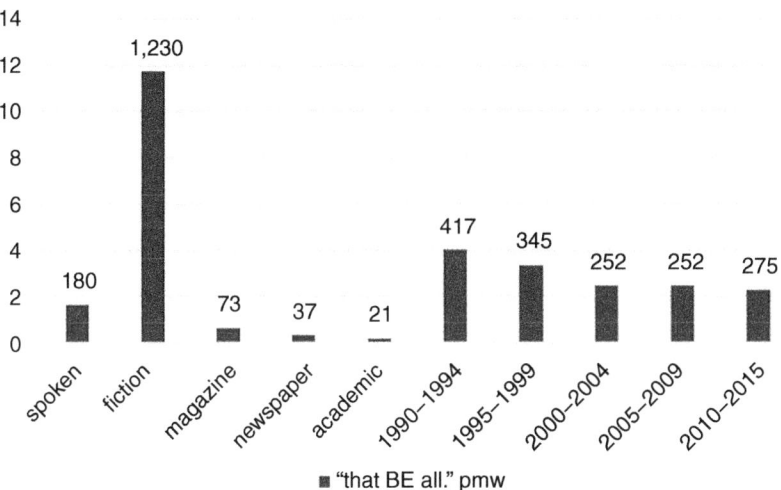

Figure 5.2 Distribution of "that BE all ." in COCA per million words (pmw) across text types and time periods
The numbers above the bars show the absolute frequencies.

cannot be rephrased literally. *That's all* ends the speaker's telling. In (9d) the literal meaning cannot be deduced from actual words in the previous sentence, but *all* refers to the entirety of things to say and meta-linguistically expresses the speaker's desire to end the conversation.

The two instances of *that is all* in (9e) appear to have different functions. The first instance is rather literal and refers directly to the content of the preceding clause, but the second instance signals the end of the broadcast segment and thus also functions as dismissal. In the corpora, ending a conversation and thereby dismissing attendees is a notable function of *that is all*. In contrast to other shades of pragmatic function of *that is all* mirrored in the use of sentence-final *is all*, we have not identified any instance of *is all* as a dismissal. Examples (9f) illustrates quite a prototypical example of the pragmatic function of sentence-final *(that) is all*, asking the addressee not to infer anything unfortunate, unwanted, or negative.

By focusing more on the speakers' needs than the listener's, examples (9b–d) appear to be more subjective, while examples (9e–f) appear to be more intersubjective, as they directly invoke the addressee, which is indicated by an explicit *you* in our paraphrases.

(9) a. I will allow a ball point pen and writing pad. **That is all**. (2014 *PennLitJournal*; COCA)
 'That is all I will allow,' 'closing the list'

b. Want to order? Alison: Nope. I am here for work – **that is all**. Can we please start with the skeletal system? (2008 AWT; SOAP)
'that is all I am here for,' 'closing the topic of having dinner'
c. If you remember everything, I can probably get you back there tonight. [...] Abigail: All right, I'll give it another try. All right. Okay, I was reaching for the music box. And it was still playing. (Music-box-playing) I looked up I [sic] and saw Nick heading to the door. Opening the door. And I heard him say – Nick: What are you doing here? Abigail: "What are you doing here?" **That's all. That's all.** (2002 AWT; SOAP)
'that is all I remember,' 'I am closing my telling'
d. perhaps you should all ask yourselves if you could be doing more. And if you can't, at least offer a word or two of thanks to the people in the room who are bearing the heaviest loads. A little appreciation can go a long way. **That's all.** (2016 *PerfectComebackCarolineJacobs*; COCA)
'that's all that needs to be said,' 'I do not want to say anything else'
e. Tell them [your political representative] you won't vote for them. **That's all. And that's all**. We'll be back. (2017 *TheView*; COCA)
'that is all you should (need to) tell them to have an effect', 'dismissal'
f. Forgive me, my Marcia. I've had a bad morning, **that is all**. (2010 *Analog*; COCA)
'do not infer that I don't love you'

Example (10), however, illustrates one of many instances in which we cannot decide whether this is a literal or pragmatic use of *that is all*. Its literal meaning would be 'that is all I had to do,' which does not seem to capture its full meaning; it also implies 'please believe me' and possibly 'don't infer that I had bad intentions'

(10) Mateo: Hey, Vanessa. You alone? Vanessa: Yes, I am. Mateo: The only reason I ask is that we're locking up here, so – Vanessa: Oh, sure, sure. I just – I had to see my son, **that's all**. Leo? Leo, darling? (2002 AMC; SOAP)

That's/is all also co-occurs with *just* but less frequently so than *is all* (see Table 5.5). It occurs in about a third of the examples in COCA. As is true for sentence-final *is all*, the co-occurrence is higher in the SOAP data than in the data from COCA and the proportions in TV and Movies lie in between.

Table 5.5 *Co-occurrence of sentence-final* that's/is all *with* just

Corpora	N *that's all*	*just ... that's all* % (N)	N *that is all*	*just ... that is all* % (N)
COCA	2598	31% (794)	120	4% (5)
SOAP	8968	63% (5,677)	72	16% (11)
TV:US/CA	1000*	48% (478)	328	7% (24)
Movie:US/CA	1000**	49% (485)	318	7% (22)

Note. * This represents a sample from more than 10,000 cases from the US/CA section of the TV corpus.
** The represents a sample from approximately 10,000 cases of the US/CA section of the Movies corpus.

In sum, we consider the relationship between *that is all/ that's all* and *is all* as an indication that *that is all* or *that's all* might be the source of sentence-final *is all*. Sentence-final (,) *is/was all* often has pragmatic function and invokes the conversational implicature "do not infer anything more/else than what has been said." The same conversational implicature can be evoked by *that is/'s all*. Section 5.3.3 investigates this derivation.

5.3 Historical Study

Because of the infrequency of sentence-final *BE all* in earlier periods, a wide variety of historical English corpora and text collections, both BrE and AmE, were consulted for this study (see Table 5.6).

5.3.1 Earliest Examples of Sentence-Final Is/Was All

Of the historical corpora searched, only COHA and Movies provide examples of sentence-final *is all*. No examples are found in the BrE historical corpora (see also Shibasaki 2019: 235).[5] The earliest examples of *is all* in AmE appear in the first quarter of the twentieth century (11), but the form does not become common until the middle of the twentieth century. The past tense construction (12), while contemporaneous, is very rare.

(11)   a.   Naw. We're fired off the reservation, **is all**. (1907 *RowdyCrossL*; COHA)
       b.   Don't swallow any, **is all**. let's weigh it out, Cash, and see how much it is, just for a josh. (1918 *CabinFever*; COHA)
       c.   "You're out to see the elephant, yourself." "I am seeking health, **is all**," I explained. (1922 *DesertDust*; COHA)

Table 5.6 *Diachronic corpora used in this study*

American Data	Dates	No. of Words
Corpus of Early American Literature (CEAL)	1690–1920	13,500,000 words
The Corpus of Historical American English (COHA)	1810–2009	400,000,000 words
British and American data		
The Corpus of English Novels (CEN)	1881–1922	26,227,428 words
The Movie Corpus (Movies)	1930–2018	325,000,000 words
British data		
Early English Books Online (EEBO)	1470s–1660s	755,000,000 words
The Proceedings of the Old Bailey (OB)	1674–1913	ca. 134,000,000 words
The Corpus of Late Modern English Texts (CLMET3.0)	1710–1920	34,386,225 words

---

[5] No examples are found in CEAL, most likely because of the small size of the corpus and the fact that the latest twentieth-century texts in the corpus date from 1919.

	d.	Oh, I – I lost my head over the girl **is all**. (1931 *The Last Flight*; Movies)
	e.	"You have affection, **is all**?" "Yes, that is all," said Lydia (1933 *FaultAngels*; COHA)
	f.	It's just that I don't like De Lautruc, **is all**. (1938 *Jezebel*; Movies)
(12)	a.	And he didn't seem to be using it. He kept it beside him, **was all**. (1912 *PluckOnLongTrail*; COHA)
	b.	It would mean a long walk, **was all** (which stretched longer by the moment). (1933 *ShiningOnes*; COHA)
	c.	I jest craved peace, **was all**." (1939 *Yearling*; COHA)

COHA provides 152 examples of sentence- or clause- final *is all* and 18 examples of *was all*, for an overall normalized frequency of 0.395 pmw. With only twelve exceptions, the examples are all parenthetical or free-standing and function pragmatically; irrelevant examples are similar to those shown in example (2).

Sentence-final *BE all* is consistently found in Fiction, where it occurs in represented speech. Only three examples are found outside Fiction, in the Magazine genre, two in represented speech (13b) but one in expository prose (13a):

(13)	a.	Calgary seems to have an unsophisticated, almost south-of-the-border Texas personality. The accent's a little different, **is all**. (1988 *Time*; COHA)
	b.	"Don't sweat it. They're just a little late, **is all**," said Graftwell. (1991 *Time*; COHA)

As in present-day English, *just* is frequently present in the clause to which *BE all* is attached (37/158 or 23 percent of the time in COHA) (see (12c)).

5.3.2   Antecedents of Sentence-Final Is All

A number of antecedents of sentence-final *is all* occur in the data, including both the complete clause – (conjunction) *that* (or *this*) *is/was all* – and more expansive forms such as *that is all I mean*.

5.3.2.1   That/This BE All   The OED (s.v. *all*, adj., pron. and n., adv. and conj., B2b) cites examples of sentence-final *that is/that's all* meaning "the full extent of the matter or question; the sum total of what there is to be said about something" from 1616 onward. In *English Books Online* (EEBO, 1470s–1660s), one finds constructions both with the distal demonstrative (*that is all* – 225 examples; *that was all* – 123 examples) and with the proximal demonstrative (*this is all* – 332 examples; *this was all* – 67 examples), dating from the mid-sixteenth century onward.[6] Examining the examples of *that is all* in more detail, we find that the vast majority

---

[6] The search string used was "that/this is/was all _y*". "y" corresponds to all punctuation marks.

already function parenthetically or are free-standing; in only eleven examples, *that is all* functions as part of a larger syntactic structure (e.g., *I think that is all, if that is all*) or *that* is a relative pronoun (e.g., *he/him that is all*). The presence of an initial conjunction (*and/but/for*) is common, especially with *that* (163 examples).[7]

The function of the examples of *that/this BE all* in EEBO, though sometimes difficult to interpret, often seems – like present-day examples – to express the meaning 'do not infer anything else from what I am saying' and they serve as means of closing off the topic ("and that is all I have to say"). Examples with *is* (14) and *was* (15) are given showing this meaning.

(14)   a.   I am not well in health, **and that is all**: (1623 *Mr. Vvilliam Shakespeares Comedies*; EEBO)
        b.   only I offer'd her the courtesie oth'Country, and she refus'd it, **that is all**: (1664 *Love's Kingdom*; EEBO)
        c.   he died too young, he died in the morning of his life, **this is all** (1664 *Joshua Redivivus*; EEBO)
        d.   ah poor candiope! I pity her, **but that is all**: (1668 *Secret-Love*; EEBO)

(15)   a.   they might heare them peradventure when they were little ones to stammer, to lispe, to spel and put syllables together, or to speake broken Greeke, **and that was all**: (1603 *The Philosophie*; EEBO)
        b.   they began to conceiue reuerently of his doctrine, and were willing to heare him; **and this was all**, (1632 *CVIII Lectures*; EEBO)
        c.   he ... calls him, good master, and desires to be instructed of him; **but that was all**: (1664 *Twenty five sermons*; EEBO)
        d.   he said there was no harm in it, **that was all**: (1684 *The Tryal of Laurence Braddon and Hugh Speke, gent.*; EEBO)

Turning to Late Modern English, we find that *that/this BE all* continues to be common. While some clearly do not have the pragmatic function of the present-day form (16a – i.e., here it means 'this is all I know'), others are quite similar in function (16b).

(16)   a.   And is that all you know of her, Wilkins?" "**This is all**. (1857 *BrotherClerks*; COHA)
        b.   I would thy faith were greater, **this is all**. Now must I bid farewell. (1871 *AdmetusOtherPoems*; COHA)

Late Modern English frequency results are given in Table 5.7. The rather disparate frequencies of *that BE all* in the different corpora can be attributed to the nature of the corpora/text collections. CLMET3.0 and COHA are both genre-balanced corpora and show comparable frequencies of *that BE all*. CEAL has a "somewhat uneven" genre distribution, with political writings,

---

[7] Using COHA data, Shibasaki (2019: 234) dates *and/but that is all* constructions from the mid-nineteenth century.

Table 5.7 That/this BE all in Late Modern English

Sentence-final/independent	CEAL (1690–1920)	CLMET3.0 (1720–1920)	COHA (1810–1919)	CEN (1881–1922)	OB (1674–1913)
that's all	173 (178)*	214 (219)	1173 (1218)	437 (451)	17 (18)
that is all	53 (54)	91 (97)	669 (712)	379 (390)	426 (436)
that was all	81 (82)	93 (97)	612 (624)	296 (300)	359 (411)
this is all	0	17 (18)	41 (52)	1 (1)	6 (8)
this was all	3 (7)	7 (9)	43 (45)	2	0 (3)
Total – parenthetical uses (raw)	310	422	2537	1115	808
Total – parenthetical uses (pmw)	23.0	12.3	14.3	42.5	6.0

Note. The search string used for COHA was "that/this is/was all _y*" and "that's all _y*". CEAL, CLMET3.0, CEN, and OB were searched using AntConc (Anthony 2018), with the search string followed by a period, a semi-colon, a comma, colon, and an exclamation point. We are grateful to Dustin Grue for the downloaded OB text files.

* Numbers in parentheses represent total numbers, including cases in which *that/this BE all* is not parenthetical.

journals, and religious texts in the first period, approximately 42 percent fiction in the second period, and 93 percent fiction in the third period (Höglund and Syrjänen 2016: 21). CEN consists entirely of fiction and is limited to twenty-five authors.[8] The overwhelmingly fictive nature of both CEAL and CEN likely leads to the higher frequency of *that BE all*. OB is a specialized genre of court records where *that BE all* does not have high frequency and functions literally to end a list of items or actions enumerated for the judge or answers an inquiry about the completeness of the witness's testimony.

Two trends are obvious from the data. The proximal demonstrative *this* falls out of use almost entirely.[9] The contracted form *that's all*, which is not found in EEBO,[10] becomes the most common form (except in OB, where transcription practices likely account for the virtual absence of the contracted form). As discussed in Section 5.3.3, the predominance of the contracted form can be seen as giving rise to *is all*. A third trend is the reduction of constructions headed by a conjunction; only 10 percent (133/1173) of the examples of *that's all* in COHA begin with a conjunction.

---

[8] A handful of authors seem to be overrepresented; see the *Corpus of English Novels* (CEN): https://perswww.kuleuven.be/~u0044428/cen.htm.

[9] On the replacement of *that* by *this* in *this/that said* and *this/that is not to say*, see Brinton (2017: 204; 2020); the change from proximal to distal demonstrative is argued to reflect expansion from scope over the proposition to scope over the discourse. Similar to *BE all*, *that is not to say* expresses "non-inference."

[10] The OED (s.v. *all*, B2b) cites one early contracted form: *Meere Essaists! a few loose sentences, and that's all.* (1616 B. Jonson, *Epicoene* II iii 49 in *Wks* I).

The following examples show *that BE all* as a pragmatic marker expressing 'do not infer anything more from this' in the eighteenth century, including examples of *that's/that is all* (17) and less often *that was all* (18).

(17) a. I have heard she has been in Bridewell, and she goes for a loose Woman, **that's all**. (1730 Trial of Edward Birch, t17350911-75; OB)
b. I know my Cousin is angry at something, and I wish you were Friends again, **that's all**. (1736 *The Female Quixote*; CLMET3.0)
c. I saw her black Marks about her Throat, after she was dead, – **that's all**. (1740 Trial of Samuel Badham t17400709-2; OB)
d. I am a sad fool! I want spirits, **that's all**. (1748 *Pamela*; CLMET3.0)
e. "I fancy," said he, "her gentle spirits were a little too much fluttered last night; **that is all**." (1751 *Amelia*; CLMET3.0)

(18) a. the lady, if she were not my wife, had been very much injured; **that was all**. (1748 *Clarissa*; CLMET3.0)
b. He was carry'd before Alderman Alexander the same day, and charg'd with stealing the grocery. He said he was in the boat, **that was all**. (1757 Trial of John Flat, t17570914-24; OB)
c. Q. At the time when he and you had agreed to go out, what was it to do. Knott. It was only to walk and wash, **that was all**. (1761 Trial of Basil Francis, t17610916-21; OB)
d. "There was no sort of cause," answered he; "the fellow did not know whom he spoke [to], **that was all**." (1782 *Cecilia*; CLMET3.0)

5.3.2.2 Other Sources As suggested by Follett (1998/1966), Ando (2005), Fujii (2006), and Shibasaki (2019) (see Section 5.1.1), it is possible that expanded forms may serve as the historical source of *is all* via ellipsis. While structures with *what* (*what I mean/I think of it/I am, that's what I mean*, etc.) are proposed, more obvious sources are ones with *all* (*that's all I mean*, etc.).

Table 5.8 presents the raw frequencies of a range of expanded forms with *all* and *what* in CEN (the corpus with the highest number of *that BE all* forms; see Table 5.7).

Expanded forms with *all* are rare; only *that's all I can say* and *that's all I have to say* (19a–b) show a noticeable presence. These are similar in function to the shorter form, *that's all*, in that they suggest that nothing further should be inferred from the previous discourse.

(19) a. well, time enough to talk about it. It's a pity, **that's all I can say**. (1886 *Demos*; CEN)
b. "I had plenty of grub" continued The Kid. "I did my best for them and helped them home. **That is all I have to say**." (1904 *The Prospector*; CEN)

That is/that's all could be derived from these longer forms by simple ellipsis of the semantically rather light relative clause (*I can say, I have to say*). However,

Table 5.8 *Expanded forms with* all *or* what *in CEN (free-standing and parenthetical forms)*

Expanded ALL forms	N	Expanded WHAT forms	N
{that is, that's} **all** I {mean, meant}	3	{that is, that's} **what** I {mean, meant}	29
{that's, that is} **all** I {think, thought}	0	{that's, that is} **what** I {think, thought}	18
{that is, that's} **all** I {say, said}	1	{that is, that's} **what** I {say, said}	34
{that's, that is} **all** there is to say	5	{that's, that is} **what** there is to say	0
{that's, that is} **all** I can say	10	{that's, that is} **what** I can say	0
{that's, that is} **all** I {have, 've got} to say	26	{that's, that is} **what** I {have, 've got} to say	0
{that's, that is} **all** I {want, need} to say	0	{that's, that is} **what** I {want, need} to say	0
that was **all** I {meant, said, thought}	0	that was **what** I {meant, said, thought}	2
that was **all** I could say	1	that was **what** I could say	0

the rarity of the longer forms in comparison to the shorter form during this period, as well as the earlier period,[11] suggests that we are more likely looking at a case of expansion rather than contraction, that is, of *that is all I have to say* being an expansion of *that is all*.[12]

Forms with *what* are more common than forms with *all*, but derivation of *that is/that's all* from forms with *what* poses difficulties as there is no easy explanation for the replacement of *what* by *all*. More significantly, however, the *what* forms seem to have a different function, being used for clarification or confirmation, as in the examples in (20).

(20) a. "It's a pity, sir, we lost that second load. **That's what I mean**," replied the captain. (1881 *Treasure Island*; CEN)
 b. "But I can see nothing," he whispered. "There is no door." "**That's what I thought**," said Mary. (1909 *The Secret Garden*; CEN)

While expanded forms with *all* are rare in the earlier period, they would appear to become more common in the present day. For example, SOAP has 85 examples of *{that's, that is}* **all** *I* [modal] *say*, 74 of *{that's, that is}* **all** *I have to say*, 37 of *{that's, that is}* **all** *I {think, thought}*, 21 of *{that's, that is}* **all** *I {mean, meant}*, 14 of *{that's, that is}* **all** *I {want, need} to say*, 10 of *{that's, that is} all I {say, said}*, 7 of *{that's, that is}* **all** *there is to say*, and 3 of *{that's, that is}* **all** *I've got to say* (for a total of 166 forms). This increase of expanded

---

[11] For example, in the first two periods of CLMET3.0 (1780–1850), we find only 21 expanded forms: 6 examples of *{that's, that is} all I {say, have to say}*, 1 example of *that was all I said*, 2 examples of *{that's, that is} what I {think, thought}*, 11 examples of *{that's, that is} what I {say, said}*, and 1 example of *that was what I said*.

[12] A similar sort of expansion is seen in the case of *that said* giving rise later to the longer forms *that being said* and *that having been said* (Brinton 2017: 205).

forms over time points to the expanded forms being a development from the shorter form rather than the reverse.[13]

5.3.3 Development of Is All

It seems clear that sentence-final parenthetical *is all* develops from *that's/that is all*, which exists in incipient form in the seventeenth century and is fully developed pragmatically in the eighteenth century. The source of *is all* in a full clause is consonant with the emergence of many other pragmatic markers that have developed from full clauses, including declarative main clauses (e.g., *I see, you know, it seems*), imperative main clauses (e.g., *mind you, look*), adverbial clauses (e.g., *if you will, as it were, if you ask me*), and nominal relative clauses (e.g., *that is to say, all I'm saying is*) (see Brinton 2017: 16–23). The full clauses undergo various kinds of reduction in their evolution as pragmatic markers.

The development of *is all* from *that is all* and of *was all* from *that was all* can follow from simple deletion of the demonstrative. Yet already in Late Modern English the more common form is the contracted *that's all*. The change from *that's all* to *is all* can be explained as a process of phonological reduction, deletion, voicing, and reanalysis, which can be schematized as follows, though the changes might occur in a different order:

/ðætˈs ɔl/ > [ðətˈsɔl] > [əˈṣɔl] > /ɪˈzɔl/ <is all>

The reduction of *that* /ðæt/ to [ə] would be a result of vowel reduction /æ/ > [ə] in an unstressed syllable, which is a natural process in English, and of the elision of /ð/ and /t/, which are the second and third most frequently deleted sounds in English after /d/ (Turnbull 2015: 222). In intervocalic position, /s/ (*'s*) is partially voiced to [ṣ]. The resulting reduced form [əˈṣɔl] is reanalyzed as *is all* and may thus be pronounced /ɪˈzɔl/. This reanalysis is potentially supported by the existence of the parallel form *that is all*.

5.4 Conclusions

Sentence-final *is/was all* often leads to a conversational implicature for the recipient not to infer more than what has been said and/or it is used to close the topic. In this function, it is more frequent in AmE than in BrE and is found first in the early twentieth century. In our data, it occurs almost exclusively in the fictional representation of spoken English rather than in spoken data as such or more formal written genres like academic. Lack of sentence-final *is/was all* in British historical corpora points to its origin and earlier occurrence in AmE,

---

[13] As shown in Table 5.2, SOAP contains 227 examples of pragmatic *that BE all*. Thus, SOAP has two-thirds as many expanded forms as short forms.

with (fairly recent) spread from AmE to BrE. The recentness of the spread of sentence-final *is/was all* to BrE is attested to by the increase of its frequency in the UK/IE (Ireland) section of the TV corpus – from no occurrence in the 1970s–1990s to a frequency of 0.69 pmw in the 2000s and to 1.17 pmw in the 2010s.

The diachronic data point to the origin of sentence-final *is all* in the construction *(and/or) that/this be all* in Early Modern English; this form is the precursor of the pragmatic non-inference meaning of the contemporary form. Three changes – loss of the initial conjunction, replacement of *this* by *that*, and contraction of the verb (in the case of *is*) – produce the most common Late Modern English forms, sentence-final *that's all* and *that was all*. Eighteenth-century examples of these forms display pragmatic meaning (i.e., the conversational implicature of *is all*) and are exclusively found in fictional representations of speech. They persist in present-day English with a wider set of functions, such as the use to dismiss attendees of a conversation.

We postulate that sentence-final *is all* and *was all* arose in the early twentieth century by phonetic reduction and reanalysis of *that's all/that was all*. Expanded constructions such as *is all I have to say/can say* were rare in the early period and hardly likely to be the source construction; rather, they represent expansions of the shorter form, making explicit the non-inference meaning.

6 "That Is Totally Not My Type of Film"
Innovations in the Intensifier System of UK English

Karin Aijmer

6.1 Introduction

In recent years, *totally* has emerged as an innovative intensifier in UK English, as illustrated in examples (1–5) from the *Spoken British National Corpus 2014* (henceforth BNC2014S) (Love et al. 2017):

(1) and it is (.) it's **totally fine** (S 3RL-S0432)

(2) I'm **totally going to** watch that cos I really really fancy him (S50 J- S0085)

(3) I imagine the kids **totally will** be really hoping school's close tomorrow (SEGL-S0155)

(4) Yeah **totally a class thing** (S0383-SDA8)

(5) Annie: don't you think you've had a bit too much wine already? Mary: **mm totally** (S632-S028)

These examples demonstrate that *totally* is used in grammatical contexts in which intensifiers are normally expected, for example, before an adjective (as in (1)), but also in less canonical positions, such as before verbs (as in (2) and (3)) and noun phrases (as in (4)). The position of *totally* points toward different functions. In (5), for example, *totally* appears to function similarly to a discourse marker. While the use of *totally* in North American English has been relatively well documented (see, e.g., Aijmer 2011), it has not been widely described as a property of UK English, despite the fact that its frequency has increased over the past two decades. The purpose of this chapter is to establish a baseline of the syntactic, semantic, and pragmatic properties of a "new" *totally* in UK English in the 2010s, as demonstrated through the BNC2014S. In addition to looking at the structural properties, the chapter also reports on social properties such as age and gender, offering information on the social meanings of *totally*. The chapter offers a short-term diachronic perspective, comparing the instances of *totally* from the BNC2014S with the original British National Corpus.

Intensifiers are a rich topic of study for scholars interested in variation and change, and there is a long tradition of studying their developments over time. Sociolinguists have generally used an apparent-time methodology whereby changes are studied as they are taking place by comparing the speech of individuals of different ages (Labov 1963, 1966). However, a number of sociolinguistic factors such as age-grading may complicate the interpretation of the data (Bailey 2004). It is therefore lucky that we can now carry out "real-time sociolinguistics" by comparing data from corpora of spoken English compiled at different periods of time through what has been called "a short-term diachronic comparative corpus linguistics" (Leech et al. 2009: 24). There is a growing body of corpora of spoken English that can now be used for studying recent or ongoing changes.

The BNC2014S consists of informal, spontaneous conversations between family members or friends representing contemporary spoken British English (Love et al., 2017). It is a sociolinguistic corpus, which makes available metadata about categories such as the speakers' age and gender. These factors, of course, have been demonstrated to be important determinants in studies of variation and change, including studies of intensifiers. The corpus has been designed along the same lines as the *British National Corpus – Demographic 1994* (henceforth BNC1994D). However, the new corpus is not a carbon copy of the original BNC. As pointed out by Love (2017: 185), "although comparable to the [BNC1994D], the approach taken to compile the 11.5 million-word [BNC2014S] differs of necessity, rather than by design, from its predecessor in several ways." The sampling methods used to compile the BNC2014S are, for example, different from those used in designing the model corpus, and the populations in the corpora are not identical with regard to the number of speakers belonging to different age groups or with regard to gender.[1]

For this investigation of *totally*, the occurrences of *totally* and its variant *totes* were extracted from the BNC1994D and BNC2014S using the Corpus Query Processor facility (Hardie 2018: 27). They were subsequently categorized with regard to their collocational properties, function, and the sociolinguistic features age and gender of the speakers.

---

[1] However, a new corpus tool, BNCLab, has recently been launched with the aim of creating a balanced sociolinguistic core from both the BNC2014S and the BNC1994D which will allow for more sophisticated sociolinguistic analyses (Brezina et al. 2018).

6.2 Background

According to Quirk et al (1985: 599), intensifiers can be divided into *amplifiers*, scaling the meaning upwards from an assumed norm, and *downtoners*, which scale downwards. Amplifiers can be further classified as *maximizers* (reinforcers), with the function to express the maximum degree of a property, and as *boosters*, involving a scalar conception and expressing a high degree of a property of an adjective (Paradis 1997: 27).

With a verb in its scope, *totally* is generally described as an "emphasizer" (Quirk et al. 1985: 583) "expressing the semantic role of modality [...] In adding to the force (as distinct from the degree of a constituent), emphasizers do not require that the constituent concerned should be gradable."

As can be seen from these definitions, the semantic picture of *totally is* complex, and its multifunctionality has resulted in a great deal of discussion. The issues debated concern the relationship between intensification and (epistemic) modality and how the interpretation of *totally* is related to factors such as the syntactic environment – for example, whether the elements targeted by *totally* are adjectives, verbs, nouns, and so forth. In addition, the semantic and pragmatic constraints associated with gradability and boundedness, in connection especially with adjectives and nouns, have been considered. Other topics concern the correlation between the functions of *totally* and sociolinguistic factors such as the age and gender of its main users. Another aspect is how the relationship between degree and modality can be described in terms of grammaticalization and subjectification.

Irwin (2014: 37–38) distinguishes between two different uses of *totally*: it can be a completive adverb like *completely* or a speaker-oriented adverb similar to *definitely, absolutely,* and *frankly*. She also suggests that speaker-oriented *totally* can be described as synonymous with "whole-heartedly" since the speaker's commitment is more emotive and less knowledge-based than *definitely* (Irwin 2014: 9).

According to Irwin (2014: 31), utterances with *totally* can be ambiguous between the speaker-oriented and the completive interpretation. For example, consider the following instances from Irwin (2014):

(6) Jamie **totally** broke up with that guy
Reading 1: Jamie broke up with that guy completely (the completive *totally*)
Reading 2: I feel strongly that it's the case that Jamie broke up with that guy (the speaker-oriented *totally*)

Beltrama (2018) concludes (in line with Irwin's suggestion) that there are two different meanings of *totally*: (a) the lexical meaning, where *totally* is a completive adverb, and (b) a non-lexical meaning, where the focus is on the speaker's commitment towards the sentence. The emphasizer use, where *totally* strengthens the speaker's commitment towards the utterance, is referred to by Beltrama (2018) as "pragmatic" or "non-lexical," in contrast to the lexical use.

Beltrama proposes a number of diagnostics to distinguish between the lexical and non-lexical functions of *totally*. The most important of these have to do with the semantic properties of the adjective or verb: in its lexical use, *totally* combines with upper-bounded predicates, operating as a maximizer and ensuring that the property denoted by the predicate holds to a maximum degree (Beltrama 2015: 19). The boundedness hypothesis predicts that totality modifiers combine with bounded adjectives, whereas verbs and emphasizers (or boosters) combine with unbounded adjectives and verbs. The following example is from Beltrama (2015: 19):

(7) The bus is totally full. (Bounded adjective)
     I totally support this movement. (Bounded verb)
     You should totally click on that link. (Unbounded verb)
     Dude, this is a totally deep hole. (Unbounded adjective)

Another diagnostic is based on the observation that lexical and non-lexical *totally* are differently encoded in grammar (Beltrama 2018: 221). According to Beltrama (2015: 19), the non-lexical or speaker-oriented *totally* cannot, for example, appear in the scope of negation (*you shouldn't totally click on that link* to be compared with occurrences of *totally* having lexical meaning: *I don't totally support you*). In its non-lexical meanings, *totally* is said to be closely associated with subjectivity; that is, it is contingent on a subjective assessment on the part of the speaker of the utterance and the unboundedness of the collocating predicate. *Totally* is, for example, used in its pragmatic meaning with evaluative adjectives such as *brilliant, nice, beautiful* (cf. Beltrama 2018: 223). Following Martin and White (2005), I regard evaluative adjectives as closely associated with registering positive and negative feelings. They can express the speaker's judgments of a person's qualities (*totally honest*) or the speaker's reaction to objects or events with regard to whether they are good or bad, as in (8):

(8) that figure might be **totally outrageous** but it's it's something mind-blowing (SNYG-S008)
     Evaluative adjectives can also express the speaker's emotions (e.g., *totally sad*).

According to Beltrama (2018: 225), *totally* does not co-occur on the lexical level with extreme (evaluative) adjectives since these are not real upper-bound predicates. *Totally* allows, for example, for another individual to instantiate the property to a higher degree (*This movie was totally amazing, but this other one is (even) better*). The special status of evaluative or extreme adjectives has also been observed by Paradis (1997: 63), who notes that extreme adjectives [evaluative adjectives] could be said to represent a mix between scalar and limit [either/or] adjectives. Extreme adjectives are not conceptualized in terms of "more or less," or in terms of "either/or," but rather have traits of both, according to Paradis.

Besides the lexical and non-lexical uses, Beltrama (2018: 249) identifies a "responsive assertion" use, illustrated in (9):

(9)   John: Did Luke get married at 25?
      Kim: yes, he TOTALLY got married at 25.[2]

In this example, *totally* has an epistemic modal meaning that can be explained in terms of a *verum focus* operator, flagging "a particular kind of focus that emphasizes the polarity of the proposition in contrast to an antecedent with different polarity" (Beltrama 2018: 250). Examples of *totally* in "responsive assertion" were not found in my material, but *totally* could be used on its own as a response marker, which Beltrama (2018: 223) denotes as a "stand-alone fragment to answer a question."

In addition to their grammatical properties, researchers have likewise taken an interest in how the semantic and pragmatic properties of intensifiers are related to social factors, such as the speakers' age and gender or the informality of the speech situation (e.g., Waksler 2012; Beltrama and Casasanto 2017). For example, Waksler (2012: 17) draws attention to how speakers use intensifiers such as *totally* in innovative ways by violating the semantic or pragmatic constraints on its use. She refers to the new uses of intensification as "over-the-top intensification," reflecting "the speaker's surpassing the usual syntactic, semantic, or pragmatic limits" (Waksler 2012: 18). In her data, such "over-the-top" intensification was found in colloquial style, and the intensifiers were used mainly by young speakers to express more subjectivity. The colloquial nature of *totally* is also mentioned in the *Oxford English Dictionary* (OED), and it is linked to various social attributes in the *Urban Dictionary* (s.v. *totally*).

To summarize, there is some consensus that *totally* is multifunctional depending on the syntax, semantics, and pragmatics of the collocating elements. *Totally* is found with many different meanings, such as "completely," "extremely," "very," and "definitely," with a great deal of ambiguity or overlap between the meanings. A distinction has been made between a lexical (maximizing) category, booster, and emphasizer (the pragmatic or speaker-oriented use). In its lexical use, *totally* can be replaced by "completely," the adjective or verb modified by *totally* is bounded and the speaker's perspective is less present. In the emphasizer function, *totally* co-occurs with an unbounded verb or adjective and it can be replaced by *certainly*. *Totally* has been regarded

---

[2] *Totally* with caps indicates focal stress.

as a booster when it combines with gradable adjectives to express a high degree of an adjectival property on a mental scale where one of the end points is to express maximum force. The most radical change is illustrated by the function of *totally* to respond to a previous utterance in the conversation.

In the following sections, I look in more detail at discourse-pragmatic variation and "innovating" uses of *totally* in the BNC2014S in different syntactic environments (modifying words or clauses), its semantic and pragmatic developments, and its functions. I also explore the age and gender of the speakers who use *totally* in different contexts and functions.

6.3 Results

As mentioned, the trigger for this study was the observation that the intensifier *totally* has become more frequent in UK English over the short time gap separating BNC1994D and the BNC2014S. *Totally* shows a fairly steep rise in frequency, from 231 examples in BNC1994D (46.06 instances per million words (pmw)) to 424 words in the BNC2014S (88.62 instances pmw).[3]

Whenever there is a shift in frequency with an innovative variant, it can be hypothesized that there is a connection between the new form and the age and gender of the speakers. However, in this case the data does not exhibit major differences in the frequency of *totally* across genders and age cohorts. This can be seen in Table 6.1, showing the number of occurrences of *totally* used by speakers in each age group on the basis of the classification scheme introduced in the BNC2014S. *Totally* was more frequently used by males (95.91 occurrences pmw) than by females (79.36 occurrences pmw). The difference was significant at the $p<0.01$ level.

In the rest of this chapter, I examine whether the age and gender of the speakers are sensitive to the semantic and pragmatic properties of *totally* in different syntactic environments. To begin, I compare the frequency and use of *totally* in different syntactic and semantic contexts in the BNC1994D and the BNC2014S.

6.3.1 Totally *in Different Syntactic Contexts*

Totally occurs in many syntactic contexts with different functions. With regard to its syntactic function, *totally* can be a modifier, a subjunct, or a disjunct. *Totally* is a modifier before adjectives and adverbs. It has the syntactic function to operate at the level of constituents rather than at the clause level. *Totally* modifying a verb, negative, noun phrase, pronoun, or prepositional phrase has been categorized

---

[3] The sample version of the BNC2014 (c. 5 million words) has been used to make it comparable with the BNC1994D which comprises c 5 million words.

Table 6.1 *Number of occurrences of* totally *used by speakers in each age group in the BNC2014S*

Age	Tokens	No. words	pmw
0–10	–	1,281	–
11–18	3	191,987	15.63
19–29	150	1,961,779	76.46
30–39	86	834,379	103.07
40–49	46	463,022	99.35
50–59	39	375,368	103.90
60–69	67	625,013	107.20
70–79	33	254,263	129.79
80–89	–	45,066	–
90–99	–	3,812	–
Unknown	–	28,271	–
Total	424	4,784,241	

syntactically as a subjunct rather than a modifier. According to Quirk et al. (1985: 566), the term subjunct is applied to adverbials "which have to a greater or lesser degree a subordinate role [...] in comparison with other clause elements." When *totally* functions as a disjunct it has "a superior role as compared with the sentence element," and it has "a scope that extends over the sentence as a whole" (Quirk et al. 1985: 613). As discussed in this chapter, *totally* has different functions at different syntactic levels. It can be an intensifier, an emphasizer, or a booster.

Table 6.2 shows the frequency pmw of *totally* with different syntactic targets in the BNC1994D and the BNC2014S.

In both the BNC1994D and the BNC2014S, *totally* was most frequent with adjectival targets. The number of occurrences increases from 26.92 cases pmw in BNC1994D to 41.17 times pmw in the BNC2014S. The higher frequency of *totally* in BNC2014S is above all due to its increase in frequency with verbal targets, from 7.78 occurrences pmw in BNC199D to 24.24 occurrences pmw in BNC2014S. *Totally* in the BNC2014S was found in a number of new syntactic contexts, where it modifies *be going to*, auxiliaries, and negatives. Moreover, *totally* occurred as a response marker with a frequency of 6.27 pmw in the BNC2014S compared with 0.40 times pmw in the BNC1994D, indicating that this function, while still quite rare, is increasing in frequency.

The high rate of use of *totally* as a modifier of adjectives is confirmed in other studies, although the use is lower here than in comparable studies. Núñez Pertejo and Palacios Martínez (2014) studied *totally* in both adolescent and adult spoken language on the basis of comparable corpora compiled in the 1990s. In their data, 80 percent of all the examples of *totally* were followed by

Table 6.2 *The frequencies of* totally *with different syntactic targets and functions in the BNC1994D and the BNC2014S*

Syntax		Function	BNC1994D	pmw	BNC2014S	pmw
Modifier						
	adjectives or participial adjectives (emphasizer)	intensifier or booster	135	26.92	197	41.17
	adverbs	intensifier	4	0.80	1	0.21
Subjunct targeting a specific word						
	lexical verb	emphasizer	39	7.78	116	24.24
	be going to	emphasizer	–		5	1.04
	auxiliary	emphasizer	–		5	1.04
	negative	emphasizer	–		4	0.84
	noun phrase	emphasizer*	5	0.99	13	2.72
	pronoun	emphasizer	2	0.40	2	0.42
	preposition phrase	emphasizer**	19	3.79	23	4.81
Disjunct						
	utterance-final discourse marker	emphasizer	6	1.20	11	2.30
	response marker	emphasizer	2	0.40	30	6.27
	unclear		19	–	17	–
	total		231		424	

Note. * There was one example where *totally* could be regarded as an intensifier. See Section 6.3.5.
** There are some examples where *totally* could also be analyzed as an intensifier. See Section 6.3.6.

an adjective, compared with only 63.8 percent in the teenage data in the Bergen Corpus of London Teenage Language (COLT), indicating that the rise in frequency is an adolescent phenomenon.

6.3.2 Totally *Modifying Adjectives*

Adjectives or participial adjectives were by far the most common forms modified by *totally* in the BNC2014S (37.38 tokens pmw). The adjectives represent seventy-six different types (Appendix A6.1a), which is a rise in frequency in comparison with the thirty-one different adjective types that occurred in the BNC1994D (thirty-one types) (Appendix A6.1ab).

Maximizers may also show semantic preference. Semantic preference "describes a phenomenon whereby a particular lexical item x collocates frequently, not with another lexical item y, but with a series of items which belong to a semantic series {S}" (Partington 2004: 150). *Totally* shows a preference for adjectives associated with lexicosemantic features such as absence of a quality (*empty, bald, devoid of*), change of state (*different*), dependence (*dependent on*), or something unpleasant or bad (*wrong, sickening*), which can be described at the level of evaluation as having an unfavorable element. According to Cacchiani (2005), *totally* is "a relatively strong negative intensifier" with a tendency to co-occur with negatively colored adjectives (Cacchiani 2005: 409).

However, *totally* may also occur in favorable contexts with positive evaluative adjectives as *totally good* (*fine, interesting, nice, awesome, weird, absorbs*) or adjectives that can be given a positive meaning (*safe, true, right*) where the adverb reinforces the favorable implications of the adjective. Semantically what is intensified is the speaker's emotional attitude such as approval or disapproval (which can be associated with *totally*'s positive or negative semantic prosody) (cf. Partington 2004: 151). The context has been analyzed as neutral when it is not possible to say if the adjective intensified by *totally* is associated with a positive or negative evaluation (*totally dark, totally English*). Table 6.3 shows the frequency of *totally* with negative, positive, and neutral adjectives in the BNC1994D and the BNC2014S.

Totally displays a preference for negative adjectives in both corpora. However, the semantic preferences of the adverb are shown to be changing over time. In its lexical (maximizing) and most frequent use, *totally* co-occurred with bounded adjectives (cf. Waksler 2012: 28; Beltrama 2015: 19). *Totally* can be replaced by *completely* and it collocates, for example, with *open*, which has a natural or definite end point (compare also, e.g., *totally full, totally different, totally wrong*).[4]

When *totally* modifies extreme (evaluative) adjectives, it is associated with subjectivity, or in other words the expression of attitudes and points of view.

Table 6.3 *The frequency of* totally *with positive, negative, and neutral adjectives*

Adjective	BNC1994D	Percent	BNC2014S	Percent
negative	112	83%	129	67.9%
positive	15	11.1%	49	25.8%
neutral	8	6%	12	6.3%
Total	135	100%	190*	100%

* In seven occurrences *totally* was doubled and counted only once

---

[4] The most frequent of the bounded adjectives was *different* (forty-five tokens in the BNC2014S). However, *wrong* is ambiguous between "limit" and evaluative (extreme).

Paradis (1997: 81) found only "the odd extreme adjective" in the London-Lund Corpus in her study of intensifiers in English. However, extreme evaluative adjectives were not unusual in the BNC2014S, which provided examples such as *bemused, bewildering, bored, boring, delicious, honest, outrageous, pathetic,* and *sickening*. Adjectives could also be placed on a scale expressing mirativity, exemplified by the extreme adjectives *bizarre, unprecedented,* and *weird*.

When *totally* co-occurs with evaluative adjectives such as *good, fine,* and *nice*, which are not superlative or extreme but scalar or comparative (Paradis 1997: 56), it is a "booster" (cf. *very, extremely*) rather than a maximizer and reinforces some value of the adjective on a scale. The modified adjectives include both common ones such as *nice* (12), *good*, or *fine* and slangy or informal ones such as *awesome, camp, insane, manic, cool,* and *chill*. The adjectives are generally positive (an exception is *sad*).

(12)   cos they're **totally nice** (S7JG-S0084)(F19–29)

In my analysis, the combinations of *totally* with a scalar adjective would represent a pragmatic clash between the maximizing meaning of *totally*, scalar adjectivity, and the positive attitude indicated by the adjective. I propose that speakers use *totally* in this unusual way in a desire to be original, to capture the audience's attention, and to demonstrate their verbal skills (cf. Tagliamonte 2008: 391). Such combinations of *totally* and scalar adjectives did not occur in the BNC1994D,[5] yet *totally fine* was a common collocation in the BNC2014S, with ten examples. In (13), the speaker is a 29-year-old café owner:

(13)   I can be rude to someone on Twitter and **it's totally fine** (SKHN-S0331)(F29)

Totally sad is uttered as a comment on an ad where mums and dads wear matching shoes of the brand Sketchers:

(14)   A: mum and dad's got a matching pair they've got his and hers sketchers
       B: yeah
       A: **totally sad** (S4YQ-S0254)(F26)

In (15), the speaker is recommending a scoop to use for the cabbage:

(15)   A: where's the scoop? The scooper (.) there we go (.) there we go (.) this is a great thing I mean it's served with spaghetti innit?
       B: um (.) no yeah
       A: **it's totally better** for cabbage (.) there we go (S7JG-S0041)(F19–29)

---

[5] An exception may be "totally mad" (one example in the BNC1994D).

Beltrama and Staum Casasanto (2017: 177) explain the pragmatic effects of such "ungrammatical" combinations as a clash between the meaning of *totally* and the expectations generated in the linguistic context, in light of which the expression is unexpected or unwarranted. They also suggest that such forms are socially salient. *Totally* also has the intersubjective function to capture the hearer's attention and to show alignment with the hearer.

The short form *totes* was used by speakers in the 25-to-34-year-old age group in four examples in the BNC2014S, each time to modify adjectives. In (16), the speaker is a 29-year-old female baker. The conversation is about members of the Hackney Council:

(16)   I reckon it's **totes normal** for them they're like UNCLEARWORD (SBM6-S0084)(F29)

Another observation is that *totes* seems to co-occur with positive adjectives, as in (17):

(17)   yeah (.) **that's totes fine** (.) er there's your statement there love (SJLT-S0084) (F19–29)

Totally adorbs can be regarded as an established collocation in adolescent speech. The *Urban Dictionary* describes *totes adorbs* as an abbreviation of *totally adorable*, "Used when one sees something that causes squealing, clapping, and overall giddyness due to something being of extreme cuteness and/or adorableness" (*Urban Dictionary*).

In (18), the speaker is a 29-year-old graduate, indicating that *totally* is a fad that is spreading from teenagers to older speakers.

(18)   A: ≫they were totally adorbs
       B: those
       C: Orbs (.) yeah and they lost anyway
       B: ah cunts
       A: those members of the board whoever **they were totes adorbs** (SUWR-S038)(F29)

The use of *totes* by speakers who are no longer in their teens suggests that it is most likely a fad that is on its way out in the teenage community.

Shifting the focus from the collocational patterns with *totally* and adjective to sociolinguistic factors, it can be observed that the speakers using *totally* with scalar adjectives are young and mainly female. Table 6.4 describes all the occurrences of *totally* with scalar adjectives, including the above-quoted examples.

In comparison to the findings highlighted in this section from the BNC2014S, in the BNC1994D corpus *totally* was likewise more frequent as a modifier of adjectives than of other words. In the BNC1994D, *totally* was

Table 6.4 *Occurrences of* totally *as a modifier of scalar adjectives produced by male and female speakers in different age categories*

Occurrence	Age bracket
A. FEMALE SPEAKER	
what what what's weird about it? like **totally fine** (S3RL)	25–34
≫and it is (.) it's **totally fine** (S3RL)	15–24
≫right **totally awesome** yeah (SKMV)	35–44
you've got ta pee (.) well that's **totally fine** (SYTD)	19–29
A: where's the scoop? The scooper (.) there we go (.) there we go (.) this is a great thing I mean it's served with spaghetti innit? B: um (.) no yeah A: it's **totally** better for cabbage (.) there we go (S7JG)	19–29
cos they're **totally nice** (S7JG)	19–29
A: mum and dads got a matching pair they've got his and hers sketchers B: yeah A: **totally sad** (S4YQ)	19–29
this guy was sort of like he was he's **totally camp** but he was more like he was just easier to get on with (SF2 F)	19–29
he was saying all of this stuff (.) er he you know he's he's **totally manic** now (SE88)	19–29
≫yeah (.) yeah and you've been a manager before so it's not **totally alien** (SDAJ)	19–29
um I will actually speak to her and see if she knows any more about it (.) because that would be like a **totally awesome** (S7Z8)	19–29
B. MALE SPEAKER	
and I because all our systems went down for an hour and a half this morning which was **totally awesome** (SBSJ)	19–29
and it's like sweet we're **totally cool** (SV49)	19–29
apparently she was just **totally chill** about it (S0383)	30–39
I could just be on the dole and just watch these videos all day and like be **totally fine** (SDJA)	25–34

found mostly with a maximizing function, usually co-occurring with extreme (evaluative) adjectives. However, it was not used as a booster with scalar adjectives that were not extreme but comparative. *Totally* was more strongly negative in the BNC1994D, where only 11 percent of the occurrences had *totally* modifying a positive adjective to be compared with about 26 percent in the BNC2014S.

In terms of the role of gender, the results here can be compared with the findings on the frequency and use by of *totally* in a study carried out by Murphy (2010), with the aim to investigate the influence of age and gender on female (and male) talk. Murphy's corpus was collected between 2003 and 2004 and consisted of three 15,000-word corpora of male and female speech representing three chronological age groups referred to as twenties, forties, and sixties. Murphy's analysis of *totally* (which she referred to as a "booster") showed that *totally* was most frequently used by male speakers in their twenties. The female speakers using *totally* were mostly in their forties. Murphy found no tokens of *totally* in the speech produced by the oldest speakers.

The study of *totally* with adjectives can now be summed up. Depending on the properties of the collocating adjective – for example, whether it is positive or negative, and depending on its boundedness and scalarity – *totally* has different meanings. *Totally* followed by an adjective can be used in a lexical way as a maximizer boosting the adjective to an end point (e.g., *totally open*). As a maximizer, *totally* can be replaced by *completely*, and it co-occurs with bounded adjectives. When *totally* collocates with extreme (evaluative) adjectives, it comes close to being an emphasizer but retains some intensifying meaning.

The instances of *totally* as a booster or emphasizer before scalar adjectives were not very frequent. However, these few instances are nonetheless interesting because of the close association between the pragmatic meaning and social meaning. The comparison between the BNC1994D and the BNC2014S showed that *totally* was more frequent before adjectives in the more recent corpus and that it was also used in innovative ways as a booster with scalar adjectives expressing that something is good or bad or to express an emotion. In addition, these few instances tended to be found in the speech of young females.

6.3.3 Totally *Modifying Verbs*

Totally before verbs had a frequency of 24.24 occurrences pmw in the BNC2014S, making it more frequent in this context in the 2014 corpus than in the BNC1994D, at 7.78 occurrences pmw. It was found with seventy-four different verb types, compared with thirty-one types of verbs in the BNC1994D.

The verbs modified or targeted by *totally* in the 2014 corpus were typically telic or more generally achievement verbs. Several of the verbs also indicate change, for example *change, transform*, and *redecorate*.[6] *Totally* was associated with negative semantic prosody in 42 percent of the occurrences and with neutral verbs in 58 percent of the examples.[7] *Totally* was not found with verbs having positive connotations.[8] The negative verbs were common ones, such as *fail, ignore, lose, neglect, ruin, ban*, and idioms such as *slip one's mind, be put off by sth, pick sth apart, knock sb off, freak out, fall apart*, and *be put on one's arse*. With telic verbs, *totally* is associated with a bounded scale that has lexical

---

[6] See Appendix A6.2a and A6.2b for a list of the verbs co-occurring with *totally* in the BNC1994D and the BNC2014.
[7] In the BNC1994D, 61 percent of the occurrences had negative prosody.
[8] A possible exception is "totally stick up for sb" where the idiomatic character of the verb phrase also can explain why *totally* is used.

meaning, for example "completely." However, there is a great deal of ambiguity between the lexical or intensifying meaning and the non-lexical or emphasizer meaning, and the speaker's intention is important for how *totally* is interpreted. Consider the following example:

(19)   ready (.) okay (.) **that totally freaked me out** (.) (SV2 V-S0084)(F19–29)

In (19), the target of intensification is the predicate "freaked me out." The verb is bounded, which suggests that there is a contrast between being completely freaked out and being only partially freaked out. Depending on the context (the speaker's intention), the construction could also have the interpretation that the speaker draws attention to her commitment to the truth of the proposition (=*definitely*).

When *totally* follows the verb, as in (20), the intensifying reading is preferred:

(20)   yeah we we have **sorted Christmas out totally** (SEPP-S0424)(M44)

According to Quirk et al. (1985: 591), maximizers in the position after the verb are more likely "to convey their absolute meaning of extreme degree."

When the verb phrase is a colorful or idiomatic expression, *totally* can be linked to an increase of subjectivity and intersubjectivity, as in (21–24).

(21)   sticking up for him I get that like cos my manager if I did something wrong she would **totally stick up** for me (SR82-S0216)(F22)

(22)   A: ≫no but you also have been trawling the charity shops so it's not like you've been
B: yes
A: you know **totally splashing the cash (SYTD-S0084)**(F19–29)

(23)   um (.) but apparently it lasted like about one round and he'd just got **totally like put on his arse** by this (SFM7-S0037)(F19–29)

(24)   ANONnameF says that she **like totally like bosses her fiancé around like** and then she's talking about this guy called – (S9E6-S0326)(M20)

Beltrama and Staum Casasanto (2017: 163) suggest that in contexts deviating from expectations, *totally* involves the hearer in the construction of the verbal exchange and can contribute "to 'create a we' grounded in the shared evaluation of the sentence as outrageous/odd. [...] For example, it is possible to use *totally* in situations in which the speaker asserts a proposition whose content is markedly odd or surprising, and as such it is likely to encounter the skepticism of the listener" (Beltrama and Staum Casasanto 2017: 161). Following Beltrama and Staum Casasanto we would then, for example, expect *totally* to be used in (25) where the verb is idiomatic and the content of the utterance refers to a situation which is "unbelievable, amusing or highly remarkable in some way, and thus worthy of 'an extra push' to be added to the Common Ground" (Beltrama and Staum Casasanto 2017: 171).

(25)   and then afterwards I'm talking away to him while I'm putting my putting my tights up and pulling them up (.) but obviously pulling them up means my dress is now around my waist so I can pull my tights up (.) I mean he was **totally copping a look** (S6J2-S041)(F19–29)

However, *totally* is also used before *see* in the same semantic field, where the intensifier would not be expected, as no exaggeration is expressed and the verb is not bounded, as in (26).

(26)   I can **totally see** it from her point of view (S3RL-S0428)(F27)

Occurrences where *totally* modifies an unbounded verb are not exceptional and may be on the rise. The following examples are taken from the complete BNC2014S (11,422,617 words). *Totally* is used as an emphasizer, equivalent to *definitely*, in examples (27–29).

(27)   de de de de cos an extraordinary happy Christmas **it totally sounds like that** as well he told me that it's gonna be a special year for you and me (S6Q6-S0595)(F18)

(28)   I'm **totally getting** all of them. or well you're **totally getting** all of them (S23A-S0032)(M28)

(29)   it's very cool but I **totally don't remember** how to do it (S23A-S0094)(F33)

Totally can be extended to many contexts with verbs. In (30), *totally* precedes an imperative to emphasize the request. The speaker is a 16-year-old girl telling her mother not to put on airs (because the mother is wearing a new hat). Again, *totally* is equivalent to *definitely*.

(30)   and **totally don't go** giving yourself airs and graces mummy (S72E-S0529)(F16)

Totally was less frequent in the BNC1994D, and it was found in fewer contexts. The verbs modified by *totally* were bounded verbs. *Totally* functioned as an intensifier expressing an absolute degree of a property. It was not found in unexpected contexts with idiomatic verbs or with unbounded verbs, favoring the interpretation of *totally* as an emphasizer.

In the BNC2014S, *totally* was found before the emphatic *going*-future with the function of intensifying subjectivity and with the intersubjective implication of fostering common ground (=*definitely, certainly*) (cf. Stange 2017). There were five examples in the BNC2014S of this type and no examples in

BNC1994D. The occurrences in my material all had a first-person subject, as shown in examples (31–34). *Totally* is apparently used to make *be going to* more argumentative by giving it an extra push.

(31)   **I'm totally going to** watch that cos I really really fancy him (S5UJ-S0085) (F19–29)

(32)   **I'm totally going to** utilise this to my advantage (S6J2-S0041)(F19–29)

In (33), the surrounding context contains the exclamation *oh god*, reinforcing the subjective meaning of *totally (gonna)*.

(33)   >oh god well **I'm totally gonna** leave it to –ANONname (SY4E–S0320)(F34)

The users of *totally+be going to* were mostly young females, accounting for four out of five examples. However, the fifth example, (34), was uttered by a middle-aged man.

(34)   I'm **totally going to** do that over the summer (SEGL-S0105)(M35)

Totally can also be extended to contexts with modal auxiliaries such as *will/ would* and *can/could*,[9] which are associated with a subjective assessment of the utterance on the part of the speaker. In all such occurrences, *totally* occurred before the modal auxiliary, strengthening the speaker's commitment.

In (35), *totally will* refers to an event in the future, emphasizing the speaker's commitment to what is said.

(35)   I imagine the kids **totally will** be really hoping school's close tomorrow (SEGL-S0155)(M42)

The speaker perspective is further indicated by *I imagine*. The speaker is a 42-year-old male, which suggests that the construction is not new. Nonetheless, no similar constructions were found in the BNC1994D.

In (36), the modal auxiliary is *can*. The interpretation is ambiguous, however, depending on whether *can* is stressed or not. In one reading, *totally* is interpreted as an emphasizer with speaker-oriented or modal meaning (="which I'm certain you can still do"). In the other reading, the speaker's intention is to emphasize what the hearer is able to do.

(36)   a tea party (.) now –ANONnameM I know you wanna do your (.) er cinema night which **you totally can** still do but I had forgotten that erm – ANONplace fitness centre where I do my or assault course racing type thing they can do parties for children you know (SZFG-S0653)(F39)

---

[9] In addition, there was one example with *have to totally*, cf. Beltrama (2018: 228): "On a broader level, it has been observed that certain modal modifiers can indeed occur before or after the modal, with no significant difference in meaning."

In (37), *totally* reinforces the assertion "could have guessed tea," which is in contrast with "I kind of guessed tea."

(37) yeah I kind of guessed tea (.) **totally could've** guessed that – UNCLEARWORD (S0032-S23A)(M28)

Totally before *be going to* or before a modal auxiliary was only found in the BNC2014S, indicating that this use is spreading to new contexts over time.

6.3.4   Totally Modifying Negatives

The BNC2014S contained five examples where *totally* was followed by a negative target such as *not* or *never*. The speakers using *totally* in this combination with a negative were all females and in the age range 19–29 or 30–39. Similar occurrences with the intensifier *so* followed by a negative have been shown to be abundant (Waksler 2012: 21). Waksler (2012: 21) found fewer examples of *totally* followed by a negative target since the new *totally* "was usually used in discourse with positive affect." The target can be *not*, followed by either an adjective, as in (38), or by a noun phrase, as in (39). In (38), two young girls are discussing whether it was rude of the teacher to tell some of the children to get out.

(38) Annie: she was like this is unacceptable get out
Maggie: yeah and they were like we have nowhere to go and she was like well why don't you just get out then?
Annie: yeah **that's totally not rude** (S5QR-S0325)(F13)

In (39), *totally* is used by the speaker to emphasize that she does not like a certain kind of film.

(39) Eve: that was well good (.) it's got Ewan McGregor and they were all like they're kind of they're told that like the world had kinda ended and it was a massive kind of contaminated bug or something like that and they literally
Anne: **that is totally not my type of film** (SPMl-S0160)(F14)

In (40), the negative word modified by *totally* is *never*. The speaker uses *totally* to underline that she is never doing it again (posting photos on Facebook):

(40) there's some really bad on there (.) really bad (.) I'm **totally never doing** that again (S6J2-S0041)(F19–29)

6.3.5   Totally Modifying Noun Phrases

Totally was followed by a noun phrase in only four occurrences in BNC1994D (0.80 times pmw), compared to thirteen occurrences in the BNC2014S (2.71

times pmw). These examples include *totally* followed by a definite or indefinite noun phrase, a clause (*totally what they think*), or nouns indicating qualities (*totally skyscrapers*). The collocation with a noun (phrase) was equally frequent in the speech of males and females. It was mostly used by middle-aged or older speakers. In (41), the speaker is complaining about the authorities granting permission to make changes to an existing building.

(41)   it was **totally the wrong way** to deal with that building (SN59-S0829)(F60+)

As in the preceding example, *totally* must be understood as an emphasizer with a modal meaning:

(42)   A: but I think a huge part of it is I mean fir- first of all it's to do with dyslexia and and and the sort of abilities in relation to certain skills but also a lot of er I mean a huge part of it which I think is where the prejudice comes from is erm (.) education and class
B: **yeah totally a class thing** (SDA8-S0383)(M30)

In (43), *totally* "targets a scale that aggregates the set of stereotypical features" associated with the noun *skyscrapers* (cf. Beltrama 2015: 17). *Totally* indicates the strength of the speaker's attitude towards the target. The speaker is young, indicating that this use of *totally* is age-related. Similar occurrences were not found in the BNC1994D.

(43)   yeah you should see what they're doing by the station I must say it looks **totally skyscrapers** (SMY3-S0326)(M20)

Totally was followed by a pronoun in only a few examples: two examples in the BNC1994D and two examples in the BNC2014S. The two occurrences in the BNC2014S had a form of *some* modified by *totally*:

(44)   ≫yeah exactly and like I said that I said to my mum yesterday I was like that is **just totally something** I'm gonna have to get used to (SFLB-S0375)(F24)

6.3.6   Totally *Modifying Prepositional Phrases*

Totally as a modifier of a prepositional phrase is not a new construction but has risen in frequency in the BNC2014S. It occurred 3.79 times pmw in the BNC1994D, compared with 4.81 occurrences pmw in the BNC2014S. In many cases, the prepositional phrase corresponds to an adjective but is more expressive. For example, in (45), *totally out of proportion* could be expressed as *totally disproportionate*, although this would not be nearly as idiomatic. Compare also *totally against the law* (=*illegal*), *totally out of the blue* (=*unexpected*), *totally out of the ordinary* (=*unusual*), and *totally out of one's mind* (=*distraught*).

(45)   but it it has got **totally out of proportion** (S4PC-S0017)(M60+)

The speaker's viewpoint is expressed more strongly when the prepositional phrase is part of an idiom, as in (46). Describing someone as not being *totally in the American pocket* is an effective and colorful means of expressing that a person is not doing something because he is told to do so by the Americans or in return for American money.

(46)   erm Zia-ul-Haq was er one of these (.) politicians in Pakistan who wasn't **totally in the American pocket** (S35 K-S0372)(M65)

The prepositional phrase targeted by *totally* was idiomatic in 82 percent of the cases in the 2014 corpus and 52 of the examples in the BNC1994D. In a little more than half of the occurrences in the BNC2014S, the preposition phrases had negative rather than a more neutral meaning – for example, *out of my mind, be off limits, out of proportion, be in the American pocket, be in the grip of*.

6.3.7   Totally *As a Discourse Marker*

Totally can be used in new functions "highlighting an interaction between discourse structure and subjectivity" (Beltrama 2015: 14). There are several factors that favor the extension of an intensifier into discourse. As we have seen so far in this chapter, *totally* as an intensifier can express a positive attitude or affect (especially in adolescent speech), and this attitude can be further reinforced when *totally* stands alone (cf. Tao 2007). Another significant factor is that *totally* has been shown to have epistemic meaning (=*definitely, certainly*) in some of its uses. Analogy with *definitely* may therefore play a role in how *totally* acquires discourse functions.

In (47), *totally* can be regarded as a discourse marker, as indicated by its position at the end of the utterance outside the propositional content. It functions as an emphasizer with modal meaning, strengthening the speaker's commitment to the preceding utterance.

(47)   I absolutely hate her (.) **like totally** (S7V3-S0016)(F19–29)

Supporting evidence of the discourse marker status of *totally* is that it can be omitted without causing any change of the propositional content and that it has the procedural function to provide a clue to the hearer about how the utterance should be interpreted. Another indication is that it combines with the discourse marker *like*.

In (48), *totally* is "backwards-looking" and has the function to emphasize the assertion *yeah totally they love it in Spain*. The function of *totally* can be compared with what Beltrama (2018) referred to as "responsive assertion."

(48)	Emily: oh my God they're bonkers about it
	Erica: they love it in Spain (.) **yeah totally** they love it in Spain
	Emily: ugh (S3PF-S0146)(F30–39)

As a response marker, *totally* is used on its own and has the function to respond to questions, requests, or uncertain assertions. In (49), it marks a response to an assertion:

(49)	it's really expensive (.) like the prices are
	Lucy: **totally** (.) and it's still a bad quality (S95D-S0018)(F30–39)

In (50), *totally* has the function to agree to a preceding request for action, in the form of a suggestion.

(50)	Anne: **let's text and say why Ballare**? It's well full of chavs on a Friday
	Margaret: **like totally**
	Anne: that's the only thing with Cambridge like where do the normal people go? Cos I feel like Revs is full of like Top Shop girls and students (STSS-S0041)(unknown age)

Totally was also used as the response to a question. The following occurrence features in the conversation between two middle-aged females.

(51)	Dawn: cos you're his mother
	Mary: I know **do you think that's what it is**?
	Dawn: **yeah totally (.) oh totally yeah**
	Mary: ≫ in that case (.) yeah so in a way it's better not to present things cos each one each time you present some possibility it gets ruled out so you're you sort of d- doing a worse job than if you didn't suggest anything really (SGFN-S0478)(F57)

Finally, *totally* was used as a "backchannel" by the listener to signal understanding or engagement with what is said without taking the conversational floor (see Eiswirth, Chapter 8, this volume). This is illustrated in (52). *Totally* is repeated, and it co-occurs with other discourse markers.

(52)	April: ≫ how are you going to decide otherwise? **someone's selling you something**
	Stacey: **totally right totally**
	April: ≫ **something as important as your wedding day**
	Stacey: yeah (S6HP-S0303)(F41)

In its function as a response marker (or a backchannel), *totally* has lost its conceptual meaning. The discourse function is assumed to emerge in dialogic contexts where the interactional work required by the speaker and hearer is as important as the exchange of information. The development is facilitated by recurrent usage and strengthened by the analogy of the functions of discourse-oriented *totally*, with similar discourse functions of the epistemic modal adverbials *certainly* and *definitely*.

The BNC2014S provided 30 occurrences of *totally* as a response marker (6.27 occurrences pmw) to be compared with 0.40 occurrences pmw in the BNC1994D. The speakers were generally female; thirty females compared to ten males. The majority of speakers using *totally* as a response marker were between the ages of thirty and thirty-nine (60 percent).

Totally as a discourse marker with the function of an emphasizer had a frequency of 6.27 occurrences pmw in the BNC2014S, compared with 1.20 occurrences pmw in the BNC1994D.

6.4 Discussion and Conclusion

Totally is a fuzzy element characterized by polysemy. It is an intensifier (maximizer) co-occurring with bounded adjectives or verbs but also an emphasizer or booster, depending on the type of adjectives or verbs with which it co-occurs. However, there is a great deal of ambiguity between the intensifier (maximizer) and the emphasizer or epistemic meaning, and both meanings can co-occur.

The differing functions as intensifier, emphasizer, and discourse marker can also be said to indicate different degrees of grammaticalization, the process by means of which "more contentful material becomes more schematic and non-referential" (Traugott 2012: 19). The most dramatic change taking place during this period is the expansion of *totally* to the area of pragmatics and discourse.

There are several indications that the grammaticalization of *totally* is grounded in conversational interaction, emphasizing "the roles of the speaker and the addressee, pragmatic and discoursal aspects, sociolinguistics, styles, and registers, subjectivity and intersubjectivity – in short, language as a means of communication" (Rissanen 2008: 345). The semantic development of *totally* from an intensifier to an emphasizer, which also relates to its functions as a stand-alone response marker, is a convincing example of a change from less to more subjectivity. According to Athanasiadou (2007), the uses of *totally* as an emphasizer with procedural rather than conceptual meaning are examples of "full attenuation," characterized by a loss of the original conceptual meaning of *totally*. They do not express degree; they retain no meaning of "completely." They are only used to express a high degree of certainty or speaker commitment (Athanasiadou 2007: 561). As a discourse marker with reactive function, *totally* becomes integrated into a paradigm of epistemic adverbials (discourse markers) such as *certainly* or *definitely* (cf. Tao 2007).

The functional perspective has been at the forefront for the discussion in this analysis. However, the corpus investigation allows us to make observations about variation and sociolinguistic aspects such as the age and gender of the speakers. For example, the findings point to a connection between the semantic or pragmatic properties of *totally* and young people, especially young females. Changes typically begin in the informal conversations among young people who use *totally* to show that they belong to a particular social group. *Totally* is generational in the sense that it can index properties associated with young people such as coolness, distancing from adult community, solidarity with the peer group, creativity, and so on. With the spread of *totally* to more and older speakers, it may lose its attraction for young speakers and be replaced by other, more expressive intensifiers.

Appendix

A6.1a   Adjectives (Types) in the BNC1994D

amazing, angelic, anonymous, ashamed, bald, bankrupt, bare, bemused, black, blank, boring, careful, completed, confused, correct, crazy, deaf, different, disastrous, disgusting, drug-oriented, embarrassed, finished off, fucked, fucked off his head, fucked up, fucked out of his head, gummed up, honest, idle, ignorable, illiterate, immaculate, Jewish, Kink, mad, missing, mixed up, non-existent, normal, opposite, outrageous, overrated, pissed, pissed off, prepared, private, rainproof, rat-arsed, red, redundant, right, satisfactory, shameless, shit, shocked, short, snowed under, strange, stupid, teetotal, transparent, true, unbelievable, unexpected, unfair, unfit, unnatural, unnecessary, unsubtle, wasted, wave-length, wild, wonderful, wrecked, wrong

A6.1b   Adjectives (Types) in the BNC2014S

adorbs, alien, arbitrary, automated, aware, awesome, bald, bemused, better, bewildering, bizarre, blanched, bland, blimey, boiling, bored, boring, brilliant, burnt, camp, chill, closed, clued up, common, confused, constrained, cool, crazy, dark, delicious, dependent, depressed, determined, devoid, different, disproportionate, dominant, empty, English, excited, famous, fine, focused, free, fucked, gone, hammered, honest, hungover, ignorant, illegal, inappropriate, incapable, incompatible, inconsequential, innovative, insane, interesting, irrelevant, loved up, mangled, manic, naive, naked, new, nice, nonsensical, normal, obsessed, outrageous, pathetic, perplexed, pissed, pointless, pure, rammed, ready, refined, rich, right, sad, safe, same, satisfied, screwed, sealed, self-contained, selfish, sensible, shit, sickening, slaughtered, spurious, stone faced, supple, sure, true, Turkish, unconditional, undraped, understandable, unnecessary, unpleasant, unprecedented, unrealistic, unrewarding, unfit, unstable, useless, weird, whack, white, worth, wrong

A6.2a   Verbs (Types) in the BNC1994D

agree, change, cover, depress, disappear, dislike, fake it, forget, give up, have it, ignore, insult, knock sb, lack, lose, make sth different, make a fool of, misconstrue, pull out of, rebuild, redecorate, refuse, relax, re-tile, ruin, split up, take over, transform, understand, worry, wreck

A6.2b   Verbs (Types) in the BNC2014S

absorb, accuse, agree, alienate, backfire, ban, be, blame, boss her fiancé around, change, choose, come, cop a look, construct, cope, determine, dismantle, disregard, draw attention to, engage with, eye up sth, fail, fall apart, forget, freak out, freeload, freeze, get sth, get fucked in the storm, get sat down, go (to my classes), Google, grant, guarantee, have got, ignore, knock sb out, know, leave evidence of, lose out, make the most of, make up, maximize, miss out, neglect, organize, perplex, pick apart, play on sth, put off, put sb on his arse, refine, remove, rip off, ruin, see, sell, slip one's mind, stick up for sth, splash the cash, sort out, split up, surprise oneself, take it, take on, think about, transform, tune out, understand, white out, wind up, work, zap

7 *Uh*, What Should We Count?

Tim Gadanidis and Derek Denis

7.1 Introduction

The "accountable" quantification of variants is likely the main methodological advancement that the variationist turn in the study of discourse-pragmatic phenomena has offered (Pichler 2010; Waters 2016). While previously applied sporadically (e.g., Dubois 1992), a movement toward applying the Principle of Accountability (Labov 1972b) in quantitative analysis of discourse-pragmatic variation over the last two decades has pushed forward the field's understanding of, among other things, the longitudinal development and grammaticalization of pragmatic markers (e.g., Pichler and Levey 2011), the social meaning of various discourse-pragmatic features (e.g., Moore and Podesva 2009), and the place of discourse-pragmatic phenomena within the grammar (e.g., Denis 2017).

An alternative method of quantification from earlier work on discourse-pragmatic variables was to use normalized frequencies of individual variants – that is, the frequency of variants per 10,000 words (e.g., Stubbe and Holmes 1995). Pichler (2010) critiques this approach. She argues first that different transcription protocols for different corpora vary with respect to the treatment of phenomena such as false starts, minimal responses (e.g., *mhm*), and cliticized morphemes (e.g., *could-n't*), and these differences affect the overall word count. Second, she argues that analyses that use this method can be affected by the fact that discourse-pragmatic variables "do not have an equal chance of occurrence throughout an interaction" and therefore normalized frequencies will be affected by varying types of interaction (Pichler 2010: 595). Lastly, she argues that normalized frequencies "do not show where in the linguistic system variables occur, nor what the social and internal mechanisms are that produce variation and change in their use" (Pichler 2010: 595).

In this chapter, we defend the normalized-frequency approach. Pichler's first critique is valid, and we back her recommendation that researchers be fully transparent about the minutiae of transcription and word counts. We suggest that Pichler's second critique, while also valid, is a problem that is not unique to the normalized-frequency approach but one that is also shared with following the Principle of Accountability. If one variant is preferred in a particular context and distribution of that context is uneven in the sample, the bias remains in proportions and the Principle of Accountability will suggest a higher relative frequency of that variant just as the normalized-frequency approach will suggest a higher normalized frequency of the variant.

However, what we focus on in this chapter is a response to Pichler's third critique. In the case study we present, we demonstrate that not only are there statistical methods for disentangling the social and linguistic constraints on variation using the normalized-frequency approach but, more importantly, this method provides a unique perspective on the development of discourse-pragmatic phenomena that the typical variationist approach does not. Moreover, we argue that an analysis combining the two approaches provides the broadest analytical perspective.

To illustrate our argument, we examine a change in twentieth-century English that has progressed under the radar of laypeople and (until recently) linguists: the rise of *um* as the predominant variant of the "filled pause" variable (UHM) at the expense of *uh* (Tottie 2011; Fruehwald 2016; Wieling et al. 2016). The variation is exemplified in (1):

(1)   **Uh** as a rule they harrowed it before they **um** drilled it. (NIA-22)

Fruehwald (2016: 43) documents this "textbook" change over more than 100 years of apparent time: *um* increases incrementally between generations and the rise is led by women. We investigate (UHM) at an early stage of this change to determine what triggered the rise of *um*. As one potential explanation, we address the hypothesis that the rise of *um* was connected to the development of a new discourse function for the variable (UHM) that *um* came to be favored with. We remain agnostic about what the function might be but follow Tottie (2016) and Fruehwald (2016), who suggest a correlation between utterance position and function; specifically, Fruehwald (2016: 46) suggests that "turn-initial *um* may be the best candidate for a new discourse function coming into use."

We begin by following essentially a variationist approach, first treating *um* and *uh* as variants of a linguistic variable and using the Principle of Accountability and proportional analysis to assess the role of social and linguistic factors. We then augment these results with an examination of the normalized frequency of the individual variants and variable itself in discourse to broaden our perspective on this change. What we find is that the results of the variationist approach are not as clear-cut as that singular perspective suggests. Instead, we must look beyond the variable context, as defined, to understand this change.

7.2 (UHM) As a Pragmatic Marker

The exact nature of (UHM) as a linguistic feature is not a trivial question. A great deal of ink has been spilled over whether the variants are produced consciously or unconsciously and what their purpose is. One common view in the psycholinguistics literature is that (UHM) is an involuntary noise uttered as a result of speech production problems. For example, according to Levelt (1989), "[*uh*] apparently signals that at the moment when trouble is detected, the source of the trouble is still actual or quite recent. But otherwise, [*uh*] doesn't seem to mean anything. It is a symptom, not a sign" (Levelt 1989: 484).

One problem with the involuntary "symptom" view is that, as Clark and Fox Tree (2002: 98) point out, speakers have some control over whether or not they produce (UHM) – for example, they note that it can be suppressed in a public speaking context (and, indeed, speakers are often advised to do so). Based on data from corpora of spontaneous speech, they argue that (UHM) is an "interjection" used to signal a delay, with *um* signaling longer delays than *uh*. This view of (UHM) as an ordinary word, which is planned and produced like any other, is broadly similar to Maclay and Osgood's (1959: 41–42) influential analysis, which characterizes (UHM) as a floor-management device – speakers insert it to indicate that they do not want to be interrupted when hesitating over what to say.

Extending this line of analysis, Tottie (2016) has put forward the argument that (UHM) is a pragmatic marker that, in speech, indicates planning. This is on the basis that (UHM) is used more frequently in contexts requiring more speaker planning, such as narratives and responses to questions. Tottie (2017) describes (UHM) as being on a "cline of lexicalization," where instances of (UHM) in forms like *and-uh* and *but-uh* are not perceived as words but *uh* and *um* alone are. Tottie (2017: 125–126) describes the former case, where the final consonant of a monosyllabic word such as *and* or *but* is immediately followed by (UHM), as cliticized forms. She goes on to argue that the use of (UHM) between words and silent pauses, rather than in these cliticized forms, causes (UHM) to be perceived as a word in the lexicon, making it available for conscious use in writing. Along the same lines, Gadanidis (2018) argues that (UHM) is consciously and agentively used in instant messaging, an interactive, text-based medium. On this hypothesis, (UHM) has transitioned from a purely interactional feature (indicating that a pause is incoming due to planning) to an interpersonal feature that indicates the speaker's stance or point of view. For example, in (2), from Tottie (2017, example 2), the writer plays on the word-search-indicating function of *uh* to draw attention to their pun:

(2) An ode to opera's, **uh, operation**. As ... Baroque-era composers become increasingly popular, more people wonder about the castrati – the emasculated singers ... (*L.A. Times* 2005; cited in Tottie 2017)

If the transition from a cliticized form to a standalone word can be taken to represent functional change in (UHM)'s diachronic development, we might expect to see an effect of cliticization at early stages. Specifically, we might expect that the variant that is more advanced in this functional change is used more often in non-cliticized forms.

As we noted in Section 7.1, (UHM) is undergoing a change in progress. The rise in relative frequency of *um* has now been described extensively in the variationist and corpus-linguistic literature, across a number of corpora and speech communities. The typical finding is that women have a higher *um:uh* ratio than men and that younger speakers have a higher *um:uh* ratio than older speakers. This pattern has been demonstrated in various speech communities and contexts in the United States (Acton 2011; Laserna et al. 2014; Fruehwald 2016; Wieling et al. 2016), as well as in England and Scotland (Tottie 2011; Wieling et al. 2016), in both real and apparent time. In other words, we see a pattern consistent with a classic sociolinguistic change – it is led by women and increasing over time and through generations – and this pattern is replicated through multiple studies and multiple regions. Moreover, Wieling et al. (2016) show that the pattern extends cross-linguistically as well, existing not only in English but in five other Germanic languages: Dutch, German, Norwegian, Danish, and Faroese.

While these accounts demonstrate that a change is underway, an explanation for the actuation of this change remains elusive. What was the trigger for the start of this "textbook" change? Fruehwald (2016) and Wieling et al. (2016) both suggest that a new meaning or function for *um* may have emerged in English. (For Wieling and colleagues, this is a possible explanation for the cross-linguistic nature of the change: a new function for *um* could have emerged in English and then spread through contact to the other Germanic languages.) While neither study is explicit about what such a function might be, some evidence adduced in support of this idea is the finding that *um* "tended to have a longer duration, was preceded and followed by longer pauses, and was more frequently found at the beginning or end of an utterance than *uh*" (Wieling et al. 2016: 228). Wieling et al. (2016) also suggest that *um*'s rise may be related to a possible increase in its frequency of use as a discourse marker (to manage turn-taking or to signal speaker stance), which was not taken into account in their analysis.

Although Fruehwald (2016) notes that *um* and *uh* appear to be trading frequencies, casting doubt on a functional expansion explanation, it is possible that the emergence of a new function at some earlier point may have played a role nearer to the beginning of the change. Accordingly, in this chapter, we investigate data from before the rise of *um* with the goal of evaluating the functional expansion hypothesis.

7.3 Data and Coding

7.3.1 Data

The data for this study are from the *Farm Work and Farm Life Since 1890* oral history collection from the Earlier Ontario English Collection (EOE) (Denis 2016, 2017). The corpus consists of oral history interviews with 155 elderly farmers, recorded in 1984. The corpus covers five regions of Ontario, Canada: Temiskaming, Essex, Dufferin, Niagara Region, and Eastern Ontario; for this study, speakers from the latter two regions were considered. Speaker birth years range from 1891 to 1919, just before *um* began to take off per Fruehwald (2016). The interviews in each region were conducted by university students local to the region: a female student (F-INT) conducted the interviews in Niagara, and a male student (M-INT) conducted the interviews in Eastern Ontario.

7.3.2 Variable Context

For the purposes of this study, we follow Fruehwald (2016), Wieling et al. (2016), and Tottie (2016), among others, in treating *uh* [ə] and *um* [əm] (also written as *er* and *erm*) as variants of one sociolinguistic variable, termed (UHM). It should be noted that this is not the only way that the variable context could be defined. In fact, we can define three general ways to set up the envelope of variation for a study of (UHM).

The most intuitive is to treat *um* and *uh* as the only two variants, on the grounds of phonetic form (both variants consist of schwa, followed optionally by the bilabial nasal). As noted by Fruehwald (2016), *um* and *uh* have also traditionally been treated as a unique phenomenon in the psycholinguistic literature. This setup allows us to conduct a traditional variationist analysis, in line with the Principle of Accountability (Labov 1972b) following an essentially derivational approach (Pichler 2013). Under such an analysis, if *um* is taking on a new function, and *uh* is not, then our hypothesis would be that *um* will be represented in a larger share of the tokens as we progress forward in (apparent) time.

Another option is to include *unfilled* pauses (i.e., silence) in the envelope of variation. This is justified under the assumption that *um* and *uh* really are "filled pauses," since we would expect them to compete directly with the "zero" variant. Setting the analysis up this way, the variable context is defined only by putative function – by including silent pauses, which per se have no phonetic realization, we would be abandoning the phonetic similarity between *um* and *uh*, instead anchoring the envelope of variation around the function of "pausing." The key issue with operationalizing the variable this way is that it is tricky to determine what would constitute an unfilled pause – how many milliseconds does a pause need to be before we consider it an unfilled pause? If a speaker pauses between two sentences or phrases, how can we be sure it is actually a fillable pause? What about a silent interval after one speaker completes the final utterance in their turn and before the next speaker begins the first utterance in theirs – is this considered a fillable pause for both speakers or neither? It is difficult to imagine nonarbitrary answers to these questions, so directly analyzing this envelope of variation according to the Principle of Accountability is likely not feasible. However, we can get an indirect view by taking the number of occurrences of each variant in a speaker's talk and normalizing it by the number of words that they uttered: we expect speakers who are filling more pauses to use relatively more (UHM) than those who are filling less. These normalized count data have largely been shied away from in variationist analysis (e.g., Pichler 2010, but cf. Fruehwald 2016), but in conjunction with standard variationist analyses, and by using Poisson regression (to be discussed in detail in Section 7.4.2), these measures can, *contra* Pichler (2010: 595), give us information about "where in the linguistic system variables occur" and "what the social and internal mechanisms are that produce variation and change in their use."

A third option, beyond the scope of this chapter, is to include all words/phrases used as "fillers" or "planners" in the envelope of variation. For instance, Tottie (2018) includes (UHM) as one element of a set including *well*, *you know*, and *like*, on the basis that all of the elements are used to indicate speech planning. We do not take up this view in depth here, but we note that *um* and *uh* are single-word constructions that, unlike *well*, *you know*, and *like*, do not appear to be derived from semantically bleached lexical items but from apparently non-lexical speech sounds and thus seem to form a separate class.

7.3.3 Extraction and Coding

We extracted each instance of *uh* and *um* from the transcripts, excluding unrelated instances such as *uh-oh*. Tokens from the two (much younger) interviewers were also extracted and analyzed separately. The transcription protocol, based on Tagliamonte (2006b), emphasized faithful reproduction of *uh* and *um*. All interviews were carefully second-passed by the second author, knowing that (UHM) would be analyzed in the data.

The data were coded for the following social factors: year of birth, gender, and region (Niagara or Eastern Ontario). Year of birth and gender were used to operationalize the change-in-progress hypothesis. Table 7.1 presents a table of speakers by gender, region, and year of birth.

We also code for two linguistic factors. To address the functional expansion hypothesis, we operationalize utterance position by coding

Table 7.1 *List of speakers*

ID	Gender	Region	Year of birth
F-INT	F	Niagara	mid-to-late 1960s
M-INT	M	Eastern Ontario	mid-to-late 1960s
NIA-1	M	Niagara	1906
NIA-9	F	Niagara	1912
NIA-11	M	Niagara	1917
NIA-12	F	Niagara	1916
NIA-20	F	Niagara	1911
NIA-22	F	Niagara	1899
NIA-23	M	Niagara	1898
NIA-24	M	Niagara	1902
NIA-27	M	Niagara	1911
NIA-28	M	Niagara	1907
NIA-32	F	Niagara	1904
NIA-35	F	Niagara	1902
NIA-36	F	Niagara	1903
EON-01	M	Eastern Ontario	1891
EON-04	F	Eastern Ontario	1907
EON-06	M	Eastern Ontario	1905
EON-12	M	Eastern Ontario	1910
EON-13	F	Eastern Ontario	1914
EON-14	F	Eastern Ontario	1899
EON-16	M	Eastern Ontario	1912
EON-19	M	Eastern Ontario	1904
EON-20	F	Eastern Ontario	1906
EON-22	F	Eastern Ontario	1915
EON-24	M	Eastern Ontario	1898
EON-28	F	Eastern Ontario	1919

each token of (UHM) for initial or non-initial utterance position. We code (UHM) as "initial" if it is the first element in an utterance, as in (3), and "non-initial" if it is not the first element in an utterance, as in (4). The exception is in the case of *and-* or *but-* cliticization, where (UHM) was classed as "initial" if the containing utterance began with *and-uh* or *but-uh*. (UHM) did not frequently occur after other conjunctions (e.g., *or*), or after other discourse markers (e.g., *well*), so these were not counted as cliticized forms.

(3)   **Um** spring time was a very busy time for everyone on the farm.
       (EON-28, F/1919)

(4)   The birthdays we'd **uh-** we'd try to- we'd **uh** remember them.
       (EON-001, F/1907)

Uh, What Should We Count?

To test for a potential effect of cliticization, per Tottie's (2017) suggestion that this may have played a role in (UHM)'s lexicalization, we code each token as "clitic" if it occurred immediately following *and* or *but*, as in (5), and as "non-clitic" otherwise, as in (6).

(5) If it was in school time I couldn't go unless it was Saturday **but-uh**, auction sales were usually on Saturday. (NIA-09, F/1912)

(6) **Um** do you know how old you were when you started? (F-INT)

7.4 Results

7.4.1 Proportional Frequency

Before turning to discussion of the specific features of our own data, we begin by showing how they compare with previous communities analyzed, as shown in Table 7.2. Note the important caveat that, as mentioned in our introduction, the different corpora use different methodologies for collection and transcription, which most likely affects word counts, and thus the normalized frequency measures (see Pichler 2010). Regardless, we still believe that comparison with other reported results in the literature can be generally informative.

The first block summarizes our data from Niagara and Eastern Ontario, as well as the two younger interviewers (F-INT and M-INT). The second block summarizes results reported in Wieling et al. (2016) based on previous work on the Switchboard corpus (Switchboard; Godfrey et al. 1992), the Fisher corpus (Fisher; Cieri et al. 2004), the Philadelphia Neighborhood Corpus (PNC; Labov and Rosenfelder 2011), and the spoken part of the British National Corpus (Audio BNC; Coleman et al. 2012). From left to right, the columns provide the raw number of *uh* tokens, the raw number of *um* tokens, the percentage of

Table 7.2 *Cross-community comparison*

Community	N *uh*	N *um*	% *um*	Mean *uh*/1000	Mean *um*/1000	Mean UHM/1000
Niagara	1,864	357	16.1	21.3	4.1	25.4
E. Ont.	1,563	168	9.7	22.6	2.4	25.0
F-INT	321	318	49.8	12.4	12.3	24.7
M-INT	255	51	16.7	13.2	2.6	15.8
Switchboard	—	—	28.3	22.1	7.5	29.6
Fisher	—	—	64.1	6.8	9.9	16.7
PNC	—	—	27.6	13.2	4.5	17.7
BNC	—	—	46.1	4.5	4.3	8.8

(UHM) tokens that were *um*, the mean normalized frequency of *uh* per 1,000 words (averaged across speakers), the mean frequency of *um* per 1,000 words (also averaged across speakers), and the mean frequency of (UHM) altogether per 1,000 words (again averaged across speakers).

As can be seen in Table 7.2, *um* is less frequent in our farmer data compared to the more recent corpora. The female interviewer uses it around half the time, while the male interviewer's rate is comparable to the farmers'. The median number of (UHM) tokens per speaker is 140, with an interquartile range of 105.5. Relative frequency of (UHM) taken as a whole is on par with other corpora, but again, such a comparison must be taken with a grain of salt because each corpus was collected and transcribed differently.

Looking at individual speakers' proportional frequencies, we can see that all speakers use both *uh* and *um*, but there is little patterning by age or gender. Figures 7.1 and 7.2 illustrate this by presenting each speaker's *um* rate, with the bars in each figure shaded by region and gender, respectively. Figure 7.1 confirms a slight skew toward increased *um* rate in Niagara, but this is not driven by any one speaker. Figure 7.2 confirms a slight skew toward increased *um* rate among female speakers, which again is not driven by any one speaker. The numbers at the top of each bar indicate the number of (UHM) tokens for that speaker.

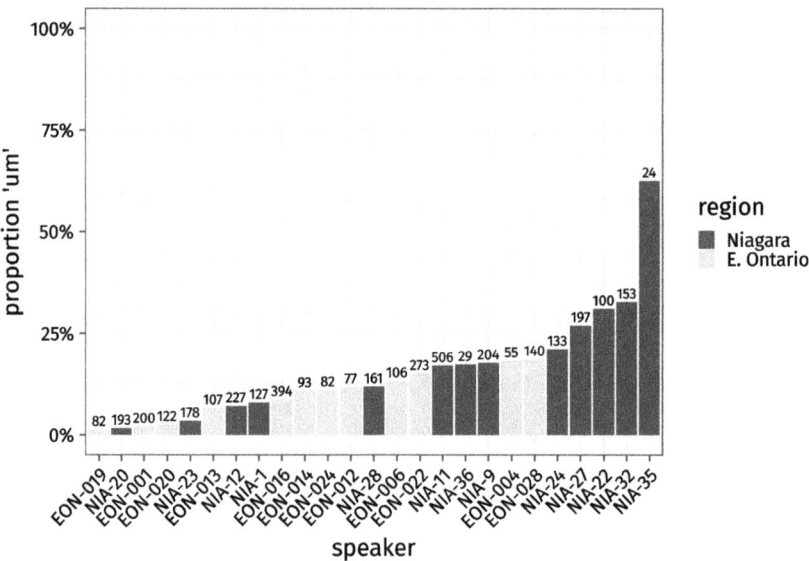

Figure 7.1 Proportion of *um* per speaker, shaded by region

Uh, What Should We Count? 159

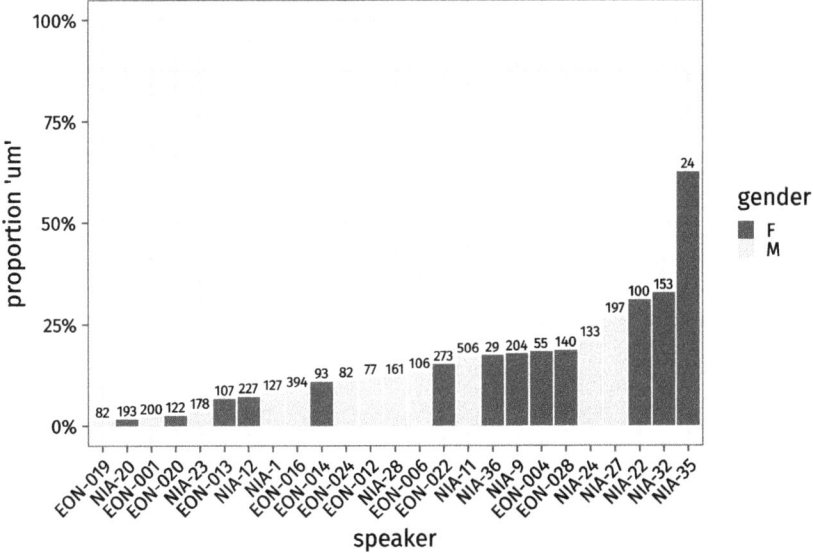

Figure 7.2 Proportion of *um* per speaker, shaded by gender

Figure 7.3 shows the proportion of *um* in apparent time, with year of birth on the x-axis and *um* rate on the y-axis. Each point represents one farmer (interviewers were excluded, other than where explicitly mentioned). In the plot to the left, year of birth is binned into five-year increments, which makes the patterns easier to see; in the plot to the right, year of birth is continuous, and the line is drawn using R's LOESS (locally estimated scatterplot smoothing) function. Because LOESS is a local regression technique, the fit at a given point is based on the data close to that point.

In both the binned and LOESS plots, there is a modest trend upward over time. To determine the possible predictors underlying this trend, in the following figures we split the data by gender, and our two linguistic conditions, position and cliticization. Figure 7.4 shows the pattern when splitting speakers by gender. Starting around 1905, women use *um* slightly less often than men do, with these two genders' *um* rates trending slightly upward over time. Figure 7.5 shows the pattern when splitting tokens by position (initial vs. non-initial). Starting around 1905, *um* is used more frequently in initial position than in non-initial position. Figure 7.6 shows the pattern when splitting tokens by cliticization with *and* or *but* and position. Comparing these figures reveals that *um*'s proportional increase appears to be limited to non-cliticized initial tokens: the increase disappears in all other contexts, as shown in Figure 7.6.

160   Tim Gadanidis and Derek Denis

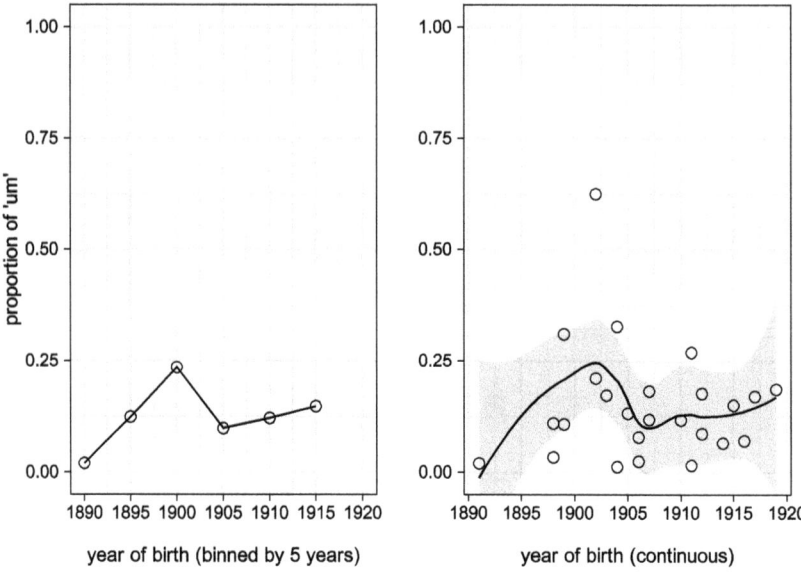

Figure 7.3 Proportion of *um* in apparent time

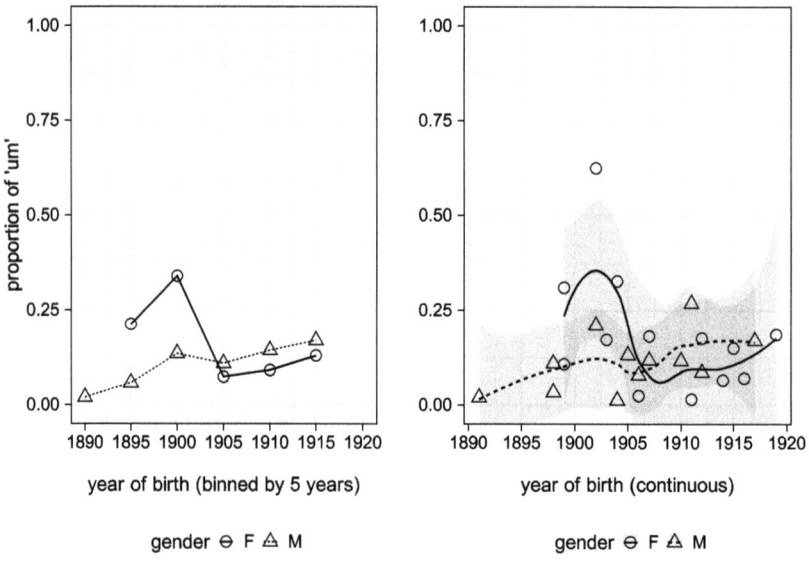

Figure 7.4 Proportion of *um* in apparent time, by gender

Uh, What Should We Count? 161

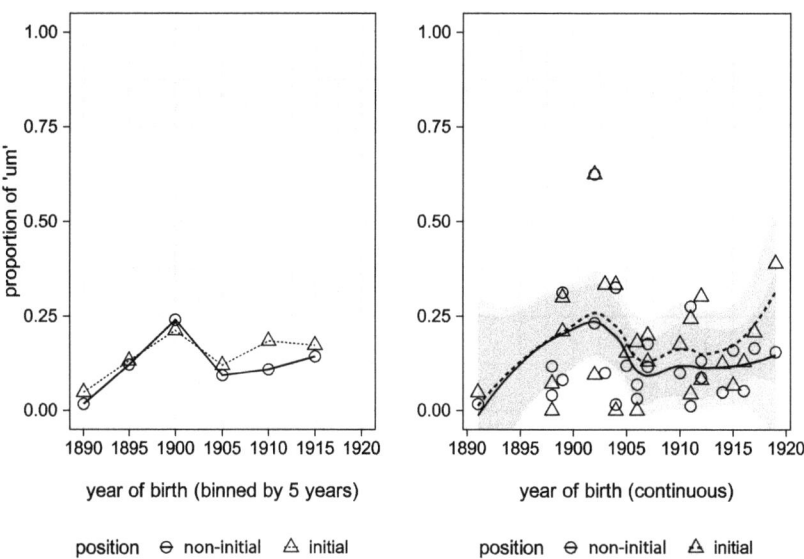

Figure 7.5 Proportion of *um* in apparent time, by position

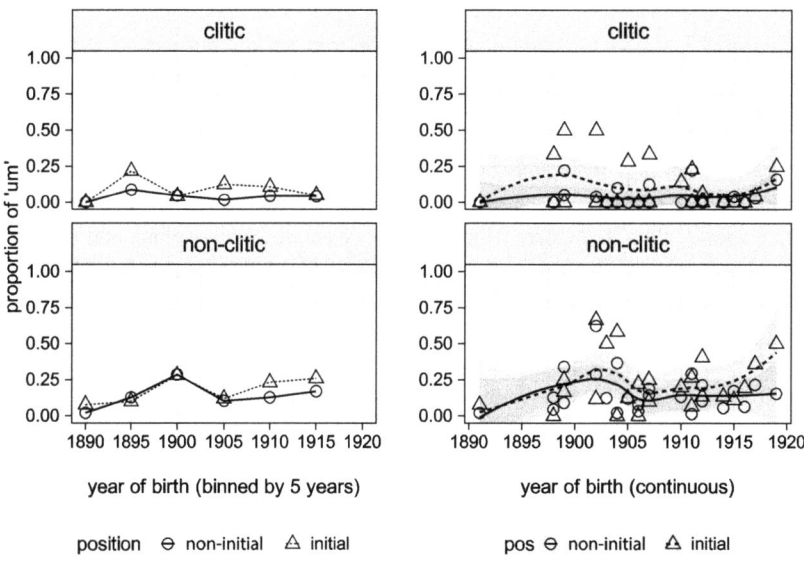

Figure 7.6 Proportion of *um* in apparent time, by position and cliticization

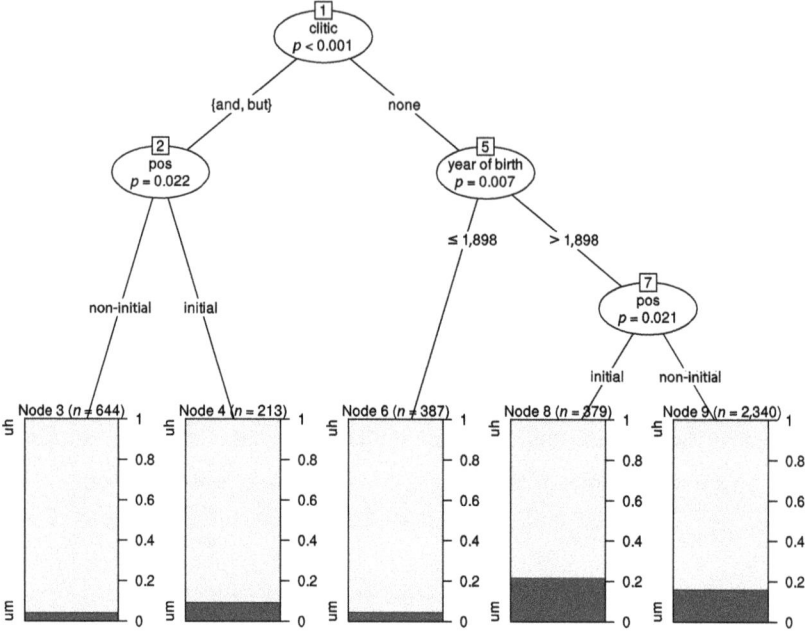

Figure 7.7 Conditional inference tree for farmers

Figure 7.7 shows a conditional inference tree for all farmers. Conditional inference trees are statistical models built by repeatedly splitting the data based on a set of covariates, using a significance test procedure to select the variables to split by (Tagliamonte and Baayen 2012). In other words, the data are divided, step by step; at each step, the variable that would create the largest difference is chosen to split by. The model in Figure 7.7 contained the predictors position ("pos"), cliticization ("clitic"), gender (which was not selected for any splits), and year of birth. The model confirms several of the patterns indicated in Figures 7.3–7.6. The tree splits first at cliticization, with cliticized (UHM) having a low overall *um* rate. Within the cliticized tokens, there is a slight difference between non-initial and initial (UHM), with initial tokens having a higher *um* rate (9.39 percent) than non-initial ones (4.35 percent). Within the non-cliticized tokens, there is an effect of year of birth: speakers born after 1898 have a much higher *um* rate in non-cliticized tokens than that of speakers born in 1898 or earlier (4.65 percent). This is especially true in initial position: non-initial cliticized tokens have a lower *um* rate (16.10 percent) than initial ones (21.90 percent).

Figure 7.8 shows a conditional inference tree for the two interviewers. The model contained position and cliticization (year of birth was not included

Uh, What Should We Count?

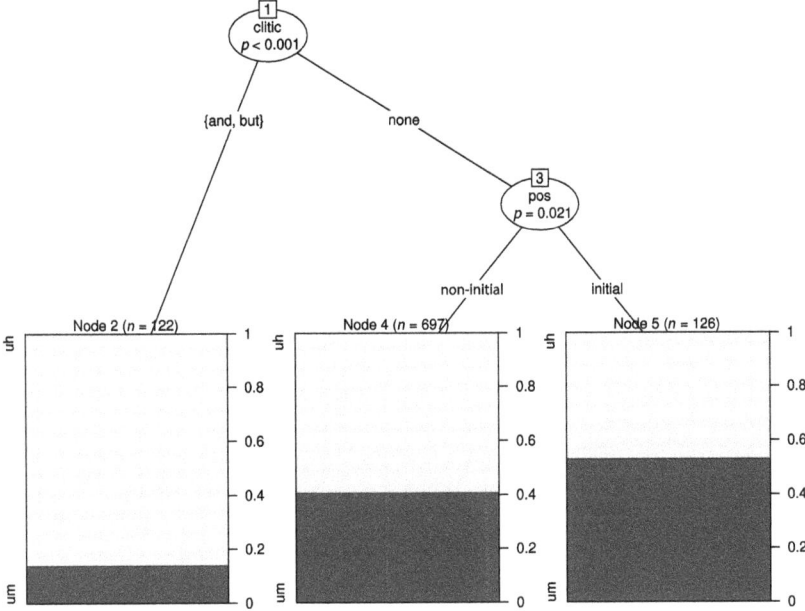

Figure 7.8 Conditional inference tree for interviewers

because the interviewers' years of birth are not known, and there are only two speakers in any case). As shown in the tree, the internal constraints are much the same, but the baseline *um* rate is much higher (due in large part to the female interviewer). *Um* is the least common in the cliticized tokens (13.90 percent). In non-cliticized tokens, there is a split by position, where initial tokens favor *um* (53.20 percent) compared to non-initial tokens (40.90 percent).

Taken together, the results presented in this section appear to show the beginning of the change toward *um* that has been observed by other researchers. While other work has shown that women lead this change, we do not find this pattern in our data. In fact, older women actually use (slightly) more *um* than do younger women. What we are likely seeing here is a stage of change before gender specialization/split (Labov 2001b: 308), similar to quotative *be like* in earlier generations (Tagliamonte and D'Arcy 2007: 208–209).

Looking at internal factors, we can see that cliticized forms, like *and-uh*, favor *uh*. There is some evidence for positional divergence, possibly consistent with a new utterance-initial discourse function that favors *um* (cf. Fruehwald 2016, who found no turn-positional difference). Conditional inference trees confirm that the internal constraints persist with the younger speakers, while their baseline *um* rate is higher. These patterns suggest that, in these early data, *um* may indeed be specializing to initial position, potentially due to the emergence of a new utterance-initial discourse-pragmatic function.

If we stopped here, having analyzed the data following the Principle of Accountability, this would be our narrative: there is evidence that a new utterance-initial discourse-pragmatic function is emerging for *um*, and this results in its rise in proportional frequency. Rather than stopping there, however, in Section 7.4.2 we further test this hypothesis using normalized-frequency data. From this perspective, we can probe the potential expansion of *um* into an additional discourse-pragmatic function.

7.4.2 Normalized Frequency

In this analysis, we follow Fruehwald (2016), who tests the hypothesis that functional expansion triggered the rise of *um* by considering changes to the relative frequency of variants over time (e.g., frequency of *um* or *uh* per 1,000 words). His logic is as follows. When a new discourse-pragmatic function emerges, we expect this function to add to the normalized frequency of the feature: the feature is used overall more frequently now because, all else being equal, it appears that many more times in the new context (Levey, Kastronic, Digesto, and Chiasson, Chapter 3, this volume). If the new function is restricted to one variant, the normalized frequency of that variant should rise, with little change to the relative frequency of the other variant. Critically, this pattern results in an S-shaped curve when we view the data following the Principle of Accountability. However, the S-shaped curve of change in proportional frequency that we observe for *um* (or at least its beginnings) could also be generated simply by one form replacing the other over time.

We illustrate this in Figure 7.9, four charts created with simulated data. Thus far, the Principle of Accountability has given us the perspective we see abstractly in both Figure 7.9(a) and 7.9(c): in both these charts, the proportional frequency of *um* is increasing over time following an S-shaped curve of change. However, the data in Figure 7.9(a) and 7.9(c) are underlyingly quite different; a similar pattern appears proportionally for two different scenarios. The underlying difference is shown in Figure 7.9(b) (which corresponds to Figure 7.9(a)) and 7.9(d) (which corresponds to 7.9(b)). Figure 7.9(b) and 7.9(d) plot the normalized frequency of *um* tokens in each decade and the normalized frequency of *uh* in each decade. In Figure 7.9b, we see a replacement pattern: one variant is taking over from another variant. *Uh*, the solid line, has a high normalized frequency at the beginning of the century and gradually its normalized frequency lowers. At the same time, the normalized frequency of *um*, the dashed line, starts low and rises over time. Figure 7.9(d) has a different pattern. Here, *uh* (solid line) still begins with a higher normalized frequency than *um* (dashed line) but remains stable over time. Meanwhile, the normalized

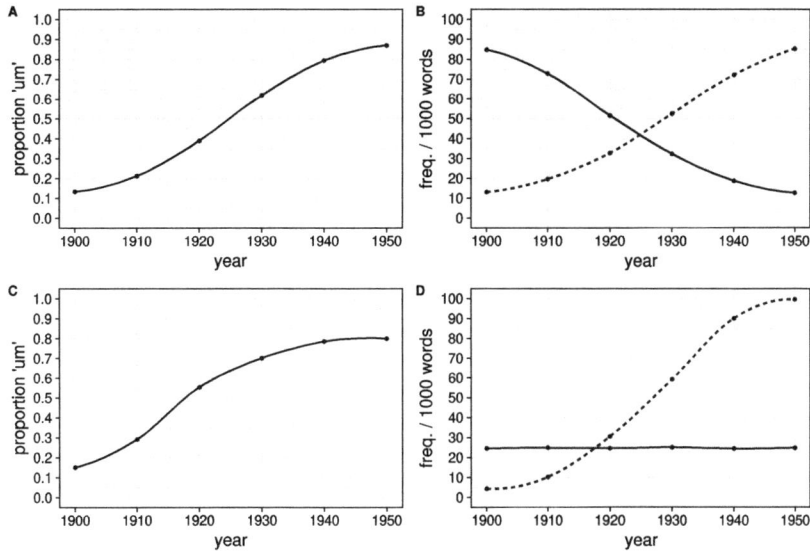

Figure 7.9 Proportional and normalized frequency of two hypothetical datasets, one where variants are trading frequencies – (a) and (b) – and one where one variant remains static and the other increases – (c) and (d). Note that the proportional plots (a) and (c) do not distinguish the two datasets, while the normalized frequency plots (b) and (d) illustrate the differences.

frequency of *um* gradually rises higher than the frequency of *uh*, then higher still. The pattern in Figure 7.9(d) is what we would expect for a functional expansion scenario: *um* is being used at a higher normalized frequency because it has expanded into a new context that *uh* does not have access to, while *uh* remains stable. From the perspective of the Principle of Accountability, these two patterns are indistinguishable, but normalized frequencies provide us with a perspective that can distinguish this scenario from a scenario in which there is expansion of usage.

Thus, if a new discourse function is what led to the rise of *um*, as hypothesized in the literature, we should expect to see a pattern in our data similar to Figure 7.9(d), with *um* rising and *uh* remaining stable. Alternatively, if *um* were straightforwardly replacing *uh*, we expect *uh* to fall in tandem with *um*'s rise.

In the interest of transparency and replicability, we illustrate here how our data are organized in order to allow us to conduct normalized-frequency analyses (as well as to do mixed-effects Poisson regression

Table 7.3 *Organization of the data*

	Speaker	Variant	Gender	Year of birth	Position	Count	Word count	Norm. freq. (per 1,000 words)
1	NO-1	uh	M	1906	initial	14	6,090	2.3
2	SG-28	uh	F	1919	initial	15	6,848	2.19
3	NO-1	um	M	1906	initial	3	6,090	0.49
4	SG-28	um	F	1919	initial	7	6,848	1.02
5	NO-1	uh	M	1906	non-initial	103	6,090	16.91
6	SG-28	uh	F	1919	non-initial	99	6,848	14.46
7	NO-1	um	M	1906	non-initial	7	6,090	1.15
8	SG-28	um	F	1919	non-initial	19	6,848	2.77
...	...	...	...	...	...	...	...	...

modeling, discussed in more detail later in this section). We organize our data as follows: for each speaker in the data, we calculate the number of times they produced *um* and *uh*, each split by initial versus non-initial position, for a total of four rows per speaker. (We do not account for cliticization in this analysis because further subdividing leads to rows with very low numbers of tokens, and the position effect is relatively constant across both cliticized and non-cliticized tokens.) We then calculate the normalized frequency by dividing the raw count for *um* or *uh* in each position by the total number of words that speaker produced and multiplying by 1,000. In other words, we calculate the normalized frequency of initial *um*, non-initial *um*, initial *uh*, and non-initial *uh* for each speaker. A slice of the data, containing just two speakers, is shown in Table 7.3.

By organizing our data in this way, we are able to address Pichler's (2010: 595) concern that the normalized-frequency approach cannot effectively consider linguistic and social constraints: our normalized-frequency data are grouped based on these constraints.

Figure 7.10 shows the frequency of *um* and *uh* per 1,000 words for each of the farmers, with year of birth on the x-axis and frequency on the y-axis. Each point represents one farmer. There is evidence of a pattern similar to Figure 7.9(d); however, the pattern is in the opposite direction as expected: it is *uh* that is increasing as *um* remains relatively stable. The pattern becomes both more extreme and more specific when we further probe the data. If we split the data by position, as in Figure 7.11, we see that in initial position both *um* and *uh* are largely stable, whereas in non-initial position *uh* alone is increasing. Splitting the data again by gender, we can see that the increase can be attributed to the female speakers – there is no apparent increase over apparent time for male speakers, but the older female speakers have

Uh, What Should We Count? 167

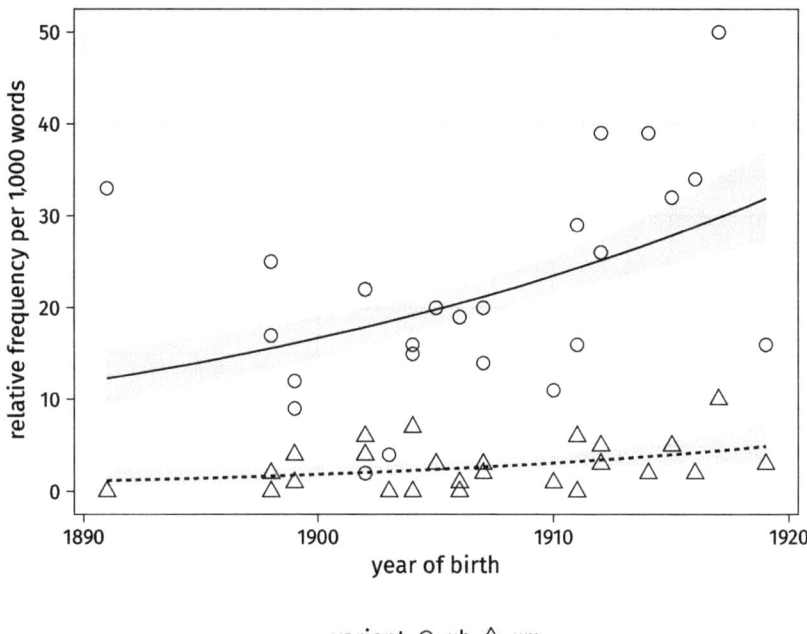

Figure 7.10 Frequency of *uh* and *um* per 1,000 words

a relatively lower *uh* rate that rises among the younger women to match the male speakers by the 1910s.

At this point, we require a statistical model to confirm these patterns. We make use of mixed-effects Poisson regression, a tool that allows us to statistically examine "the social and internal mechanisms [...] that produce variation and change" from a normalized frequency perspective (cf. Pichler 2010: 595; see also Eiswirth, Chapter 8, this volume).

Poisson regressions are used when the dependent variable is a count: the range of possible values of the dependent variable is limited to zero and all positive integers, and the assumption of normality is not required. In addition to counts, Poisson regression models also allow us to examine *rates* by including an offset variable in the model. This is critical because, in naturally occurring language data, the raw counts of any given feature will be affected by the size of the data source (hence why we normalize frequency counts). By including each speaker's overall word count from their interview as an offset for the count of *uh* and *um*, we essentially normalize the frequencies in the model.

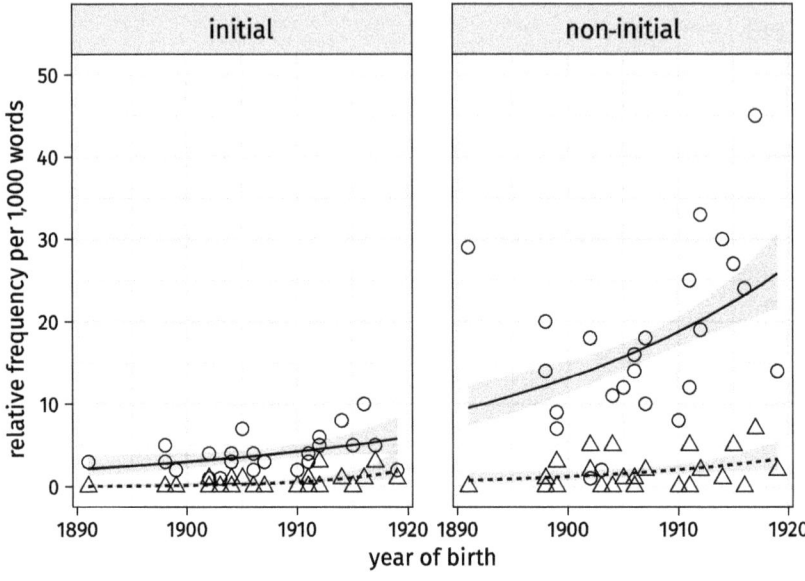

Figure 7.11 Frequency of *uh* and *um* per 1,000 words, by position

To confirm the interactions we observe in the distributional analysis in Figures 7.10–7.12, we run a mixed-effects Poisson regression model using the lme4 package in R.[1] We limit the dataset to only non-initial position because this is where the relevant interaction between variant, gender, and year of birth seems to be. The model is shown in Table 7.4.

The dataset fed to the model is organized like in Table 7.3. It includes each speaker's *um* and *uh* raw counts in non-initial position, which was the dependent variable; year of birth, gender, and variant (*uh* or *um*) were the predictors, along with a random intercept for speaker and a random slope for variant by

---

[1] The code for the model is as follows:
```
glmer(formula = token_count ~ year_of_birth * variant * gender + (1
+variant|speaker_code),
          data    = dat,
          family  = "poisson",
          offset  = log(word_count))
```
where "token_count" is the number of tokens produced by a speaker, "year_of_birth" is centered year of birth, "variant" is whether the token was "um" or "uh," "gender" is whether the speaker was coded as "male" or "female," "speaker_code" is the speaker code, "word_count" is the total number of words produced by the speaker in the interview, and "dat" is the name of the dataframe containing the data.

Table 7.4 *Mixed-effects Poisson regression model on non-initial (UHM) counts*

Predictor	Estimate	Std. error	z	p
(Intercept)	−6.22	0.25	−25.20	0
year of birth	0.08	0.036	2.30	0.02
variant (*uh*)	2.22	0.27	8.08	0
gender (female)	−0.24	0.35	−0.68	0.50
year of birth : variant	−0.07	0.04	−1.89	0.06
year of birth : gender	−0.07	0.05	−1.30	0.19
variant : gender	−0.30	0.39	−0.78	0.43
year of birth : variant : gender	0.14	0.06	2.55	0.01

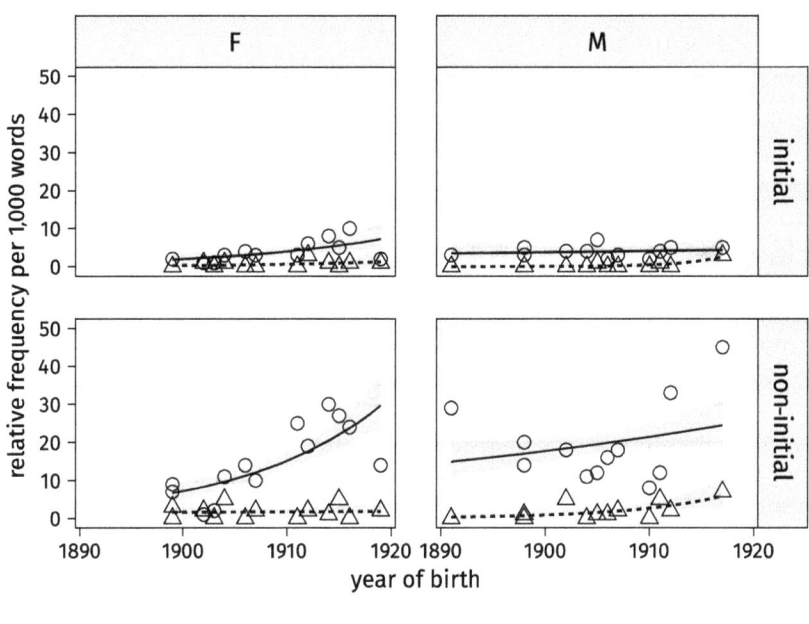

variant ⊖ uh △ um

Figure 7.12 Frequency of *uh* and *um* per 1,000 words, by position and gender

speaker. The reference level for gender was male, and the reference level for variant was *um*. As just described, the logarithm of each speaker's word count was used as an offset in order to normalize across speakers. Positive estimates in the output table indicate that the model predicts to observe a higher count in the given category. For example, the positive *uh* estimate indicates that *uh* tokens are predicted to be more frequent than *um* tokens, and the positive year of birth estimate indicates that (UHM) tokens are more frequent as year of birth increases (i.e., nears the present day). To get at differences between variants, therefore, we examine interactions between the variant factor and other independent variables in the model.

In fact, the final estimate in Table 7.4 shows that there is an interaction between year of birth, variant, and gender. The relevant coefficient, 0.14, indicates that, in non-initial position, the slope for year of birth for *uh* is predicted to be greater for women than for men. In other words, women's non-initial *uh* frequency (compared to *um*) is increasing over time to a greater extent than men's is. This confirms the gender-position interaction shown in the bottom-left and bottom-right facets of Figure 7.12.

7.5 Discussion

Exploring data from before the rise of *um* has yielded ambivalent results. On one hand, using the variationist framework and the Principle of Accountability to look at proportional frequency, we find that, for the younger farmers, *um* appears more frequent than *uh* in initial position, and the same is the case for the two (much younger) interviewers. Alone, this could be taken as suggestive evidence in favor of a new, initial-position function for *um* as hypothesized in the literature (Fruehwald 2016; Wieling et al. 2016). Looking at the normalized-frequency data, however, we see that the pattern does not appear to be driven by an increase of *um* in initial position. Like Fruehwald (2016), we do not find strong evidence that a new, utterance-initial function for *um* is behind the rise of *um*. The question as to what the trigger for the rise of *um* was remains unanswered. However, we find evidence of a different change: *uh* seems to have expanded its functional range in this time period, becoming more frequent in non-initial contexts, especially among women.

We tentatively suggest that this observed expansion of *uh* may be because *uh* was recruited by speakers to fill erstwhile unfilled pauses, particularly in non-initial position. Such an increase in pause-filling using *uh* would lead to an increase in its normalized frequency. We illustrate this hypothesis using (7) and (8): two passages of about the same length from NIA-11, a younger woman in the dataset born in 1916 (NIA-11), and an older woman born in 1903 (NIA-36). In the transcriptions, (UHM) is bolded, and unfilled pauses are indicated using (.) or (...), depending on the length of the pause. In her extract, NIA-11 uses (UHM) eight times – all but one of which are *uh*. In sharp contrast, NIA-36 does not use (UHM) once, opting instead for lengthy, unfilled pauses. With respect to (UHM), the two speakers employ fundamentally different discourse strategies.

(7)   INT: And what types of fruit (.) did you grow?
NIA-11: Well the **uh** (.) originally **uh** when they came- **uh** grandfather bought the property in nineteen hundred and **uh** (.) **um** (.) to begin with there was very- there were very few fruit trees on it and they planted (.) **uh** (.) our orchard of **uh** (.) peaches. And **uh** waiting- while they waited for the peaches to come into bearing, they planted raspberries between the rows, so it started out as principally a raspberry farm I suppose but (.) it evolved into a farm that **uh** principally grew peaches and cherries, mainly sweet cherries.

(8)   INT: Okay. And how much (.) older was the very oldest?
NIA-36: The oldest was born (...) in eighteen ninety two (...) and then my sister Lianne, eighteen ninety four (...) Greg, eighteen ninety eight (.) Sally nineteen hundred and one (...) I was born nineteen hundred and three (.) and that's it.
INT: Okay, and how old was your dad when you were born? At-
NIA-36: (...) I- (...) how old was my dad when I was born? Oh.
INT: I think we had figured out that he was probably somewhere around forty five.
NIA-36: Oh yes.
INT: And your mom was?
NIA-36: Thirty (.) five?
INT: Thirty- oh-
NIA-36: Is that it?
INT: Yup. Good.

This hypothesis is tentative, and testing it goes beyond the scope of the present chapter. However, it may be a piece of the puzzle when it comes to the competition between *uh* and *um* and *um*'s eventual rise in the twentieth century. While our data are too early to shed much light on the rise of *um*, and it is important to be careful when generalizing across corpora and speech communities, it is possible that the *uh*-led shift from unfilled to filled pauses played a role in the competition between *um* and *uh* in the years to come. For example, *uh* may have specialized to non-initial position, which often appears to indicate what Tottie (2016, 2017) has called the "word-search" function, as in (9), adapted from Tottie's (2016: 107) example 11, in which the speaker searches for the word "sheet" when describing how to make fudge.

(9)   Then you pour that out on a uh... sheet.

A specialization to the word-search function may have caused *uh* to become a less desirable variant, since frequent word-search potentially gives the impression of disfluency. This could lead to *uh* being used less frequently – which would also appear as a rise in the proportional frequency of *um*.

Moreover, this mid-utterance word-search function may previously have been linked with unfilled pauses. Notice that, in (7), (UHM) tends to appear when the speaker is recalling information, such as what was planted (the family's orchard) and what grew in the family's orchard (peaches) in the following snippet: "they planted (.) **uh** (.) our orchard of **uh** (.) peaches." This is the same sort of context in which lengthy unfilled pauses, marked by "(...),‍" are used in (8), when the speaker is recalling years of birth for her family members. Our data thus provide tentative support for the hypothesis that *uh* may have become associated with this function, explaining its rise in overall frequency among women in our data. However, we must stress again that more work would be needed for us to be able to go beyond this kind of speculation.

7.6 Conclusion

Our case study analyzed both proportional and normalized-frequency data, in an attempt to identify potential triggers for the rise of *um* that has been described over the last decade by Fruehwald (2016), Tottie (2016), and several others. While one perspective suggests that there may indeed be a new discourse function that *um* came to fill, the view from normalized frequencies suggests a different understanding of the kind of discourse-functional changes that went on at the turn of the twentieth century. Our goal was to highlight the importance of viewing discourse-pragmatic variation and change from multiple angles: the two quantitative perspectives we employ here provide complementary information about the functional expansion hypothesis. Considering only the proportional data might suggest that a new function for *um* is emerging, but the relative frequency data indicate that the relevant change is actually one that we had not considered, and one that falls outside our original envelope of variation: a change from unfilled pauses to *uh* in non-initial position.

While the variationist turn in discourse-pragmatic variation has been illuminating, we want to emphasize that a limited quantitative perspective can limit our ability to interpret our data. In this way, we echo and extend Waters's (2016) argument that a "bespoke" approach is necessary to the study of discourse-pragmatic variables – not just with respect to how we define the envelope of variation but also with respect to how we quantitatively analyze our data. No single approach is right for all variables or for all questions; the choice of quantitative and statistical approach should not be axiological but rather should come about in response to the specific questions being asked about the specific phenomenon.

8 Modeling Listener Responses

Mirjam Elisabeth Eiswirth

8.1 Introduction

The traditional definition of the sociolinguistic variable – different ways of saying the same thing – is based on phonological structure (Labov 1963). Presences and absences of the variable can be counted, and structural constraints analyzed, before considering the social stratification of the variable. This is notoriously challenging when it comes to variables above the level of the phoneme. A number of approaches based on semantic, formal, functional, or derivational equivalence have been proposed to address these issues (Lavandera 1978; Dines 1980; Buchstaller 2009; Pichler 2010, 2013; Tagliamonte 2016; D'Arcy 2017). However, it remains difficult, first, to assess structural constraints on variation and, second, to fulfill the Principle of Accountability. This is because it is not always possible to describe all places in which a variable should accountably occur; optionality is part of their very definition. Many discourse-level features fall into this category of open-set variables, including listener responses (LRs), the variable introduced in this chapter.

LRs are an interactional phenomenon – the listener giving (non)vocalized feedback to the main speaker – that has attracted attention from psychologists, sociologists, corpus linguists, and, broadly speaking, variationist sociolinguists. For the purposes of this analysis, I define LRs as the vocalized responses listeners can do during an ongoing (multi-unit) turn of the other speaker without taking over the floor. They are thus defined and operationalized as structurally couched in ongoing talk. The approach I present here builds on Pichler (2013), who explicitly called for an integration of conversation analysis (CA) and variationist methods in order to address the challenges outlined at the start of the chapter. While Pichler introduces core CA tools and concepts to her analysis and uses them to describe different variants, she does not go as far as defining the variable itself based on interactional structure, nor to quantify it with respect to interactional structure. The present chapter does this for LRs as a discourse-organizational variable. This chapter illustrates that we can use CA to (1) define and delimit the variable, (2) quantify its frequency by taking into account interactional structure, and (3) describe interactional constraints. This forms the basis for (4), which is statistically exploring how these constraints impact on frequency for different social groups. Gender is operationalized as a social variable in this study because the majority of quantitative work on LRs has focused on either gender or culture, and gender is better represented in the present corpus.[1]

In the remainder of this chapter, I first present the data and methods. I then propose a qualitative definition of LRs by drawing on existing CA work on listenership and discuss the quantitative work on the phenomenon. I show that the qualitative studies have had little interest in quantifying, while the quantitative perspective rarely takes the results from these qualitative studies into account. I then discuss how the issues in the quantitative analysis of LRs reflect the more general challenges sociolinguists face when defining variables above the level of the phoneme. The quantitative analysis shows that turn length is the only statistically significant factor impacting the number of LRs produced, and that the structural constraints (presented in Section 8.3.1) impact the production of LRs in a systematic way. Finally, I discuss the results of the analysis with respect to LR frequency and structural constraints and return to the theoretical and methodological contribution this chapter aims to make with respect to defining a variable above the level of the phoneme.

8.2 Methodology and Data

The analysis is based on 5,202 LRs from 24 dyadic interactions between 16 participants. The data were collected as part of a research project based at the University of Edinburgh, where participants were invited to talk about their experiences of living with or caring for someone with type 1 diabetes. Such topic-focused conversations are extremely fruitful for sociolinguistic analyses because the participants' attention is focused on the content and the interaction rather than their way of speaking. Further, these conversations are highly involved and engaged, reducing the observer's paradox. This offsets the disadvantage that it was not possible to create a fully gender-balanced sample. All but one participant were native speakers of English: ten Scottish English speakers; three Southern British English speakers; one Irish English speaker; one native Polish speaker who had been living in Scotland for a decade at the time of recording; and one Finnish American speaker (bilingual from childhood) who had been living in Scotland for seven years at the time of recording. Conversations lasted on average 26 minutes (SD=6:20 min), ranging from 15:40 to 40 minutes. There were ten all-female dyads, thirteen mixed dyads,

---

[1] The theoretical and methodological implications of operationalizing "gender" as a binary variable are discussed in the methodology.

Table 8.1 *Cross-tabulation showing how often each participant takes the speaker and listener role, depending on the gender of their interlocutor*

Listener	Speaker	Number
Female	Female	20
Female	Male	13
Male	Female	13
Male	Male	2
Total		48

Table 8.2 *Cross-tabulation of raw token counts of LRs by listener and speaker gender across all interactions*

	Female speaker	Male speaker	Total by gender
Female listener	2,291	1,557	3,848
Male listener	1,100	254	1354

Note. Tables 8.2, 8.3, 8.4, and 8.5 appeared in a different format in Eiswirth (2020b).

and one male-only dyad, resulting in the role distribution summarized in Table 8.1.[2] Because there was only one all-male pair, it is important not to generalize to "(all) men do listening in this way." It is important to keep in mind that this chapter primarily aims to present a methodological innovation, not to make claims about gendered behavior at large.

Table 8.2 illustrates the distribution of the 5,202 LRs that are produced by male and female listeners towards male and female speakers.

Inter-coder reliability for the identification of LRs was extremely high, with an F-Measure of 0.97, based on a Precision of 0.99 and a Recall of 0.96. Krippendorff's alpha (Krippendorff 2004a, 2004b, 2011) was used to calculate inter-coder reliability for coding the types of responses based on structural constraints.[3] The analysis that follows explains in detail how LRs are defined and thus how the tokens summarized here were identified.

---

[2] Both participants take the role of the speaker at some points and that of the listener at others. This means that each dyad contains four roles: each participant as the speaker and each participant as the listener, respectively. Consequently, in twenty-four conversations with two participants each, this results in forty-eight speaker roles and forty-eight listener roles.

[3] The Krippendorff alpha metric assesses how likely the *dis*agreements between coders are due to chance. Again, agreement across action types was high, with *alpha*=0.74 and thus above the threshold for reliability suggested by Krippendorff (2004a: 241).

8.2.1 Quantitative Approaches

The first step of the quantitative analysis is understanding how frequently listeners produce vocalized responses. I propose an extension and refinement of the frequency operationalization by Duncan and Fiske (1977), which is based on the number of LRs in any given turn relative to the number of words in the turn. This rate is calculated for each turn and multiplied with 100 (words), the mean turn length. Consequently, the response frequency for a single turn can be 0 if there is no LR at all in this (multi-unit) turn. Some of the absences of LRs are due to listening not being relevant, but there might also be moments in which producing a vocalized LR was potentially relevant.

Zero-inflated Poisson regression models are a tool to inferentially model variation in the frequency at which listeners respond, and how their responses are affected by structural constraints. In previous studies, they have been used to interpret count data with a high number of zeros, which could be related to different predictor variables (Lo and Andrews 2015; Winter and Wieling 2016; Coupé 2018; Eiswirth 2020a, 2020b; Gadanidis and Denis, Chapter 7, this volume). The model consists of two parts: a logit (or zero inflation) model and a count model. The logit model predicts whether we expect an LR to be present by estimating the number of "excess zeros" in the data. The count model predicts how many LRs are expected. The model was fit using the `glmmTMB` package (Brooks et al. 2017), for overall frequency, and the `brms` package (Bürkner 2018), which also takes into account structural constraints, specifically how strongly any given response is interactionally in the hands of the listener or the speaker (or both). Turn length was centered around the median of seventy-five words and then log-normalized. The model formulas are given in the respective analysis sections and explained in more detail in context.

There are two quantitative questions: First, are there significant differences between how frequently listeners respond, based on their own and the speaker's gender? Second, are there significant differences between these gender-based groups in terms of how the structural constraints impact on the production of LRs? Before these questions can be answered, it is necessary to supply a definition of the variable, which is rooted in interactional structure in such a way that enables quantification. This definition is developed in the following section.

8.3 Introducing LRs as a Variable

8.3.1 Qualitative Perspectives on LRs: The Basis of a Structural Definition

Listenership has been of interest to CA from the inception of the field, with a strong focus on the negotiation of how an interaction, often specifically a story, develops based on the listener's behavior (Goodwin 1984; Sacks 1995). Quantifying how many or which kinds of responses listeners do was never a key concern. Based on this interactional perspective, Schegloff (1982) criticized the first quantitative treatments of what was then called backchannels (Yngve 1970; Duncan and Fiske 1977). Schegloff pointedly critiques that "disengaging the listener behavior from its local sequential context not only undercuts the possibility of understanding what it is doing; it can remove an important basis for understanding what is going on in the discourse itself" (Schegloff 1982: 86).

This criticism relates to the core of CA, namely the assumption that interaction is organized sequentially: every question invites an answer, and every greeting a response. Whether something is a question is determined based not on its form but on how the recipient treats it: If they give a response (or an excuse for not giving one), they have treated it as a question. If they do not, and the person who formulated it follows up and pursues a response, this too indicates that the contribution was a question. This line of reasoning, which is called the next-turn proof procedure,[4] is a crucial tool in the analysis and methodology I propose. Furthermore, CA upholds that every bit of talk is conditioned by and fitted to the talk that precedes it by being a relevant next action (or accounting for not being one), while at the same time fitting into the ongoing talk lexically, phonetically, prosodically, and morpho-syntactically.

Drawing on this understanding, I define LRs as a variable based on their sequential position and impact, as visualized in Figure 8.1 and described as follows:

- LRs *tend* to be placed at so called transition-relevance points (TRPs) (see Clancy et al. 1996; Ford and Thompson 1996).
- However, they *do not have to be* produced at every possible point of occurrence, and their occurrence is not restricted to TRPs.
- LRs are followed by more same-speaker talk.

In terms of their form, LRs tend to be brief and unobtrusive, but they can also be longer and more elaborate. Furthermore, listeners can do a number of different actions in this sequential slot. The examples presented in (1)–(4) illustrate several different types of LRs, which share the structure previously described; they are couched in the main speaker's ongoing talk and support it, sometimes in overlap with ongoing speech, and sometimes in the clear. Example (1) is a prototypical acknowledgment. It occurs between two turn constructional units (TCUs) of PuzzleB's

---

[4] Of course, there are prototypical questions, or prototypical greetings, that are recognized as such even in the absence of a response or a second greeting. When such a response or second greeting are not provided, they are usually pursued, which shows that they would have been interactionally relevant. Examples are provided later in the chapter.

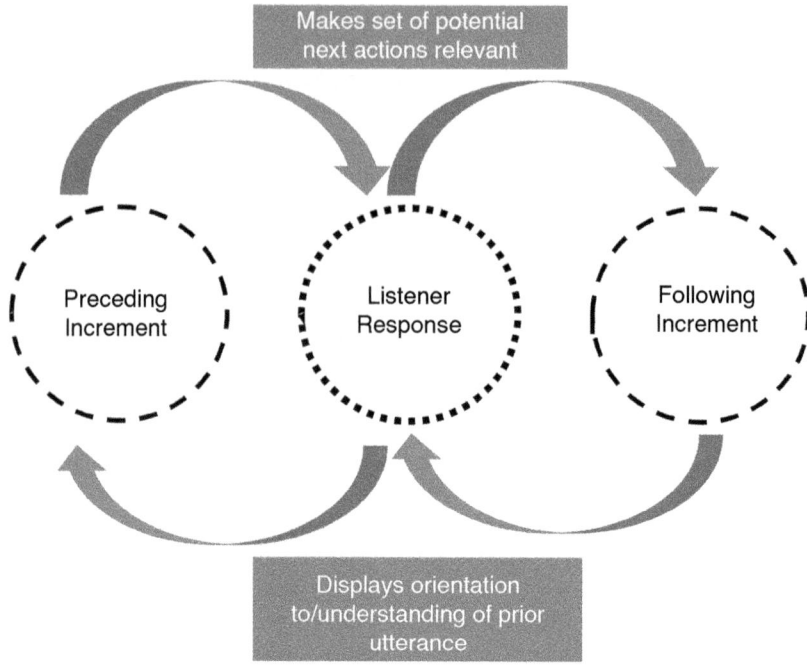

Figure 8.1 Structural definition and sequential position of LRs
Note. Figure 8.1 originally appeared in Eiswirth (2020a).

talk,[5] is very brief and quiet, and Donna makes no move to take the floor by producing any further talk.

(1) Acknowledgment, Donna and PuzzleB, Diabetes Camp and DAFNE, minutes 16:15–18:00
```
20  PuzzleB:  but I think a lot of them'd been sent-
21  Donna:    °mhm°.
22  PuzzleB:  because they weren't controlling- (.)
```

Example (2) is called a *self-initiated other-repair* in CA (Kitzinger 2012). It can be regarded as a *word-supply*. Tomek, the main speaker, signals word-search trouble by repeating different versions of a word that might be "quinoa," cutting off and self-correcting several times. In line 4, Velominati offers a possible candidate for the word with which Tomek is struggling. This candidate word is uttered quietly and with rising intonation, framing it as a suggestion and not as taking the floor. Tomek immediately confirms that this is the word for

---

[5] Participants were allowed to choose their own pseudonyms.

which he is searching (line 5 "yeah that's the one, sorry"), and Velominati produces a prototypical and again very quiet LR "yeah" in overlap with Tomek's talk. This can be taken as an indication that Velominati has no intention of taking the floor, and the 0.7 second lapse (represented on line 7) is further evidence that both "quinoa" and "yeah" were LRs supporting Tomek's talk and maintaining the current speaker–listener relationship, rather than an attempt to take the floor. In line 8, Tomek continues his multi-unit turn.

(2) Self-initiated Other-repair, Tomek and Velominati, Quinoa, minutes 16:10–16:20

```
1    Tomek:        so:: uh things like (.) uh-
2    Tomek:        (.4)
3    Tomek:        quini- qui- uh no not quini- qu- ↑quoina (.) quina,
4 →  Velominati:   °er quinoa°,
5    Tomek:        yeah that's the [one sorry-
6    Velominati:                   [°yeah°-
7    Tomek:        (.7)
8    Tomek:        and uh-

     TOMEK CONTINUES
```

The third type of LR – *collaborative construction* (Lerner 2004) – is illustrated in example (3). Velominati is talking about glucose monitoring options dating back several decades, and towards the end of his TCU in line 12, when the content of the rest of his turn is projectable from context, Tess produces a possible completion "urine dip" (line 13) in overlap with Velominati's own completion "urine analysis." The contribution from Tess is marked with turn-final falling intonation and not followed by more talk from her side. As soon as Velominati continues, integrating her suggestion with a "yeah" in line 14 and moving to further describe the testing procedure, Tess produces the prototypical *acknowledgment* "yeah" (line 15, and again in line 17) instead of making any move to take over the floor.

(3) Collaborative Completion, Tess and Velominati, Urine Analysis, minutes 2:55–3:10

```
10    Velominati:   [!] so the only way of self-monitoring was uh-
11    Velominati:   the delightful-
12    Velominati:   urine an[alysis.
13 →  Tess:                 [urine dip.
14    Velominati:   [yeah (.) you know-
15    Tess:         [yeah.
16    Velominati:           [with a little test tube and some-
17    Tess:                 [yeah-
```

"Yeah" and "mhm" are highly frequent *acknowledgments*, but they can also be used to signal incipient speakership and take over the floor rather than serving as an LR (Drummond and Hopper 1993; Jefferson 1993). Example (4) illustrates this. PuzzleB is evaluating her daughter's experience at a diabetes camp, and Donna responds with a positive first assessment in line 29. This assessment is quiet and not followed by more talk from Donna. PuzzleB's turn, represented in line 30/31, ends with "and," projecting continuation, but is initially followed by a 0.5 second-long pause. Donna then continues with a "yeah," which, based on its lexical form, might be taken as an LR and signal of continued listenership. However, this "yeah" is immediately followed by more talk from Donna. Therefore, it interactionally functions as a signal of incipient speakership. It acknowledges the preceding talk, while also preparing to launch a new speaker-turn and reverse the listener and speaker roles.

(4) First assessment and incipient speakership, Donna and PuzzleB, Diabetes Camp and DAFNE, minutes 16:15–18:00.

```
28     PuzzleB:    but she still enjoyed it just that (.)
                   [relaxation you know=
29 →   Donna       [°that's good°.
30     PuzzleB:    =it's just like 'oh being with other people who
31                 understand this and-'
32     PuzzleB:    (.5)
33 →   Donna:      yeah cause I'd never-
34     Donna:      well I'd met people-
35     Donna:      but I never knew anybody-
```

Examples (1)–(4) show that LRs can be defined based on interactional structure using the next-turn proof procedure. This means that LRs are not constrained nor defined in terms of their form (not all "yeah"s are LRs, and not all LRs are "yeah"s) and that listeners can do a number of different actions by uttering LRs.

For the purposes of this chapter, I propose distinguishing three groups of LRs that are differentially constrained by the interaction, specifically by the preceding talk: listener-driven responses, speaker-driven responses, and responses driven by both speaker and listener to similar degrees. Drawing on the vast literature in the field of CA and on the analysis of 5,202 LRs, I argue that the relevance of an LR can be constrained by the interactional structure.

Listener-driven responses are always potentially relevant – listeners can do them almost at any point in the interaction. Schegloff (1982) notes that these are *acknowledgments* and *repair-initiations*, taking the form, for example, of asking a question for clarification. The listener can potentially treat everything that is being said as repairable, based on trouble hearing or understanding something in the previous talk. The *acknowledgments* presented in examples (1)–(3) are listener-driven responses: listeners can produce them without being strongly constrained by what the speaker does in their talk.

Speaker-driven responses are directly made relevant by the speaker in the preceding talk. A *word-supply* like the one presented in (2), for example, is only relevant if the speaker has signaled word-search trouble. Without this preceding context, providing a candidate completion might be part of a *collaborative completion* or a grab for the floor. I consider actions such as word-supply or second assessments as constrained by the speaker's actions because there is a strong orientation to *word-supply* being interactionally preferred (see Pomerantz 1984 on preference organization). In many cases, the speaker will continue with their word-search until they receive a word-supply option from the listener, or they will abandon their current turn and restart.

The third set of LRs are driven by both the speaker and the listener to similar degrees. The speaker provides the opportunity for these responses, but there is no strong preference for the listener to take up these opportunities. A *collaborative completion*, like the one presented in (3), is not always possible, but if there is an opportunity, this does not *have* to be taken up by the listener. Similarly, not everything in the speaker's ongoing talk can be assessed, but when this is the case, the listener *can* but does not *have to* produce a *first assessment*, as seen in (4) (Pomerantz 1984; Goodwin 1986).

I thus propose a definition of LRs that is rooted in interactional structure and takes into account the preceding and following talk produced by the speaker. This definition proposes a set of structural constraints on whether an LR is produced based on the interactional roles of speaker and listener in constructing such an action. Thus, this section does the sort of "intuitive quantification" that is part of CA (see Schegloff 1993; Stivers 2015; Kendrick 2017) even though CA scholars do not focus on such questions of quantification and often reject the very notion.[6] Accordingly, LRs have not been quantitatively analyzed from a CA perspective. While there are numerous studies of LR frequency from a quantitative perspective, they do not integrate the interactional aspects described here. The definition and the constraints presented in this chapter form a useful basis for quantitatively analyzing LR variation.

---

[6] See Schegloff (1982) and his original critique of quantitative treatments of LRs but also more general discussions on CA and quantification by Schegloff (1993), Steensig and Heineman (2015), and Stivers (2015).

8.3.2 Quantitative Perspectives on LRs

I use the term LRs to draw attention to their dynamicity and interactional situatedness, in contrast to a number of different quantitative perspectives on the same phenomenon. Quantitative studies have referred to LRs as "backchannels" (Yngve 1970), "minimal responses" (Fellegy 1995; Reid 1995), "reactive tokens" (Clancy et al. 1996), or "response tokens" (O'Keeffe and Adolphs 2008). These terms and definitions zero in on the product at the expense of the process; they are "responses," but who produced them, in which context, and why, is not accounted for. Moreover, as I illustrate in the remainder of this chapter, with different labels come different definitions, delimitations, and approaches to quantifying frequency.

Previous definitions of LRs have been based on (lexical) form (Fellegy 1995; Gardner 1998), length, and/or their placement without overlap with ongoing talk (Schweitzer and Lewandowski 2012). Only placement has the potential to take interactional structure into account. However, "placement without overlap with ongoing talk" as a definition is not rooted in the structure of the interaction and excludes many LRs that in fact do stand in (partial) overlap, as seen in examples (1)–(4).

Previous approaches to quantifying frequency are similarly variable and largely disregard the speaker–listener role distribution and interactional context in which the responses were produced. In corpus linguistics, the frequency of backchannels is traditionally calculated per million words (see O'Keeffe and Adolphs 2008; Murphy 2012), while other studies consider the number of LRs per minute (Tottie 1991; Bavelas et al. 2000) or per three minutes (Maynard 1990). Other scholars orient more strongly to Labov's (1972b) Principle of Accountability by defining what they consider *opportunities* to produce an LR and noting how often these opportunities are (not) taken (Brunner 1979; White 1989). A similar approach is comparing the number of speaker changes that are floor changes to the number of what is called "supportive changes" to do LRs (Clancy et al. 1996).

Murphy (2012) illustrates why it is problematic not to take interactional structure into account when operationalizing frequency. Based on the corpus linguistic metric "per million words," she finds that women produce far fewer responses than men in her data. Murphy then demonstrates that this gender effect is explained by the fact that the speaker roles are not evenly distributed in the conversations, with women doing more talking and men doing more listening. This means that the men in this corpus had far more opportunities to produce LRs than women, and hence the number of LRs by men relative to all talk in the corpus supersedes the number of responses produced by women. What looks like a social effect is thus largely due to interactional role distribution. This critique fully applies to the other studies cited in this chapter, which operationalize LR frequency based on metrics that are blind to interactional constraints and context.

Social psychologists have proposed a frequency operationalization that can be built on to resolve the issue outlined by Murphy (2012), as well as Fellegy (1995) and Reid (1995), who note similar challenges. Duncan and Fiske (1977) and Duncan and Niederehe (1974) normalize backchannel frequency relative to 100 interlocutor words in the interaction, thus taking the distribution of speaker and listener roles into account. When applied to the turn-level, this metric allows for a careful, turn-by-turn, interactionally rooted quantification of frequency, and thus a basis for statistical analysis (for an in-depth discussion, see Eiswirth 2020b). It is this normalization that I draw on in my quantitative analysis, after a brief discussion of how the issues that are typical for quantitative work on LRs relate to the concept of the sociolinguistic variable overall.

As was made clear earlier in this section, not all LRs are made equal, and they are structurally constrained by the preceding talk. Thus, we can only understand what an LR does if we also consider what comes before it (see Schegloff 1982: 88). There are three key challenges when quantitatively analyzing variation in LRs: (1) defining and delimiting them as a variable, (2) quantifying them in an interactionally accountable way, and (3) describing and quantitatively accounting for structural constraints on their production. These issues also apply to other variables above the level of the phoneme, such as quotatives (Buchstaller 2006, 2014) and negative tag questions (Pichler 2016b). The interactionally and structurally rooted definition of LRs as a variable, as proposed here, has the potential to address these issues. The following quantitative analysis demonstrates how this approach enables a more interactionally accountable quantitative analysis of variation.

8.4 Quantifying Overall LR Frequency

LR frequency is operationalized in this analysis as (number of LRs in any given turn)/(number of words in this turn) and multiplied by 100 – the mean turn length – in order to make turns of different lengths comparable (see Eiswirth 2020b). The inferential statistical model presented in this section takes normalized counts of both LRs and words in turn as input, but the output is given as the number of LRs the model predicts for a 100-word-long turn. As outlined in Section 8.2, zero-inflated Poisson regression models (Eiswirth 2020b, Gadanidis and Denis, Chapter 7, this volume) consist of two parts, a zero-model that in this case predicts how long a turn needs to be to receive an LR and a count model that predicts how many LRs are expected for a turn of length X. The model formula takes speaker gender and an interaction between the number of words in the turn and listener gender as fixed effects and treats the listener and the dyad as random effects. These random effects account for individual or dyad-specific variation, while the interaction allows turn length to have a different effect based on the gender of the person producing the turn. The model formula is as follows:

glmmTMB (number of responses ~ number of words in turn * Speaker gender + Listener gender + (1|Listener) + (1|Dyad))

The full model output is given in the chapter appendix. Table 8.3 shows the predicted minimum turn length at which an LR is produced. A female listener listening to a female speaker is predicted to produce the first response after 11.4 words in a turn, and after 14 words if she is listening to a male speaker. A male listener listening to a male speaker is likely to produce the first response after 14.8 words, and when listening to a female speaker after 12.2 words. Turn length ($p<0.001$) as well as the interaction between turn length and speaker gender ($p=0.003$) are statistically significant, suggesting that these differences are not only driven by random effects.

Table 8.4 shows the predicted number of responses normalized relative to the mean turn-length of 100 words by speaker and listener gender. Only turn length is statistically significant in this part of the model ($p<0.001$). Speaker gender is just below the threshold of statistical significance ($p=0.048$). Thus, the count model predicts (1) the longer a turn, the more responses it will receive and (2) male speakers tend to receive fewer responses than female speakers.

Table 8.3 *Minimum turn length at which the first LR is predicted based on the zero-model*

	Female speaker	Male speaker
Female listener	11.4	14
Male listener	12.2	14.8

Table 8.4 *Predicted number of responses to a 100-word turn based on speaker and listener gender*

	Female speaker	Male speaker
Female listener	6 (7.8)	5.1 (6.2)
Male listener	5.6 (5.8)	4.7 (4.5)

The observed numbers of LRs are given in brackets for comparison. Based on the observed numbers, there seems to be a stronger difference based on both speaker and listener gender, with the highest number of responses in all-female dyads and the lowest number in all-male dyads, as well as evidence for cross-gender accommodation; that is, male listeners produce more responses towards female speakers, while female listeners produce fewer responses towards male speakers. However, the statistical model that takes listener and dyad into account as random effects shows that the only clearly statistically significant factor predicting the number of LRs in any given turn is turn length, with longer turns receiving more responses.

8.5 Quantifying Variation Based on Interactional Constraints

As discussed in Section 8.3, what happens in the talk preceding a response can be considered and operationalized as a structural constraint. Based on this, there are three types of LRs: listener-driven responses, speaker-driven responses, and responses driven by both the speaker and the listener to similar degrees. A Bayesian zero-inflated Poisson regression model that takes preceding context into account shows that the impact of speaker and listener gender varies depending on how much structural influence the speaker and listener respectively have on this action getting done. The model, which was fit with `brms` (Bürkner 2018) in a Bayesian paradigm, predicts how many responses a male/female listener is likely to do based on the constraints outlined in Section 8.3. Just as in the count model, this is based on the amount of talking the other person does. The model formula developed based on this qualitative understanding of the data is:

`brm (number of responses ~ structural constraint * (Listener gender + Speaker gender) + (1 | structural constraint + Listener) + (1 | structural constraint + Dyad) + offset = log (number of Speaker words in conversation), family = zero_inflated_poisson, prior = priors)`[7]

Table 8.5 shows the output from this model. The structural constraint is called "main actor" based on the notion that the listener is the "main actor" for listener-driven responses and the speaker is the "main actor" for speaker-driven responses.

---

[7] Priors were specified with the get_prior() function, which is part of the brms package. The steps outlined here are described in more detail in the brms package documentation and relevant literature (Bürkner 2017, 2018; Carpenter et al. 2017).

Table 8.5 *Fixed effects of the zero-inflated Poisson model predicting how many actions listeners do based on which party has how much impact on the action from a qualitative perspective*

	Estimate	Est. Error	CI 2.5%	CI 97.5%
Intercept	−5.227	0.218	−5.676	−4.799
Effect of Main Actor				
Listener	2.020	0.218	1.588	2.446
Speaker	**−1.151**	**0.204**	**−1.556**	**−0.751**
Effect of Listener and Speaker Gender				
Listener gender (male)	**−0.947**	0.387	**−1.700**	**−0.188**
Speaker gender (male)	0.138	0.106	−0.071	0.342
Interaction Main Actor × Listener gender (male)				
Listener × male Listener	0.621	0.376	−0.121	1.374
Speaker × male Listener	0.421	0.321	−0.221	1.050
Interaction Main Actor × Speaker gender (male)				
Listener × male Speaker	−0.138	0.134	−0.405	0.123
Speaker × male Speaker	**−0.524**	0.230	**−0.986**	**-0.074**

Note. CI=credible interval.

The model takes the third condition of LRs constrained by the listener and the speaker to similar degrees as a baseline and compares the other two groups to it. The credible intervals (CIs) show the range within which the possible estimate results might fall. In this model, 95 percent of all possible results of the estimates for the effect of the main actor being speaker fall between −1.556 and −0.751, suggesting that the overall estimate of −1.151 is a good representation of the effect. The first tier, "Effect of Main Actor," confirms that there are more listener-driven responses (i.e., acknowledgments and repairs) and fewer speaker-driven responses (i.e., word-supplies or second assessments). This interpretation is based on the negative estimate for the main actor being the speaker. The second tier, summarizing the effects of listener and speaker gender shows that, overall, listener gender has a greater impact than speaker gender, and male listeners do a smaller number of responses overall than female listeners. This is in line with the overall frequency results presented in Section 8.4.

The most important parts of the regression table are the two sets of interaction effects at the bottom, showing the interactions between main actor (i.e., the type of LR) and listener gender and between main actor and speaker gender, respectively. For listener-driven responses, listener gender has a clear effect: male listeners are predicted to produce more of these responses than female listeners. Furthermore, male listeners are more likely to do listener-driven responses (*estimate*=0.421, 95% CIs −0.221 to 1.050). The output for the interaction between main actor and speaker gender shows that the number of speaker-driven responses is indeed more strongly predicted by the speaker's gender than by the listener's gender (*estimate*=−0.524, 95% CIs −0.986 to −0.074). This suggests that, even when accounting for individual and dyad-related variability, listeners produce fewer instances of speaker-driven responses when listening to male speakers rather than female speakers. Given the strong effect of listener gender across all models and conditions, this is not surprising.

Overall, this model shows that the type of LR interacts with gender: the frequency of occurrence of speaker-driven responses is lower with male speakers, and the frequency of listener-driven responses is higher with male listeners. In both cases, the gender of the interlocutor has a small effect with a large degree of uncertainty, including the direction of the effect (see the bottom two tiers of the model output in Table 8.5).

8.6 Discussion

Here, I briefly contextualize and discuss the findings reported in this chapter with respect to LR frequency and gender, before returning to their relevance to the overall conceptualization of the sociolinguistic variable above the level of the phoneme. The only clearly significant factor predicting the number of LRs in any given turn was turn length, with longer turns receiving more responses. Listener gender was not statistically significant, and speaker gender was very close to the threshold for statistical significance (p=0.048), with male speakers tending to receive fewer responses than female speakers. These results contrast with Murphy (2012) as well as Stubbe (1998), who both found men to produce more LRs than women. They are in line with Oreström (1983), who reports no difference based on listener gender in overall response frequency, and with Reid (1995), who finds female speakers receive more responses than male speakers. In the present study, there is a significant effect of speaker gender in the same direction: female speakers received more LRs. However, the results also highlight the contrast between the purely descriptive statistics, which suggest a strong gender difference, and the inferential statistics, which show these differences are not significant. This underlines the importance of statistical tools like the zero-inflated Poisson regression models used in this study, given that the random effects of individuals and dyads account for most of the variation. Factors beyond gender, such as age, variety of English, or conversational style, might also play an important role in explaining LR frequency. Previous work has shown that L1 and even the particular variety of English impact how frequently listeners respond (White 1989; Ward and Tsukahara 2000; O'Keeffe and Adolphs 2008), and investigating these factors further would be a worthwhile avenue of future work.

The definition I propose of LRs based on interactional structure allows us to formulate structural constraints on variation, and the quantitative analysis demonstrates that these structural constraints are statistically significant. Listener-driven responses are statistically constrained by listener gender while speaker-driven responses are statistically more strongly influenced by the speaker than by the listener.

It would, however, be rash to deduce underlying gendered behavioral patterns from these results. A more in-depth interactional analysis of both speaker-driven and listener-driven responses is needed in order to understand how this variation plays out. To give one example, the observation that men receive fewer speaker-driven responses could be related to three different interactional patterns:

1 The male participants simply *provide fewer opportunities* for those responses to be produced.
2 The male participants here *provide just as many opportunities* for those responses to be produced as women do, *but listeners do not take them up* (this is unlikely, because, as we have seen, when a speaker signals word-search trouble the structurally preferred response is for the listener to provide a candidate word).
3 If a male participant provides such an opportunity, it is taken up but leads to a floor change, that is, the listener turns into the new speaker, rather than the male speaker continuing. These instances would therefore not be counted as LRs based on the definition provided here, but would rather be examples of incipient speakership, as seen in example (4).

These are three very different explanations for the same pattern, and further qualitative analyses and potentially additional coding are needed in order to understand which one underlies the overall observation at each individual point.

8.7 Conclusion

This chapter has illustrated that bringing CA tools and perspectives into analyses of variation not only helps in defining and delimiting the variable and formulating structural constraints but also impacts how we interpret the results. A CA perspective is a constant reminder that these actions are negotiated on an utterance-by-utterance basis, and, as famously stated by Schegloff (1982: 88), "the treatment of them [LR] in the aggregate, separated from the talk immediately preceding them, loses what they are doing."

This perspective also informs critiques of essentialist interpretations of gender differences in other linguistic phenomena. Tag questions, overlap, high-rise terminals, hedges, compliments, turn-taking, and the distribution of speaking time in an interaction have all been shown to be contingent not only on one participant's behavior but also on the other person(s) in the conversation and on the interactional projects these participants embark on together (Dubois and Crouch 1975; Cameron et al. 1989; Holmes 1995; Meyerhoff 2014; Wilkinson and Kitzinger 2014; Meyerhoff and Ehrlich 2019). Accordingly, we need to consider both parties' contributions to the phenomenon to provide an interactionally accountable interpretation of any group or individual differences observed, rather than concluding that women or men behave in a particular manner.

This chapter has illustrated that drawing on CA makes it possible to delineate a variable that is rooted in interactional structure at the level of turn-taking. Drawing on CA also allows us to formulate structural constraints, two of the "most useful properties of a sociolinguistic variable" (Labov 1963: 279), that are nonetheless challenging to pin down above the level of the phoneme. Squarely situating variation in the interaction rather than in each individual participant's system of behavior changes our perspective on quantifying frequency and on interpreting the results. Frequency is calculated relative to the *other's* talk. Likewise, variation based on interactional constraints needs to be interpreted carefully, with respect to the individual local context of the interaction. A further contribution is the introduction of zero-inflated Poisson regression models, common in other areas of research, as a useful tool to statistically model phenomena such as LRs. The methodology presented here could be transferred to other variables above the level of the phoneme. Pichler (2016c) has already moved in this direction with her analysis of *innit*. Other tag questions or hedges would be interesting candidates for future research along the lines demonstrated here.

To summarize, this chapter has introduced LRs as a discourse-organizational variable that illustrates a fruitful integration of CA and variationist sociolinguistic methods. The chapter makes theoretical and methodological contributions to sociolinguistic, pragmatic, and discourse-pragmatic work by demonstrating how such an integrated analysis can be done.

Appendix

Model Output of the Zero-Inflated Poisson Model for Overall LRs Frequency

Fixed Effects of the Logit Model

Fixed effect	Estimate	Std. error	Z-value	p-value
(Intercept)	−8.14	1.64	−4.97	<0.001
Words in turn (centered)	−1.12	0.05	−24.47	**<0.001**
Listener (male)	1.90	1.91	0.99	0.32
Speaker (male)	1.02	1.79	0.57	0.57
Words in turn (centered) × Listener (male)	−0.23	0.08	−2.96	**0.003**

Note. The longer the turn, the more likely there is to be an LR. This effect is somewhat less strong for male than female listeners.

Fixed Effects of the Count Model

Fixed effect	Estimate	Std. error	Z-value	p-value
(Intercept)	1.54	0.08	19.64	<0.001
Words in turn (centered)	0.57	0.004	138.18	**<0.001**
Listener (male)	−0.07	0.11	−0.63	0.53
Speaker (male)	−0.16	1.08	−1.98	**0.048**
Words in turn (centered) × Listener (male)	−0.01	0.01	−1.39	0.17

Note. The number of LRs increases with turn length, and male speakers receive fewer responses than female speakers.

Part III

Language Contact Settings

9   *You Know* in L1 and L2 English

Chloé Diskin-Holdaway

9.1   Introduction: A Variationist Approach to Discourse-Pragmatic Markers

This chapter investigates the distribution of the discourse-pragmatic marker (DPM) *you know* in two L1 varieties of English – Irish English (IrE) and Australian English (AusE) – and two L2 varieties consisting of Polish and Chinese L1 speakers residing in Ireland. DPMs are characterized by many defining features, including orality, high frequency, stylistic stigma, phonological reduction, semantic shallowness, and optionality (Brinton 1996: 33). It is generally understood that they do not carry much lexical import on their own but instead function as integrated parts of an utterance. They are far more flexible, creative, and semantically rich than their surface lexical meanings. Their function has been defined as the following:

They [DPMs] signal transitions in the evolving process of the conversation, index the relation of an utterance to the preceding context and indicate an interactive relationship between speaker, hearer and message. (Fung and Carter 2007: 411)

Despite the wealth of description, categorization, and analysis of the functions and pragmatic significance of DPMs (see Östman 1981; Schourup 1985; Erman 1987; Schiffrin 1987; Andersen 2001; Erman 2001; Aijmer 2002, 2004), variationist studies of discourse-pragmatic features are proportionally rare. This is surprising considering the fact that they, "like other features in the grammar, evince orderly heterogeneity and a capacity for change" (Pichler 2010: 582). However, the flexibility, multifunctionality, and optionality of discourse features make it difficult to circumscribe the variable context in an accountable way (see Schleef and Mackay, Chapter 2; Eiswirth, Chapter 8; Gadanidis and Denis, Chapter 7, this volume). Other issues such as methodological heterogeneity have resulted in a lack of generalizability, replicability, and extension of findings (Pichler 2010).

Nonetheless, DPMs have been found to be "an important means for indexing social identities" (Pichler 2013: 10) and are a worthy area of investigation within the context of L2 speakers in particular, and L1–L2 contact, since they are good indicators of socio-pragmatic competence (see Diskin 2017) and offer insights into potential differences in intercultural communication. Recent variationist research into the DPM *like* in particular (Andersen 2001; Levey 2006; D'Arcy 2008, Tagliamonte 2012; D'Arcy 2017; Diskin 2017) has begun to fill the aforementioned gap. As argued by Pichler (2013: 15–16), a "systematic, exhaustive, and accountable" quantitative study of DPMs can provide "numerical evidence" about the multifunctionality of DPMs and the "sensitivity of discourse-pragmatic features to external constraints."

9.1.1 Discourse-Pragmatic Markers and L2 Speakers

There are few studies that bring together both the quantitative, variationist analysis of DPMs and the study of second language acquisition (SLA). The field of interlanguage pragmatics, for example, focuses on the pragmatics of L2 speech but does not encompass a variationist approach and tends to take speech acts as its focus of investigation, rather than the sociolinguistic variable (see Kasper and Blum-Kulka 1993). Other large-scale, quantitative investigations examine frequencies and distributions of individual DPMs, but the majority, according to Müller (2005: 1), only focus on L1 speakers. The relative lack of research is surprising, considering the fact that DPMs provide insights into language acquisition on an interpersonal and communicative level and thus can be used as an accurate measure of different kinds of competence: "pragmatic competence, in terms of knowing the cultural values of the second language [...] is recognized as being essential for successful communication" (Müller 2005: 1). Svartvik had a similar argument when he wrote:

If a foreign language learner says "five sheeps" or "he goed," he [*sic*] can be corrected by practically every native speaker. If, on the other hand, he omits a "well," the likely reaction will be that he is dogmatic, impolite, boring, awkward to talk to etc., but a native speaker cannot pinpoint an "error." (Svartvik 1980: 171)

Echoing this view, Aijmer (2002: 3) claims that infrequent or incorrect use of DPMs by L2 speakers may lead to misunderstandings, and Mosegaard Hansen (1998: 199) notes that this can be "less significant but certainly far less easy to resolve than the incorrect use of a content word."

Language instruction and testing for English as Second Language learners tends to be skewed towards the acquisition of phonology, content words, and grammar, whereas discourse-pragmatic aspects of language such as DPMs do not tend to be taught as explicitly, especially those considered to belong to the informal, "spoken" domain, such as *like* and *you know* (Hellermann and Vergun 2007). However, without this explicit instruction, L2 speakers may have difficulties in interpreting the intentions of speakers correctly in naturalistic, spontaneous L1 speech. It has been argued that the quantitative study of DPMs is an ideal measure of successful SLA, particularly because it can be indicative of level of contact with L1 speakers (Liao 2009: 1314).

Previous studies of DPMs and L2 speakers have shown that, in general, the frequency patterns of L2 speakers do not mirror those of L1 speakers. Fung and Carter (2007) found *you know* to be more frequent among L1 as compared to L2 speakers. Fuller (2003) found that German, French, and Spanish L1 participants (highly proficient academic staff in American universities) used a range of DPMs less frequently than their L1 counterparts, especially when it came to *you know*, *like*, and *I mean*. Only their frequency of *oh* and *well* mirrored that of English L1 speakers. Müller (2005) found that L2 speakers (exchange students from Germany in the United States) used *you know* and *like* far less than American English L1 speakers; whereas they used *well* and *so* proportionately more often. Buysse (2010) found similar results, whereby his participants (Flemish university students) used *you know*, *like*, *kind of*, and *I mean* significantly less than British English (BrE) L1 speakers, but they used *so* and *well* significantly more. He attributes this trend to the stigma surrounding the more "informal" and "interpersonal" DPMs, such as *you know* and *I mean* (see also Schiffrin 1987; Underhill 1988).

Neary Sundquist (2014) found that, as proficiency increased among L2 speakers, so too did their frequency and variety of DPMs. *You know* was found to be used ten times more frequently among high proficiency speakers as compared to low proficiency speakers (Neary Sundquist 2014: 650). This suggests that the DPM *you know* is acquired relatively late among learners of English. Romero Trillo (2002) found that L2 speakers (with Spanish L1) were capable of acquiring "operative markers" (*look* and *listen*), but "involvement markers" (*you know*, *I mean*, *well*) presented more difficulty. Nestor et al. (2012) focused on the acquisition of the DPM *like* among Polish migrants in Ireland. They found that, whereas L1 Irish English speakers had high proportions of *like* in clause-final position, which is an idiosyncratic feature in the dialect and also has pragmatic applications, L2 speakers had more *like* in clause-initial position. Truesdale and Meyerhoff (2015) found that Polish teenagers in Edinburgh had lower frequencies of *like* than their local peers and that they had a more restricted set of discourse-pragmatic functions for *like* at their disposal, as compared to L1 speakers. Hellermann and Vergun (2007) also focused on migrant L2 speakers and found that, among adult beginner learners of English, proficiency and exposure to native speakers (NS) increased their use of the DPMs *like*, *you know*, and *well*. More "acculturated" non-native speakers (NNS) were more likely to use a higher frequency of DPMs (Hellermann and Vergun 2007: 168).

Hasselgreen (2004) examined fluency among Norwegian NNS of English, conducting a quantitative analysis of 19 DPMs or "smallwords" (including *like*, *you know*, and *I mean*). She found that young Norwegians with high proficiency in English used DPMs at a rate closer to that of L1 speakers (although L1 speakers still used them the most). She also observed that "smallwords may be an area of vocabulary where learners most need the comfort of familiar words and phrases – the 'lexical teddy bears' of speaking" (Hasselgreen 2004: 177). Overall, there is a general consensus within the literature that DPMs pattern unsystematically in L2 speech and that, while they can be affected by factors such as proficiency or acculturation, there are also high degrees of individual variation (Liao 2009).

9.1.2 The Discourse-Pragmatic Marker You Know

The DPM *you know* fulfills a variety of functions, including requesting acknowledgment (Schourup 1985) or reassurance (Holmes 1986); appealing to shared knowledge and achieving intimacy (Östman 1981; Schiffrin 1987); and introducing consequence, background information, or clarification (Erman 1987). *You know* is reported to be a salient stylistic marker (Östman 1981: 20) and to be subject to sociolinguistic variation (Stubbe and Holmes 1995; Macaulay 2002). Investigations such as Macaulay (2002), found that, in Scotland, *you know* was more likely to be used by female speakers and that middle-class speakers were more likely to use it clause-medially for self-repair or elaboration, whereas working-class speakers were more likely to use it clause-finally. Stubbe and Holmes (1995) revealed that *you know* was significantly correlated with young, male working-class speech and informal speech styles in New Zealand.

Within popular discourse, *you know* has been reported to be "irritating" and "unnecessary" within speech, functioning merely as a filler in conversation (Stubbe and Holmes 1995: 63). However, linguistic studies into *you know* have focused on the degree to which it is "addressee-oriented" or of "sympathetic circularity," as opposed to "speaker-oriented" DPMs or "opinion openers" such as *I mean* (Stubbe and Holmes 1995; see also Schleef and Mackay, Chapter 2, this volume). Fox Tree and Schrock (2002) claim that the addressee-oriented nature of *you know* results in speakers of "higher status" (e.g., in the workplace) being less likely to use *you know* for requesting agreement, in order to distance themselves from (lower status) addressees.

In one study of *you know* among L2 (defined in the study as English as a Lingua Franca – ELF) speakers, House (2009: 171) argues that the use of *you know* by ELF speakers is "critically different" from that of L1 speakers of English, in that ELF speakers use *you know* predominantly as a "self-serving strategy" to create coherence and buy time, rather than to avail of its pragmatic uses, such as establishing common ground with an interlocutor. Other studies have examined merely the frequency of *you know* in L2 speech and results have been somewhat inconsistent. Neary Sundquist (2014) found that high proficiency Chinese and Korean L2 speakers of English used more *you know* than the L1 (American English) speakers in her sample. However, Müller (2005) found the opposite: her L1 speakers (Americans) used *you know* five times more than the L2 speakers (Germans) in her study.

Despite the aforementioned previous work that has examined *you know* in different varieties of English, little work has looked at *you know* comparatively across different dialects simultaneously. One known exception is Kallen (2005), who found that within IrE spoken interactions, the proportion of *you know* (3.27 instances per 1,000 words) was higher relative to *I mean* (1.26 instances per 1,000 words). Quite the opposite was found for BrE, where *I mean* (4.43 instances per 1,000 words) was preferred to *you know* (3.6 instances per 1,000 words). The present chapter fills a gap in cross-dialectal work by examining *you know* among two L1 English communities that are geographically distant from one another: IrE and AusE. In fact, generally little is known about *you know* in these two varieties.

9.1.3 Rationale and Research Questions

As a research rationale, *you know* was selected for analysis due to its high frequency in the everyday speech of L1 speakers of English (see Östman 1981; Crystal 1988; Erman 2001; Fox Tree and Schrock 2002; Buysse 2017: 40), its reported presence in the speech of L2 speakers of English (see Aijmer 2004; Müller 2005; Fung and Carter 2007; Hellermann and Vergun 2007; House 2009), and its equivalents in the L1s of the L2 speakers in this study (Polish and Chinese). Its deployment for sociostylistic purposes also offers ample pathways for investigations of stratified use across groups that differ by L1. The following research questions guided the present study:

1 Does *you know* differ across two varieties of English (that are geographically very isolated from one another)?
2 Does *you know* differ in frequency between:
   2a L1 and L2 speakers?
   2b L2 speakers with different L1s (Polish and Chinese)?
   2c L2 speakers with different proficiency levels in English, overall levels of education, or lengths of residence in an English-speaking country?
3 Is *you know* more likely to be used for certain discourse-pragmatic functions over others?
4 Does *you know* tend to co-occur with other DPMs, such as *I mean*, and does this differ across two varieties of English?

9.2 Methodology

9.2.1 Participants and Data Collection

This chapter presents a quantitative analysis of the frequency and function of a total of 1,511 tokens of *you know* across two L1 (IrE and AusE) and two L2 varieties of English (Polish and Chinese migrants in Ireland). The data originates from two corpora of sociolinguistic interviews with a total of fifty-nine individuals collected in Dublin, Ireland, in 2012 and in Melbourne, Australia, in 2017 (Table 9.1). It is worth noting that the Dublin L1 speakers constitute a proportionately smaller sample than the Melbourne L1 speakers and the L2 speakers; however, since the Dublin L1 group have the lowest numbers of standard deviation of rates of *you know* (Table 9.4), the data still constitutes a reliable source for comparison.

All participants were interviewed using the method of the semi-structured sociolinguistic interview, where the main aim is to allow spontaneous conversation, with minimal interviewer intervention, but with an ancillary aim of gathering attitudinal and demographic information about participants' and their daily lives (see Labov 1972b). In Dublin, participants were interviewed one-on-one by the author (with the exception of two participants interviewed together as a dyad) in their own homes or in public spaces such as cafés. In Melbourne, participants were interviewed by the author and a native AusE speaker in a sound-attenuated studio on a university campus. Five AusE participants were interviewed alone and six were interviewed in three dyad pairs.

In Dublin, participants' level of education was ascertained via a question in the semi-structured interview ("How many years of school did you have a chance to finish?" – from Tagliamonte 2006b), and in Melbourne it was recorded via a tick-box question in a background questionnaire filled out by participants ("What is your highest educational qualification?"), although the Melbourne education data is not examined in the present chapter.

At the end of the Dublin interviews with the L2 participants, they were administered a written questionnaire based on the Common European Framework of Reference for Languages (CEFR) (Council of Europe 2001).

Table 9.1 *Participants in the Dublin and Melbourne corpora*

L1/L2 status	Nationality	Place of residence	Female	Male	Total
L1	Irish	Dublin	4	3	7
	Australian	Melbourne	6	5	11
L2	Chinese	Dublin	8	12	20
	Polish	Dublin	10	11	21

Table 9.2 *Proficiency levels from the Common European Framework of Reference for Languages (CEFR)*

Proficiency levels	N (overall)	N (Chinese)	N (Polish)
A1 (Basic user)	0	–	–
A2 (Basic user)	2	2	–
B1 (Independent user)	14	7	7
B2 (Independent user)	11	6	5
C1 (Proficient user)	13	4	9
C2 (Proficient user)	1	1	0

The questionnaire requested participants to self-assess their level of English by selecting statements that best corresponded to their proficiency in five areas: listening, reading, spoken interaction, spoken production, and writing. The participants' scores in the five areas were averaged so that each speaker was assigned a general score based on the CEFR labels (Table 9.2). The average assessment was close to a B2. There was an even spread across the B1 and B2 categories, but there were more Polish ($N=9$) than Chinese participants ($N=4$) in the C1 category. All the participants had had some degree of English instruction prior to arrival in Ireland, normally within the formal school system. The lack of A1 users is due to the fact that one of the prerequisites for participation in the study was that participants be proficient enough to engage in a conversation in English.

The Dublin participants were aged between 19 and 49 (average age: 29.7; $SD=6$) and, for the migrants, their length of residence in Ireland ranged from 1 to 11 years, with an average of 4.5 years. It should be noted that, among the L2 speakers in Dublin, proficiency and residency were not collinear, as many migrants received schooling in English prior to migrating. The Melbourne participants were aged between 26 and 43 with an average age of 31 ($SD=5$). Thus, the average age across both corpora was comparable and age was not included as a sociolinguistic variable in the study.

9.2.2 Coding

For the analysis of the Dublin data, a 20-minute segment from the middle portion of every interview was coded, whereas the entirety of the Melbourne corpus was coded. This procedure was followed so that both corpora would be somewhat commensurate in terms of the total hours of speech and words in the overall analysis. This came to a total of approximately 16 hours of speech (100,853 total words) in the Dublin corpus and approximately 11 hours of speech (64,599 total words) in the Melbourne corpus. This then resulted in the extraction of 1,075 tokens of *you know* and 55 tokens of *I mean* for analysis from the Dublin corpus and 436 tokens of *you know* and 79 tokens of *I mean* from the Melbourne corpus.

9.2.3 The Variable Context

The DPM *you know* cannot be considered a sociolinguistic variable, *sensu stricto*, as it does not constitute "two or more ways of saying the same thing" (Weiner and Labov 1983: 30) – this presents a challenge for variationist analyses of discourse-pragmatic features more generally (see Pichler 2010). Nonetheless, DPMs can and have been approached using rigorous quantitative methodologies (see, e.g., D'Arcy 2005, Müller 2005; Levey 2006; Nestor et al. 2012; Labelle-Hogue 2013; Schweinberger 2015; Waters 2016; D'Arcy 2017; Diskin 2017). Furthermore, methodological developments in variationist sociolinguistics more broadly are being addressed by the gradual replacement of variable rule analysis, which is best suited to the analysis of binary variables, with fixed- and mixed-effects regression analyses, which are more conducive to the analysis of non-binary variables, including DPMs.

In the present chapter, a normalization procedure is adopted, where the frequency of *you know* per 1,000 words is examined, thus accounting for differences such as variability in the number of words per speaker (see Macaulay 2002: 750; Walker 2010: 76). The approach is not, strictly speaking, a variationist one and does not include all instances where *you know* could have occurred but did not. This was the method underpinning D'Arcy (2005) and Kastronic (2011) for their analyses of *like*, but this type of variationist approach results in an overwhelming number of potential contexts for occurrence, which can become unwieldy when coding manually (see Diskin 2017: 148). D'Arcy (2005) overcame this by using a randomly selected subsample. In doing so, however, one might argue that this process creates an "artificial overall rate" that may, in fact, render such analyses not strictly accountable either (Walker 2010: 77).

The analysis here takes a "form-based" approach, whereby the variable context includes all instances of the DPM *you know* (but no other "competing" variants). It operationalizes *you know* according to Pichler's general definition that regards discourse-pragmatic features as "formally heterogeneous," "syntactically optional," and not contributing to "truth-conditional meaning" (Pichler 2013: 4). *You know* in the Dublin and Melbourne datasets was investigated by first extracting all instances of *you know* from the orthographic transcriptions and examining each one manually, in order to ascertain its eligibility as a DPM (e.g., instances of *you know* where "know" was clearly used as a verb, were excluded), and then coded for a variety of linguistic and sociolinguistic factors. *You know* was operationalized as "those instances that can be analyzed as consisting of a combination of the subject and predicator of a clause" (Buysse 2017: 41) and collocations including *you know*, such as *you know that way* or *like you know* were excluded, as were constructions preceded by "do," such as *do you know what I mean*.

With regards to linguistic factors, *you know* was examined for its discourse-pragmatic function as outlined in Table 9.3 (note that, owing to time constraints, this was only conducted for the Dublin data). This table was compiled on the basis of a compendium of previous research on *you know* and operationalized via a pilot study on the functions of *you know* from the Dublin corpus (see Diskin 2015). Some functions of *you know* can present overlap, such as the "illustrate" and "exemplify" categories (see Table 9.3, where the example for "exemplify" could also be viewed as the provision of background information or clarification). For the purpose of the present analysis, these were kept

Table 9.3 *Functions of* you know *in the Dublin corpus*

Code	Function	Examples
Illustrator	Introduce consequence, background information, or clarification (Erman 1987); create coherence; highlight certain elements in the discourse (Erman 2001); introduce explanation (Müller 2005)	**You know** *Poland is between East and West in a way* (Magda, Polish L1)
Filler	Staller for time (Erman 1987, 2001); lexical/content search (Östman 1981; Müller 2005)	*What the hell's going on there, people is just afraid go* **you know** *even for a walk!* (Marcin, Polish L1)
Exemplifier	Exemplification (Erman 1987)	*I'd rather to go out for a walk,* **you know** *to meet someone, or just to go for a walk without a reason* (Michał, Polish L1)
Invite response	Turn-yielding; invite a response (with rising intonation) (Östman 1981); ask for acknowledgment (Schourup 1985); appeal for reassurance (Holmes 1986); "cajoler" (House 2009); appeal for listener to have patience (Holmes 1986; Erman 1987); appeal for understanding (Müller 2005)	*I would like to feel like I am home,* **you know**? (Beata, Polish L1)
Reference to shared knowledge	Pretend shared knowledge and achieve intimacy (Östman 1981); reference to shared knowledge (Müller 2005), either between speaker and hearer (Stubbe and Holmes 1995) or in general (Schiffrin 1987)	*We can uh see something in television, we can uh read uh magazines,* **you know?** (Eliza, Polish L1)

separate to start with (in line with Diskin 2015) but, later, following House (2009), collapsed into a broader "coherence" category along with the "filler" function (Table 9.5). The function of *you know* can also correlate with certain syntactic positions and prosodic patterns, such as the "invite response" function typically occurring clause-finally and with a rising intonation (see Diskin 2015); however, these aspects are not examined here.

Three main types of statistical analysis were run. First, for the analysis of the frequency of *you know*, a fixed-effects regression was run using the lm function in R (R Core Team 2013), with each speaker as the dependent variable. The independent variables were each speaker's frequency of *you know* per 1,000 words and six sociolinguistic variables: L1/L2 status; variety for the L1 speakers (IrE/AusE); speaker gender; level of education (Dublin only); and length of residence and English proficiency for the migrant groups. Second, for the analysis of the functions of *you know*, a series of mixed-effects regression analyses were run using the lme4 package (Bates et al. 2015) in R (R Core Team (2013), where each individual function of *you know* (see Table 9.3) was the dependent variable. The independent variables were the speaker (included as a random effect) and L1/L2 status, nationality, and proficiency in English. Third, for the analysis of the co-occurrence of *you know* with another DPM, *I mean*, a Pearson correlation analysis was run. As cited in Levshina (2015: 115, 139), a correlation analysis is used to investigate the relationship between two quantitative variables (in this case, the frequency of *you know* and *I mean* per 1,000 words), whereas a regression analysis tests the relationship between a response (dependent) variable and an explanatory (independent) variable). Since the interest lay not in whether *I mean* could explain rates of *you know*, or vice versa, but simply in whether their co-occurrence was not down to chance, a Pearson correlation analysis was deemed more suitable in this instance.

9.3 Results

This section features the results of the analysis of the frequency (Section 9.3.1) and function (Section 9.3.2) of *you know* in L1 and L2 speech. Section 9.3.3 discusses the co-occurrence of *you know* with other DPMs in both corpora.

9.3.1 Frequency of You Know *among L1 and L2 Speakers*

To start, the frequency of *you know* per 1,000 words was calculated across both the L1 groups (IrE and AusE) and the L2 groups in Dublin (Table 9.4). Among the L1 speakers, the average rate of *you know* in Melbourne (6.75 per 1,000 words) was more than twice the rate of that of the IrE speakers in

Table 9.4 You know *among L1 and L2 speakers*

L1/L2 status	Variety	Speakers (N)	Total words	Total *you know*	Avg. *you know*/1,000 words (all speakers)	SD	Avg. *you know*/1,000 words (females)	Avg. *you know*/1,000 words (males)
L1	IrE	7	8,236	28	3.1	2.1	2.62	3.73
	AusE	11	64,599	436	6.75	6.26	8.1	5.81
L2	Polish L1	21	51,333	782	14.86	14	19.23	10.05
	Chinese L1	20	41,284	265	6.12	8.16	4.52	8.51

Dublin (3.1 per 1,000 words); however, following a fixed-effects linear regression analysis, these differences were not found to be significant ($F=2.56$, $p=0.13$). It is also of note that there were high degrees of individual variability in both corpora, indicated by the high standard deviations (6.26 in Melbourne and 2.1 in Dublin). One IrE speaker had no *you know* at all.

Following fixed-effects linear regression analyses, differences between the L1 and L2 corpora were found to be only near significant. However, when the four speaker groups were compared with one another, the Polish group was found to be significantly more likely to use *you know* (at 14.86 average *you know*s per 1,000 words) as compared to the three other speaker groups ($F=3.84$ on 3 and 55 DF, $p<0.01$). This is visualized in Figure 9.1. While the boxplot indicates no outliers in the Polish group, it should again be noted the high degrees of individual variation in this group, with a standard deviation of 14.

When sociolinguistic factors were included in the analyses, gender did not have any significant effect, despite some variability by gender as presented in Table 9.4, particularly among the L2 speakers.

Focusing in more detail on the L2 groups in Dublin, following a fixed-effects regression analysis, the only sociolinguistic factor that was found to have an effect was level of education ($F=3.42$ on 3 and 44 DF, $p<0.02$). The frequency of *you know* per 1,000 words by migrants' level of education (and as compared to the L1 IrE group) is visualized in Figure 9.2, showing that those whose highest level of education was secondary school (high school) were more likely to use *you know* than those educated to tertiary level ("3rd level" and "Postgraduate"). Neither length of residence nor proficiency in English was found to have significant effects, even when both were also run as separate regression models. Residence length and proficiency were also examined as both categorical and continuous variables and in both cases had no effect.

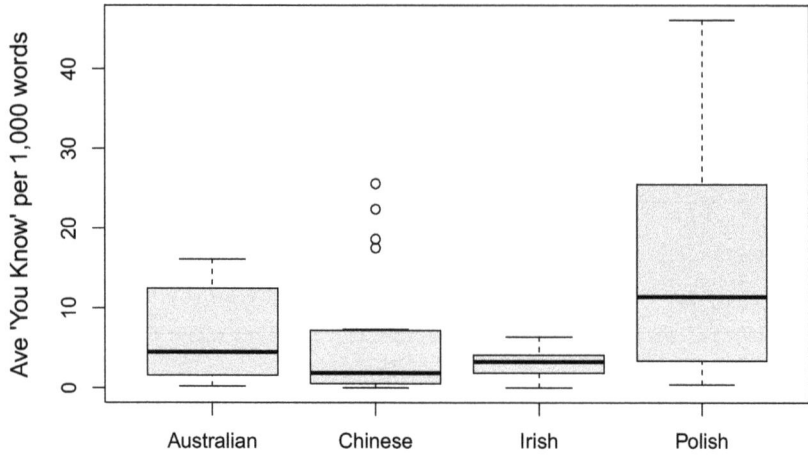

Figure 9.1 Average rates of *you know* per 1,000 words across four speaker groups

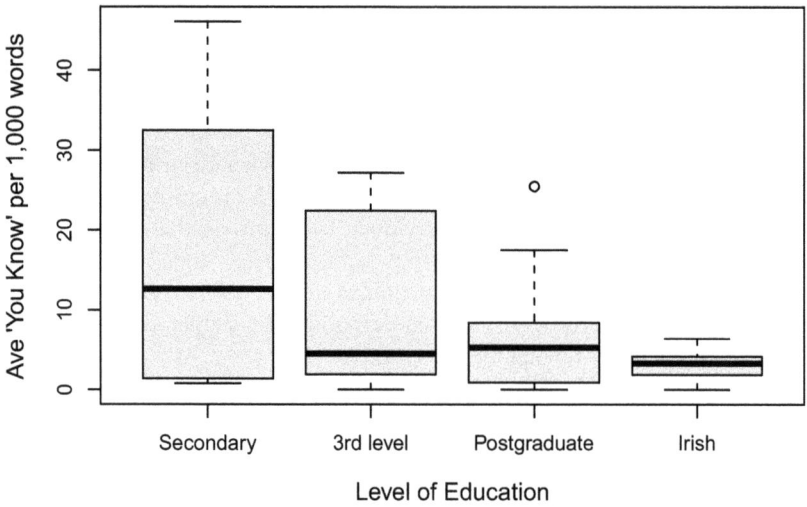

Figure 9.2 Frequency of *you know* by migrants' level of education in the Dublin corpus

9.3.2 Function of You Know among L1 and L2 Speakers (Dublin)

Table 9.5 shows the distribution of the functions of *you know* in the Dublin corpus. It shows the predominance of *you know* as used as an illustrator

Table 9.5 *Breakdown of* you know *by function (House 2009): Dublin corpus*

Functional category	Function	L1 (Dublin)*		L2 (Polish)		L2 (Chinese)	
		N	% of total	N	% of total**	N	% of total
Coherence	Illustrate	12	44.44%	462	60.7%	152	58.91%
	Filler	2	7.41%	110	14.45%	31	12.02%
	Exemplify	3	11.11%	39	5.12%	7	0.71%
Interpersonal	Invite response	8	29.63%	80	10.51%	53	20.54%
	Reference to shared knowledge	2	7.41%	70	9.20%	15	5.81%

Note. * A total of 29 tokens from the Dublin corpus were excluded from the present analysis of functions due to them occupying functions not listed here, such as floor opener (which occurred at rates too low to consist of a category in its own right); or due to their function being ambiguous.
** Owing to rounding, total percentages may not add up to 100%.

Table 9.6 *Mixed-effects regression output for* you know *as illustrator by L1 speakers (Intercept) and L2 speakers in the Dublin corpus*

	Estimate	Std. error	Z-value	Pr(>|z|)
(Intercept)	−0.256	0.4462	−0.566	0.5713
L2 speakers	0.7738	0.4622	1.674	**0.0941**
Log Likelihood	−696.1			

Note. Random intercept: Speaker. Figures in bold indicate significance or near significance; $*p \leq 0.05$; $**p \leq 0.01$; $***p \leq 0.001$.

(between 45 percent and 60 percent of the time) and the comparatively low proportion of *you know* as used as a filler (between 7 percent and 14.5 percent of the time).

The proportion of use of *you know* as a filler, exemplifier, and to refer to shared knowledge (e.g. Table 9.7) did not differ significantly by any of the independent variables. However, near significance was found for the L2 speakers to favor *you know* as a illustrator (Table 9.6).

The L1 speakers were also found to significantly favor the invite response function (Table 9.8) over the L2 speakers, although the low token count for the L1 speakers in this case (N=8) means only indicative conclusions can be drawn.

Table 9.7 *Mixed-effects regression output for* you know *to refer to shared knowledge by L1 speakers (Intercept) and L2 speakers in the Dublin corpus*

	Estimate	Std. error	Z-value	Pr(>|z|)
(Intercept)	−2.5774	0.7591	−3.396	0.000685***
L2 speakers	0.1108	0.7703	0.144	0.885634
Log Likelihood	−298.9			

Note. Random intercept: Speaker. Figures in bold indicate significance or near significance; *p ≤ 0.05; **p ≤ 0.01; ***p ≤ 0.001.

Table 9.8 *Mixed-effects regression output for* you know *to invite response by L1 speakers (Intercept) and L2 speakers in the Dublin corpus*

	Estimate	Std. error	Z-value	Pr(>|z|)
(Intercept)	−0.8738	0.5518	−1.583	0.1133
L2 speakers	−1.3225	0.5854	−2.259	**0.0239***
Log Likelihood	−396.6			

Note. Random intercept: Speaker. Figures in bold indicate significance or near significance; *p ≤ 0.05; **p ≤ 0.01; ***p ≤ 0.001.

Following these indicative trends, the different functions of *you know* were collapsed into two "macro" categories taken from House (2009). The reason for using these were that they were specifically designed for a comparison of L1 and L2 speakers and they made a clear distinction between "discourse" and "pragmatic" uses, unlike, for instance, Holmes (1986), which focused more squarely on pragmatic/interpersonal uses of *you know* and only investigated L1 speakers. This subsequent analysis drawing on House (2009) divided *you know* into the two broad categories of "coherence" (the illustrate, filler, and exemplify functions) and "interpersonal" (the invite response and reference to shared knowledge functions). Following this categorization, near significance ($p=0.05$) was found for the L2 speakers to favor *you know* for coherence and for the IrE speakers to favor *you know* for interpersonal aims.

9.3.3 You Know *and Other Discourse-Pragmatic Markers*

You know, like many DPMs, is commonly found in co-occurrence with other DPMs. In the Dublin corpus alone, more than 100 tokens of *you know* were found in co-occurrence with *like*: as collocations such as *like you know* ($N=82$) or *you know like* ($N=28$). Owing to the ambiguity of the category and function of these collocations, they were excluded from the quantitative analyses presented thus far in the present chapter. However, all tokens of *I mean* were extracted, as previous research found important differences in how *you know* and *I mean* were used cross-dialectally, where BrE was found to have a higher proportion of I mean to you know, whereas in IrE the opposite was the case (Kallen 2005).

There were seventy-nine tokens of *I mean* extracted from the Melbourne corpus and fifty-five from the Dublin corpus. The use of *I mean* appeared to be specific to the usage of particular individuals: in Melbourne, eight of the eleven participants used *I mean*; and, in Dublin, only eighteen of the forty-eight participants (and two of the six L1 speakers) used it. This is, of course, not merely a question of personal stylistic preference but also the degree to which discourse contexts potentially favoring *I mean*, such as reinforcing the illocutionary intent of a speaker (Kallen 2005), or opening the floor, emerged in the one hour or so during which participants spoke during their sociolinguistic interviews. While an operationalized account of these different potential discourse contexts was beyond the scope of the present analysis, a comparative analysis of the average usage of *I mean* per speaker and per 1,000 words was conducted in order to test its proportion of occurrence vis-à-vis *you know* in both IrE and AusE.

In Melbourne, the average rate of use of *I mean* was 1.29 per 1,000 words (as compared to 6.75 per 1,000 words for *you know*). In Dublin, *I mean* occurred at 0.47 (0.16 for L1 speakers) per 1,000 words, and *you know* at 9.51 (3.1 for L1 speakers) per 1,000 words. These findings therefore lend support to the findings of Kallen (2005) and show similarities between IrE and AusE (both having a preference for *you know* over *I mean*) as compared to BrE. Furthermore, the results in Section 9.3.2, where the interpersonal functions of *you know* were found to be preferred by L1 speakers in the Dublin corpus, corroborate at least somewhat Kallen (2005), who wrote that *you know* is used as a downgrader, which is an interpersonal usage. A qualitative analysis of *you know* in the Melbourne corpus found that it was also being used for interpersonal reasons, such as referring to shared knowledge (as in (1)), where, at times in tandem with the DPM *I mean* and other expressions such as *of course*, speakers deployed *you know* in instances where they took the floor to state their opinion or stance on a particular issue.

(1)   I-(.) I mean but, **you know** of course the posts are also quite heavily moderated so (.) **you know** there's sorts of those sorts of issues. (AU_029_F, Melbourne)

Indeed, following a Pearson correlation analysis, it was found that, in Melbourne, uses of *you know* and *I mean* were highly correlated (r(11)=0.76, $p<0.01$). In Dublin, however, no such correlation was found (r(48)=0.23, p=0.08).

Other DPMs that were used in instances of self-disclosure in the Melbourne corpus included the DPM *look*, which in the literature is often reported as an "attention-getter" (Romero Trillo 2002: 77). However, in the eleven instances where it appeared in the Melbourne corpus, it was used most often in instances of the sharing of personal stories or establishment of intimacy. Half of the time it was used in conjunction with other DPMs, such as *you know, I mean, oh*, or *well* and with filled pauses (*uh* or *um*) (as in (2)). The Dublin corpus had just five tokens of *look* and they were all used by the L2 speakers, for the most part in the "attention-getting" sense, which was bolstered by co-occurrence with expressions such as *come on* (3).

(2) Uh, **look** (.) uh, yeah I- at-at-at times, yeah I mean, you know, different times, I've got on better with them than- than others (AU_007_F, Melbourne).

(3) I was observing others and come on, **look**, someone is saying something, it's not rocket science, you heard that in-in some movie like a thousand times (Paweł, Polish L1).

9.4 Discussion

This section presents the frequency and function of *you know* in L1 speech (Section 9.4.1) and L2 speech (Section 9.4.2).

9.4.1 You Know *in L1 Speech*

This study sought to compare the use of the DPM *you know*, a highly attested and frequent feature of oral discourse, in two L1 varieties of English (IrE and AusE) that have never before been examined comparatively in the discourse-pragmatic literature and that are geographically about as distant as two communities can be from one another. The present investigation, albeit small-scale, showed remarkable similarities across both communities in the frequency of use of *you know*. This provides some evidence towards a claim that *you know* is relatively robust and stable across these two varieties, although similarities in form and frequency, of course, do not necessarily map onto similarities in function (see Waters 2016). Future work on the function of *you know* in AusE could provide a fruitful avenue of investigation.

Indeed, initial forays into analysis of the clustering of DPMs and their co-occurrence with other discourse-pragmatic features (e.g., filled and unfilled pauses; *look, I mean, of course, come on*) indicated that it is unlikely that the use of a DPM in one variety will be identical to that of another. For example, it was shown that IrE and AusE pattern similarly in their preference for *you know* over *I mean* – a trend that sets them apart from trends previously found for BrE (Kallen 2005). However, by looking at correlations between uses of DPMs, it was found that AusE differs from IrE in the sense that *I mean* and *you know* are correlated and thus pattern more closely in their distribution than they do in IrE. Other qualitative differences emerged in uses of DPMs such as *look*, which in AusE was found to emerge in contexts of self-disclosure and intimacy and among L2 speakers in Ireland was found to be used in a more conventional, attention-getting sense. This opens up wide scope for future study of the co-occurrence and clustering of DPMs, which may in turn shed light on their inherent multifunctionality (see Cheshire 2007: 158). Indeed, while, for the purposes of the present study, collocations such as *like you know* were excluded, future work could go far in elucidating the mechanisms underpinning such constructions and their illocutionary force, as well as their potential cross-dialectal variability.

9.4.2 You Know *in L2 Speech*

Another aim of the present study was to compare the use of *you know* between L1 and L2 speakers of English, as well as between two L2 groups (Polish and Chinese L1). Some important differences emerged, including a strong preference for Polish L1 speakers to use *you know* in English at significantly higher rates than IrE speakers or Chinese L1 speakers. These findings are in opposition to those of a number of studies that report L2 speakers to use DPMs less than L1 speakers (e.g., Fuller 2003) and most notably and recently that of Buysse (2017), who found that L2 speakers used *you know* significantly less than L1 speakers. Similar findings were also reported by Müller (2005) for *you know*. It must be noted, however, that the L2 speakers in these studies had different L1 backgrounds than those reported here (in the case of Buysse (2017), their backgrounds were Dutch, French, German, and Spanish; in Müller (2005), it was German).

The notable presence of *you know* in the speech of the Polish L1 group in the present study could be the effect of positive transfer, since Polish has a DPM that could be considered, in both its core semantic meaning and its discourse-pragmatic functions, to be synonymous with *you know (wiesz)* (cf. Degand, Broisson, Crible, and Grzech, Chapter 4, this volume), whereas in Chinese there is no such equivalent. That is not to say that Chinese does not have DPMs that function as illustrators or response-inviters; however, since less advanced L2 speakers tend to privilege meaning before form (VanPatten 2004: 7), it follows that L2 speakers may find DPMs more challenging to acquire when there is no direct equivalent in the L1 (see also Diskin and Levey 2019). This claim about less advanced L2 speakers holds somewhat less weight, however, when it is taken into consideration that neither proficiency in English nor length of residence was found to have a significant effect on use of *you know* among the L2 speakers in the present study. Furthermore, both Buysse (2017) and

Müller (2005) suggested that negative transfer can come into play when L2 speakers encounter a form that is overly similar to a form in the L1 and may thus avoid it. However, in the case of the Polish L1 speakers here, positive transfer appears to be at least one of the more likely explanatory factors for the patterns observed.

Some results also indicated an effect of function and/or discourse types in governing variability in the use of *you know*. It was found that *you know* was significantly less likely to emerge in the speech of L2 speakers educated to university level, whereas it was preferred by those with a secondary education only (cf. Schleef and Mackay, Chapter 2, this volume). While such findings could be interacting with factors such as social class (see Stubbe and Holmes 1995), it could also be the case that, since *you know* is associated with informality and orality, it may be less likely to be a feature of those exposed to academic discourse. The high degrees of interspeaker variability overall support the arguments put forward by Hasselgreen (2004; see also Schleef and Mackay, Chapter 2, this volume) that DPMs in particular may be subject to some degree of personal preference, which can arguably become more fossilized in the speech of L2 speakers, once they find a DPM that meets their conversational needs. The lack of effect of either length of residence or proficiency in English suggests that *you know* is relatively straightforward to acquire and may thus be variable among L2 speakers for stylistic purposes. This, however, warrants much more detailed, qualitative investigation.

A further important finding that emerged from analysis of the L1 and L2 speakers in Dublin was the fact that uses of *you know* for "coherence" (i.e., discourse/structuring functions) were more likely to be used by L2 speakers, whereas uses of *you know* for "interpersonal" reasons (i.e., "pragmatic" uses) were more likely to be used by L1 speakers. This supports previous findings for L2 speakers and *you know* in House (2009). While the small sample size of IrE speakers restricts the possibility of making too strong a claim, this does corroborate findings from previous work on DPMs and L2 speakers, which shows that, while DPMs as surface forms may be easily acquired (and, presumably, noticed) by L2 speakers, specific pragmatic uses of them may be more challenging than others. This supports the interface principle of Sorace (2005), as cited in Meyerhoff and Schleef (2014), which suggests that variable structures that require interface knowledge are difficult to acquire. This was also the case argued in Diskin (2017), where DPM *like* was used less as a mitigator or hedge by L2 speakers than by L1 speakers. The challenging nature of pragmatic uses of DPMs was also presented in Truesdale and Meyerhoff (2015), who found that L2 speakers' acquisition of DPMs tended to have a more restricted functional range than that of L1 speakers.

The present findings also lend support to a usage-based theory of SLA, in the sense that *you know* as an illustrator was by far its most common use among the

L1 speakers. It holds, then, that L2 speakers would be more likely to acquire and use these forms first, before using *you know* for interpersonal reasons, to which they have had less exposure. Indeed, the salience and prevalence of *you know* may contribute to its rapid adoption by L2 speakers, but more nuanced inspection reveals potential challenges for them to acquire the full range of functions of DPMs in spoken discourse. The salience of *you know* is also likely to be influenced by its syntactic position and its prosodic aspects, which offer promising avenues for future research of this feature among L1 and L2 speakers.

9.5 Conclusion

The present chapter has highlighted the importance of examining both frequency and function of DPMs in language contact situations. Since similarities in frequency and form may mask underlying differences in function, it is crucial that such a multipronged approach be taken. The relative underrepresentation of DPMs in speech as compared to, for example, phonological features, presents an ongoing challenge for variationist approaches to discourse-pragmatic features. Nonetheless, the present study, although limited in its size and scope, has gone some way to opening up potentially fruitful lines of inquiry in a number of domains, including cross-dialectal variability in discourse-pragmatic features; clustering and co-occurrence of these features (and the implications of this for variationist approaches); and the acquisition of discourse-pragmatic features by L2 speakers, who themselves are exposed to different varieties of English. The study of DPMs in language contact situations also provides more potential for the study of the emergence and grammaticalization pathways of DPMs. Future work taking, for example, a construction grammar or usage-based approach could also provide useful methodological alternatives or supplements for investigating DPMs from a variety of perspectives.

10 General Extenders in Bilingual Speech

Joseph Kern

10.1 Introduction

General extenders are discourse-pragmatic features that consist of a conjunction and a noun phrase and usually appear clause-finally in spoken discourse (Overstreet 1999; Cheshire 2007; Tagliamonte and Denis 2010). Examples of general extenders extracted from recorded conversations in English and Spanish between young adult Spanish–English bilingual friends from Southern Arizona are shown in (1) and (2).

(1) She just comes over to eat, like dinner **and stuff** and she just goes back or she just stays over there (8B1).

(2) *Estaba saliendo con una muchacha de allí de X pero era bonita, era inteligente, era muy buena **y todo**. Pero era demasiado así de esas que se creen muy maduras, era demasiado estricta **y todo eso*** (7B1).
He was going out with a girl from there from X, but she was pretty, she was smart, she was hot **and all**. But she was too much like those (girls) that think they are really mature, she was too strict **and all that** (7B1).

General extenders have been studied extensively across varieties of English in the United States (Overstreet and Yule 1997; Overstreet 1999; Overstreet and Yule 2002), Canada (Tagliamonte and Denis 2010), England (Aijmer 2002; Cheshire 2007; Pichler and Levey 2011), Ireland (O'Keeffe 2004), Scotland (Macaulay 1991), Australia (Dines 1980), and New Zealand (Stubbe and Holmes 1995; Terraschke 2010). They have also been called "approximation markers" (Erman 1995), "extension particles" (Dubois 1992), "generalized list completers" (Jefferson 1991; Lerner 1994), "set-marking tags" (Dines 1980; Ward and Birner 1993), and "vague category identifiers" (Channell 1994).

Studies of general extenders in English have explored their use and development according to form and function. Although the forms of general extenders have been found to vary among dialects of English (Aijmer 2002), their phonetic reduction in length of words appears to be a sign of their grammaticalization across varieties (Cheshire 2007; Wagner et al. 2015), with shorter forms representing a later stage in their development. The phonetic reduction of discourse-pragmatic features was also seen in the development of *is all* (Kolbe-Hanna and Brinton, Chapter 5, this volume). Corresponding to their phonetic reduction, the semantic bleaching of the referential function of general extenders has also been hypothesized as a sign of their development, with longer forms showing a preference for fulfilling a function of extending a set of items (Wagner et al. 2015).

Although general extenders have been studied in other languages, including Spanish (Cortés 2005, 2006a, 2006b; Gille 2006; Gille and Häggkvist 2006; Alvarado Ortega 2008; Gille and Häggkvist 2010; Fernández 2015), French (Secova 2014), German (Overstreet 2005; Terraschke 2010), and Persian (Parvaresh et al. 2012), these studies are limited in number. Previous studies of general extenders in Spanish have only documented their use in Peninsular Spanish, while other dialects of Spanish have not been explored. Moreover, general extenders have not been analyzed in contact situations.

The present study analyzes the use of general extenders in English and Spanish in the speech of eighteen young adult Spanish–English bilinguals from the US Southwest. Building on previous studies in both languages, 325 tokens of general extenders were analyzed quantitatively. The forms of general extenders in English and Spanish in the speech of these bilinguals were identified and compared with previous studies in non-contact varieties. The length in words of these forms and their functions (referential vs. non-referential) were also explored in both languages to assess hypotheses of their development. The following section reviews previous studies of general extenders in English and Spanish. This is followed by a discussion of the methods of data collection in this study. Finally, the analysis of the forms and functions of general extenders in English and Spanish is presented. As the first study to analyze the use of general extenders in both languages in the speech of bilinguals, the results of this study add to previous studies of general extenders in US English, document the use of general extenders in the unstudied variety of US/Mexican Spanish, and contribute to our knowledge of discourse-pragmatic features in contact situations.

10.2 Previous Studies of General Extenders in English and Spanish

The prototypical form of general extenders in English consists of a connector (*and*, *or*), quantifier (*all, every, some, any, the odd, the whole, no*), generic (*thing(s), stuff, people, one, where, shit, crap, baloney*), and a comparative (*like that, sort of, kind of, type of, of that kind, of that sort, of that type, around there, to that effect*) (Tagliamonte and Denis 2010: 336–337). A connector is required, a quantifier and/or a generic is required, and a comparative is optional (Tagliamonte and Denis 2010: 336). General extenders that begin with *and* as a connector have been identified as "adjunctive," whereas those that begin with *or* as a connector are considered "disjunctive" (Overstreet and Yule 1997; Cheshire 2007; Tagliamonte and Denis 2010). Cheshire (2007: 187) proposes that adjunctive and disjunctive general extenders should be analyzed separately since they often fulfill distinct pragmatic functions and have different distributions across varieties.

Adjunctive and disjunctive general extenders have also been identified in Peninsular Spanish. Cortés (2006a, 2006b) identifies four categories of general extenders in Peninsular Spanish, including adjunctive forms beginning with *y* 'and'; disjunctive forms beginning with *o* (*or*); forms that begin with the connector *ni* 'nor' including *ni nada* 'not anything' and *ni eso* 'not even that'; and forms without a connector including *cosas así* 'stuff like that' and *todo eso* 'all of that'. Fernández (2015: 4) classifies the forms that begin with the connector *ni* 'nor' as negative adjunctive general extenders that "cancel" items from a list rather than include them. Furthermore, she proposes that general extenders without a connector are adjunctive or disjunctive forms that have been "reduced" in cases in which the "conjunction does not surface lexically" (Fernández 2015: 4). General extenders in Peninsular Spanish have also been discussed by Gille (2006: 159) and Gille and Häggkvist (2006: 65–66) who denote them as *apéndices de categorización generalizada* (generalized category extenders) and group them along with four other categories of *apéndices conversacionales* (conversational extenders) on the right periphery including *creo yo* 'I believe,' *¿sabes?* 'you know,' *por decirlo así* 'to say it like that,' and *pues* 'well, so.'

The most frequent forms of adjunctive and disjunctive general extenders have been identified in previous studies in both English and Spanish. Although the most frequent forms of general extenders in English vary socially within and between dialects (Aijmer 2002), the adjunctive *and stuff* and the disjunctive *or something* have been found to be common forms in several varieties. In American English, Overstreet and Yule (1997) found that *or something* was the most frequent general extender followed by *and stuff*. Wagner et al. (2015) concluded that *and stuff* (18%) was the most frequent general extender followed by *or something* (17%) in the Fisher corpus of telephone conversations, *but* and *everything* (22%) and *and things like that* (16%) were the most frequent variants in the Language Change and Stabilization (LCS) corpus of sociolinguistic interviews. In Canadian English, *and stuff* was the most frequent form of general extenders (Tagliamonte and Denis 2010; Wagner et al. 2015) and *and stuff* has been found to be increasing in British English (Cheshire 2007; Pichler and Levey 2011).

In Peninsular Spanish, adjunctive general extenders have been found to be more frequent than disjunctive general extenders (Fernández 2015). Cortés (2006b) found that the most frequent general extenders were *etcétera* 'etcetera', *y todo eso* 'and all that', and *y eso* 'and that' in a corpus of sociolinguistic interviews from Almería, Spain (El corpus del habla de Almería). In the Corpus Oral de Referencia del Español Contemporáneo (COREC) of Peninsular Spanish, Fernández (2015) concluded that the most frequent general extender was *y tal* 'and such' (30%; 224/738), followed by *y eso* 'and that' (13%; 96/738) and *y todo* 'and all' (8%; 56/738). Echoing Aijmer (2002), Fernández (2015) argues that the forms of general extenders vary across dialects of Spanish. Although she did not analyze the use of general extenders in other varieties of Spanish, Fernández (2015: 12) notes that the most frequent general extender in the COREC corpus *y tal* 'and such' was not found in the Corpus Oral de Lenguaje Adolescente from Buenos Aires.

In addition to the forms of general extenders, the pragmatic functions of general extenders have been analyzed in both English and Spanish. Wagner et al. (2015: 707) propose that the prototypical pragmatic function of general extenders is to extend an inferable set of items. Overstreet (1999, 2014) finds that adjunctive general extenders express the existence of more items while disjunctive general extenders signal the possibility of other items. Fernández (2015) confirms that adjunctive and disjunctive general extenders in Spanish can fulfill the same referential function of extending a list. In addition to a referential function, general extenders can also fulfill non-referential pragmatic functions in both English (Overstreet 1999) and Spanish (Fernández 2015). In both languages, adjunctive general extenders have been found to hedge the quality of information and mark positive politeness, while disjunctive general extenders can hedge the accuracy of information and mark negative politeness (Overstreet 2014; Fernández 2015;). Aijmer (1985: 378) identifies even more non-referential functions of general extenders in English including the use of adjunctive general extenders to summarize, fumble, create rapport, establish common ground, and provide foreground information, and disjunctive general extenders to soften and approximate. Similarly, Fernández (2015) outlines additional non-referential functions of general extenders in Spanish including creating solidarity between interlocutors, closing sequences, and reporting speech. Cheshire (2007: 158) cautions that non-referential pragmatic functions of general extenders can overlap and should not be prioritized in their analysis. Doing so, she argues, "overlooks the flexibility and multifunctionality that is the most salient characteristic of these linguistic forms."

The analysis of the forms and functions of general extenders has shed light on their development. Cheshire (2007) explores the grammaticalization of general extenders in English by assessing four key characteristics of their forms and functions: phonetic reduction, decategorization, semantic change, and pragmatic shift. Also observed by Overstreet (1999) and Wagner et al. (2015) in English, and Fernández (2015) in Spanish, the phonetic reduction of general extenders involves the shortening of longer forms (e.g., *and stuff like that > and stuff*) (Cheshire 2007: 167). The decategorization of general extenders occurs in situations in which they are used without an anaphoric relationship to a preceding noun (Cheshire 2007: 168). Finally, semantic change and pragmatic shift refer to the use of general extenders to fulfill non-referential functions that do not correspond to the prototypical, referential function of extending an inferable set of items (Cheshire 2007; Wagner et al. 2015). Pichler and Levey (2011: 452) propose four stages in the development of the pragmatic functions of general extenders on a continuum of referential to non-referential: Stage 0: Set marking; Stage 1: Set marking and interpersonal/textual; Stage 2: Interpersonal/textual; and Stage 3: Devoid of referential/pragmatic meanings.

The semantic change and pragmatic shift of general extenders has been found to correspond with their phonetic reduction. Wagner et al. (2015) concluded that general extenders that fulfilled referential functions were longer in form (three or more words) than general extenders that fulfilled non-referential functions. Cheshire (2007) also found that the shorter forms such as *and that*, *and everything*, and *or something* demonstrated more evidence of decategorization and semantic change than the longer forms *and stuff like that*, *or something like that*, and *and everything like that*. However, some studies of general extenders have not found evidence of their grammaticalization, notably Pichler and Levey (2011), who did not find systematic change in the form or functions of general extenders.

Building on previous studies of general extenders in English and Spanish, the present study explores their use in both languages in the speech of bilinguals from Southern Arizona. Although general extenders have not been explored in the speech of bilinguals, several other discourse-pragmatic features have been found to prone to pragmatic borrowing (Andersen (2014: 17), including discourse markers (Brody 1987; Salmons 1990; Brody 1995; Matras 1998, 2000; de Rooij 2000; Fuller 2001; Hlavac 2006; Dajko and Carmichael 2014; Blondeau, Mougeon, and Tremblay, Chapter 11, this volume), interjections (Treffers-Daller 1994; Andersen 2014), politeness markers (Peterson and Vaattovaara 2014, Andersen, Chapter 12; Peterson, Hiltunen and Vaattovaara, Chapter 13, this volume), and curse words (Andersen 2014). Previous studies of other discourse-pragmatic features in Southern Arizona among the same bilinguals in this study, including the discourse marker *like* (Kern 2020a) and the quotative *be like* (Kern 2020b), have found limited pragmatic borrowing. In addition to assessing the use of general extenders in contact, this study adds to our previous knowledge of the forms and functions of general extenders in US English and contributes to our knowledge of general extenders in Spanish as the first study of a non-Peninsular variety. The following section turns to the methods of data collection in this study.

10.3 Methods of Data Collection

The general extenders analyzed in this study were extracted from informal conversations in English and Spanish between nine pairs of young Spanish–English bilingual friends. The conversations were approximately one hour in length and were recorded one week apart. At the time of each conversation, participants were instructed to speak as they would normally speak to their friend in each language. If participants needed a topic to sustain their conversation, fourteen optional questions were provided in both languages on relevant topics for college students such as "What has been your favorite vacation?" and "What class have you most enjoyed taking?" The conversations have an informal register, demonstrated by overlapping turns, expletives, code-switching, and the use of discourse-pragmatic features including general extenders. A total of eighteen hours of recorded conversations were analyzed, nine hours in each language.

The eighteen participants in the study were comparable in age and dialect of Spanish. All of the participants were college students between eighteen and twenty-four years old. This age group was chosen for this study since several previous studies have found that younger speakers use general extenders more frequently than older speakers (Dubois 1992; Stubbe and Holmes 1995; Tagliamonte and Denis 2010; Pichler and Levey 2011). In addition, all of the participants were second- or third-generation Spanish–English bilinguals of Mexican descent who were born and raised in Southern Arizona. Although Spanish is spoken in many homes in Southern Arizona because of its geographic location north of Mexico and the immigration of new monolingual Spanish speakers, English is the majority language in the community. In a study of the maintenance of Spanish in Southern Arizona, Jaramillo (1995) found a generational shift towards English monolingualism.

Since English is replacing Spanish among second- and third-generation bilinguals in Southern Arizona, the language dominance of each participant was calculated using the Bilingual Language Profile (Birdsong et al. 2012). Scores from the Bilingual Language Profile range from −218 to +218 with positive scores representing English dominance, negative scores indicating Spanish dominance, and a score of 0 corresponding to the idealized "balanced bilingual."[1] The average score of the participants was 3.20 with a range of −60.57 to 49.952, which permitted language dominance to be used as a social factor in the study.

The other extralinguistic factor chosen for this study was the gender of participants. Although many previous studies have not found gender to be significant in the use of general extenders (Cheshire 2007; Tagliamonte and Denis 2010), Pichler and Levey (2011) found a higher frequency of general

---

[1] The term "balanced bilingual" is written in quotation marks since it is a problematic term.

extenders among young male speakers. The participants in the present study were equally divided by gender. With the exception of one pair of female bilinguals and another pair of male bilinguals, the remaining participants were female–male pairs. Female bilinguals had an average dominance score of 1.34 while male bilinguals had an average dominance score of 5.06. The analysis of the use of general extenders in the speech of these bilinguals is presented in the next section.

10.4 Analysis

The analysis of general extenders in the present study begins by exploring their relative frequencies in English and Spanish in the speech of the bilinguals. Table 10.1 presents the frequency of general extenders in each language per 10,000 words for each participant. Female and male bilinguals are arranged in

Table 10.1 *Frequency of general extenders in Spanish and English per 10,000 words according to participant, gender, and language dominance*

Participant	General Extenders in English	General Extenders in Spanish
Female Bilinguals		
5B1	19.89	28.66
12B2	30.40	30.07
3B2	3.71	7.37
1B1	13.86	7.23
15B2	20.09	18.11
8B2	2.26	2.56
1B2	10.80	18.52
16B2	21.32	27.41
17B2	16.39	3.44
Average Female	*15.41*	*15.93*
Male Bilinguals		
5B2	70.53	41.84
16B1	39.21	16.49
12B1	12.22	2.66
7B2	32.75	58.32
7B1	12.60	36.51
3B1	12.82	4.95
15B1	17.53	24.07
17B1	26.45	14.44
8B1	39.40	12.95
Average Male	*29.28*	*23.58*
Overall Average	*22.35*	*19.76*

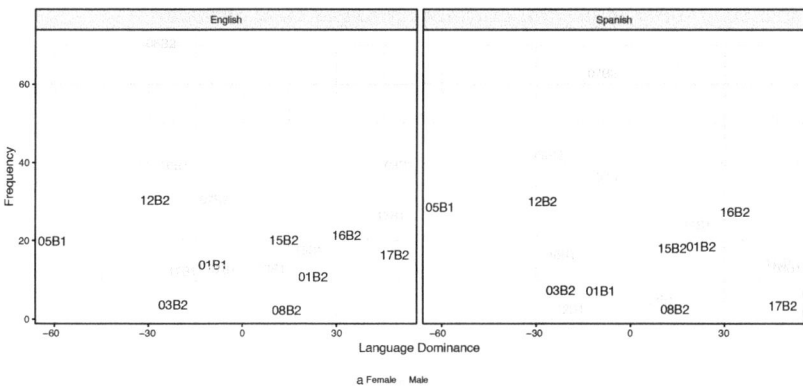

Figure 10.1 Frequency of general extenders in Spanish and English per 10,000 words according to participant, gender, and language dominance

the table from most Spanish dominant to most English dominant. The numbers assigned to each participant correspond to each pair of friends. This table is presented visually in Figure 10.1, with each point corresponding to a participant.

As shown in Table 10.1 and Figure 10.1, the frequencies of general extenders are similar across participants and languages with only a few outliers. They were used an average of 22.35 times per 10,000 words in English and 19.76 times per 10,000 words in Spanish. This data was analyzed using a linear mixed-effects model. Frequency was fit as a function of language (English, Spanish), gender (male, female), and language dominance. The fixed effects were dummy coded with English and female as the reference levels, and the model included by-participant random intercepts. The main effects of language, gender, and language dominance were tested through nested model comparisons in R (R Core Team 2013) using the lme4 package (Bates et al. 2015). Goodness-of-fit was assessed using marginal R^2 (R^2 m), which excludes random effects and conditional R^2 (R^2 c), which includes them. There were no main effects of language ($\chi^2(1)=0.37$; $p>0.05$), gender ($\chi^2(1)=3.19$; $p>0.05$), or language dominance ($\chi^2(1)=1.74$; $p>0.05$), and the model was best fit when including the random effects (R^2 $m=0.20$ and R^2 $c=0.53$). Consequently, the model did not find a difference in the frequency of general extenders between languages or according to gender or language dominance.

After assessing the frequencies of general extenders, the forms of general extenders in each language were documented. Since connectors are not always present in Spanish, the forms of general extenders were identified in the English and Spanish conversations by their required generics, which included *stuff*,

Table 10.2 *Forms of general extenders in English and Spanish*

General Extenders in English		General Extenders in Spanish	
Adjunctive General Extenders		Adjunctive General Extenders	
and STUFF	31% (57/185)	*y todo (eso)* ('and all (that)')	49% (69/140)
and everything (like that)	15% (27/185)	*y así* ('and that')	10% (14/140)
and THINGS	5% (9/185)	*y COSAS* ('and THINGS')	8% (11/140)
and shit	5% (9/185)	*y eso* ('and that')	3% (4/140)
and (all) that	1% (2/185)	Other Adjunctive GEs	1% (2/140)
Other Adjunctive GEs	2% (3/185)		
Adjunctive GEs Total	*58% (107/185)*	*Adjunctive GEs Total*	*71% (99/140)*
Disjunctive General Extenders		Disjunctive General Extenders	
or something (like that)	28% (52/185)	*o algo (así)* ('or something (like that)')	16% (23/140)
or anything	8% (14/185)	*o cosas así* ('or things like that')	2% (3/140)
or whatever	4% (7/185)	Other Disjunctive GEs	1% (2/140)
Other Disjunctive GEs	1% (2/185)		
Disjunctive GEs Total	*41% (75/185)*	*Disjunctive GEs Total*	*20% (28/140)*
Other General Extenders		Other General Extenders	
this and that	2% (3/185)	*algo así* ('something like that')	6% (8/140)
		todo eso ('all that')	1% (2/140)
		Other	1% (2/140)
Other GEs Total	*2% (3/185)*	*Other GEs Total*	*9% (12/140)*
Overall GEs	100% (185/185)	Overall GEs	100% (140/140)

thing, things, shit, that, and *whatever* in English and *todo* 'all', *así* 'this', *cosas* 'things', *eso* 'that', and *algo* 'something' in Spanish. Table 10.2 presents the forms of general extenders in each language that were identified in this study.

In the English conversations, adjunctive general extenders beginning with *and* (58%; 107/185) were more frequent than disjunctive general extenders beginning with *or* (41%; 75/185). The most frequent general extender in English was *and STUFF* (31%; 57/185). The *and STUFF* variants included 51 tokens of *and stuff*, four tokens of *and stuff like that*, and one token each of *and a lot of stuff* and *and a bunch of other stuff*. The second and third most frequent general extenders in the English conversations were *or something (like that)* (28%; 52/185) and *and everything (like that)* (15%; 27/185). The general extenders *and stuff, or something (like that)*, and *and everything (like that)* were also found to be common in previous studies of general extenders in American English. The general extenders *and stuff* and *or something* respectively were the most frequent in the Fisher corpus of telephone conversations analyzed by Wagner et al. (2015), while *and everything* was the fourth most frequent variant. The general extender *and everything* was the most frequent in the

LCS corpus of sociolinguistic interviews in American English, also analyzed by Wagner et al. (2015), while *or something* and *and stuff like that* were the third and fifth most frequent variants respectively. In Overstreet and Yule's (1997) study, *or something* was the most frequent general extender followed by *and stuff*.

Several other general extenders were documented in the English conversations. These include the adjunctive general extenders *and THINGS* (5%; 9/185), *and shit* (5%; 9/185), and *and (all) that* (1%; 2/185). The *and THINGS* variants include six tokens of *and things like that* and one token each of *and all these things* and *and all those things*. The other adjunctive general extenders in English include one token each of *and this and that*, *and whatever*, and *and whatnot*. Other disjunctive general extenders found in the English conversations include *or anything* (8%; 14/185), *or whatever* (4%; 7/185), and one token each of *or shit like that* and *or someplace like that*. The Other GEs category in English consists of three tokens of *this and that*.

In the Spanish conversations, adjunctive general extenders beginning with *y* 'and' (71%; 99/140) were much more frequent than disjunctive general extenders beginning with *o* 'or' (20%; 28/140), mirroring Fernández's (2015) analysis in Peninsular Spanish. The most frequent general extender in the Spanish conversations was *y todo (eso)* 'and all (that)' (49%; 69/140), followed by *o algo así* 'or something like that' (16%; 23/140) and *y así* 'and that' (10%; 14/140). This is the first study of general extenders in a variety of US Spanish – Mexican Spanish – so direct comparisons with the same dialect cannot be made. In Peninsular Spanish, *y todo eso* 'and all that' was the second most frequent general extender in a corpus of sociolinguistic interviews from Almería (Cortés 2006b). In Fernández's (2015) study of part of the COREC corpus of Peninsular Spanish *y todo* 'and all' was the third most frequent variant. The general extender *o algo así* 'or something like that' was documented in Peninsular Spanish by Cortés (2006b) and Fernández (2015), but was relatively infrequent. The most frequent general extender in Cortés' (2006b) study, *etcétera* 'etcetera', was represented by only one token in the present study, while the most frequent general extender in Fernández's (2015) study, *y tal* 'and such', was not found in this study. The differences in the forms of general extenders in the Spanish of the bilinguals of this study and previous studies in Peninsular Spanish are interpreted as normal variance between dialects previously discussed by Aijmer (2002) in English and Fernández (2015) in Spanish.

Several other forms of general extenders were found in the Spanish conversations of the current study. These include the adjunctive general extenders *y COSAS* 'and THINGS' (8%; 11/140), *y eso* 'and that' (3%; 4/140), and one token each of *y todo así* 'and all that' and *etcétera* 'etcetera'. The *y COSAS* variants included three tokens of *y cosas así* 'and things like that' and several other combinations of the connector *y* 'and' and the generic *cosas* 'things' with distinct quantifiers and comparatives. Other disjunctive general extenders in Spanish include *o cosas así* 'or things like that' (2%; 3/140) and one token each of *o así* 'or that' and *o todo eso* 'or all that'. The Other GEs category in Spanish includes *algo así* 'something like that' (6%; 8/140), *todo eso* 'all that' (1%; 2/140), and one token each of *todo ese rollo* 'all those things' and *cosas así* 'things like that'.

Potential language contact in the speech of the Spanish–English bilinguals in this study does not appear to influence the forms of general extenders. Although English is the majority language in the community, no English forms of general extenders were used in the Spanish of these bilinguals (and no Spanish forms of general extenders were used in the English of these bilinguals). This result differs from studies of other discourse-pragmatic features in the speech of these same bilinguals who occasionally incorporated the discourse markers *like* (Kern 2020a) and the quotative *be like* (Kern 2020b) in Spanish discourse even though they were instructed to speak in each language on different occasions. Accordingly, general extenders do not appear to behave like other discourse-pragmatic features that have been shown to be prone to borrowing. The repertoire of general extenders in Spanish of the bilinguals in this study shows minimal dialectal differences from Peninsular Spanish.

A defining characteristic of the forms of general extenders is their potential to be reduced into simpler forms. The phonetic reduction of the forms of general extenders has been explored in previous studies by assessing their length in words (Cheshire 2007; Fernández 2015; Wagner et al. 2015). Following Wagner et al. (2015), general extenders in the present study were classified as long if they consisted of three or more words and short if they consisted of two words. Table 10.3 presents these results.

The majority of general extenders consisted of fewer than three words in both English (81%; 150/185) and Spanish (66%; 92/140). This preference for shorter forms was also found in previous studies in English (Aijmer 2002) and Spanish (Fernández 2015). This data was analyzed using a logistic mixed-effects regression model in R. The length (long, short) of general extenders was fit as a function of language (English, Spanish) and the social factors of gender (male, female) and language dominance. The fixed effects were dummy coded

Table 10.3 *Length of general extenders in English and Spanish regardless of function*

Length	English	Spanish
Long (3 or more words)	19% (35/185)	34% (48/140)
Short (2 words)	81% (150/185)	66% (92/140)

with English and female as the reference levels, and the model included by-participant random intercepts. The main effects of language, language dominance, and gender were tested through nested model comparisons. There was a main effect of language ($\chi^2(1)=10.26$; $p<0.002$) but not gender ($\chi^2(1)=1.24$; $p>0.05$) or language dominance ($\chi^2(1)=0.07$; $p>0.05$). The model was best fit when including the random effects (R^2 $m=0.07$ and R^2 $c=0.25$). These results suggest that there is a difference in the length of general extenders in English and Spanish, and general extenders are longer in Spanish than in English. Perhaps this difference in the length of general extenders in English and Spanish is due to internal linguistic constraints within each language; nevertheless, it is present in the speech of these bilinguals who reproduce the subtleties in the forms of general extenders in both languages.

The length of general extenders has been found to correspond with pragmatic function. Wagner et al. (2015) propose that general extenders that are longer in length, three or more words, fulfill a referential function of extending a list of items more frequently than shorter, two-word general extenders. In order to test this hypothesis, the general extenders that fulfilled referential functions in the conversations were identified. Wagner et al. (2015) classified general extenders as referential if two or more referents could be located within the speaker's turn. In (3), the general extender *and things like that* fulfills a referential function because it is extending an inferable set of items with two referents: "good like English skills" and "good like art skills."

(3) But with guys it's like they reinforce the math and science, but they won't reinforce like <u>good like English skills</u> and <u>good like art skills</u> **and things like that** (12B2).

In contrast, the general extender *and things like that* in (4) fulfills a non-referential function because two referents cannot be identified.

(4) We were gonna hang out over winter break, but that's when the shop is like the busiest obviously cuz it's like, Christmas **and things like that** (16B1).

Differing from Wagner et al. (2015), the context for identifying referents of general extenders was expanded from the speaker's turn to the entire conversation. Although this decision is supported by a detailed qualitative analysis that recognizes the role of both interlocutors who co-construct a conversation, it led to a classification process that was less conservative than Wagner et al. (2015), hampering comparability. For example, the bilingual participant in (3) originally only mentions one referent, "pictures," for the general extender *and stuff* but later mentions "journal" as a second referent. The general extender *and stuff* in this example was therefore classified as fulfilling a referential function in this study but would not have been classified as referential according to Wagner et al.'s (2015) criteria.

(3)   16B1: I'm gonna have to go back, and look through all like, my stuff.
       16B2: Your pictures?
       16B1: My pictures **and stuff**.
       16B2: Or do you have a diary that says it all.
       16B1: Maybe.
       16B2: ((laughs)) Do you really?
       16B1: It's a journal, ok? (16BE).

The general extender and *all those things* in (4) is interpreted by the interlocutor as referential who adds a second referent and was therefore classified as referential in this study, although it would not have been classified as referential in Wagner et al.'s (2015) analysis. Later in the conversation, the participants refer to these same referents with another general extender *and stuff*, which was also classified as referential in this study.

(4)   5B2: Hmm. I feel like the, like, if by feeling peer pressure, I guess, you know in high school, like those, it's like those kinda times where like some students or kids start like smoking weed **and all those things**.
       5B1: Yeah, drinking.
       (...)
       5B2: You still might have those friends that smoke weed **and stuff** but they, they don't really peer pressure anyone (5BE).

Although expanding the context for identifying referents to the entire conversation was a less conservative approach, any cases in which two or more referents could not be identified were classified as non-referential. In (5), it is not clear according to the context of the conversation if the actions of sitting down and listening to albums are referents of the general extender *and stuff*, so it was classified as non-referential.

(5)   I like the music I've heard, but it's not like I've sat down and listened to his albums **and stuff** (15B2).

Non-referential functions of general extenders often overlap (Cheshire 2007; Pichler and Levey 2011) and general extenders can even be completely devoid of pragmatic meaning (Pichler and Levey 2011). In (5), the general extender *and stuff* could hedge the quality of the participant's familiarity with the music or mark positive politeness to avoid threatening the interlocutor's taste in music, or both. In (6), the general extender *and shit* does not have a clear pragmatic function.

(6)   They're like Irish **and shit**, so they're just totally like family oriented (17B1).

With these complications in mind, the analysis of the non-referential functions of general extenders will be reserved for a future study.

General extenders in the Spanish conversations were also similarly classified as referential or non-referential. The general extender *y todo* in (7) was classified as referential because it has at least two referents: "el carro se movía con el viento" and "todas las parabrisas llenas de agua."

(7) *Una vez estábamos manejando mi- mi toda mi familia en- de X a Y y empezó a llover súper fuerte y así tanto que <u>el carro se movía con el viento</u>, y <u>todas las parabrisas llenas de agua</u>* **y todo** *y así mi papá siguió manejando (3B1).*
One time we were driving, me- all of my family from X to Y and it began to rain really strongly so that <u>the car moved with the wind</u>, and <u>the windshield full of water</u> **and all** and like this my dad kept driving (3B1).

In (8), two referents "cosas de Bate Papo" and "un artículo" bookend the referential general extender *y esas cosas.*

(8) Y en otra cosa en la página de Facebook de la del Departamento de Español y Portugués cuando ponen <u>cosas de Bate Papo</u> **y esas cosas**, pusieron <u>un artículo</u> de que Google está contratando a gente que hablara portugués para mandarlas a Irlanda, a Nueva York y no sé qué otro país (12B2). And in another thing on the Facebook page of the Department of Spanish and Portuguese when they put things about Bate Papo **and these things**, they put an article that Google was hiring people who speak Portuguese to send them to Ireland, to New York and I don't know what other country (12B2).

The Spanish conversations also presented some examples in which two or more referents were not explicitly mentioned but clearly implied. These general extenders were also classified as referential. In (9), the plural "unos memes" before the "así de" of exemplification implies multiple referents and the general extender y cosas así was therefore classified as referential.

(9) 5B1: *Fiesta de divorcio ((risas))*
5B2: *Haz de cuenta que imprimí <u>unos memes</u>,*
5B1: *Sí*
5B2: *así de soltería* **y cosas así** *(5BS).*
5B1: Divorce party ((laugher))
5B2: Realize that I printed some memes.
5B1: Yes
5B2: about being single **and things like that** (5BS).

In (10), the use of *mucho* before the *como* of exemplification also implies multiple referents even though only one referent was mentioned. The general extender *y todo eso* in this example was classified as referential.

(10) *Me dieron mucho como las barbies* **y todo eso** *(15B2).*
They gave me a lot like Barbies **and all that** (15B2).

Table 10.4 *Distribution of referential and non-referential functions of general extenders in English and Spanish according to participant, gender, and language dominance*

Participant	General Extenders in English		General Extenders in Spanish	
	Referential	Non-Referential	Referential	Non-Referential
Female Bilinguals				
5B1 F	33% (1/3)	67% (2/3)	27% (4/15)	73% (11/15)
12B2 F	35% (6/17)	65% (11/17)	52% (12/23)	48% (11/23)
3B2 F	100% (1/1)	0% (0/1)	67% (2/3)	33% (1/3)
1B1 F	40% (2/5)	60% (3/5)	0% (0/2)	100% (2/2)
15B2 F	6% (1/16)	94% (15/16)	67% (6/9)	33% (3/9)
8B2 F	0% (0/1)	100% (1/1)	100% (1/1)	0% (0/1)
1B2 F	50% (2/4)	50% (2/4)	17% (1/6)	83% (5/6)
16B2 F	22% (2/9)	78% (7/9)	38% (3/8)	63% (5/8)
17B2 F	9% (1/11)	91% (10/11)	0% (0/1)	100% (1/1)
Overall Female	*22% (14/65)*	*79% (51/65)*	*43% (29/68)*	*57% (39/68)*
Male Bilinguals				
5B2 M	55% (23/42)	45% (19/42)	35% (7/20)	65% (13/20)
16B1 M	38% (6/16)	63% (10/16)	50% (3/6)	50% (3/6)
12B1 M	33% (1/3)	67% (2/3)	100% (1/1)	0% (0/1)
7B2 M	43% (6/14)	57% (8/14)	29% (4/14)	71% (10/14)
7B1 M	50% (3/6)	50% (3/6)	53% (9/17)	47% (8/17)
3B1 M	25% (1/4)	75% (3/4)	100% (1/1)	0% (0/1)
15B1 M	0% (0/4)	100% (4/4)	80% (4/5)	20% (1/5)
17B1 M	25% (3/12)	75% (9/12)	67% (2/3)	33% (1/3)
8B1 M	24% (4/17)	76% (13/17)	40% (2/5)	60% (3/5)
Overall Male	*39% (47/120)*	*61% (73/120)*	*46% (33/72)*	*54% (39/72)*
Overall Average	*34% (63/185)*	*66% (122/185)*	*44% (62/140)*	*56% (78/140)*

Table 10.4 presents the distribution of general extenders in English and Spanish according to whether they fulfill a referential or non-referential function. Female and male bilinguals are arranged from most Spanish dominant to most English dominant. The numbers assigned to each participant correspond to each pair of friends. Figure 10.2 illustrates the percent of use of general extenders in English and Spanish to fulfill referential functions according to participant, gender, and language dominance.

Compared to Wagner et. al (2015), the majority of general extenders used in this data are used to fulfill non-referential functions in both English (66%; 122/185) and Spanish (56%; 78/140). The data in this study was further analyzed using a linear mixed-effects model. The percent of referential general extenders was fit as a function of language (English, Spanish), gender (male, female), and language dominance. The fixed effects were dummy coded with English and

General Extenders in Bilingual Speech 227

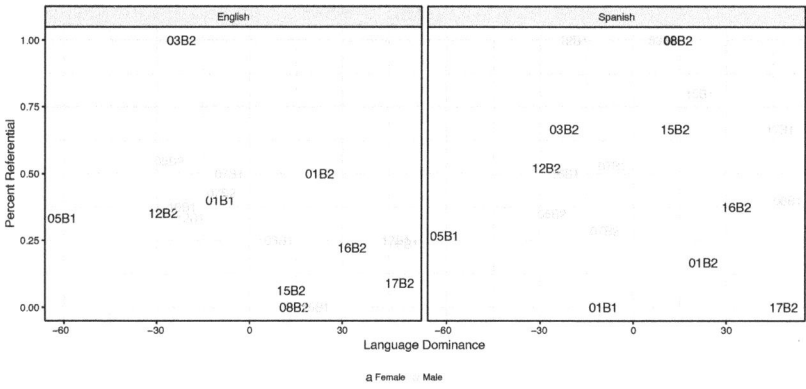

Figure 10.2 Percentage of general extenders that fulfill a referential function in English and Spanish according to participant, gender, and language dominance

female as the reference levels, and the model included by-participant random intercepts. The main effects of language, gender, and language dominance were tested through nested model comparisons. There was a main effect of language ($\chi^2(1)=3.94$; $p<0.05$) but not gender ($\chi^2(1)=1.28$; $p>0.05$) or language dominance ($\chi^2(1)=2.02$; $p>0.05$). The model was fit the same with and without random effects ($R^2\ m=0.11$ and $R^2\ c=0.11$). These results suggest that there is a difference in the referentiality of general extenders in English and Spanish. A larger proportion of general extenders in Spanish are referential than in English.

In summary, general extenders are not only longer in Spanish than in English but also used more often to fulfill referential functions more frequently in Spanish than in English in the speech of the same bilinguals. This result is consistent with Wagner et al.'s (2015) findings that longer general extenders fulfill referential functions more frequently than shorter general extenders. In order to corroborate Wagner et al.'s (2015) hypothesis, a final linear mixed-effect model was carried out. In this model, the percent of referential general extenders was fit as a function of length (long, short) and language (English, Spanish). The fixed effects were dummy coded with long and English as the reference levels, and the model included by-participant random intercepts. The main effects of language and length were tested through nested model comparisons. There was a main effect of length ($\chi^2(1)=21.76$; $p<0.001$) and no main effect of language ($\chi^2(1)=1.22$; $p>0.05$). The model was fit the same with and without random effects ($R^2\ m=0.08$ and $R^2\ c=0.08$). These results suggest that there is a difference in the referentiality of general extenders according to their length. Longer general extenders of three or more words are used to fulfill referential functions more frequently than shorter general extenders ($\beta = 0.42$, se = 0.22, z = 1.85, *p*<0.07). These results confirm Wagner et al.'s (2015) findings for English and provide evidence that this same pattern is present in the use of general extenders in Spanish.

Although this study is limited in scope, the conclusion that longer general extenders of three or more words fulfill referential functions more frequently than shorter forms in both English and Spanish is consistent with Cheshire's (2007) hypothesis on the grammaticalization of general extenders. As predicted by Cheshire's hypothesis and supported by Wagner et al. (2015) in English, longer general extenders are used to fulfill the prototypical function of extending a list of items more often in both English and Spanish than shorter forms. Additionally, general extenders in Spanish were longer and used to fulfill referential functions more frequently than their counterparts in English. More research on general extenders in Spanish is necessary to assess if these differences provide further evidence of the lack of influence of English on the Spanish of these bilinguals. If phonetic reduction and semantic change are indeed indicators of later stages of the development of general extenders, the results of this study suggest that general extenders in Spanish are less grammaticalized than general extenders in English in the speech of the same bilinguals.

10.5   Conclusion

This study has analyzed the forms and functions of general extenders in English and Spanish in the speech of bilinguals from Southern Arizona. General extenders were used with approximately the same frequency in both languages (22.35 times per 10,000 words in English and 19.76 per 10,000 words in Spanish). The most frequent form of general extenders in English was *and stuff* followed by *or something (like that)*. These forms were also found to be frequent in previous studies of general extenders in American English (Overstreet and Yule 1997; Wagner et al. 2015). In the Spanish of these bilinguals, the most frequent forms were *y todo (eso)* 'and all that' and *o algo (así)* 'or something (like that)', which have also been documented in Peninsular Spanish (Cortés 2006b; Fernández 2015). Adjunctive general extenders beginning with *and* were more frequent than disjunctive general extenders beginning with *or* in both English and Spanish.

Language contact in the speech of bilinguals does not appear to influence the use of the general extender forms. Although English is the majority language in Southern Arizona, there were no English forms of general extenders in Spanish. Consequently, general extenders do not appear to behave like discourse markers and other discourse-pragmatic features that are prone to "pragmatic borrowing" (Andersen 2014) in contact situations. The differences in the forms of general extenders between US/Mexican Spanish and Peninsular Spanish can be explained by expected variation between dialects.

The phonetic reduction and semantic change of general extenders was explored by analyzing their length in words and their referentiality. The bilinguals in the present study showed a preference for shorter forms of general extenders of two words in both English and Spanish, but general extenders were longer in Spanish than in English. General extenders were also used most often to fulfill non-referential functions in both languages that did not correspond to the prototypical pragmatic function of general extenders of extending a set of items, but general extenders were used to fulfill referential functions more frequently in Spanish than in English. These results are consistent with hypotheses of the grammaticalization of general extenders discussed by Cheshire (2007) and Wagner et al. (2015) regarding phonetic reduction and semantic change (see also Kolbe-Hanna and Brinton, Chapter 5, this volume). Longer general extenders of three or more words were used to fulfill the prototypical extending function more often than shorter forms in both English and Spanish. If this hypothesis is accurate, the results of this study also provide evidence that general extenders in English show more signs of development than general extenders in Spanish in the speech of the same bilinguals.

More investigation is needed to continue to explore the use of general extenders and hypotheses of their development across languages. Although there are many studies of general extenders in several varieties of English, there is particularly a need for studies of general extenders in more varieties of Spanish for comparative research in both contact and non-contact situations. For now, this study adds to previous studies of general extenders in US English and contributes to our knowledge of the use of general extenders in Spanish, specifically Southern Arizona Spanish, and in the speech of bilinguals.

11 The Diverging Paths of Consequence Markers in Canadian French

Hélène Blondeau, Raymond Mougeon, and Mireille Tremblay

11.1 Introduction

This chapter is the first real-time study of change in the grammatical and discursive uses of consequence markers in Canadian French. Our study is based on data collected in the 1970s and 2010s in Montreal, Quebec, and in Welland, Ontario, a city whose French-speaking population originates primarily from Quebec. While there is a genetic link between Welland French and Montreal French, there are marked differences in the status of French in both communities and in the provinces where they are located. In Montreal, francophones represent a majority of the population, but in Welland, they are a small minority. In Quebec, French is the official language and francophones constitute close to 80 percent of the population. However, Francophones represent only 5 percent of the population in Ontario, and although French receives some measure of governmental support, it is not an official language. French comes into much closer contact with English in Welland than in Montreal.

The Montreal French corpora (Montreal 1971, Montreal 1984, and Montreal 1995) have allowed the study of sociolinguistic variation and change in both apparent and real time (Sankoff 2018, 2019). In addition, the corpus of Welland French collected in 1975 has documented variation in the context of intense contact with English (Beniak et al. 1985). The present study, which is based on new corpora collected in these same communities in the 2010s, allows us to deepen our understanding of the temporal dimension of linguistic change by documenting the evolution of the use of consequence markers over a forty-year period. The originality of our study lies in (1) its diachronic depth (forty years), (2) the crossover between trend studies, and (3) the fact that it focuses on two varieties of Canadian French that are related but spoken in different sociolinguistic contexts. By examining variation and change in French with real-time data collected from a representative sample of the different social strata and age groups in the community, our study fills a gap in sociolinguistic research on these varieties of French.

Previous comparative research examined two sociolinguistic variables other than the consequence markers in Welland French and in Montreal French, namely *m'as* versus *je vas* versus *je vais* 'I'm going to' (Mougeon et al. 2010) and *rien que* versus *juste* vs *seulement* versus *ne ... que* 'only' (Mougeon et al. 2016). These two studies were based on the corpora collected in the 1970s. They found that there was a high degree of intercommunity convergence in relation to the repertory of variants, their frequencies, and the internal and external constraints on variation.

Previous research on the use of consequence markers in Montreal (Dessureault-Dober 1974) and in Montreal and Welland (Blondeau et al. 2019; Martineau 2019) has revealed that speakers of Montreal French use three consequence markers, namely *(ça) fait (que)*, *alors* and *donc*, and that speakers of Welland French use these markers, as well as the conjunction *so* borrowed from English. These studies had several limitations: (1) there is no study of the use of consequence markers by Welland francophones in the 1970s; (2) Dessureault-Dober's (1974) study is based on a limited speaker sample drawn from the 1971 corpus, and (3) Blondeau et al. (2019) and Martineau (2019) are based only on the 2010s corpora. Our study addresses these limitations.

In the present study, the comparison of the 1970s corpora with the 2010s corpora reveals that the two communities had already started to diverge in the 1970s in relation to the inventory of variants, their frequencies, and the internal and external constraints on variation. Furthermore, our study has found that, over the last forty years, intercommunity divergence has intensified. Among the most striking manifestations of divergence, one can mention the emergence of connector *so* in Welland in the 1970s and its subsequent vigorous growth, largely at the expense of traditional vernacular variant *(ça) fait (que)*. This stands in contrast with a marked increase in the use of *(ça) fait (que)* and its diffusion to all social groups in Montreal from the 1970s to the 2010s. Our analysis of the evolution of standard variant *alors* reveals another facet of intercommunity divergence. In Montreal, this connector has undergone a sharp decline from the 1970s to the 2010s and is becoming obsolescent in the speech of the younger generations; however, in Welland, *alors* evidences stability from the 1970s to the 2010s.

The fact that our study has adduced clear evidence of intercommunity divergence not only in the 2010s but also in the 1970s stands in contrast with the patterns of convergence documented by Mougeon et al. (2010) and Mougeon et al. (2016). We discuss some of the factors that may account for these opposite results, including, primarily, (i) the fact that minority speech communities experiencing intense language contact have often been found to borrow discourse markers – a factor that favors the emergence of *so* in Welland French and (2) the standardizing impact of the French-medium schools on the speech of the younger generations who, for the most part, tend to disuse French in the informal and/or private domains of society – a factor that favors the maintenance of *alors*.

11.2 Background

Montreal is a large and diverse metropolis located in the Province of Quebec, where French is the only official language. In 2011, 54.3 percent of residents of Montreal spoke mostly French at home, 25.3 percent spoke mostly English, and the remaining 20.4 percent spoke other languages.[1] Over the last forty years or so, Montreal has undergone a sociolinguistic transformation. In the 1970s, the National Assembly of Quebec adopted the French Language Charter (also known as Bill 101). This measure has reduced the pressure of English by increasing the use of French in the workplace and its visibility in the linguistic landscape and by compelling immigrants to send their children to the French-language schools. Furthermore, globalization has increased contact with other varieties of French, while also maintaining the pressure of English due to its status in Canada and its role as a lingua franca on the world stage.

Welland is located on both sides of a major canal linking Lake Ontario and Lake Erie along the Ontario side of the Niagara River. Welland underwent considerable industrial expansion from 1914 to 1928 and from 1939 to 1969. During these two periods of growth, French-speaking migrants originating mostly from rural Quebec settled in Welland. According to the 1971 Canadian census, there were 7,555 French–mother tongue individuals in Welland, who represented 17 percent of the local population. At that point in time, francophones in Welland had reached a demographic apex. During the following decades, Welland has lost much of its industrial base. This economic downturn curtailed the inflow of French-speaking migrants and, by the end of 1970s, it had come to an end.

The 1971 census revealed that 25 percent of the French–mother tongue population had already shifted to English at home, due in part to rising linguistic exogamy and to limited French-medium education in the local state-funded schools. During the ensuing decades, state-funded French-medium schools became available, but this development has been unable to reverse linguistic assimilation. According to the 2011 census returns, the local French–mother tongue population had dropped to 5,430 people, representing less than

---

[1] These proportions are based on the 2011 national census returns. It is worth noting that in Greater Montreal individuals who speak French at home represent 69.9 percent of the population, and in the province, 85.2 percent.

11 percent of the local population. Moreover, the shift to English at home had reached an alarming level of 65 percent. In sum, the two varieties of French examined in this study have evolved in divergent sociopolitical and demolinguistic contexts. Since the 1970s, Bill 101 has eased the pressure of English on French in Montreal. In contrast, the pressure from English in Welland has intensified considerably over the past forty years. This has led to an increase in the bilingualism of individuals and a penetration of English into the social spaces that once ensured the linguistic reproduction of the community (Mougeon et al. 2018). This chapter seeks to measure the linguistic impact of these differences based on a longitudinal study of consequence markers in the two communities over a forty-year period.

11.3 The Variable

Previous research on the use of consequence markers in Montreal (Dessureault-Dober 1974) and in Montreal and Welland (Blondeau et al. 2019; Martineau 2019) has found that speakers of Montreal French use three consequence markers, namely *(ça) fait (que)*, *alors*, and *donc*, and that speakers of Welland French use these markers and the English borrowing *so*. These connectors can fulfill a grammatical or a discursive function. The grammatical function, exemplified for each marker in (1)–(4), is that of inter-sentential consequence.

(1) *Elle restait sur la rue Mercier dans ce temps-là **fait que** probablement qu'elle a pris euh le tramway* 'She lived on Mercier street then **so** she probably took uh the streetcar' (FRAN-Montréal HOMA12 907M89)

(2) *On doit aller dans un restaurant **alors** évidemment le coût est plus élevé* 'We have to go to a restaurant **so** it is more expensive' (FRAN-Welland 113M62)

(3) *La prof m'avait demandé de sortir **donc** le surveillant il pouvait pas lui expliquer* 'The teacher had asked me to step out **so** the supervisor could not explain it for her' (FRAN-Montréal HOMA12 032M21)

(4) *La plus vieille elle joue au hockey **so** on suit les parties de hockey* 'My oldest [daughter] plays hockey **so** we watch hockey games' (FRAN-Welland 029F61)

The discursive function corresponds to cases where the connector is used to engage a turn of speech or introduce a new topic ((5)–(7)) or to mark the end of a speech turn (8).

(5) *Fait-que c'est ça pis tu vois le/ donc le primaire ou le secondaire c'est pas loin là sixième secondaire un.* '**So** that's it and you see the/ so primary or secondary school it's not far like Grade six secondary one'. (FRAN-Montréal HOMA12 012F53)

(6) Euh ma blonde voyage en métro. Euh **donc** c'est ça pis comme je le dis au besoin si on a/ si on veut sortir une fin de semaine on loue une auto. 'Uh, my girlfriend takes the subway. Uh **so** that's it and as I said if we need to if we have/if we want to get out for a weekend we rent a car'. (FRAN-Montréal HOMA12 001M29)

(7) En tout cas euh // **alors** non j'adore Welland je suis // interviewer: Oui 'Anyways uhm // **so** no I love Welland I am // interviewer: Yes' (FRAN-Welland 020F64)

(8) Mon mari prend des traitements à la dialyse **so** // interviewer: C'est-tu à Welland ça? 'My husband is on dialysis **so** // interviewer: Is it in Welland?' (FRAN-Welland 029F61)

In the next section, we provide a brief review of the main sociolinguistic studies of consequence markers in Laurentian French (see Blondeau et al. 2019 for a more detailed review).[2]

11.4 Previous Research

The first sociolinguistic study of consequence markers in Laurentian French is Dessureault-Dober (1974). It is based on a sample drawn from the 1971 corpus of Montreal French. It documented three markers, *(ça) fait (que)*, *alors*, and *donc*, which were used either to express the notion of consequence or to fulfill discursive functions; however, in her study this linguistic factor turned out to have little statistical influence on variant choice. Furthermore, Dessureault-Dober (1974) found that speakers of lower socioeconomic status (SES) were using the vernacular *(ça) fait (que)* almost categorically. However, among the high SES speakers, the older speakers used standard *alors* 97 percent of the time and the younger speakers were more evenly split between *alors* (48 percent) and *(ça) fait (que)* (45 percent), suggesting that the younger higher SES speakers were moving in the direction of the lower SES speakers. *Donc* was seldom used in her sample.

Thibault and Daveluy (1989) continued the analysis of consequence markers in Montreal based on the entire corpus from 1971 and a new corpus collected in 1984. The new corpus included sixty of the speakers who had been interviewed in 1971. They focused on the trajectory of *alors* over time and found that these sixty speakers increased their use of *alors* from 1971 to 1984. The authors interpreted this result as an age-grading phenomenon that went against Dessureault-Dober's (1974) hypothesis of a decline of *alors* at the community level.

---

[2] Laurentian French refers to the varieties of Canadian French whose origins lie in the colony of New France, which was in the St. Lawrence valley. To our knowledge, no variationist studies have explored this socio-stylistic dimension in Hexagonal French.

Blondeau et al. (2019) investigated the use of consequence markers in Montreal and Welland in corpora collected in the 2010s. Speakers in Montreal use the same three markers they used in the 1970s. In Welland, they use these same markers and the English borrowing *so*. In Montreal, the linguistic function of the markers still has only a modest influence on variant choice. This is also the case in Welland for *(ça) fait (que)*, *alors* and *donc* but not for *so*, which is strongly associated with the discursive function. In Montreal, the use of *(ça) fait (que)* is still rising, driven by lower SES speakers and women, *alors* is showing signs of obsolescence, and *donc* seems to have stopped growing. In contrast, in Welland, *so* is showing signs of steady progress at the expense of *(ça) fait (que)*, driven by intermediate and lower SES speakers, women, and speakers who are either dominant in English or are balanced in both French and English. The decline of *(ça) fait (que)* is most noticeable among high SES speakers, females, and English-dominant bilinguals. The marker *alors* evidences only a relative decline whereas *donc* is increasing, especially among high SES speakers, men, and English-dominant bilinguals. Blondeau et al. (2019) concluded that consequence markers in Montreal and Welland French in the 2010s were exhibiting markedly divergent evolutions.

Martineau (2019) compared the use of consequence markers by speakers aged 15–34 with that of older speakers using samples drawn from the Montreal and Welland 2010s corpora. She arrived at results like those of Blondeau et al. (2019). She found notably that, while among the younger speakers in Montreal *alors* had undergone a markedly sharp decline, in Welland it had maintained itself. In interpreting these findings, she argued (1) that in Montreal the stylistic formality of *alors* is not strong enough for this form to withstand the vigorous rise of *(ça) fait (que)*, which has become the default marker, and (2) that in Welland *alors* is not even a marker of formal style but, in fact, is a "French" equivalent of vernacularizing *so*.

Regarding other communities, Mougeon and Beniak (1991) examined consequence markers in a corpus collected in Ontario in 1978 among adolescents in Hawkesbury, a strong majority community, and in Cornwall, North Bay, and Pembroke, three minority communities. The effect of speaker SES on *(ça) fait (que)*, *alors*, and *donc* was the same as what had been found by Dessureault-Dober (1974) for Montreal French. As for *so*, it was used almost only in the minority communities, was strongly associated with balanced and English-dominant bilinguals, and tended to be avoided by the high SES speakers.

Mougeon et al. (2009) reexamined the consequence markers using a new adolescent corpus collected in 2005 in Hawkesbury and Pembroke. In Hawkesbury, *alors*, which was infrequent in 1978, was absent in 2005. Concomitantly, the frequency of *donc* had increased substantially. *So*, which was almost absent in 1978, was used 8 percent of the time. In Pembroke, the frequency of *alors* and *donc* had increased significantly. This change was ascribed to the fact that, in 2005, most of the Pembroke adolescents were English-dominant speakers. As such, they tended to be cut off from the vernacular and hence were more influenced by the standardized French of school. The authors also found that the frequency of *(ça) fait (que)* had dropped markedly, a change that they also attributed to the rise of English-dominant bilingualism. That said, some of the sociolinguistic patterns found in 1978 remained stable over time: *alors* and *donc* were still associated with higher SES speakers and *(ça) fait (que)* with lower SES ones. As for *so*, the high SES speakers were still disinclined to use it.

Although the use of the consequence markers in Quebec and Ontario French has been examined by an appreciable number of variationist studies, there is still a need for further research that will address the limitations of previous studies. Thus, in relation to the 1970s, the present study will analyze the entire Montreal corpus of 120 speakers and assess the influence of not only age and SES but also gender, a factor not considered by Dessureault-Dober (1974). Our study will also examine the use of *donc* more systematically than Dessureault-Dober (1974) and Mougeon and Beniak (1991) were able to do. Further, the present study will investigate sociolinguistic change in the use of the consequence markers in Montreal and Welland via a comparison of the 1970s and 2010s corpora and not just an analysis of apparent time as in Blondeau et al. (2019). Such a comparison sheds light on the evolution of intercommunity convergence versus divergence since previous research on this topic was based on data gathered in either the 1970s or the 2010s.

11.5 Study Design

11.5.1 Corpora

The present study is based on corpora collected first in the 1970s by two teams of sociolinguists and a second time in the 2010s in the context of *Le français à la mesure d'un continent*, a Major Collaborative Research Initiative (MCRI) directed by France Martineau and funded by the Social Sciences and Humanities Research Council of Canada (SSHRC) from 2011 to 2017. These corpora were recorded using similar protocols via face-to-face interviews and were conducted by interviewers from the community.

As shown in Figure 11.1, the study design allows us to test the validity of the apparent-time model by comparing real-time changes at Times 1 (1970s) and 2 (2010s) in majority (Montreal) and minority (Welland) contexts.

Speakers in each of the corpora have been categorized according to age, SES, gender, and language dominance (for Welland). This information is presented in Table 11.1.

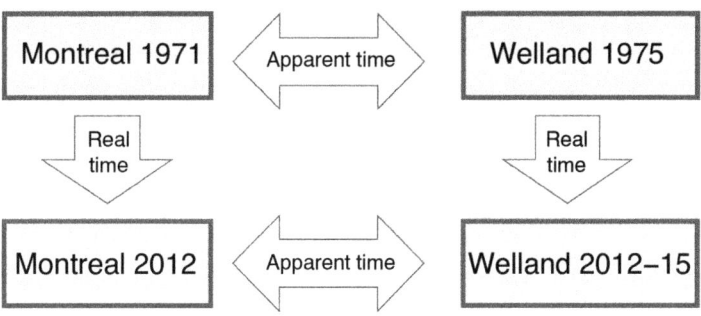

Figure 11.1 Study design

Table 11.1 *Corpora*

		Montreal 1971	Montreal 2012	Welland 1975	Welland 2012–2015
Age					
	15–31	59	21	35	16
	35–64	52	17	26	27
	65–85	9	12	10	25
	TOTAL	120	50	71	68
SES					
	Higher	28	14	16	27
	Intermediate	34	18	27	26
	Lower	58	18	28	15
	TOTAL	120	50	71	68
Gender					
	Female	58	23	36	38
	Male	62	27	35	30
	TOTAL	120	50	71	68
Language dominance					
	French Dom.			32	27
	Balanced			15	19
	Engl. Dom.			24	22
	TOTAL			71	68

11.5.2 Analyzing Variation

11.5.2.1 Extraction and Exclusions The analysis included only the connectors that could be used to fulfill either a grammatical or discursive function as assessed by native speakers. We thus excluded other uses such as *alors que* 'while' (9) and the intensifier *donc* [dɔ̃] (Bertrand 2014) (10). The total number of tokens analyzed in this study is 12,547: 3,292 from Montreal in 1971, 4,120 from Montreal in 2012, 1,166 from Welland in 1975, and 3,969 from Welland in 2012–2015.

(9) *C'est quelqu'un qui nous avait montés l'un contre l'autre **alors qu**'on avait pris un petit coup* 'It was someone who had set us against each other when we were a little drunk' (FRAN-Montréal HOMA12 018M51)

(10) *Ben voyons **donc** papa vous êtes **donc** ben pessimiste* 'Come on dad you are so pessimistic' (FRAN-Montréal HOMA12 002F52)

11.5.2.2 Statistical Analyses In the following subsections, we present the results of multivariate analyses conducted with the variable rule program GoldVarb Lion (Sankoff et al. 2005). To examine the lexical effect of variation, we first analyzed the choice of connector according to linguistic function for each community and time period. Results of distinct multivariate analyses of the effect of social factors are also presented for each community and time period. Patterns of variability for each connector are presented in terms of variant frequencies, factor effects, range, and the level of significance of the results[3]. Such patterns provide an indication of change within the community. They can also be compared across the two communities to shed light on convergent or divergent evolutions.

11.6 Results

11.6.1 General Tendencies

Figure 11.2 provides the general frequencies found for each of the four markers in Montreal and Welland at the two points in time. The vernacular variants *(ça) fait (que)* and *so* (for Welland) are grouped together alongside the standard variants *alors* and *donc*. If we compare the frequencies of each community in synchrony, we see that there was a moderate level of divergence between the two communities in the 1970s. The variant *(ça) fait (que)* was used at quite similar levels of frequency, *so* was absent in Montreal and was used less than 5 percent of the time in Welland, *alors* was the second most frequent variant in both communities but was used somewhat more frequently in Montreal than in Welland, and *donc* was used marginally in Montreal and somewhat more than 10 percent in Welland. In the 2010s, intercommunity divergence has increased

---

[3] Owing to the low representation of the youngest speakers in the second Welland corpus, there were several cases of factor interactions in the GoldVarb analyses. Such interactions have, to some extent, limited our ability to determine with optimal accuracy the order of factor influence. With GoldVarb, interactions are signaled by discrepancies between the hierarchy of frequency differences and the hierarchy of factor weights. Owing to space limitations, in the presentation and discussion of the results, for the most part, we do not discuss these interactions.

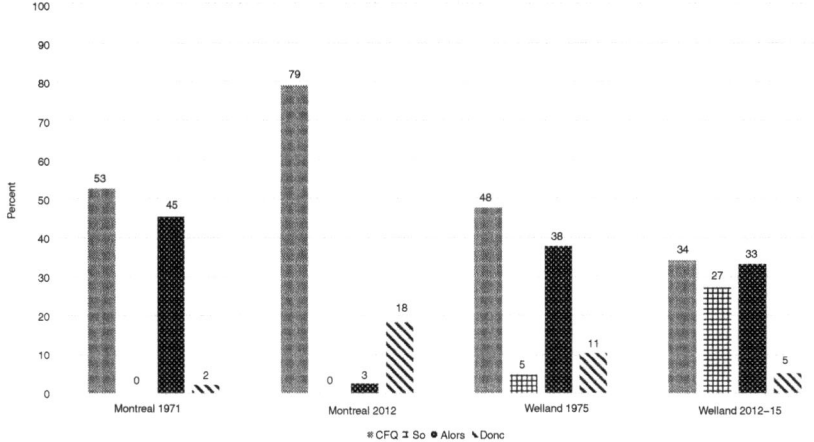

Figure 11.2 Variant frequencies in the 1970s and 2010s in Montreal and Welland

markedly. *(Ça) fait (que)* is twice more frequent in Montreal than in Welland, *so* is still absent in Montreal, but is used more than a quarter of the time in Welland, *alors* is used less than 5 percent of the time in Montreal and more than a quarter of the time in Welland, and *donc* is used close to 20 percent of the time in Montreal but only 5 percent of the time in Welland.

Given that there are differences in the proportion of speakers according to age and SES within and across the corpora and the methodologies used to collect the four corpora were not fully identical, the patterns of convergence or divergence revealed by the overall variant frequencies ought to be taken with some caution. In the remainder of this chapter, we discuss the issue of inter-community divergence versus convergence when we focus on the linguistic and extra-linguistic constraints of variation via GoldVarb analyses. These analyses also allow us to identify the social groups in the vanguard of linguistic change and those that, in contrast, lag behind it. Additionally, the analyses test the apparent-time model in real time.

11.6.2 Montreal and Welland in the 1970s

11.6.2.1 Influence of Connector Choice According to Linguistic Function A first step was to assess the use of each connector according to a grammatical or discursive function in the Montreal and Welland 1970s corpora. To do so, we conducted GoldVarb analyses with the function (grammatical or discursive) as

Table 11.2 *Influence of connector choice according to linguistic function in Montreal 1971 and Welland 1975*

	Montreal 1971 (N = 3292) Input = 0.64			Welland 1975 (N = 1166) Input = 0.13		
Connector	% *Discursive*	N total	Weight	% *Discursive*	N total	Weight
CFQ	62.4	1,727	0.485	11.3	556	0.465
So				50.9	55	0.876
Alors	67.0	1,493	0.534	12.2	433	0.487
Donc	30.6	72	0.200	12.3	122	0.488
Range			33			41

the dependent variable. Table 11.2 provides the results with the application value as the discursive function.

Table 11.2 shows that the connectors are used much more frequently to fulfill a discursive function in Montreal than in Welland. This difference is indicated by the frequency percentages and the input values (0.64 in Montreal vs. 0.13 in Welland). Table 11.2 also includes the factor weights computed by GoldVarb. In Montreal, we see that *(ça) fait (que)* slightly disfavored the discursive function (0.485) and *alors* slightly favored it (0.534). In contrast, *donc* clearly disfavored the discursive function (0.200). In Welland, *(ça) fait (que)*, *alors*, and *donc* slightly disfavored the discursive function, but *so* strongly favored it. In sum, the use of *(ça) fait (que)* and *alors* according to function are similar between communities, but the strong disfavoring of the discursive function of *donc* in Montreal presents a sharper difference. Our analysis of the 1970s data provides some evidence of a moderate level of intercommunity divergence in relation to connector choice.

11.6.2.2 Influence of Social Factors Table 11.3 presents the influence of social factors on the use of consequence markers in Montreal in the 1970s. Age has an influence on all three connectors; however, the hierarchy of the factor weights for *(ça) fait (que)* and *alors* is puzzling. While the preference of the middle-aged speakers for *alors* might reflect an age-grading phenomenon (Thibault and Daveluy 1989), the fact that the overall frequencies show a sizable increase of *(ça) fait (que)* between 1971 and 2012 suggests that the age pattern could reflect two processes: either two subsequent changes – the replacement of *(ça) fait (que)* by *alors* followed by a reversal of this trend – or an age-grading phenomenon. Concerning *donc*, we see that this form is favored by the younger speakers and somewhat disfavored by the middle-aged and older speakers. Regarding the effect of SES, vernacular *(ça) fait (que)* and standard *alors* are in complementary distribution. While *(ça) fait (que)* is

Table 11.3 *Influence of social factors in Montreal 1971*

	Montreal 1971 (N=3292)								
	(ÇA) FAIT (QUE)			ALORS			DONC		
	N	%	Wt	N	%	Wt	N	%	Wt
Age									
Young*	1,497	60.8	0.69	1,497	35.9	0.30	1,497	3.3	0.64
Mid*	1,524	39.1	0.28	1,524	59.7	0.74	1,524	1.2	0.38
Old*	271	81.5	0.73	271	17.0	0.27	271	1.5	0.43
	Range: 46			Range: 47			Range: 26		
SES									
High	1,278	11.7	0.10	1,278	85.4	0.90	1,278	2.9	[0.59]
Inter.	1,004	72.7	0.68	1,004	25.1	0.33	1,004	2.2	[0.48]
Low	1,010	84.0	0.89	1,010	14.8	0.11	1,010	1.3	[0.41]
	Range: 79			Range: 79			Range: NA		
Sex									
Female	1,862	54.3	[0.50]	1,862	43.5	[0.50]	1,862	2.2	[0.51]
Male	1,430	50.1	[0.50]	1,430	47.8	[0.51]	1,430	2.2	[0.49]
	Range: NA			Range: NA			Range: NA		
	Input: 0.507 Si: 0.000			Input: 0.449 Si: 0.000			Input: 0.019 Si: 0.000		

Note. * Young refers to speakers aged 18–31, Mid refers to speakers aged 35–64 and Old refers to speakers aged 65–85

favored by the lower and intermediate SES speakers, *alors* is favored by the higher SES speakers. The higher SES speakers have the highest rate of *donc*, but the intergroup differences are not significant (non-significant results are presented in square brackets). Lastly, the effect of gender is not significant for all three forms.

Turning now to the Welland results, Table 11.4 shows that the younger speakers disfavor *(ça) fait (que)*, the middle-aged speakers favor it slightly, and the older speakers favor it somewhat more than the middle-aged speakers. As for *so*, the young speakers are clearly in the vanguard of *so* use in terms of percentage and factor weight. The standard connectors *alors* and *donc* are not influenced by age. Concerning SES, we see that *(ça) fait (que)* is favored by the lower and intermediate SES speakers, and *so* is strongly favored by the intermediate SES speakers and disfavored by speakers from the other two categories. In contrast, *alors* is strongly favored by the higher SES speakers and clearly disfavored by speakers from the other two SES categories while *donc* is also preferred by the higher and intermediate SES speakers. With respect to gender, we see that males favor *(ça) fait (que)* and females strongly prefer *so*. The standard forms *alors* and *donc* have opposite gender effects: *alors* is preferred by females and *donc* by males. As for language dominance,

Table 11.4 Influence of social factors in Welland 1975

	(ÇA) FAIT (QUE)			SO			Welland 1975 (N=1166) ALORS			DONC		
	N	%	Wt	N	%	Wt	N	%	Wt	N	%	Wt
Age												
Young*	424	31.1	0.38	424	12.5	0.95	424	44.6	[0.49]	424	11.8	[0.46]
Mid*	616	55.5	0.55	616	0.2	0.11	616	33.4	[0.52]	616	11	[0.56]
Old*	126	65.6	0.60	126	0.8	0.66	126	30.3	[0.43]	126	3.3	[0.35]
	Range: 22			Range: 84			N.A.			N.A.		
SES												
High	401	4.7	0.07	401	0.2	0.08	401	82	0.92	401	13	0.58
Inter.	509	67.4	0.76	509	9.4	0.87	509	10.2	0.19	509	13.5	0.61
Low	256	75.8	0.84	256	2.3	0.48	256	20.3	0.28	256	1.6	0.20
	Range: 77			Range: 79			Range: 73			Range: 41		
Sex												
Female	624	40.2	0.38	624	8.3	0.78	624	42.9	0.61	624	8.5	0.39
Male	542	56.3	0.64	542	0.6	0.19	542	30.4	0.37	542	12.7	0.63
	Range: 26			Range: 59			Range: 24			Range: 24		
Dominance												
Fr. Dom	426	69.7	0.60	426	0.5	NS	426	27.9	0.53	426	1.9	0.19
Balanced	389	37.8	0.49	389	9.5		389	35.5	0.40	389	17.2	0.73
En. dom.	351	31.9	0.39	351	4.6		351	50.1	0.54	351	13.4	0.66
	Range: 21						Range: 14			Range: 54		
	Input: 0.39 Si: 0.000			Input: 0.02 Si: 0.000			Input: 0.325 Si: 0.001			Input: 0.059 Si: 0.000		

Note. * Young refers to speakers aged 18–31, Mid refers to speakers aged 35–64 and Old refers to speakers aged 65–85

the French-dominant bilinguals favor *(ça) fait (que)*, the balanced bilinguals slightly disfavor it, and the English-dominant bilinguals disfavor it somewhat more. Language dominance does not seem to have much of an effect on *alors* (factor weights close to the 0.50 neutral value), but *donc* is the clear preference of the balanced and English-dominant bilinguals (cf. Kern, Chapter 10, this volume).

We can now compare the Welland results with Montreal and look for evidence of sociolinguistic divergence or convergence in the 1970s. In relation to the external constraints on variation, the general trend is that the two communities had already started to follow divergent paths in their use of the consequence markers. This is supported by two main bits of evidence: *(ça) fait (que)* is favored by the younger speakers in Montreal and disfavored by them in Welland; and gender has no influence on *(ça) fait (que), alors* and *donc* in Montreal but has an impact on all three forms in Welland. That said, the comparison also reveals that the two communities were sharing similar SES constraints in relation to *(ça) fait (que)* and *alors*.

11.6.3 Montreal and Welland in the 2010s

11.6.3.1 Influence of Connector Choice According to Linguistic Function
Table 11.5 provides the results of the analysis of the influence of the choice of connector according to a grammatical or discursive function in the 2010s. In Montreal, we see that as *(ça) fait (que)* continues to grow and now somewhat favors the discursive function. *Alors* now disfavors the discursive function, perhaps due to the move of the other standard variant *donc* towards this function. In comparison to the 1970s, *donc* is much less favorable to the grammatical function (effects of 0.20 vs. 0.49). A possible interpretation of this change is that *donc* entered local speech via the grammatical function but moved away from it as its frequency greatly increased.

The Welland results show that *(ça) fait (que)* was neither favorable nor unfavorable to the discursive function in 1975, and it is now only slightly unfavorable to it. *So* does not favor the discursive function as strongly as it did in 1975, a change that may reflect its sizable rise in local speech. The two standard variants *alors* and *donc* also evidence relatively little change. In 1975, they did not show a preference for function, and they now moderately disfavor the discursive function.

Turning to the significance of the results for the issue of intercommunity convergence versus divergence, a comparison of the factor weights found for *(ça) fait (que)* and *alors* in both communities shows that they are relatively similar. Furthermore, since the use of *donc* to fulfill a grammatical function has weakened in Montreal, intercommunity convergence has somewhat increased; consequently, there is no evidence of an increase of intercommunity divergence in the 2010s concerning the influence of linguistic functions.

Table 11.5 *Influence of connector choice according to linguistic function in Montreal 2012 and Welland 2012–2015*

Factor	Montreal 2012 Input = 0.569; Significance: 0.000 N=4120			Welland 2012–2015 Input = 0.335; Significance: 0.000 N=3969		
Connector	% discursive	N total	Weight	% discursive	N total	Weight
CFQ	59.3	3,251	0.525	33.5	1,355	0.498
So				44.2	1,081	0.609
Alors	37.6	109	0.314	27.6	1,325	0.428
Donc	48.9	760	0.421	25.2	208	0.400
Range			22			21

11.6.3.2 Influence of Social Factors Table 11.6 provides the results of the analyses of the influence of extra-linguistic factors on variant choice in Montreal in the 2010s. In Montreal, *(ça) fait (que)* and *alors* are no longer in complementary distribution. *Alors* is now an obsolescent variant, only used by the older speakers, and it has been replaced by *(ça) fait (que)* and *donc*. Age is not a significant factor for *(ça) fait (que)* – all age groups use this variant at rates greater than 75 percent – and this vernacular variant is favored by the lower SES speakers and women. However, age has an influence on *alors* and *donc*, reflecting the replacement of standard *alors* by *donc*, a change led by men. A plausible explanation for this change resides in the fact that they are both features of Standard French. The fact that age does not influence *(ça) fait (que)* is puzzling since it seems to indicate that this form has become the default form for the younger generations. Although the form is socially conditioned by SES and gender, one may wonder how young females index stylistic shift if they rarely use *alors* and *donc*,[4] a question that would require a closer analysis of the respective roles of men and women in the rise of *donc* and *(ça) fait (que)*.

Turning to the Welland findings (Table 11.7), influence of age on *(ça) fait (que)* and *so* reveals that the rise of *so* is occurring at the expense of *(ça) fait (que)* and that the younger and middle-age speakers are in the vanguard of this shift. In contrast, as in 1975, the older speakers still strongly favor *(ça) fait (que)*. As for the influence of speaker SES on *(ça) fait (que)* and *so*, we see that the two forms are disfavored by the higher SES speakers and favored by speakers from the other two SES categories. The results for the influence of speaker gender and language dominance suggest that the replacement of *(ça) fait (que)* by *so* is driven by

---

[4] An anonymous reviewer pointedly commented that this demographic group may experience no particular need to style shift and that not every linguistic item or construction has stylistic variants. We think that, if it were indeed the case, this could indicate that consequence markers are on the verge of losing their sociolinguistic marker status in Montreal French.

Table 11.6 *Influence of social factors in Montreal 2012*

	Montreal 2012 (N=4120)								
	(ÇA) FAIT (QUE)			ALORS			DONC		
	N	%	Wt	N	%	Wt	N	%	Wt
Age									
Young*	1,716	77.5	[0.51]	1,716	0.1	0.074	1,716	22.4	0.55
Mid*	1,968	80.5	[0.51]	1,968	2.7	0.81	1,968	16.8	0.49
Old*	436	77.3	[0.43]	436	12.4	0.97	436	10.3	0.35
Range: NA				Range: 89			Range: 19		
SES									
High	1,597	70.8	0.35	1,597	2.9	0.64	1,597	24.3	0.66
Inter.	1,291	75.1	0.41	1,291	2.9	0.45	1,291	22.0	0.62
Low	1,232	93.3	0.77	1,232	2.1	0.37	1,232	4.5	0.20
Range: 42				Range: 27			Range: 46		
Sex									
Female	2,368	84.8	0.592	2,368	2.4	[0.47]	2,368	12.8	0.40
Male	1,752	71.0	0.376	1,752	2.9	[0.54]	1,752	26.1	0.63
Range: 22				Range: NA			Range: 23		
Input: 0.82 Si: 0.000				Input: 0.006 Si: 0.000			Input: 0.14 Si: 0.000		

Note. * Young refers to speakers aged 18–31, Mid refers to speakers aged 35–64 and Old refers to speakers aged 65–85

women and the balanced and English-dominant bilinguals (all three groups favor *so*); men and the French-dominant bilinguals lag behind this change (both groups favor *(ça) fait (que)*). Let us now examine the results for the two standard variants. With respect to the influence of age, we see that, in the 2010s, *alors* is favored by the middle-age speakers, who use this form almost two-thirds of the time, and is disfavored by both the youngest and oldest speakers. As for *donc*, it is favored quite strongly by the younger speakers, disfavored by the middle-age speakers, and, unexpectedly, is favored by the older speakers. However, these latter speakers use this form less than 3 percent of the time. With respect to SES, we see that both *alors* and *donc* are favored quite strongly by the higher SES speakers and disfavored by the intermediate and lower SES speakers. Gender does not exert a statistical effect on *donc* and has a very modest influence on *alors*. Lastly, regarding the influence of language dominance, we see that, in the 2010s, the French-dominant bilinguals disfavor *donc* and favor *alors*. As for the English-dominant bilinguals, they not only favor *alors* but also, as we have just seen, clearly disfavor the traditional vernacular form *(ça) fait (que)* and favor the innovative form *so*. Lastly, the balanced bilinguals, stand in between the other two groups of bilinguals inasmuch as they show a strong preference for *donc* and, at the same time, as we have seen, they are not disinclined to use *(ça) fait (que)* and *so* (cf. Kern, Chapter 10, this volume).

Table 11.7 Influence of social factors in Welland 2012–2015

	(ÇA) FAIT(QUE)			SO			ALORS			DONC		
	N	%	Wt	N	%	Wt	N	%	Wt	N	%	Wt
Age												
Young*	754	6	0.36	754	38.7	0.72	754	37.3	0.31	754	18	0.81
Mid*	1,737	20.6	0.35	1,737	36.2	0.62	1,737	41.4	0.63	1,737	1.8	0.16
Old*	1,478	64.7	0.74	1,478	10.9	0.26	1,478	21.8	0.44	1,478	2.6	0.76
	Range: 39			Range: 46			Range: 32			Range: 65		
SES												
High	1,572	8.7	0.15	1,572	20	0.31	1,572	59.4	0.87	1,572	11.8	0.88
Inter.	1,722	43.8	0.76	1,722	32.8	0.57	1,722	22.4	0.49	1,722	1	0.26
Low	675	69.2	0.73	675	30.1	0.75	675	0.3	0.01	675	0.4	0.12
	Range: 61			Range: 44			Range: 86			Range: 76		
Sex												
Female	2,653	29.6	0.37	2,653	32.4	0.56	2,653	34.6	0.52	2,653	3.4	[0.43]
Male	1,316	43.5	0.75	1,316	16.9	0.38	1,316	30.6	0.47	1,316	9.0	[0.64]
	Range: 38			Range: 18			Range: 5			Range: NA		
Dominance												
Fr. dom	1,414	54.5	0.63	1,414	10	0.35	1,414	32.9	0.60	1,414	2.5	0.29
Balanced	1,151	37.2	0.69	1,151	31.9	0.58	1,151	19.2	0.26	1,151	11.7	0.89
En. dom.	1,404	11.3	0.24	1,404	40.8	0.63	1,404	45.3	0.62	1,404	2.6	0.30
	Range: 45			Range: 28			Range: 36			Range: 60		
	Input: 0.27 Si: 0.000			Input: 0.22 Si: 0.000			Input: 0.19 Si: 0.02			Input: 0.008 Si: 0.000		

Note. * Young refers to speakers aged 18–31, Mid refers to speakers aged 35–64 and Old refers to speakers aged 65–85

We can now turn our attention to the issue of intercommunity divergence versus convergence. The general trend is that both communities have moved farther on the path of sociolinguistic divergence than they had done in the 1970s. This is supported by several bits of evidence. Regarding age, all three groups in Montreal exhibit a very strong propensity to use *(ça) fait (que)*, but in Welland this form is now favored only by the older speakers and it is close to reaching obsolescence in the speech of the younger speakers. In Montreal, speakers still do not use *so*, but in Welland the frequency of this form has greatly increased even in the speech of the older speakers. In Montreal, *alors* has been leveled out in the speech of the younger generation, but in Welland it is still used more than one-third of the time by the same generation. Regarding gender, women play a leading role in the continued growth of *(ça) fait (que)* in Montreal, while men disfavor this form; however, in Welland, women disfavor *(ça) fait (que)* and men show a strong preference for it. That said, even at this more advanced stage of sociolinguistic divergence, the two communities still share some sociolinguistic constraints. In both communities, the higher SES speakers show a strong inclination to use *alors* and *donc* and the younger speakers use *donc* more often than the middle-aged and older speakers.

11.7 Discussion

Let us now briefly interpret and discuss the main findings of the present study, starting with the analysis of the 1971 Montreal corpus. In basing our analysis on the entire corpus of 120 speakers, we have been able to advance our understanding of variation farther than what Dessureault-Dober was able to do in her (1974) study. Firstly, by including *donc* in the analysis of the use of the variants according to a discursive or grammatical function, we have highlighted the strong association of this form with the grammatical function, a finding that may reflect *donc*'s early entry in local speech. Secondly, in distinguishing three age groups instead of two, we have brought to light the curvilinear fluctuation of *alors* with age, a finding that lends credence to Thibault and Daveluy's (1989) hypothesis that the frequency of *alors* varied across the lifespan of individuals (i.e., age-grading during the 1970s and 1980s). Thirdly, by including gender as a factor, we arrived at the unexpected finding of a lack of a statistical effect of this parameter on the frequency of all three variants in the 1970s in spite of their exhibiting clear patterns of social stratification. This finding is in contrast with the emergence of a strong impact of gender in the 2010s.

Turning now to the Welland findings, our evaluation of the use of the variants according to the discursive function in the 1970s is an original contribution of the present study, since this research issue was not examined in Mougeon and Beniak (1991). The strong association of the English borrowing *so* with the discursive function as it was beginning to enter local speech stands in contrast with the association of the other variants with the grammatical function. In the 1970s, there was a complementary distribution of functions between *so* and the other variants. The finding of the dual effect of gender and SES on all four variants is not only generally in line with the results of Mougeon and Beniak (1991) but also is one of several indications of the early divergent evolution of Welland French. Finally, the results of the evaluation of the effect of language dominance on the use of *so* are in keeping with those of Mougeon and Beniak (1991), as well as those of studies that documented the borrowing of discourse markers (including connector *so*) in situations of intense language contact (Goss and Salmons 2000; Torres 2006; Hickey 2009).

When comparing the Welland results with Montreal to look for evidence of sociolinguistic divergence or convergence, the general trend is that the two communities had already started to follow divergent paths in their use of the consequence markers in the 1970s. This finding differs from the results of Mougeon et al. (2010) and Mougeon et al. (2016), who examined, respectively, the *m'as/je vas/je vais* 'I'm going to' and the *rien que, juste, seulement*, and *ne ... que* 'only' sociolinguistic variables and found that Welland and Montreal French shared the same inventory of variants and the same set of linguistic and extra-linguistic constraints in the 1970s. According to these authors, their findings reflected in part the fact that the bulk of the inflow of Quebecers into Welland occurred relatively recently (i.e., from the beginning of the 1940s to the beginning of the 1970s). The present study's finding of divergence in the 1970s suggests that the demographic factor invoked by Mougeon and colleagues may not necessarily entail intercommunity convergence and that certain sociolinguistic variables may have structural properties that make them especially conducive to sociolinguistic divergence. That said, one should not lose sight that the present study has also found that the two communities were sharing similar SES constraints in relation to *(ça) fait (que)* and *alors* in the 1970s.

The analysis of the 2010s corpora arrived at results on the influence of the linguistic and extra-linguistic factors on variation that were generally in line with those of Blondeau et al. (2019). The chief merit of the analysis of the 2010s corpora is that its results can be compared with those of the analysis of the 1970s corpora to document the trajectory of each variant over a period of about forty years. Such a comparison sheds light on the story of *donc* in Montreal French, an aspect that was barely touched upon by previous studies. We saw that *donc* was marginal and associated with the younger speakers in the 1970s, which was an apparent-time indication of its role as an incoming standard variant. In the 2010s, *donc* is still favored by the younger speakers but also by men and higher and intermediate SES speakers, and its frequency has greatly increased, overtaking the obsolescent *alors* to become the chief standard variant competing with *(ça) fait (que)*. Martineau (2019) suggests that, in comparison to *donc, alors* lacked stylistic saliency and thus was unable to withstand the rising tide of *(ça) fait (que)*. To verify this hypothesis, one would have to independently assess the stylistic saliency of each standard variant since *alors* likely exhibited a pattern of age-grading between 1971 and 1984.

A comparison of the Welland results in the 2010s with the 1970s sheds light on the competition of *(ça) fait (que)* with *so* and the unexpected resilience of *alors*. Interestingly, while the younger speakers already disfavored *(ça) fait (que)* in 1975, they still used this variant three times more often than its rival *so*; however, *so* has clearly overtaken *(ça) fait (que)* in the speech of the younger generations in the 2010s. That said, in contrast with the Montreal younger speakers who use *(ça) fait (que)* more than 75 percent of the time in the 2010s, the younger speakers in Welland have not massively shifted to *so*. They use this variant less than 40 percent of the time, and in their speech *alors* and *donc* have respective frequencies of 37 percent and 18 percent. One factor that probably contributes to the maintenance of *alors* among the younger generations is that most of the younger speakers in the Welland sample and the community at large are English-dominant bilinguals who prefer this variant strongly. Variation in the speech of the younger generations primarily manifests itself as a contrast between *so*, the new vernacular variant, and the standard variants *alors* and *donc*. The findings of the increased strength of *alors* and *donc* in the speech of the younger generations are in line with those of Mougeon and Beniak (1991) and Mougeon et al. (2009) and underscore the fact that French speakers in minority Franco-Ontarian communities increasingly rely on French-medium schools for their linguistic reproduction as French is receding in the informal and private domains of society (e.g., the home). Jones (1998) also documented the standardizing impact of Welsh-medium schooling in communities where Welsh is losing out to English.

11.8 Conclusion

Our research contributes to the evaluation of one of the leading hypotheses put forward by Labov (2001a, 2001b), namely that synchronic variation (linguistic and social) is at the basis of diachronic variation. The longitudinal nature of the present study allowed us to go beyond the predictions of language change based on the apparent-time model of previous research using the 1970s or 2010s corpora. By exploring the issue of intercommunity divergence or convergence at the two points in time under study, we arrived at two main findings. First, the two communities were already exhibiting divergent patterns in the 1970s in the use of consequence markers: *so* was absent in Montreal and several linguistic and extra-linguistic constraints on variation were not shared between the two communities. Second, in the 2010s, intercommunity divergence intensified. This latter finding is understandable given that over the period of forty years examined by our research there have been profound changes in the status of French and the demolinguistic vitality of francophones in both communities. Future comparative research on additional sociolinguistic variables should allow us to gain a better sense of the magnitude and evolution of intercommunity convergence and divergence and to make further progress in our understanding of the social and linguistic factors that lie behind these two processes.

12 What Governs Speakers' Choices of Borrowed vs. Domestic Variants of Discourse-Pragmatic Variables?

Gisle Andersen

12.1 Introduction

Contact linguistics is a specific branch of sociolinguistics that studies the effects of multilingualism manifested as code-switching, translanguaging, borrowing, and other practices. Among the significant developments of this branch in the last few decades has been a shift towards more pragmatically oriented studies. As formulated by Auer and Eastman (2010) in the *Handbook of Pragmatics*:

> The enormous interest code-switching and related practices have found in linguistics over the last three decades is at least in part (i.e., in addition to internal developments in linguistics) due to the demise of the monolingual national ideologies which have become less and less realistic in the age of globalization, transnationalism, and migration. (Auer and Eastman 2010: 84)

While code-switching concerns alternating use of language systems (languages, dialects, or styles) in individual situations, the study of linguistic borrowing concerns itself with the more permanent effects of language contact. Traditionally, studies of borrowing have explored the transfer of vocabulary as an effect of close contact within bi- or multilingual communities, such as French loanwords in the Dutch spoken in Brussels (e.g., Treffers-Daller 1994) or English loanwords in francophone Canada (Poplack et al. 1988). In the last few decades, there has been a surge of studies that investigate the effect of language contact in situations referred to as "remote" (Meyerhoff and Niedzelski 2003), "weak" (Zenner et al. 2014), and "non-contiguous (Sayers 2014) contact scenarios" (Peterson 2017) or as "foreign language contact" (Peterson and Beers Fägersten 2018: 105). The most conspicuous case of such globalism-induced contact scenarios is the omnipresence of English in contexts connected with international business, travel, mass media, and technology. The growing interest in research on the effects of remote contact from

English has manifested itself as a range of studies of lexical borrowing. Thus, it makes sense to speak of Anglicism research as a specific branch of sociolinguistics that encompasses Anglicism dictionaries (Carstensen and Busse 1993–1996; Graedler and Johansson 1997; Görlach 2001), monographs (Graedler 1998; Plümer 2000; Prćić [2005] 2011; Onysko 2007), collective volumes (Fischer and Pułaczewska 2008; Furiassi et al. 2012; Furiassi and Gottlieb 2015), special issues of journals (Andersen et al. 2017; Peterson and Beers Fägersten 2018), and an international research network dedicated to the study of Anglicisms (GLAD).[1]

In a more recent article, Andersen et al. (2017) argue that studies of linguistic borrowing have taken a "pragmatic turn" congruous with a more general shift towards usage-based as opposed to structuralist approaches to language contact (Backus 2014). This means that there is somewhat less focus on inventory issues and more focus on how borrowing is constrained by cultural, social, or cognitive factors, on how discourse items get borrowed (e.g., politeness formula, expletives, discourse markers), and on how longer stretches of discourse including phraseology are transferred from one language to another. The current study places itself within this more recent line of research and explores cases of borrowing of discourse-pragmatic variants that originate in English but that are used in Norwegian alongside their domestic alternatives.

The account of pragmatic contact phenomena should be interpreted against the backdrop of previous studies. The earliest study to document what today would be labeled pragmatic borrowing from English to Norwegian is Haugen ([1953] 1969). He noted that interjections are noticeable – albeit comparatively infrequent – among the loanwords in his data of the language of Norwegian immigrants to the United States. In his material, the interjection *nå* 'no' had largely replaced the Norwegian *nei*, and interjections such as *sjur* 'sure', *vell* 'well', and *gudbai* 'goodbye' were universally used in place of their Norwegian equivalents (Haugen [1953] 1969: 92).[2] Other relevant observations were that adverbs such as *ennivei* 'anyway', *ætål* 'at all,' *iven* 'even,' and *kårs* 'of course' were regularly used by his informants, in ways that we today would associate with discourse marker functions. In general terms, Haugen's groundbreaking research strongly suggests the pervasiveness of several English-based interjections and discourse markers in this language contact variety.

A crucial question in studies of pragmatic borrowing is, do the borrowed items "do the same thing" in the language they are borrowed into (the recipient language, RL) as in the source language (SL) from which they are borrowed? Although not the prime focus of Haugen's work, subsequent research has shown that pragmatic borrowings can be expected to undergo functional

---

[1] Global Anglicism Database Network (GLAD): www.gladnetwork.org.
[2] These forms are Haugen's transcriptions as they appeared in spoken data.

adaptations upon transfer from the source to the recipient language (Andersen 2014). An early study that illustrates such effects of pragmatic borrowing from English is Meyerhoff's (1999) account of *sori* 'sorry' in Bislama, an English-based creole language spoken in the Pacific Island of Vanuatu. She shows that this form has been adopted by Bislama speakers and has undergone post hoc pragmatic adaptation. This amounts to an adjustment of its functional range from functions that are coexistent with the SL, namely expressing an apology or an emphatic stance, to adapted functions of expressing empathy without overtly mentioning the "theme" towards which empathy is expressed. In this adjusted function, *sori* operates textually as a kind of emphatic backchannel, akin to English "Oh no!" and "oh dear." Meyerhoff also observes an entirely new function of *sori* as a verbal and propositional expression of missing someone or something, which is developed from the politeness functions.

In an article pertinently entitled "What happens to politeness markers when they are borrowed across languages?," Terkourafi (2011) looks into the use of a set of English-based politeness markers in Cypriot Greek, notably *thank you*, *sorry*, and *please*. The strength of commitment of their associated speech act function of thanking, apologizing, or requesting is generally much lower for these imported forms than for their domestic competitors. Further, the borrowed forms are shown to perform additional discourse-structural functions such as marking a conversational closing (*thank you*) and self-repair (*sorry*).

Similar observations are made by Peterson and Vaattovaara (2014) regarding the use of *pliis* 'please' in Finnish (see also Peterson, Hiltunen, and Vaattovaara, Chapter 13, this volume). The pragmatic borrowing is "associated with settings where solidarity and positive politeness are either present or strived for" (Peterson 2017: 121), which notably contrasts with its domestic alternative *kiitos*, and with *please* in the SL, which would be considered a more general marker of negative politeness (Brown and Levinson 1987: 101).

Also addressing the topic of post hoc adaptations of pragmatic borrowings, Andersen (2014) investigates different instantiations of the expletive *fuck* in Norwegian. His data show that the most salient functional adaptation concerns the illocutionary force of this expletive. Compared to its English etymon, "the expletive appears substantially less coarse and is not necessarily associated with strong illocutions" (Andersen 2014: 28).

Balteiro (2018) looks into the phrase *oh wait* used as a discourse marker in Spanish in an online setting, namely spontaneous synchronic comments in a forum for football fans. The most notable aspect of this marker is its ironic overtones. The marker "is restricted to ironic uses, probably conditioned by its presence in oralized written discourses like chats; neutral non-ironic occurrences have not yet been found or recorded in spoken language, as is the case in English" (Balteiro 2018: 131).

Common to these previous studies is that all share an element of post hoc adaptation of the functional range of the borrowed pragmatic items. In the framework of Andersen (2014), different aspects of functional adaptation can be regarded as narrowing (e.g., the restriction of apologetic *sorry* to minor offenses or the specialization of *oh wait* as a marker of irony), broadening (e.g., the development of new discourse functions such as marking a conversational closing), or shift (e.g., the change from negative to positive politeness seen with *pliis* in Finnish). The previous studies cover a relatively narrow range of pragmatic functions – restricted to politeness, thanking, and apologizing – expletives, and marking of discourse structure. However, it is clear that a wider range of discourse-pragmatic features may be subject to borrowing and deserve scholarly attention, including greetings and leave-taking formulas, vocatives, general extenders, tags, quotatives, and even intonation, symbols, and gestures (Andersen 2014: 23). An interesting case in point is provided by Mišić Ilić (2017), who shows that borrowing is not necessarily restricted to linguistic elements that perform a function that already exists in the language but even to the importation of discourse formulas that are "a novel communication and cultural pattern from the Anglo-American globalizing culture" (Mišić Ilić 2017: 103). Her article shows that localized variants of *Thank you for your understanding*, *Can I help you?*, and *Here's your change* represent English-induced acts of communicative behavior that, qua borrowings, go under the radar, so to speak. Filling a "discourse gap" in Serbian, this usage shows that the notion of pragmatic borrowing goes well beyond the transfer of individual word forms.

The current chapter aims to explore what happens to discourse markers that are borrowed from English into Norwegian. This is done through an investigation of four corpora of spoken Norwegian. I investigate two discourse-pragmatic variables whose envelope of variation includes borrowed and domestic forms. These include requests that are realized by the borrowed form *please*, or one of a set of domestic variants including *vær så snill*, and *sorry* used in apologies alongside the domestic variants *(jeg) beklager* and *unnskyld*. The two Anglicisms have a relatively long history in Norwegian (Görlach 2001). A search in the National Library's text archive shows that tokens of non-quotational/code-switching use start to appear around 1950 for *sorry* (cf. *Du tror visst jeg skal slå meg ned her, du, tenkte jeg, og sa jeg var sorry* 'You think that I'm going to sit down here, I thought, and said I was sorry'; *Stavanger Aftenblad* Jan. 30, 1950) and *please* (cf. *Og arabere: please bruk ikke arabisk skrift!* 'And Arabs, please do not use Arabic writing'; *VG* (newspaper) Jan. 12, 1951).[3]

---

[3] National Library, Norway: https://www.nb.no/.

Exploring the variation between the borrowed forms and their alternating domestic forms in spoken corpora entails a function-based conceptualization of discourse variables, in the variationist fashion of Pichler (2010). I address two specific research questions. The first question is whether the borrowed variants covary with domestic forms in all of the corpora or whether they can be seen to replace domestic forms. The second question is to what degree the borrowed and domestic variants are equivalent in terms of their speech act functions and illocutionary strength. Given the previous literature, we can expect functional adaptation to occur post hoc, such as the loss of illocutionary strength and the development of new discourse functions in the way that has been described with similar instances of borrowing in the literature outlined in this section. Although not the prime focus here, I also briefly also discuss variability in terms of the age and gender of speakers that instigate the use of the borrowed variants.

12.2 Material and Methods

Unfortunately, there is no large corpus of spoken conversation in Norwegian. However, many studies have utilized data collected in various research projects. Table 12.1 gives an outline of the four corpora that this study is based on.

It should be pointed out that only one of the datasets, UNO, is a "corpus" in the traditional sense used in corpus linguistics. This is a teenage language corpus whose sampling strategy was modeled on the Corpus of London Teenage Language (COLT), also collected in the 1990s. UNO contains audio-recorded and highly informal conversation between teenagers from the Oslo area. The BBc contains conversation from the first season of the

Table 12.1 *Corpora used in this study*

Corpus	Date of collection	No. words	Content/speakers
Ungdomsspråk i Norden (UNO)	1997	450,000	Conversation, Oslo, age 13–17
Big Brother Corpus (BBc)	2001	440,300	Conversation from reality TV show; Oslo (and other dialects), age 23–36
Norsk talemålskorpus (NoTa)	2004–2006	957,000	Sociolinguistic interviews and dyadic conversation, Oslo, all ages
Nordic Dialect Corpus (NDC)	2007–2008	2,800,000	Sociolinguistic interviews and dyadic conversation, whole country, all ages

TV reality show, broadcast on Norwegian television in 2001. In contrast, the NoTa and NDC corpora do not contain unsolicited conversation but interviews and dyadic conversation recorded in a studio in connection with research projects in sociolinguistics. Owing to this difference, and for simplicity, I refer to UNO and BBc collectively as the "conversational" corpora and NoTa and NDC as "sociolinguistic" corpora. Note also that this latter group of corpora contains speakers of all ages, unlike UNO and the BBc, where the speakers are adolescents and young adults. As it is not my intention to contrast the usage of the discourse variable between the corpora by comparing frequencies, these differences in composition are not a major issue.

The two discourse-pragmatic variants I focus on here can be exemplified as in (1) and (2).[4] The example in (1) shows *please* as a politeness marker in a request. The example in (2) shows *sorry* as a politeness marker in an apology.

(1) Anette: *kanskje vi skal ## finne på et eller annet lurt i dag . . . # please da* 'maybe we should ## do something smart today . . . # please <particle>' (BBc: Anette)

(2) Anette: *oi **sorry** # jeg visste ikke dere var her jeg skal bare ha noe som tilhører Lars* '<interjection> sorry # I didn't know you were here I was just going to get something that belongs to Lars' (BBc: Anette)

The case studies that follow in the next section are based on analyses of tokens such as (1) and (2), where an illocutionary act is performed (request or apology) either by means of the borrowed forms *please* or *sorry* or by means of an equivalent domestic expression. For each token of the discourse variable, I evaluate the illocutionary force and strength of commitment to the feeling expressed. In doing so, I am following the method of Terkourafi (2011), but I also apply some explicit criteria directly observable in the transcription (repetition, co-occurrence with boosters, etc.) or audible in the audio/video file (intonation, emphatic stress). Although manifestations of the speech acts of request or apology are possible through other linguistic or non-linguistic means, I have chosen to focus exclusively on explicit realizations that involve the selection of one of the equivalent variant forms. I disregard tokens that occur as part of quotations or longer stretches of code-switching.

---

[4] I have retained the notations used in the original transcriptions. See the chapter appendix for transcription conventions.

12.3 Results: Anglicisms Used as Markers of Politeness

12.3.1 Requests with Please and Domestic Alternatives

Table 12.2 gives an overview of the use of *please*-requests in the spoken corpora vis-à-vis its equivalent domestic expressions.

There are, of course, many ways of making a request more polite. The use of discourse markers such as *please*, *vær så snill*, literally 'be so kind', or the adverbial *vennligst* 'kindly' is an explicit marking that adds to politeness by mitigating the face threat induced by the request. Other means may be modal expressions such as "could you," "it would be nice if...," by intonation, and so on. Since my main objective is to evaluate the use of the Anglicism vis-à-vis its direct domestic competitors, I decided to set aside modal expressions and intonation. Altogether sixty-one tokens of such explicit politeness marking were found in the corpora.

Table 12.2 demonstrates that the Anglicism is outnumbered by the domestic variants in all four corpora and for the dataset as a whole. Of the two domestic variants, *vennligst* is rare and generally outnumbered by *vær så snill*. It should be pointed out that these variants are not stylistically equivalent, as *vennligst* would be regarded as a relatively formal variant, especially associated with formal letters.

With only six tokens, *please* can be considered a marginal politeness marker in the four corpora. Seen from the total corpus frequencies in parentheses in Table 12.2, there were some tokens that were discarded for being part of longer stretches of code-switching into English (e.g., *somebody help me please*; BBc: Anette). The low frequency makes an interesting parallel with the marker's marginality in Cypriot Greek (Terkourafi 2011: 230). Previous corpus-based research has shown that *please* occurs primarily in indirect requests and mitigated commands but only secondarily in responses to offers, as in *yes please* and *please do*

Table 12.2 *Use of* please *and equivalent domestic polite expressions in requests (total corpus token frequency in parenthesis)*

Corpus	please	vær så snill	vennligst	total domestic	% please	% domestic
UNO	1 (6)	17	1	18	5.3%	94.7 %
Big Brother corpus	5 (8)	28 (30)	0 (1)	28	15.2%	84.8 %
NoTa Oslo	0	7	0 (1)	7	0.0%	100.0 %
Nordic Dialect Corpus	0 (1)	2	0	2	0.0%	100.0 %
Total	6	54	1	55	9.8%	90.2%

(Wichmann 2005: 239). There was one such token in the BBc, which was set aside.

The remaining tokens of *please* share an important qualitative feature: they all seem to be used in requests with a noticeable insistent and begging quality, as in example (3).

(3)   Ramsey: *du du har nå litt lyst til å bli Ramseyifisert har ikke du det?*
Anita: *ikke så veldig*
several unidentified speakers: _latter_
Roy: ramma _latter_
Ramsey: *jo*
Anita: *lengste jeg kan gå er å synge Guns and Roses-sanger med deg _latter_*
Ramsey: *litt sokking ?*
Anita: *nei*
Ramsey: *litt **please** kom igjen litt*
Roy: * *nei kom igjen da* *
(BBc: Ramsey)
Ramsey: you you do want to be ramseyfied a little, don't you?
Anita: not particularly
several unidentified speakers: <laughing>
Roy: rammed <laughing>
Ramsey: yes
Anita: the furthest I'll go is to sing Guns and Roses songs with you <laughing>
Ramsey: a little sucking?
Anita: no
Ramsey: a little, please, come on, a little
Roy: no, come on

Ramsey's offer of *litt sokking* as an exemplification of what it means to be "ramseyfied" is not an ordinary Norwegian verb, but it can be interpreted as a phonetically adapted version of the English verb "sucking." Again, signifying the sexual innuendoes of much of the talk in this corpus, Ramsey uses *please* to increase the insistence and tenacity of his efforts to get Anita to accept his invitation. Thus, the borrowed discourse marker seems to have a strengthening effect on the illocutionary act in which it is used (see Peterson, Hiltunen and Vaattovaara, Chapter 13, this volume). In fact, this is a qualitative feature of *please* in Norwegian that seems consistent across the (albeit few) tokens in the corpora. It is seen perhaps even clearer in (4) (the extended context of example (1)).

(4)   Anette: *kanskje vi skal ## finne på et eller annet lurt i dag*
Lars Joakim: *kanskje ikke?*
Anette: *jo_da*
Lars Joakim: *nei*
Anette: *jo_da # **please** da _fremre_klikkelyd_*

Lars Joakim: *nei*
Anette: * _latter_
Anette: **please**
several unidentified speakers overlapping: *hva som helst liksom | sånn som _uforståelig_*
Lars Joakim: *sånn som jeg har sagt jeg altså jeg veit du jeg veit du liker meg Anette men det det kommer ikke til å skje # du må jobbe litt mer*
(BBc: Anette)
Anette: maybe we should ## do something smart today
Lars Joakim: maybe not?
Anette: yes <particle>
Lars Joakim: no
Anette: yes <particle> please yes <particle> <click>
Lars Joakim: no
Anette: <laughing>
Anette: please
several unidentified speakers overlapping: like, anything | such as <unclear>
Lars Joakim: as I have told you <particle> I know you I know you like me Anette but it it is not going to happen # you have to work a bit more

Anette's two tokens of *please* are part of a longer strategy to convince Lars Joakim to spend time with her and probably also to gain his affection. The request is reinforced by the marker *please* alongside the particle *da*, which contributes on equal footing to strengthening the illocutionary force of these requests.

So how does this compare with the equivalent domestic expressions? The first thing to note is that one variant, *vennligst*, is only used once as a genuine request in the corpora, as shown in (5).

(5) Thomas: *klesklipern% kliperne mine, **vennligst** lever dem tilbake. har <utyd> du </utyd> ikke råd til klesklipere selv, nei*
Mari: (latter)
Michael: (latter)
(UNO: Thomas)
Thomas: the clothes peg- my clothes pegs, please give them back, can <unclear> you </unclear> not afford clothes pegs yourself, no
Mari: <laughing>
Michael: <laughing>

The context suggests that Thomas' request is to be interpreted as jocular, mirroring a stylistic level that seems over-formal and thus unfit for this conversational setting between adolescents. As seen from the total corpus tokens in Table 12.2, the form does appear with a token in the BBc and in NoTa too. These are in (unmarked) quotations, for instance, in narratives and are therefore disregarded from the percentage counts. In other words, in the varieties represented by the investigated spoken corpora, *vennligst* does not seem to be a genuine contestant to *please* and *vær så snill*.

Another point to be observed concerns the degree of syntactic freedom of the variants. Collectively, (3)–(5) show that *please* can tag onto propositional material as in Ramsey's *litt please* 'a little please' in (3) or as stand-alone utterances as in Anette's second *please* in (4), or with other discourse markers as in her first *please*-token in the same extract. The domestic variant *vær så snill* is equally flexible as it could replace the Anglicism in all of these contexts. This does not apply to *vennligst*. With the syntactic function of a sentence adverbial, this variant does not occur as a stand-alone utterance but needs to be syntactically integrated with propositional material that denotes the desired verbal action, as seen with Thomas' *vennligst lever dem tilbake* 'please give them back' in (5).

As for the more flexible domestic variant, it is clear that *vær så snill* can be used with the same insisting force as observed for *please* above, as in example (6).

(6)   Rodney: *nei men du du du du du e # _sukking_*
Rodney: *Anette du har aldri noensinne sagt # hva du føler for meg # hva v-_uforståelig_ nei hør hør på meg hør _uforståelig_ nei nei nei nei nei # nei men hør på meg # hør*
Anette: * *nei men _uforståelig_ vi har vært her i fjorten dager # vi har vært her i fjorten dager*
Rodney: * *_latter_* **vær så snill** *og hør på meg da # hør på meg hør på meg* **vær så snill** *# jeg mener det helt ærlig*
Anette: * *ja*
(BBc: Rodney)
Rodney: no but you you you you you e # <sighs>
Rodney: Anette you have never ever said # what you feel about me # what v- <unclear> no listen listen to me listen <unclear> no no no no no # no bu listen to me # listen
Anette: we have been here for fourteen days # we have been here for fourteen days
Rodney: <laughing> *please listen to me* <prt> # *listen to me listen to me please # I mean it honestly*
Anette: * yes

However, it is clear that the domestic variant has a wider spectrum of usage than what seems to be the case with *please*. This is seen from several utterances such as (7) where there is clearly a much lower degree of illocutionary force associated with the requests than evidenced in (6).

(7)   Anette: *å herregud det var morsomt eller? _latter_ herregud Anne Mona kan du hjelpe meg* **vær så snill***?*
Lars_Joakim: nei

several speakers: _latter_
Anne_Mona *hvorfor skal jeg å- hjelpe deg?*
(BBc: Anette)
Anette: *oh my god that was funny or?* <laughing> *oh my god Anne Mona can you help me please?*
Lars_Joakim: *no*
several speakers: <laughing>
Anne_Mona *why should I help you?*

The relative illocutionary strength of requests with *please* or a domestic variant can be evaluated according to a set of objective criteria that are observable through contextual and auditory cues in the discourse. These include the repetition of the requestive utterance; repetition of the discourse marker itself or another variant of it; co-occurrence with a strengthening discourse marker/ interjection or boosting adverb; co-occurrence with another variant of the discourse variable; or prosodic, and phonological cues such as vowel lengthening, emphatic stress, and/or rising intonation. Repetition of the requestive utterance as well as of the discourse marker *vær så snill* is illustrated by Rodney's request *hør på meg* in example (6). Repetition in the form of co-occurrence of two different variants is seen in (8).

(8)   Karoline: # *jeg vet. men eh= = nei nå glemte jeg hva jeg skulle si gitt,* #
        Eva: # *ja men hallo.* **vær så snill, please.**
        (UNO: Eva)
        Karoline: I know. but eh == no now I forgot what I was going to say <prt>
        Eva: yes but hello. please. please

Co-occurrence with an interjection or discourse marker is illustrated by Iren's utterance *åh vær så snill a* in (9), while co-occurrence with a boosting adverbial is evident in Rodney's *helt ærlig* 'honestly' in (6).

(9)   Iren: *hyggelig det ja.*
        Helene: *hyggelig det ja, hva mener du med det*
        Iren: **åh= vær så snill a**. *det er bare et uttrykk*
        (UNO: Iren)
        Iren: *that's nice yes*
        Helene: *that's nice yes, what do you mean by that*
        Iren: *oh please* <particle>. *it's just an expression*

It seems clear that such repetition and use with co-occurring strengthening adverbial and discourse marker adds to the illocutionary force of the request. For instance, Iren's request would be perceived as somewhat less forceful without the interjection *åh* 'oh' or the particle *a* in (9). While *please*-requests invariably display at least one of these features, and usually more than one, their absence is noticeable in the request with *vær så snill* in (7). This suggests

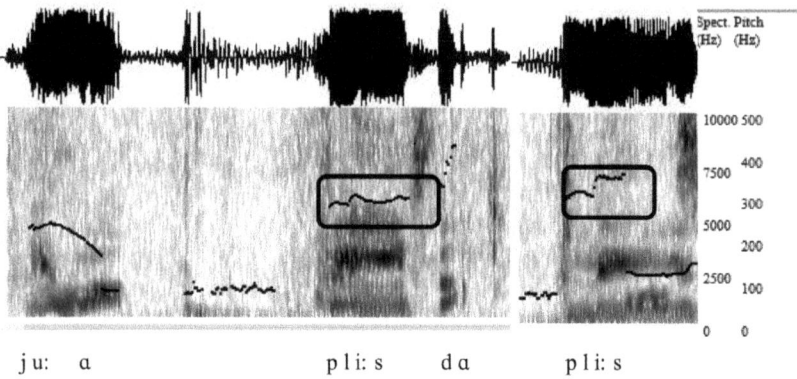

j u: a   p l i: s   d a   p l i: s

Figure 12.1 Waveform and spectrogram with *please*

that *vær så snill* can be used with relatively strong and relatively weak illocutionary force, while *please* appears to be restricted to the former of these two contexts in the corpora investigated. Although not directly observable from the transcriptions, the speakers commonly add to the insistency of requests using prosodic means. A considerably elongated vowel, additional stress, and a markedly raised intonation is used in several of the *please*-requests reported in this section, as well as in some of the tokens of *vær så snill*. For example, elongation and raised tone is illustrated by Anette's *jo_da # please da please* ['j u: a 'p l i: s d a 'p l i: s] in example (4), seen as a waveform and spectrogram in Figure 12.1 (the first token of *da* is pronounced without the stop but conveniently transcribed in its full form in the corpus).

In summary, setting aside the stylistically marked adverbial *vennligst*, it is the domestic variant *vær så snill* that displays the greater variability vis-à-vis its English-based competitor *please* in the corpus data at hand. Although the two would appear as largely interchangeable, *please* is invariably used with one or more of the strengthening discourse-contextual and auditory cues, while this is not the case for *vær så snill*. As regards interpretation, *please* is invariably used with a certain degree of insistency that is not necessarily felt with all tokens of *vær så snill*. Hence, I conclude that the illocutionary force of *please* is mostly greater than that of its domestic competitor variant. The latter, on the contrary, is readily used in joking, playful contexts where there is clearly a low degree of commitment towards the sincerity of the request, most notably seen in example (10).

(10)   Terese: *jeg har aldri før klatra på den= ribbeveggen her før.*
       Anette: *nei heng deg og så tar du:=*
       Una: *heng deg ja* <utyd/>

Una: *nå skal du henge deg Terese **vær så snill**.*
Elisabeth: (latter)
(UNO: Una)
Terese: I have never climbed these wall bars before
Anette: no hang yourself and then you take=
Una: hang yourself yes <unclear/>
Una: now you must hang yourself Terese, please.
Elisabeth: <laughing>

The observation that *please* is associated with relatively strong illocutions contrasts with Terkourafi's findings in Cypriot Greek, where *please* is the variant that expresses the least "strength of commitment to the feeling expressed (desire)" (Terkourafi 2011: 232). However, my study does corroborate her observation that "[t]he close association of 'please' with directive speech acts thus leaves little margin for it to develop additional discourse-marking functions" (Terkourafi 2011: 232). *Please* in Norwegian seems to invariably convey its core meaning of minimizing imposition between interlocutors as a "formulaic, conventionalized expression of courtesy, acknowledging varying degrees of indebtedness in conjunction with a request" (Wichmann 2005: 236–237). However, it could be argued that *vær så snill* serves an additional function in extract (9) in Iren's utterance *åh= vær så snill a. det er bare et uttrykk*. Uttered as a reaction to Helene's previous utterance, this is not a request in the ordinary sense, but it provides an attitudinal meta-comment conveying that Iren is critical as to the relevance of Helene's previous utterance *hyggelig det ja, hva mener du med det*. This invoked attitude of 'exasperation' could be captured by English expressions such as "Oh please!" (Wichmann 2005: 242) or "Give me a break!" The degree to which this attitudinal and discourse-marking function of *vær så snill* is conventionalized would require additional data than what has been considered here.

12.3.2 Apologies with Sorry *and Domestic Alternation*

Table 12.3 gives an overview of the use of *sorry* in apologies in the spoken corpora vis-à-vis its equivalent domestic expressions.

Analogous with requests, I set aside tokens where an apology is realized by other means than a borrowed or domestic variant. Three domestic expressions can be regarded as equivalents to *sorry*. None of these would be stylistically odd in conversation in the way that was described for *vennligst* in Section 12.3.1. However, the variants are only partly comparable with regard to their syntactic freedom or potential for syntactic integration. The markers *beklager* 'regret' and *er lei meg* 'am sorry' constitute verb phrases that enter into formulaic polite expressions when used with a first-person singular

Table 12.3 *Use of* sorry *and equivalent domestic polite expressions in apologies (total corpus token frequency in parenthesis)*

Corpus	sorry	beklager	er lei meg	unnskyld	total domestic	% sorry	% domestic
UNO	15 (16)	8 (9)	0	36 (50)	44	25.4%	74.6 %
Big Brother corpus	40 (52)	4 (12)	0	20 (46)	24	62.5%	37.5 %
NoTa Oslo	4 (8)	2 (5)	0	24 (37)	26	13.3%	86.7 %
Nordic Dialect Corpus	7	2 (8)	0	15 (20)	17	29.2%	70.8 %
Total	66	16	0	95	111	37.3%	62.7 %

pronoun and in the present tense. A clausal object denoting the theme, that is, explicating the offense that led to the apology (as in 'I am sorry that...') could accompany the formula, but this is not obligatory. In terms of word class, the apology marker *unnskyld* could be classified as an interjection, although its lexical source is the verb *unnskylde* 'apologize'. The interjection is usually not syntactically integrated or part of a verbal apologetic formula (**Jeg unnkylder at* 'I am sorry that'). However, it is conceivable to have a thematic clausal object denoting the reason for the apology (*unnskyld for at*..., lit. 'sorry for that...').

We observe from Table 12.3 that the Anglicism is outnumbered by the domestic variants in three of the four corpora and for the dataset as a whole. Again, a set of tokens were disregarded due to occurrence in longer code-switching contexts or in quotations (especially in narratives). The overall use of the Anglicism *sorry* in apologies amounts to 37.3 percent, in contrast to requests with *please* with a mere 11.3 percent. The borrowed form outnumbers domestic forms in the Big Brother corpus, with a ratio of 62.5 percent. We also observe that *unnskyld* is clearly the preferred choice of domestic marker in all the four corpora, *beklager* is quite rare, and *er lei meg* does not occur in the data investigated.

The differences between the corpora with regard to the use of apologies is closely tied to their different conversational dynamics. Recall that UNO and BBc are conversational corpora recorded in natural settings in the case of UNO and in the, admittedly artificial, studio setting of the Big Brother reality TV concept. Nevertheless, these corpora bear the hallmarks of conversation to a degree not found in NoTa or NDC. These sociolinguistic corpora are recorded in contrived studio settings in which two speakers sit quietly conversing at a table, of which some have assigned roles as interviewer and interviewee. Not only are apologies much more frequent overall in the two conversational corpora but, in the two sociolinguistic corpora, there is a strong tendency to use (non-quotational) apologies not for true offenses that significantly affect the relationship between the speakers but for metadiscoursal maneuvering. The controlled dyadic setting does not lend itself to the expression of sincere apologies for real transgressions, but it is a fertile ground for apologizing for slight situational offenses. These include apology for minor incidents such as clearing one's throat, coughing, or forgetting to turn off a cellphone, as in example (11); apology relating to turn-taking, for instance having unduly spoken at length or for interrupting, as in example (12); apology for the choice of a wrong word (self-repair) or a potentially unfitting or offensive word, as in example (13); and apology for a slight digression from the main topic.

(11) AMB: *men e du sa at du bodde b- på Bøler til du var ti*
AMB: *oi nå er det en telefon som ringer* <int>
123: *ja * det er min telefon yes *
AMB: *å ja*
123: *jeg skal skru av den det **beklager** jeg at jeg glemte den*
(NoTa: 123)
AMB: *but eh you said that you used to live at Bøler until you were ten*
AMB: *now there is a phone ringing*
123: * * it is my phone*
AMB: *ah yes*
123: *I'll turn it off sorry that I forgot it*

(12) 112: *ja * på en måte ... * altså det **unnskyld** at jeg avbryter deg men e ... * ja* yes * in a way ... * <particle> it sorry for interrupting you but eh ... * yes (NoTa: 112)

(13) 058: *jo det var alle de derre forbaskete tøsene det # **unnskyld*** yes it was all those damned bitches # sorry (NoTa: 058)

Self-repair is a related type of use that was singled out as a separate function by Terkourafi (2011). It is clear from the Norwegian data that apology markers also perform this function, as seen in example (14).

(14) 02: *nei jeg tenkte på lyden jeg da veldig kraftig her er øverste etasje det ville si det at # regnet lander rett oppå hodene våre # rett ovom hodet vårt **sorry** # ja* no I was thinking about the sound I <particle> very loud here is the top floor which meant that # the rain falls just on top of our heads # just above our head sorry # yes (NDC: namdalen_02uk)

The kinds of metadiscoursal negotiation illustrated in examples (11)–(14) are characteristic of the apologies in the sociolinguistic corpora. Such negotiation is observable in the two conversational corpora also, sometimes taking the shape of (near-formulaic) apologetic phrases such as *unnskyld uttrykket men* 'pardon the expression but' and *sorry at jeg sier det altså* 'sorry to say so' with a discourse function relating to the appropriateness of an expression, question, or statement.

Another notable and repetitive fixed phrase is *unnskyld meg* 'excuse me'. This is rarely used as a genuine apology for an offense but tends to appear in conflict-laden sequences as a quite forceful expression of the speaker attitude, as in the BBc participants' discussion about sexual debuts seen in example (15).

(15) Rebekka: *atten år på en barkrakk med sjefen min # ferdig med det*
Roy: *barkrakk?*
Rebekka: * *ja for jeg jobba på en bar*
Ramsey: *kvinnfolk de er så knulle sjef-greie*
Rodney: *ja # hva er det med sjefer?*
Ramsey: * *_lydmalende_ord_ det er standard* <*nonverbal sound*>
Ramsey: *ja # det er sånn knulle sjefer*
Rebekka: *jammen altså det er jo ikke det er ikke # du **unnskyld meg unnskyld meg** her du # du **unnskyld meg** # du hallo pause*
(BBc: Rebekka)
Rebekka: eighteen years on a bar stool and done with it
Roy: bar stool?
Rebekka: yeah cos I was working in a bar
Ramsey: women they are such fuck-their-bosses kind of thing
Rodney: yeah # what's the thing about bosses?
Ramsey: <nonverbal sound> it's typical
Ramsey: yeah # it's a kind of fuck the bosses
Rebekka: yeah but <particle> it's <particle> not it isn't # you excuse me excuse me here you # you excuse me # you hello pause

Although uttered in a context where she is grappling for the floor, Rebekka's utterance cannot be construed as an apology. Rather, the phrasal *unnskyld meg* expresses a sentiment of indignation and negative evaluation of the male speakers' generalization about women wanting to have sex with their bosses. This usage mirrors English non-apologetic use of 'I'm sorry, but' or 'Excuse me, but', for example as discussed by Borkin and Reinhart (1978) and Margerie and Muller (2019). As can be expected, this level of conflict does not characterize any of the dialogues in the sociolinguistic corpora; nevertheless, this marker of indignation does occur sporadically here also.

However, the most notable difference that sets the conversational corpora apart from the sociolinguistic ones, is the respective occurrence versus absence of sometimes strongly articulated genuine apologies that pertain to the relation between the speakers for states-of-affairs outside of the speech situation, as seen in examples (16), (17), and especially (18).

(16) *Per Morten: men poenget er at jeg vil bare si **unnskyld** for at ### e jeg reagerte sånn som jeg gjorde # på slutten # for det syns jeg var dumt* but the point is that I just want to say sorry for # reacting like I did # in the end # cos I think that was stupid (BBc: Per Morten)

(17) Anita: hei **sorry** jeg må bare ta på lyset litt jeg # jeg må hente en ny genser hey sorry I just need to put on the lights a little # I must pick up a new sweater
(BBc: Anita)

(18) Ramsey: *ja men denne der spydige holdninga kan du spare meg for # nå har jeg spart deg for spydige holdninger i to tre dager og nå kan du spare meg for den der spydige holdninga di*
Monica: * *det var ikke sp- # det var ikke spydig ment # det var ikke spydig ment ## det var ikke spydig ment det **beklager** jeg det var ikke spydig ment*
(BBc: Ramsey)

Ramsey: yeah but this here sarcastic attitude you can spare me from # now I have spared you from sarcastic attitudes for two three days and now you can spare me from that sarcastic attitude of yours
Monica: * it wasn't sar- # it wasn't meant sarcastically ### it it wasn't sarcastically meant I am sorry it wasn't sarcastically meant

So what do the data tell us about possible differences between domestic and borrowed variants of the discourse variable? We have seen from the examples so far that both *sorry* and the domestic variants *unnskyld* and *beklager* can serve either in metadiscoursal negotiation as illustrated in examples (11)–(14) or with genuine apologies as in examples (16)–(18). In other words, there is no categorical association between an individual form and a particular function.

This major divide between the conversational corpora UNO and BBc on the one hand and NoTa and NDC on the other has a bearing on illocutionary strength. It is inconceivable that a speaker would apologize for a sneeze, digression, or word choice in a way that signifies particularly strong apologetic illocutionary force. Therefore, virtually all tokens in the sociolinguistic corpora are classified as weak. This is very different from the conversational corpus data where situations are commonly connected with genuine apologies and sometimes communicated with strong illocutionary force, as seen especially in example (18). I applied similar criteria for evaluating strength as with requests in Section 12.3.1. A relatively strong illocutionary force is indicated by repetition of the theme of the apology or the apology marker; co-occurrence with a strengthening discourse marker/interjection or boosting adverb (e.g., *beklager så meget* 'I sincerely apologize'); co-occurrence with another variant of the discourse variable; or prosodic and phonological cues such as vowel lengthening, emphatic stress, and/or raised intonation. Thus, a sequence such as *det glemte jeg sorry sorry det glemte jeg* (BBc: Rodney) 'I forgot that sorry sorry I forgot that' is considered to have strong illocutionary force. I also considered the additional criterion of whether the utterance concerned a minor discourse-related offense such as sneezing or a genuine apology caused by a prior discourse-external event. The former group were virtually always associated with weak illocutionary force. Further, illocutions were considered as weak in contexts where the informants are clearly fooling around and half-ironically expressing apologies for actions that are mutually recognized as non-offensive.

What emerges from this analysis is a semi-consistent picture of division of labor: *sorry* has a weak illocutionary force in most contexts; in a mere twelve out of sixty-six contexts it was classified as strong (18.2 percent). This can be illustrated by the fact that, while *sorry* works fine in Anita's genuine apology for the mild offense of switching on the lights in example (17), it would seem unfitting in the strongly communicated apology in example (18). Further, *unnskyld* is used with strong illocutionary force in thirty of out ninety-five cases (31.6 percent), while *beklager* is used evenly with a strong and weak illocutionary force (strong in seven out of sixteen cases, i.e., 43.7 percent). These findings thus empirically corroborate the earlier work that shows the reduction of illocutionary force of borrowed pragmatic items such as expletives and apology markers (Galinsky 1967; Hilgendorf 1996; Graedler 1998; Onysko 2007, Andersen 2014). For instance, Andersen (2014: 28–29) suggests that *sorry* is mostly associated with low-stake contexts and not with sincere apologies for grave matters. It also mirrors Terkourafi's (2011: 230) observations regarding Cypriot Greek that the borrowed form is the weaker of the alternate forms. We note, however, that although *sorry* in Norwegian is clearly associated with minor inconveniences such as speech interrupted by coughing or the like, such contexts are not a categorical prerequisite for its usage.

A final point concerns the phraseological context of *sorry*. As has been pointed out by Andersen (2015), the form sometimes occurs in phrases that have been imported wholesale. In the data investigated here, this is manifested as *sorry guys* and *sorry Mac*. While *sorry guys* can be an apology addressed towards a plural audience, the expression *sorry Mac* readily occurs in contexts where there is no expression of regret towards a co-interlocutor.

(19)   Roy: *det er ikke meg sa jeg # jeg kan ikke synge det # **sorry Mac*** it's not me I said # I can't sing it # sorry Mac (BBc: Roy)

Rather than an apology, Roy's utterance is a statement of an inescapable fact for which he takes no blame. In this type of use, the marker sometimes takes on senses akin to the English expressions "sorry pal," "sorry Charlie," or even "your loss" or "fix it!" In such phrasal contexts, there is no interchangeability between the borrowed form and the domestic variants.

12.4   Concluding Discussion

The two case studies have shown that for both discourse-pragmatic variables – requests and apologies – domestic and borrowed variants are used interchangeably. This was the case in all the four spoken corpora investigated, with the exception that *please* did not occur in NoTa. The Anglicism variants were outnumbered by the domestic forms for both discourse variables. As was expected, it is the two conversational corpora UNO and BBc that provide the most fertile environment for these pragmatic variables generally and for the borrowed variants. There was a major difference between the corpora in that apologies are only used for minor situational offenses in the sociolinguistic corpora but, additionally, for genuine apologies in the conversational corpora. This is an important methodological point to be acknowledged when studying apologies across corpora collected with different sampling methods.

How do these findings compare with the observations about similar contact phenomena in earlier studies? Using corpora available in the form of audio and video data, this study in some respects corroborates earlier studies and in other respects leads to new insights. Both borrowed and domestic forms are used with strong and weak commitment to the illocutionary act they perform. The qualitative inspection of individual tokens of discourse markers has led to two contrasting observations regarding their function. The (albeit few) tokens of non-quotational use of the request marker *please* share an association with the speaker's insistence and tenacity in their efforts to convince the hearer to perform the desired action. The illocutionary force of *please* is mostly greater than that of its domestic competitor variants and it is mainly associated with a relatively strong commitment to the illocutionary act of requesting. This finding is surprising since it contrasts with the general observation in studies of pragmatic borrowing that illocutionary force is usually reduced during transfer from the SL to the RL (for instance, with borrowed swearwords). It runs counter to the behavior of *please* noted by Terkourafi (2011), which had a generally weak illocutionary force in Cypriot Greek. Further, there were no observable traces of the positive politeness functions observed with *pliis* in Finnish by Peterson (2017).

The apology marker *sorry* is mostly associated with weak commitment to the illocutionary act of apologizing. Thus, this part of the study corroborates observations made impressionistically by Andersen (2014) about the relative illocutionary force of *sorry* vis-à-vis its domestic variants, and it aligns with Terkourafi's (2011) observations in Cypriot Greek. However, there were no signs of the functional shift to an expression of emphatic stance seen with *sori* in Bislama (Meyerhoff 1999). The function of self-repair – performed by *sorry* in Cypriot Greek but not by domestic forms – is served by the borrowed as well as the domestic forms in Norwegian (see example (14)).

The study has also shown that the domestic and borrowed variants are not interchangeable in all contexts. For request markers, it was pointed out that *vær så snill* was used where no request was intended but where it invoked an attitude of exasperation akin to the English "Oh please!" (Wichmann 2005: 242). I have found no signs that the borrowed variant *please* is used to perform this function in Norwegian. Similarly, the apology marker *sorry* enters into a phrasal context such as *sorry Mac* where none of the domestic forms could have been used. It was also argued that the variants of the request variable were not interchangeable on stylistic grounds, since the formality of one variant, *vennligst*, seems to prevent non-ironic/non-quotational use in most conversational contexts. For the discourse variable of apology, no similar stylistic constraint was observed.

The study has mainly focused on assessing the interchangeability of the variants and the possible specialization of functions. It has not concerned itself with identifying the speaker groups that seem to be the instigators of the innovation towards English-based forms. The total number of tokens of *please* is too small to make any meaningful statistical comparison, but it can be added briefly here that, as expected, it is predominantly the younger speakers who use *sorry* (only one token uttered by a speaker in the oldest age group), while the gender distribution is equal (59 percent female).

I have argued that the domestic and borrowed forms can be construed as variants of two discourse-pragmatic variables. The discourse-pragmatic variationist method seems to have a lot to offer with regard to the analysis of borrowed versus domestic forms. The main observation to be drawn from the case studies is that we should not consider the English forms as replacing their domestic equivalents, but they may eventually develop distinct functions, traces of which have been identified in this chapter. The qualitative assessment of the discourse function of individual tokens revealed important findings with potentially more general implications for other markers and in other languages. For both cases, there are pragmatic factors at play that lead to divisions of labor between the borrowed and domestic variants. The borrowed variant *please* tends to convey the speaker's insistence and tenacity, while the domestic variants have a wider range of use. The borrowed variant *sorry* tends to be used in speech situations that are less offensive, while domestic forms are preferred where there is a greater need for face-threat mitigation. Investigating a larger and more updated dataset could shed more light on such pragmatic conditioning.

Appendix

Transcription Conventions

BBc/NoTa/NDC	UNO	Explanation
hvi-	hvi%	cut-off word
	<utyd> ... </utyd>	metalinguistic feature (e.g., unclear)
latter	(latter)	non-linguistic event (e.g., laughter)
#		short pause
##		medium pause
...	author's omission	author's omission
*		overlapping speech

13 A Place for *pliis* in Finnish

A Discourse-Pragmatic Variation Account of Position

Elizabeth Peterson, Turo Hiltunen, and Johanna Vaattovaara

13.1 Introduction

Pliis 'please', a borrowing from English into Finnish, has become an established part of everyday Finnish discourse. Although first attested in spoken form already in the 1940s (Paunonen and Paunonen 2000), systematic research on *pliis* – and on pragmatic borrowings in general – is relatively scarce in Finnish. Based on firsthand observations, Taavitsainen and Pahta (2012: 200) suggested that *pliis* is an "in-group identity marker in teen-age peer group talk," offering initial support to the hypothesis that, in terms of social values, *pliis* is a relatively stigmatized, context-sensitive feature. Subsequent accounts of *pliis*, including Peterson and Vaattovaara 2014, demonstrate that *pliis* is perceived to be used across different social and age groups, though it is typically associated with urban, young, and feminine styles.

Through our previous perceptual research on *pliis* (reported in Peterson and Vaattovaara 2014), we gained initial understanding of the form's social meaning potentials (see Eckert 2008). What remains to be accounted for are the grammatical characteristics of this form, for example how it has been incorporated into Finnish syntax and morphology and how the borrowed form relates to other forms of Finnish politeness, especially the heritage lexical politeness marker *kiitos* (see Andersen, Chapter 12, this volume).

Our aims with the current investigation are twofold. First, we wish to reassess the findings of our previous study, which suggest that, unlike the heritage lexical politeness marker *kiitos*, *pliis* is preferred in a clause-internal position. Like several chapters in this volume, the present chapter addresses one of the main challenges of discourse-pragmatic variation studies: the question of accountability when dealing with linguistic variables that are by

---

* The authors thank their research assistant, Katariina Pyykkö. We also thank Dr. Tapani Kelomäki for reading an early draft of the chapter.

definition functionally ambiguous (see Wiltschko et al. 2018). In our treatment of this challenge, we wish to explore and underscore the need for studies of discourse-pragmatic variables to make use of multiple datasets (data triangulation), even when addressing what appears to be a straightforward question – such as that of clausal position. This question is especially pertinent for a language like Finnish, which, due to its structural properties, in principle has a relatively free word order compared to languages such as English.

The second aim is to contribute to the research on Finnish requests. We limit our exploration to requests for two reasons. First, although *pliis*, like *please* in English, can be found in a number of linguistic constructions, we need to limit our dataset within a comparable set of parameters. In addition, *pliis*, like *please*, is naturally connected to requests. As pointed out in some of the earlier work of House (1989), for example, *please* is associated with requests, prompting House even to use the term *requestive marker* to refer to *please*.

Finally, our chapter contributes to the work on what has been called "opportunistic data," or in other words data that is not collected per se, nor is it part of a corpus, but is there for the taking (McEnery and Hardie 2011: 11). We return to methodological concerns with this type of data at the end of the chapter.

13.2 Discourse-Pragmatic Variation and Pragmatic Borrowing

There are two central research areas informing our investigation of *pliis* in Finnish. One is *pragmatic borrowing*, understood as the phenomenon whereby pragmatic elements are incorporated from one language (in this case, English) into another (in this case, Finnish). Other chapters in this volume investigating pragmatic borrowing include Kern (Chapter 11) and Andersen (Chapter 12). Pragmatic borrowings have only recently begun to attract scholarly interest as a language contact phenomenon. This is surprising, because, as Andersen (2014: 19) observes, borrowed pragmatic features are highly noticeable (i.e., *salient*) and are frequently incorporated into everyday speech. Following what has been termed a "pragmatic turn" (see Andersen et al. 2017; Andersen, Chapter 12) in language borrowing research, we focus on how the borrowed form enters into the recipient language, where it takes on specific meanings, patterns, and social functions (cf. Andersen 2014). The process of borrowing politeness markers tends to follow a common path of evolution, where the borrowed markers are "gradually bleached of their speech-act signaling potential" Terkourafi (2011: 218) and instead function as discourse markers.

The second main research area informing our perspective is the main theme of this volume, *discourse-pragmatic variation*. Methodologically, our investigation has benefited from recent contributions to discourse-pragmatic variation analysis (e.g., Levey et al. 2013; Pichler 2013; Andersen 2014; Pichler 2016a; D'Arcy 2017; Wiltschko et al. 2018). Of relevance to us are previous studies on other discourse markers (e.g., *just, like*) and intensifiers (e.g., *so*), as they provide information about functions and preferred clausal positions. Our investigation offers information on Finnish and serves as a relatively rare example of an investigation of the variation of a lexical politeness marker.

It is well established in the study of discourse-pragmatic variation that the variables we work with are context-sensitive (Degand, Broisson, Crible, and Grzech, Chapter 4; Eiswirth, Chapter 8; Schleef and Mackay, Chapter 2, this volume). With this in mind, it is clear that any one method is unlikely to offer representative and accountable findings to justify claims of any one principal function of *pliis*. This is because discourse-pragmatic variation analysis is confronted with several issues related to the complexity of the forms in question, which are summarized in Pichler (2013: 21): discourse-pragmatic features eschew easy definition as linguistic variables, identifying all contexts and competing variants for discourse-pragmatic features is difficult, and discourse-pragmatic features are variable and changeable with respect to both form and function. These issues have remained relevant as the field of inquiry has grown during the past decade or so.

Wiltschko et al. (2018: 570) present three main challenges confronting researchers of discourse-pragmatic variation: (1) How do discourse-pragmatic researchers handle the question of equivalency? (2) In the face of functional ambiguity, how can accountability be maintained? (3) How can the principal function of a form be determined? With *pliis*, which as a lexical politeness marker has a rather limited range of functions compared to other discourse-pragmatic variables (e.g., *like, you know, innit*) our main concern lies with issue (2), accountability, although clearly the three issues overlap.

An overarching question driving our investigation of *pliis* has been: Why borrow the English form *pliis* when a functional equivalent, *kiitos*, also a lexical politeness marker, already exists in Finnish? Our basic premise is that *pliis* accomplishes pragmatic and social functions that *kiitos* and other heritage forms in Finnish do not.

Our previous research investigated the preferred clausal position of *pliis* in *conventionally indirect requests* (Blum-Kulka et al. 1989), here meaning request clauses containing the modal verb *voida* 'to be able/can'. The findings indicated that *pliis* was preferred between the modal verb and the main verb, while the preferred position for *kiitos* in the same sentence was at the end of the clause (Peterson and Vaattovaara 2014: 257–258). This initial finding raised the question of impenetrability of the clause: Why would a pragmatic borrowing, a politeness marker, behave differently in the clause than a heritage politeness marker?

Our aim to address issues of accountability has been informed by the principle of triangulation: building on a pilot study for the current study, establishing baseline data, and exploring multiple related datasets. In this chapter, we first offer an overview of the linguistic situation in Finland (Section 13.3) and the system of requests and politeness of Finnish (Section 13.4). Section 13.5 presents our analysis of the preferred clausal positions in different sentence configurations, drawing on the "transit data" (Section 13.5.1) and the computer-mediated communication (CMC) data (Section 13.5.2). Finally, in Section 13.6, we discuss the complementary and conflicting findings suggested by each dataset. In the conclusion, we address the aims of the study in light of our findings.

13.3 Contact with English

The relationship between English and Finnish is one of unidirectional "weak" language contact (see Andersen, Chapter 12), one where the influence of English does not stem from so-called "strong" contact between native speakers of the two languages. For the majority of the Finnish population, English is introduced through formal means and as a consecutive or third language. English does not have official status in Finland in the same sense as the two national languages, Finnish and Swedish (see, e.g., Leppänen et al. 2008). However, between formal and informal input, the end result is that, in the present day, the average Finn has a reasonable command of English. English is the first foreign language of the majority of Finnish students (OSF 2015, 2016), and approximately 70 percent of the population are able to carry on a conversation in English (self-reported, European Commission 2012). The domains of use for English range from entertainment to academia, and the attitudes towards it are generally positive (Leppänen et al. 2011). In Thøgersen's (2004: 25) comparison of the "linguistic climate" in the Nordic societies, Finland occupies a middle position between the Faroe Islands and Norway (most purist) and Sweden and Denmark (most open to outside influence) (see also Svavarsdóttir et al. 2010).

Following Hickey (2010) and a tradition dating back to Bloomfield (1933), we refer to the type of borrowing stemming from such contact situations as *cultural*; the key factor in the modern era is the hegemony of English in (perceived) cultural influence and international communication. Discourse-pragmatic markers are a recognized borrowing phenomenon in such language contact situations, and there are plenty of English-sourced features in contemporary Finnish (see Peterson 2017). Along with *pliis*, the forms *jees* 'yes', *okei* 'ok', *kamoon* 'c'mon', and *all right* are used in colloquial Finnish, among many others (Taavitsainen and Pahta 2012).

13.4 Finnish Politeness and Earlier Work on *Pliis*

The Finnish politeness system has been described as "withdrawing and evasive" (Yli-Vakkuri 2005: 191), which is manifested, for example, in the tendency for direct reference to the addressee to be avoided in favor of other syntactic perspectives. In general, it has been said that less is more when it comes to

Finnish politeness (Sorjonen et al. 2017; Isosävi 2020), although this is not meant to imply that Finnish lacks resources when it comes to demonstrating linguistic politeness (see Lappalainen 2008; Tanner 2010). For example, while both Finnish and English make use of conventionally indirect requests (Blum-Kulka et al. 1989), Finnish is unlike English when it comes to the use of lexical politeness markers in requests. In English, the lexical politeness marker *please* is commonly used to mitigate requests. While Finnish has the lexical politeness marker *kiitos* 'please/thank you', it is relatively infrequent in everyday language (Yli-Vakkuri 2005; Markkanen 1985) and tends to mark formality in discourse (VISK, the online version of *Iso suomen kielioppi* '*The Big Finnish Grammar*'; see also Peterson and Vaattovaara, 2014). Rather than lexical politeness markers, Finnish commonly utilizes grammatical resources to mitigate the force of a request, including question particles, negation, clitics, and the use of specific cases, tenses, and moods (Yli-Vakkuri 2005: 199–200). This general tendency makes for an interesting question regarding the borrowing of the lexical politeness marker *pliis*: If Finnish speakers tend to disprefer lexical politeness markers, why have they borrowed *pliis* into Finnish discourse?

Our initial investigation of *pliis* (Peterson and Vaattovaara 2014) set out to address this question: How is *pliis* perceived to behave in variation with other lexical politeness markers in Finnish, in particular *kiitos* 'please/thank you', which, as part of Standard Finnish, is the default, unmarked variant? As *kiitos* is a multifunctional politeness marker, used for both thanking and requesting, we tested the possibility that *pliis* could be taking on some of the requesting functions of *kiitos*. To this end, we conducted a grammatical acceptability test and a joint attitude and perception test on *pliis* compared to *kiitos*, which showed that our initial hypothesis was too simplistic: we did not find evidence that *pliis* was overtaking the requesting functions of *kiitos*. Rather, *pliis* appears to be associated with specific contexts or types of social relations, social groups, and styles, notably young, urban females. As a social group, it is young (urban) women who often lead linguistic change, but this change likely carries social stigma (Labov 2001b; Peterson 2017). The findings of Peterson and Vaattovaara (2014) suggested that *pliis* fills a pragmatic gap in Finnish: it serves as a lexical politeness marker that offers the possibility to index informality, solidarity, and intimacy (cf. *positive politeness*).

In the same survey we also asked respondents to assess where in a conventionally indirect request the politeness markers *pliis* or *kiitos* would seem "most natural." The findings are presented in Table 13.1. Example (1) offers a gloss of the base sentence shown in Table 13.1.

(1) *Voitko   antaa   sen*
     Can-2SG-CON-Q give-INF   it-GEN
     'Can you give me that?'

Table 13.1 *Preferred position of* pliis *and* kiitos *on a Likert scale of 0 to 3: Can you give me that?*

	mean		mean
<u>Pliis</u> voitko antaa sen?	1.43	<u>Kiitos</u> voitko antaa sen?	1.98
Voitko <u>pliis</u> antaa sen?	1.67	Voitko <u>kiitos</u> antaa sen?	1.9
Voitko antaa sen, <u>pliis</u>?	1.5	Voitko antaa sen, <u>kiitos kiitos</u>?	2.71

Adapted from Peterson and Vaattovaara (2014)

The results in Table 13.1 emphasize that *pliis* is a dispreferred form in Finnish: in no syntactic position does it rate as high as *kiitos*. That said, the preferred slots to emerge for the respective forms are after the modal *voitko* 'can you (2SG)' for *pliis* and in clause-final position for *kiitos*. In light of previous accounts of Finnish, this finding for *kiitos* was expected, but it muddies the waters for *pliis*: the borrowed politeness marker appears to behave grammatically in a way that distinguishes it from the heritage form.

Because our initial investigation of *pliis* was limited to testing only one type of request through an acceptability test, the findings had to be treated with caution, with an obvious need for further, non-elicited empirical data. What follows is an overview of request types in Finnish and our continued investigation for possible positions of *pliis* in Finnish requests.

Within the context of cross-cultural pragmatic studies, it has been pointed out that, in Finnish, the request that seems neither too formal nor too impolite contains a conditional form, but not necessarily a modal, and no politeness marker (Markkanen 1985; see also Peterson 2004), as demonstrated through the following examples.[1]

(2) *Sulkisitko   ikkunan?*
     Shut-2SG-CON-Q window-GEN
     Would you shut the window?

(3) *Voisitko   sulkea   ikkunan?*
     Can-2SG-CON-Q shut-INF window-GEN
     Could you shut the window?

(4) *Voisitko   sulkea   ikkunan   kiitos?*
     Can-2SG-CON-Q shut-INF window-GEN   PM
     Could you shut the window, please/thank you?

---

[1] *Ole hyvä* is the form of *please* used in the context of offering something in Finnish, for example *Ota kahvia, ole hyvä* 'Take some coffee, please'. Because *ole hyvä* overlaps in the functions of *please* only in this type of speech act, we do not consider it in our analysis.

In other words, the optimally polite request for many circumstances in Finnish is a form like (2), which contains a conditional verb inflected in the second person, posed as an interrogative. The request in (3) is considered perhaps unnecessarily polite in that it contains a modal verb, in this case in the conditional mood. The request in (4), then, could often be considered too formal (see Peterson 2004). Thus, grammatical equivalence between two languages clearly does not equate pragmatic equivalence. This means that just because a grammatical structure exists in two separate languages does not mean the structure has the same pragmatic function or social meanings in both languages. Empirical data on Finnish (Yli-Vakkuri 2005) reveals that the most frequently occurring type of request in everyday discourse is, in fact, an imperative.

Obviously, there is no feasible means of listing every possible request type in Finnish, but Table 13.2 presents an overview of seven representative request types in Finnish and those we deal with in this study. The list is compiled based on Finnish grammars (e.g., VISK) and research on Finnish requests. The request

Table 13.2 *Representative request types in Finnish (non-comprehensive)*

	Explanation	Example + gloss
request type 1	elliptical; noun phrase	*Suolaa!* salt-PAR 'Salt!'
request type 2	imperative	*Heitä suolaa!* throw-2SG-IMP salt-PART 'Give me the salt!'
request type 3	interrogative	*Annatko suolaa?* Give-2SG-Q salt-PAR? 'Will you give me the salt?'
request type 4	negative imperative	*Älä huuda!* Don't-2SG shout-CONEG 'Don't shout!'
request type 5	negative present indicative	*Ethän huuda.* NEG-2SG-hAn shout-CONEG '(You) don't shout.'
request type 6	conventionally indirect	*Voisitko antaa suolaa?* can-CON-2SG give-INF salt-PAR 'Could you give the salt?'
request type 7	third-person statement	*Täällä ei saa huutaa.* here NEG-3SG can-CONEG shout-INF 'No yelling here.'

Note. In fact, the possible directive types in Finnish would be difficult to describe in one list, including passive, zero-person constructions, both positive and negatives indicatives, and so on (see VISK; Jokela 2012).

types presented here in numbered order are used as labels throughout the remainder of the chapter.[2]

Request type 1, consisting of a noun phrase, is the minimum amount of linguistic material that can be interpreted in our datasets as a request (equivalent to English verbless directives; see Huddleston and Pullum 2002: 945). Request type 2 is a classic unmitigated imperative, whereas the request type 3 is already minimally mitigated through the use of question marker *-ko*. Request types 4 and 5 offer a contrast in how negative commands can be formed in Finnish, with form 4 containing the Finnish equivalent of 'don't' and form 5 containing a negated verb in the present indicative. Both of these request types are best translated into English as 'Don't –' but the grammatical distinction in Finnish is meaningful, as demonstrated further in Section 13.5.1. Request type 6 shows the Finnish means of expressing a conventionally indirect request (Blum-Kulka et al. 1989), in this example with a verb in the conditional mood. The 'can' verb could also occur in the present indicative. Finally, request type 7 is an example of a zero-person clause expressed in a third-person perspective.

These request types offer a number of possible positions for lexical politeness markers. This is not to say that all positions are equally idiomatic or carry the same pragmatic weight and (social) meaning. To establish a baseline for comparison to our non-elicited datasets, we gained grammatical acceptability input on *pliis* and *kiitos* from five different groups of university students (N=135), who were instructed to add the target politeness marker (*pliis* or *kiitos*) to sample requests like those shown in Table 13.2. Following Wiltschko et al. (2018), our aim was first to establish the envelope of variation through baseline data, which we saw as a necessary step to lend a lens of interpretation to our eventual quantitative observations. After establishing the envelope of variation, we then wanted to determine how people actually use these lexical politeness markers. Tables 13.3 and 13.4 show the positional preferences of *kiitos* and *pliis* in the baseline tests.

The Finnish examples in Tables 13.3 and 13.4, numbered 1–7, are the same as in the representative request types presented in Table 13.2. In Tables 13.3 and 13.4, the columns headed with the notation "PM" (standing for *politeness marker*, shaded in gray) refer to possible slots for a lexical politeness marker. The numbers offered in each of these PM columns represent the total number of responses from the baseline tests. The respondents to the baseline tests were instructed to fill in one example of either *kiitos* or *pliis* in the request types 1–7. Opting out of using a lexical politeness marker was not an option. In some cases, respondents either did not answer a question or answered the same question more than once, which is why the numbers in the "total" column are

---

[2] In this chapter, we use the term *request type* to refer chiefly to a grammatical structure that forms a request. We use the term *request strategy* to refer to the pragmatic function of a request, as found in the discourse that comprises our empirical data.

Table 13.3 Baseline (elicited) positions for kiitos in seven request types.

	PM1	adv	PM2	neg	PM3	aux	PM4	verb	PM5	obj	PM6	Total
RT1	0	—	×	—	×	—	×	—	×	Suolaa!	57	57
RT2	0	—	×	—	×	—	×	Heitä	12	suolaa!	38	50
RT3	2	—	×	—	×	—	×	Annatko	8	suolaa?	49	59
RT4	13	—	×	Älä	8	—	×	huuda!	×	—	41	59
RT5	7	—	×	Ethän	12	—	×	huuda.	×	—	38	57
RT6	2	—	×	—	×	Voisitko	8	antaa	1	suolaa?	49	60
RT7	10	Täällä	0	ei	3	saa	3	huutaa.	×	—	41	57

Note. The information in this table is meant to be a heuristic/illustrative device to help illustrate our request prototypes and the clausal positions available in them; it is not intended in any way as a theory-bound syntactic description of Finnish requests.
RT=request type.

Table 13.4 *Baseline (elicited) positions for pliis in seven request types.*

	PM1	ADV	PM2	NEG	PM3	AUX	PM4	V	PM5	OBJ	PM6	Total
RT1	13	—	×	—	×	—	×	—		*Suolaa!*	73	86
RT2	11	—	×	—	×	—	×	*Heitä*	41	*suolaa!*	35	87
RT3	17	—	×	—	×	—	×	*Annatko*	42	*suolaa?*	28	87
RT4	27	—	×	*Älä*	50	—	×	*huuda!*	×	—	11	88
RT5	23	—	×	*Ethän*	51	—	×	*huuda.*	×	—	14	
RT6	6	—	×	—	×	*Voisitko*	38	*antaa*	2	*suolaa?*	39	85
RT7	53	*Täällä*	2	*ei*	10	*saa*	6	*huutaa.*	×	—	14	85

Note. The positions indicated for *pliis* are most likely possible slots for adverbials and placement in Finnish clauses is yet to be conducted. To our knowledge, a study of types of adverbials and placement in Finnish clauses is yet to be conducted.
RT=request type.

not equal. This further baseline data partially overlaps with our previous survey data (presented in Table 13.1), namely that *kiitos* is preferred in final position, whereas the preferred position for *pliis* is more mixed.

With baseline data offering us some hypotheses for consideration, the next stage is to attest these findings in a quantitative fashion by looking at empirical, unelicited data. Specifically, the hypotheses in place for our naturalistic, unelicited data are that *pliis* is dispreferred in clause-final position, *kiitos* is preferred in clause-final position, and *pliis* is more likely than *kiitos* to be used clause-medially or at least as a clause-internal element. The two datasets used to test our claims comprise the remainder of the chapter.

13.5 Analysis

Discourse-pragmatic features are notoriously difficult to observe in adequate number in spoken language corpora to allow for variationist analysis, yet the aims of this study call for a variationist approach. A politeness marker like *pliis* is even further limited due to its narrow set of functions compared to more ubiquitous discourse-pragmatic features such as *like*, *you know*, and *innit*. Indeed, our investigations of the wide breadth of currently available collections of Finnish speech data revealed there are far too few instances of *pliis* to provide a basis for any type of quantitative analysis. To circumvent the issue of availability, yet with a need to use data featuring informal language use, we turned to CMC. Although it varies widely, depending on the format and users, CMC is characterized as blurring the division between written and spoken language (see, e.g., Herring et al. 2013).

Two different CMC datasets were used in the investigations. The first is an opportunistic, experimental collection, while the second is a corpus compiled from web-scraped text. In addition to being empirical, non-elicited, and quantitative, the two datasets present other assets, as well. The opportunistic dataset was a boon for our purposes in that it was a large set of data comprised almost exclusively of requests, as well as thousands of tokens of the lexical politeness markers *kiitos* and *pliis*, presenting a unique opportunity for obtaining quantitative data about the variation in the use of these elusive discourse-pragmatic features of Finnish. As such, we were able to analyze the entire dataset as examples of requests. With the web-scraped text, our method was necessarily different: owing to the sheer magnitude of the data, it was impossible to delineate only requests for analysis, so our tactic was to retrieve stretches of discourse that included the lexical politeness markers *kiitos* or *pliis*. There is thus a different type of logic applied to the two datasets. For the opportunistic transit data (see Section 13.5.1), the data was considered requests because of the forum in which they appeared. For the web-scraped data (see Section 13.5.2.), tokens were determined by virtue of containing either *kiitos* or *pliis*. Because of these datasets, we have additional insights to offer about methodological issues, which we return to in Section 13.6.

13.5.1 Transit Data

From January to May 2012, Helsinki Transit Company (Helsingin Seudun Liikenne, HSL in Finnish) sponsored a campaign called *Matkarauhaa* 'Travel Peace'. The campaign featured posters displayed around the greater Helsinki region, a reggae song performed a Finnish pop singer, and an online component that allowed commuters to write on a website their wishes and concerns about local travel. It is this online component that we refer to as the *transit data*.

The campaign entailed use of the slogan *Ethän pliis*, which best translates into English as 'Please don't' (example (5); see also request type 5 in Table 13.2). This slogan was featured in the refrain of the campaign's theme song as well as the introductory text on the campaign posters, and it was incorporated into many of the subsequent customer responses on the campaign's website. For the five months the campaign ran, there were 5,614 online text entries (containing a total of 41,000 words) anonymously logged into the campaign's website via a public Facebook link. These entries comprise our "opportunistic corpus" (see also McEnery and Hardie 2011: 11).

The language used in the campaign slogan merits attention. The formation of the slogan, *ethän pliis* is comprised of a negated verb in the present indicative, as in (5).

(5) Ethän   pliis
     NEG-SG2-HAN   PM
     'Please don't'

The construction in (5) consists of the verbal negator *et* 'you don't'.[3] The inflected negator can occur without a verb, as seen in (5), or it can co-occur with a verb in the connegative form, as seen in request type 5. The clitic particle *–han/hän* co-occurs in (5) with the verbal negator *et*. The *-han/hän* clitic particle, widespread in Finnish discourse, mostly occurs with second-person constructions. It has a number of functions, which include addressing a social equal or someone of lower social power, or emphasizing known information (VISK §1673). The second-person singular form, along with *-han/hän*, highlights the quest for solidarity (see Yli-Vakkuri 2005) and appeal to shared local norms in the advertising campaign.

The expected outcome with the transit dataset was that the respondents would show orientation toward perceived Helsinki style, demonstrated through content but also through localized variants of verbs, nicknames for public transportation, and through use of the word *pliis*, which our studies have

---

[3] Verbal negation is inflected in Finnish according to person and number, rendering the negator an auxiliary verb (VISK §108). The complete verbal negator paradigm is as follows: *en* 'I don't', *et* 'you sg. don't', *ei* 'he/she/it doesn't', *emme* 'we don't', *ette* 'you pl. don't', *eivät* 'they don't'.

shown to be associated with Helsinki via particular styles (see also Lehtonen 2015: 134, 294). In feedback from native speakers of Finnish, the *ethän pliis* slogan has been characterized for us as targeting a local Helsinki audience and as somewhat contrived or unnatural, clearly made for advertising purposes. Indeed, in ordinary signage about how to behave on Helsinki public transport, requests are expressed using the lexical politeness marker *kiitos kun* 'thanks when', which, as demonstrated in this section, was also the preferred choice among respondents to the 2012 Travel Peace campaign.

The entries in the transit data ranged in length from three to approximately thirty words. The entries were downloaded from the transit company website, saved in a spreadsheet format, and categorized according to syntactic structure, positive or negative verbs, the presence or absence of a politeness marker, and the verbs used in the main clause. Obvious duplicate entries were removed, and entries in languages other than Finnish were not included in the analysis. After pruning, the transit data comprise 5,319 requests, of which 736 featured *pliis* and 1,054 the heritage politeness marker *kiitos*.

There were seven main request types apparent in the transit data, listed in Table 13.5, demonstrating a range of directness and grammatical composition.

A number of points emerge in Table 13.5. First, this data does not, for the most part, feature the request types presented in our baseline data in Tables 13.3 and 13.4, based on previous research on Finnish requests. Further, the most

Table 13.5 *Most frequent request strategies in transit data + lexical politeness markers*

	Transit data request strategy	N	kiitos	pliis
1.	*Kiva kun / Mukava kun ...*[*] 'It's nice/great when ... '	1,551	0/1,551	0/1,551
2.	*Ethän / Ethän kiitos / Ethän pliis ...* '(Please) don't' [present indic.][**]	944	14/944	712/944
3.	*Älä / Älä kiitos / Älä pliis* '(Please) don't ... ' [imperative]	828	679/828	22/828
4.	*Toivon / Toiveeni on / Toivoisin ...* 'I wish / My wish is / I would wish ... '	623	1/623	0/623
5.	*Tykkään ettei ...* 'I like when there is no ... '	515	0/515	0/515
6.	*Kiitos kun/ Kiitos että ...* 'Thank you when / Thank you that ... '	344	344/344	0/3
7.	an imperative inflected with a positive verb, e.g., *Ole hiljaa* 'Be quiet'	226	6/226	0/226

Note. * Other adjectives were also used in this general pattern, although *mukava* 'pleasant' and *kiva* 'nice' were the overwhelming majority. Other examples are *hieno* 'fine' and *kliffa* 'pleasant, chill'.
** In both request strategies 2 and 3 the position of *pliis* is fixed in the transit data.

frequent strategy was not the phrase *ethän pliis,* primed by the ad campaign, but a declarative statement, mirroring our request type 7 like in Tables 13.3 and 13.4. A full example of this request type is demonstrated in example (6).

(6) *On   mukava   kun   kukaan   ei   meuhkaa   tai*
    be-3SG   great   when nobody   NEG-3SG make-CONEG or
    uhkaile   bussissa
    threaten- CONEG bus-SG-INE
    'It's great when no one gets upset or threatens on the bus.'

In the baseline data, the preferred slot for the statement request type *Täällä ei saa huutaa* 'No yelling here' was clause-final for *kiitos* and clause-initial for *pliis*. The results from the transit data offer a reality check in terms of lexical politeness markers and their relation to this request type: despite having been prompted to use a lexical politeness marker (specifically *pliis*) by the campaign, in 1,507 user-generated instances of this type of request, there was not a single use of either *kiitos* or *pliis*.

The formula supplied through the ad campaign, *ethän pliis*, was, however, the second most preferred strategy, appearing in 713 of the responses (see example (7)). *Ethän pliis* accounts for 75 percent of the responses where the clitic particle is used; *kiitos* only occurs fourteen times in this construction.

(7) *Ethän   pliis ahdistele tai huuda   bussissa*
    NEG-SG2-hAn   PM   harass   or shout-CONNEG-2SG bus-SG-INE
    'Please don't harass others or shout on the bus.'

There is little doubt that this type of request would not, in fact, be preferred in more naturalistic (i.e., non-primed) conditions. Notwithstanding, when it comes to position of *pliis*, example (7) seems accurate: when forced to choose for the baseline data, a majority of the respondents (57 percent) chose the same position for our sample request type 5, as shown in Section 13.4. *Kiitos*, on the other hand, was clearly preferred in clause-final position in this type of request.

The third most frequent request type in the transit data was the negative imperative form *älä*, as shown in example (8) and as reflected in our baseline request type 4.

(8) *Älä   kiitos straidaa   tai skragaa   metrossa*
    don't-2SG   PM   urinate (colloq.) or fight (colloq.) metro-SG-INE
    'Please don't urinate or fight in the metro.'

In the transit data, moreover, 81 percent of the tokens of *kiitos* appeared in the position shown in (8), directly after *Älä* 'don't'. *Pliis* appeared only twelve times in this construction, underlining the fact that, unless prompted to do otherwise, *kiitos* is clearly a more natural or preferred choice than *pliis*. The position of *kiitos* in this construction casts doubt, however, on our previous assumptions about *kiitos* and its position in a clause. With (8), we see clear evidence that *kiitos* is, in this data sample, overwhelmingly preferred in a clause-internal position. This outcome is addressed further in Section 13.6.

Finally, it should be noted that the imperative (request type 2) was moderately frequent in the transit data, occurring a total of 380 times. What is interesting from the perspective of this chapter is that neither of the lexical politeness markers in focus were particularly common in imperatives: twelve imperatives contained *kiitos* (all in clause-final position) and only three contained *pliis* (all positions). Further, conventionally indirect requests (*Voisitko* ...? 'Could you ...?'), a canonical request type in the literature on requests – and the request type used as a prime in our previous studies – appeared only three times in the transit data.

In sum, there are three main findings from the transit data. First, the data demonstrates that requests or directives made from a neutral, third-person perspective seem to be an unmarked or natural choice for native speakers of Finnish (see also Yli-Vakkuri 2005; Peterson 2010). Second, there is a seeming contradiction in that the transit data shows a preference for *ethän pliis* but also for *älä kiitos*, indicating that position is not a telling enough factor on its own – a topic returned to in Section 13.6. A further curious point is the seeming conflict between the findings in the baseline data, where *kiitos* was routinely favored in clause-final position, and the transit data, where *kiitos* was favored within a clause.

13.5.2 Corpus Data

The corpus data comes from the 112 million-word FinnishWAC corpus, currently subsumed under the larger FiTenTen corpus and available through the SketchEngine platform (Kilgarriff et al. 2014). The corpus consists of web-scraped text, which has been cleaned up by removing boilerplate and duplicate texts and annotated for parts of speech (for details, see Kilgarriff et al. 2010). Like the transit data, the FinnishWAC corpus derives from CMC but is not prompted by any ad campaign or slogan and as such offers balance to address some of the shortcomings of the transit data.

Owing to the breadth of this data, the method of data retrieval necessarily differed from the transit data: we narrowed the scope of our analysis to just the elements that contained tokens of *pliis* and *kiitos*. To this end, we carried out an exhaustive retrieval of all instances of *pliis*, including spelling variants such as *pliiiis* (where the elongated vowel shows emphasis). The total number of instances of *pliis* in FinnishWaC was 559. By contrast, *kiitos* is functionally and socially more versatile, occurring some 25,000 times in the corpus, the majority of tokens being used for thanking. To obtain a comparable dataset, we extracted a randomly selected sample of 2,500 instances of *kiitos*, from which

Table 13.6 *Distribution of request types for* pliis *and* kiitos *in FinnishWaC*

request strategy	pliis	kiitos
Imperative	261	18
NP	183	66
As the only element	51	0
Interrogative	30	8
Declarative sentence (indicative mood)	14	6
toivon että ('I wish that')	3	5
other	17	3
Total	559	106

Note. NP=noun phrase.

we manually selected those occurring in requests, for a total of 106 tokens.[4] Finally, we classified the request strategies containing *pliis* and *kiitos* according to the criteria laid out in Section 13.4. The distribution of different request strategies co-occurring with *pliis* and *kiitos* in the FinnishWaC is shown in Table 13.6.

The most distinct outcome of the corpus analysis is that the repertoire of patterns differs from the transit data. In the FinnishWAC data, the main request type for *pliis* is an imperative, baseline request type 2, as illustrated in example (9).

(9)   *Pliis   keksikää   jotain   uutta*
       PM   invent-IMP-2PL   something   new-PAR
       'Please, come up with something new.'

The 261 occurrences of this strategy make up almost half of all the occurrences of *pliis* in the corpus data (46.7 percent), but it only occurs 18 times in the transit data (3.0 percent of the total). Moreover, the corpus data exhibits a significantly (χ^2=95.5, df=4, p<.001) higher proportion of clause-initial *pliis* (43 percent) than either our baseline data (12 percent) or transit data (22 percent).

The second most frequent pattern in the corpus data was *pliis* in conjunction with a verbless elliptical request consisting of a noun phrase, as in (10), which mirrors our baseline request type 1:

(10)   *Silti,   kamoon,   vähän   tilannetajua,   pliis.*
         Still   come on   a little   discretion-PAR   PM
         'Still, come on, (show) a little discretion, please.'

---

[4] This sample can be used for analyzing the co-occurrence preferences of the markers but not their raw frequency in the data.

With 183 occurrences (32.8 percent of the total number of occurrences of *pliis*), this pattern is only slightly less frequent than the imperative construction in the transit data. As predicted by the baseline data, the final position is also clearly preferred in this construction.

Given the frequent occurrence of these two request types in FinnishWAC, it is surprising that neither is common in the transit data, as shown in the previous section. The request type in (11) is attested in the transit data but is only marginal, whereas the type illustrated in (12) does not occur at all. Further, the FinnishWAC data does not show that *pliis* is primarily used clause-internally.

From the 106 applicable tokens of *kiitos*, two similar patterns emerged: an imperative (request type 2) and a verbless construction with a noun phrase (request type 1) as shown in example (11).

(11)   *Hieman   perusteluja,   kiitos!*
       some   reason-PL-PAR PM
       '(Give) some reasons, please/thank you!'

There were sixty-six instances of this request strategy in the corpus data, in which *kiitos* occurred in clause-final position. Our data show, then, that both *pliis* and *kiitos* are preferred clause-finally in this request type.

The second most frequent request type in the corpus data containing *kiitos* likewise mirrors the findings with *pliis*. Here, as shown in (12), an imperative request type occurs with *kiitos* in final position.

(12)   *Kerro   minulle tiedätkö   mitä   käsite   meioosi*
       tell-IMP-2SG me-ALL   know-2SG-Q what-PAR concept meiosis
       tarkoittaa, kiitos.
       mean-3SG   PM
       'Tell me if you know what the concept meiosis means, please/thank you.'

In the corpus data, *pliis* tended to occur in initial position in the same type of request as shown in example (12). This seeming contradiction points towards a pragmatic distinction that exists aside from – or in addition to – request type, a topic that is addressed in the next section.

13.6   Discussion

Our focus in this chapter has been on the clausal position of lexical politeness markers in Finnish requests, in an effort to shed light on the properties of the pragmatic borrowing *pliis* in Finnish. There are several reasons for the seemingly narrow focus on clausal position. First, an unanswered question remained from an earlier phase of our research, which we needed to reassess. Second, position was a reasonable question we could explore from the data types we have, given the challenges of obtaining adequate numbers of this type of variables for quantitative analysis. In addition, to maintain a measure of accountability, we needed a narrow focus to ensure that the research questions we pursued were valid for the type of data available to us.

The results are telling in that they contradict each other. Phase one of our study (Peterson and Vaattovaara 2014), as well as our elicited baseline data, demonstrated that *pliis* could be expected in a clause-internal position in requests, whereas *kiitos* would likely occur at the end of a clause. This expectation was not borne out in the data investigated for this chapter. Rather, we have opened up questions about Finnish that are probably best addressed through a formal syntactic overview – our main questions no longer appear to be a matter of variation based on a borrowed form versus a heritage form. For example, it would be crucial to address the relationship of *pliis* to other adverbial forms and their clausal behavior. In addition, an uninvestigated question here is that of word order: as a morphologically rich language, Finnish word order is relatively free compared to, for example, English, a factor which must be addressed. At the moment the relationship of these structural properties and the observations of Terkourafi (2011) about the bleaching of borrowed politeness markers remain somewhat ambiguous, although our findings do point in this general direction.

There are a number of lessons learned from this study and our application of multiple datasets on one small area of variation. Foremost, it is critical that we followed up on our initial perceptual data findings concerning *pliis* and its apparent infiltration of the Finnish clause. Such a claim was in no way borne out in our subsequent datasets, which showed that the same kinds of clause-internal slots are available for *kiitos* as for *pliis*, as evidenced by the request type 4 *älä huuda* 'don't shout'.

A point to emerge from the data is that length of utterance may be a critical feature to explore when it comes to position of lexical politeness markers. This possibility came about by accident from our data: shorter requests, like those tested in our baseline data, appear to attract lexical politeness markers in a final position, whereas longer and more complex utterances seem to invite such features in the left periphery. This possibility needs to be tested with further research.

A final and important point is not surprising, considering the type of variable in focus. Our study has demonstrated the overall challenges of disambiguating the structural versus interpersonal functions of discourse-pragmatic particles. We chose to focus on clausal properties, because, given the data we had to work with, this was the only possibility; social and pragmatic information was not available to us. However, the outcome of our study clearly shows that position and pragmatic function cannot (and should not) be treated in isolation (see Crible and Degand 2019b; see also Degand, Broisson, Crible, and Grzech,

Chapter 4, this volume). While the analysis presented in this chapter was a necessary stage of our overall work on the nativization of *pliis* in Finnish, it demonstrated that an investigation of discourse-pragmatic variables needs to view syntax and pragmatics as intertwined features. For this reason, the next stage of our study is set to explore the pragmatic function of lexical politeness markers in relation to placement within in a clause (as per Sato 2008 on the pragmatic meaning of different positions of *please* in English requests).

13.7 Conclusion

This chapter offers a perspective on foreign language contact and pragmatic borrowing (Kern, Chapter 11; Andersen, Chapter 12, this volume). The chapter offers an account of how a borrowed politeness marker, *pliis*, interacts with the heritage Finnish form, *kiitos*, as well as how an English-sourced pragmatic particle interacts with the grammatical structure of Finnish, namely Finnish requests. We wished to offer an optimally disciplined account of this question, keeping in mind that accountability in such studies is a challenge that must be built in from the design stage (Wiltschko et al. 2018).

As mentioned numerous times in this volume, one of the inherent challenges of working with discourse-pragmatic variables is their functional diversity. In addition, because these highly interactive elements are context-sensitive, we are bound to gain a different set of outcomes for each dataset we explore. For this reason, researchers are obliged to explore multiple datasets with the expectation that those datasets can and will contradict each other. For us, establishing the boundaries of claims we could make about language contact were especially important. Our initial investigations of *pliis* in Finnish requests led us to believe that, as a borrowing from English, *pliis* behaved in the clause in a different fashion than the heritage form *kiitos*. As demonstrated through our further investigations, this does not appear to be the case.

With the aim of achieving optimal accountability, our starting point for this analysis was to gain elicited baseline data. We were then able to contrast the baseline data with non-elicited CMC data. Our choices with regard to the CMC data were twofold. First, we found an opportunity in an unusual dataset that was gathered for advertising purposes. A challenge with this data was restructuring it for analysis: this so-called opportunistic data took an enormous amount of time to transfer and clean up, and in the end, it was not satisfactorily naturalistic for our purposes. A related point is that embarking on a quantitative research study with a data-driven approach presented numerous challenges. The challenges we faced offered good support to starting a quantitative investigation with a sound study design. Still, the opportunistic data proved useful in demonstrating general tendencies of Finnish requests, and it offered insights into the behavior of *kiitos* and *pliis*. To counter the inadequacies of the

A Place for *pliis* in Finnish 291

opportunistic data, we turned to more naturalistic, non-elicited corpus data. The main problem with this dataset was its sheer breadth, which provided challenges in narrowing in on structures we could compare to our baseline and opportunistic data.

The investigation of the data in this chapter lent credibility to our initial findings that *pliis* is associated with certain style(s) that are perceptually connected with urban Helsinki as well as related issues such as solidarity, community, and positive politeness. It is clear also from the transit data that *pliis* is context-sensitive; it belongs only with a specific style – no speaker of Finnish would consistently use *pliis* as the default lexical politeness marker (Peterson and Vaattovaara 2014). In terms of clausal position, *pliis* might be more variable than *kiitos*, but our findings indicate that variation is not satisfactorily described by request type and clausal position. Further investigations must explore the relationship of position, request type, and pragmatic meaning.

Appendix

Key for Glossing Symbols (Adapted from Sorjonen 2001)

1 1st person ending
2 2nd person ending
3 3rd person ending

Case	Ending	Abbreviation	Approximate meaning
ablative	-lt(a/ä)	ABL	'from'
accusative	no ending, -n, -t	ACC	object
adessive	-ll(a/ä)	ADE	'at, on'
allative	-ll(e)	ALL	'to'
essive	-n(a/ä)	ESS	'as'
genitive	-n, -den, -tten	GEN	possession
elative	-st(a/ä)	ELA	'out of'
illative	-Vn, -seen, -siin	ILL	'into'
inessive	-ss(a/ä)	INE	'in'
instructive	-n	INS	(various)
nominative	no ending	NOM	subject
partitive	-a/ä, -ta/ä, -tta/ä	PAR	partitiveness
translative	-ks(i)	TRA	'to,' 'becoming'

Other Abbreviations

colloq	colloquial, informal
CON	conditional
CONEG	connegative
INF	infinitive
PL	plural
PM	lexical politeness marker
POS	possessive
PRO	pronoun
Q	interrogative
SG	singular

Afterword
Future Priorities in Discourse-Pragmatic Variation and Change Research

Heike Pichler

Introduction

This volume demonstrates that the field of discourse-pragmatic variation and change research is coming into its own. After a slow and protracted start, there has been a steady growth over recent decades in the number of researchers and publications dedicated to the quantitative corpus study of discourse-pragmatic features. Yet there remains a lot of work still to be done to expand the field. In this volume, the editors have brought together a series of chapters that effectively illustrate several dimensions of expansion needed: the languages, discourse-pragmatic features, and data sources studied as well as the methods and analytical frameworks employed. In this Afterword, I elaborate on some of the future priorities of discourse-pragmatic variation and change research that I have identified from reading this volume.

Language Diversity and Language Contact

A major strength of this volume is its inclusion of several chapters that adopt and promote contact- and cross-linguistic analyses of discourse-pragmatic features, with individual chapters pursuing very different empirical and theoretical questions. Kern (Chapter 10) explores the use of Spanish and English general extenders by Spanish–English bilinguals in southern Arizona. He notes striking parallels in their composition and functionality.[1] Andersen (Chapter 12) and

---

[1] Kern's suggestion that, in southern Arizona bilingual communities, Spanish extenders are less grammaticalized than English extenders or that their distribution is at all a product of grammaticalization must remain tentative. Changes associated with grammaticalization do not, by definition, unfold concurrently (e.g., Croft 1990: 244); short extenders being associated with non-referential functions is therefore insufficient basis for a grammaticalization scenario. Nor can evidence of grammaticalization be derived from analyses of synchronic data from a single age group of young adults (see Pichler and Levey 2011).

Peterson, Hiltunen, and Vaattovaara (Chapter 13) explore how pragmatic borrowings from English, such as *sorry* and *please/pliis*, compare and compete with their Norwegian- and Finnish-language alternatives (*unnskyld, vennligst/kiitos*) – the former focusing on functional, the latter on positional constraints. Levey, Kastronic, Digesto, and Chiasson (Chapter 3) examine quotative strategies in Brazilian Portuguese, Italian, and different varieties of French, demonstrating the value of comparative sociolinguistic methods for testing contact effects on linguistic change as well as claims about inter-variety or inter-language parallelisms in change. Degand, Broisson, Crible, and Grzech (Chapter 4) introduce a functional annotation scheme for enhancing understanding of discourse markers as a linguistic category. Its application to spoken corpora of British English, European French, Peninsular Spanish, and Polish reveals that polyfunctionality and polysemy are a shared property of discourse markers across these languages, and that the frequency and distribution of (semantically equivalent) discourse markers across discourse domains may vary across languages.

The contact- and cross-linguistic focus of these chapters highlights two interlinked future priorities for discourse-pragmatic variation and change research. First, we need more studies that explore contact effects in discourse-pragmatic variation and change. For example, Kern (Chapter 10) notes that the bilingual speakers in his data occasionally use discourse *like* and quotative BE *like* in their Spanish discourse, but they never borrow English general extender forms. Comparative analyses of the syntactic-semantic distribution of general extenders in the English and Spanish data or experiments testing speakers' perceptions of English and Spanish discourse-pragmatic features could potentially establish whether pragmatic borrowing is blocked by linguistic constraints (i.e., close syntactic-semantic ties between general extenders and their antecedent) or perceptual salience (e.g., heightened prominence of general extenders compared to discourse *like* or quotative BE *like*). Explorations of this kind have the potential to produce nuanced explanations for the presence versus absence of contact effects in discourse-pragmatics. The recently launched project "Dynamics of Discourse Organisation in Language Contact" (2021– 2024), led by Shanley Allen (Kaiserslautern), Christoph Schroeder (Potsdam), and Heike Wiese (Berlin), will no doubt make major contributions here.[2]

Second, we need more studies that explore discourse-pragmatic variation and change in languages other than English. The greater availability of both public and private English-language corpora has, inevitably, yielded more studies into the properties of discourse-pragmatic features, constraints on their synchronic distribution, or details of their evolutionary pathways conducted on English than on any other language (e.g., Schiffrin 1987; Brinton 2008; D'Arcy 2017). This

---

[2] Allen, Shanley, Christoph Schroeder, and Heike Wiese. 2021–2014. "Dynamics of Discourse Organisation in Language Contact." Project funded by the Deutsche Forschungsgemeinschaft.

imbalance needs to be addressed urgently because it risks development of English-dominant models of discourse-pragmatic variation and change that – judging by the cross-linguistic dissimilarities described by authors in this volume – may not adequately or comprehensively reflect the full complexity of discourse-pragmatic variation and change (see also Evison et al. 2007: 156).

A better cross-linguistic understanding of the use and distribution of discourse-pragmatic features will in turn facilitate the first priority, that is, exploration of contact effects in discourse-pragmatic variation. For example, Degand, Broisson, Crible, and Grzech (Chapter 4) found that Polish *wiesz* 'you know' is used in both the interpersonal and sequential domains, while British English *you know* is used only in the former. These findings caution us against assuming cross-linguistic functional consistency in the use of features that share the same core semantic meaning. If Polish *wiesz* and (British) English *you know* are not functionally equivalent, we must not uncritically attribute the frequent use of sequential *you know* by Polish-heritage L2 speakers of Dublin English to positive transfer, without first studying how Irish-heritage L1 speakers of Dublin English use *you know* (see Diskin-Holdaway, Chapter 9).

In Pichler (2021), I sought to establish whether multiple language contact may have played an ancillary role in the development of *innit* from dependent to invariant tag in London English. My endeavor was hampered by the scarcity of quantitative corpus studies that describe the composition, distribution, or functionality of question tags in the languages and varieties widely spoken in those multiethnic, multilingual London boroughs where the development of *innit* was most advanced. I could not be sure that the grammar books I consulted on question tag use in the presumed contact languages did in fact reflect current vernacular usage. Quirk et al. (1985: 811) and Huddleston and Pullum (2002: 894–895), for example, offer much narrower functional descriptions of English dependent tags than corpus-based studies of their use. My contact proposal therefore has to remain tentative until such times where it can be supported with relevant cross-linguistic corpus evidence. (Of course, contact effects in discourse-pragmatic change ought to be established by comparing the structure of variation in the proposed source and recipient languages, as demonstrated in Levey et al.'s (2013) meticulous analysis of quotative *être comme* in Canadian French. However, in multiple language contact settings, such as London at the start of the century, this requirement is impractical, especially absent available corpora of relevant contact languages.)

Perception Experiments

Schleef and Mackay's (Chapter 2) experimental study examines listeners' evaluation of the discourse-pragmatic feature *you know*. The authors constructed audio-matched guises with and without clause-internal *you know* and asked listeners to rate the guises on scales associated with prestige, solidarity, and determination. Compared to guises without *you know*, those with *you know* were rated lower in terms of formality, trustworthiness, professionalism, precision, fluency, and experience. Schleef and Mackay propose that *you know*-users' perceived social traits are a function of the linguistic imprecision signaled by *you know* in clause-internal position. When individual evaluative scales were conflated into three factors – status, solidarity, determination –, guises with *you know* were rated significantly lower only on the determination factor, a result the authors attribute to the low social salience of clause-internal *you know*. Listeners in their experiment had not associated the use of *you know* in internal position with specific social groups. With its careful research design, this study provides a valuable model for future perception experiments in discourse-pragmatics.

A small number of studies have explored the social evaluation of discourse-pragmatic features. They broadly converge in demonstrating that discourse-pragmatic features are socially and perceptually salient and in suggesting that it is their salience and/or perceived functionality that gives rise to negative evaluations of their use and users (e.g., in terms of intelligence, education, articulacy). Yet, as alluded to by Schleef and Mackay, results of some studies have to be interpreted with caution. Several studies (e.g., Dines 1980; Dailey-O'Cain 2000; Buchstaller 2006; Davydova et al. 2017) elicited listener evaluations using written transcripts. Because features such as discourse *like* are ubiquitous in speech and largely absent in (formal) writing, written stimuli may have exacerbated negative responses. Other studies (e.g., Watts 1989; Beeching 2016) directed participants' attention to the features of interest. This technique may not have elicited participants' spontaneous or subconscious evaluative reactions, especially where features are stigmatized and participants reluctant to offer negative judgments. Maddeaux and Dinkin (2017) used audio guises to explore participants' subconscious evaluations of discourse *like* (see also Hesson and Schellgren 2015). However, D'Arcy (2017) questions the reliability of their findings because in many guises discourse *like* occurred in syntactic contexts that disfavor its use in natural speech (e.g., in PPs or with modals).

Schleef and Mackay overcome many of these limitations. They used empirical facts about the usage and distribution of *you know* (and other speech phenomena) to construct manipulated audio stimuli that are tightly controlled for factors potentially impacting listener evaluative reactions. Schleef and Mackay limited their investigation to *you know* in clause-internal position where it typically serves to signal linguistic imprecision. Their focus on what is the most frequent position of *you know* in empirical data (see Diskin 2015: 193) facilitated construction of short, natural stimuli that contain enough *you know* tokens to trigger listener evaluative reactions. Based on typical disfluency rates reported for conversational data, this meant inserting three *you know* tokens in each of their 75-odd word guises. Because the function of *you know* varies across position (see Beeching 2016: 98–104), the focus on clause-internal tokens also mitigated confounding effects of functional variability on listener evaluations. The between-subject design of their survey moreover reduced the chance of listeners' attention being drawn to *you know*. Finally, that both the reenactors of the audio stimuli and the listeners were from Manchester, UK, precluded potential regional effects on listener evaluations; in the absence of empirical information about how the distribution of *you know* varies across the English-speaking world (see Pichler & Cheshire, in press), this control is important.[3]

Schleef and Mackay's study is a timely reminder that perceptual questions and methods must become more central in discourse-pragmatic variation and change research. We know, for example, that the presence of discourse-pragmatic features can affect social judgments of speech samples and language users, and that these judgments can lead to language-based discrimination (see Parton et al. 2002; Russell et al. 2008). What we need more of are studies that explore the source of these judgments. Discourse-pragmatic features are variable across multiple dimensions, such as their frequency, functionality, prosodic and pragmatic prominence, positioning, and so on. At present, we do not know which of these variable properties give rise to negative (or positive) evaluations of the use and users of discourse-pragmatic features. Is it the frequency with which they occur? Is it their role in constructing different interactional styles (e.g., non-assertive, competitive)? Is it their regular occurrence in prosodically and pragmatically prominent positions? Or is it the way some features seemingly disrupt the syntactic structure of utterances? Schleef and Mackay demonstrate how we can address these questions by carefully delimiting the focus of experimental studies and systematically controlling competing effects on evaluative reaction.[4] Only by establishing exactly which (variable) properties of discourse-pragmatic features give rise to negative evaluations can we develop targeted interventions to challenge widespread prejudices about the use and users of discourse-pragmatic features and combat attendant language-based discrimination.

---

[3] It remains unclear whether the insertion of internal *you know* tokens before APs, NPs, and PPs was guided by empirical findings. That the naturalness of the stimuli was confirmed in pre-experiment focus groups marginally addresses this concern.

[4] I have one reservation about Schleef and Mackay's study: they do not acknowledge the possibility that it is the positioning of clause-internal *you know* – possibly in combination with its functionality – that triggers the negative evaluations they report. Because they are referentially and syntactically optional, clause-internal tokens of *you know* may be perceived as superfluous, a-grammatical disfluencies. It may be this perception that gives rise to negative evaluations (for example, on the fluency scale) rather than, or in addition to, the tokens' function *per se*.

Expansion of Methods and Data

Several other chapters in this volume introduce fresh perspectives for analyzing discourse-pragmatic variation and change that have the potential to advance the field in new and important directions. Eiswirth (Chapter 8) uses her analysis of vocalized non-turn-taking listener responses to advocate the integration of conversation analysis with variationist methods. She defines listener responses as a variable based on their sequential positioning and interactional impact, and situates their analysis in the sequential organization and temporal development of talk-in-interaction (e.g., Schegloff 2007). This allows her to explore both social and structural constraints on variable frequency and use. Eiswirth's approach could be usefully extended to other interactional devices whose occurrence is conditioned by sequential context, such as the English turn-taking signals *ah* or *oh* (e.g., Fischer 2000). Its wider adoption could thus address a pressing and persistent issue in the field: diversifying the range of discourse-pragmatic variables studied (see Pichler 2013: 234–235).

Gadanidis and Denis (Chapter 7) investigate variation between the filled pause variants *um* and *uh* in oral history interviews collected in Ontario, Canada. Analysis of proportional variant frequencies reveals a rise of *um* in utterance-initial position; analysis of normalized frequencies reveals that women's use of *uh* in non-initial position is increasing over time more than men's – a change the authors tentatively attribute to the variant's recruitment for pause-filling or word-search functions. The authors' contribution convincingly demonstrates how normalized frequency analyses can be configured to explore and disentangle social and linguistic mechanisms underpinning discourse-pragmatic change. It is a powerful demonstration in defense of normalized frequencies in discourse-pragmatic variation and change research (contra Pichler 2010), and in support of combining multiple, bespoke perspectives in data analysis to test alternative hypotheses about variant distribution (see also Pichler 2016c, Waters 2016). The presentation and explanation of Gadanidis and Denis's quantitative procedures (and justification for their envelope of variation) are exemplary in clarity, facilitating their future replication and contributing to quantitative progress in the field.

While quantitative progress is to be applauded and embraced, we must not ignore or downplay the value and importance of qualitative data analysis in discourse-pragmatic variation and change research (e.g., Cheshire 1981; Fox 2012; Ilbury 2019; Pichler 2021). Speakers use discourse-pragmatic features not to communicate propositional content but to signal speaker stance, build social rapport, and guide utterance interpretation. Quantitative analyses can uncover shifts in variant and variable distribution and frequencies, but qualitative analyses are needed to explain such shifts, as acknowledged by Gadanidis and Denis and compellingly demonstrated by Kolbe-Hanna and Brinton

(Chapter 5) in their nuanced investigation of the emergence of sentence-final *is all*. Attributing the rise of a variant or variable to functional change without analyzing its use in context does little to further our understanding of the interactional mechanisms yielding variation and change on the level of discourse-pragmatics.

Peterson, Hiltunen, and Vaattovaara's (Chapter 13) analysis of *pliis* and *kiitos* across elicitation, opportunistic, and corpus data yields conflicting results about the forms' preferred clausal positions, which they attribute to the context-sensitivity of discourse-pragmatic features.[5] To ensure reliable descriptions and results, they therefore advocate analysis of discourse-pragmatic features across multiple data sources, including computer-mediated communication (CMC) data. Extension of discourse-pragmatic variation research to CMC data is a positive and welcome development, supported by earlier research demonstrating the structured heterogeneity of discourse-pragmatic features in CMC (Tagliamonte and Denis 2008). As pointed out by Peterson and colleagues, it can serve as a check on conclusions drawn from analysis of other data sources. Furthermore, it allows scholars to investigate, for example, discourse-pragmatic variables that are infrequent in speech data, such as the tag *amirite* on Reddit and Twitter (e.g., Brook & Pichler 2021. Grieve et al. 2016); dimensions of discourse-pragmatic variation not relevant in speech data, such as the variable spelling of "though" as <though>, <tho> or <doe> on Reddit (e.g., Flesch 2019); or graphic symbols that share functional and distributional properties with discourse-pragmatic features, such as emoji on Whatsapp (e.g. Wiese & Labrenz 2021). Analysis of discourse-pragmatic variation beyond sociolinguistic interviews or dyadic conversations will enable scholars to diversify the range of variables studied, explore new dimensions of discourse-pragmatic variation (e.g., spelling variation), and establish whether the distribution of graphic symbols is constrained by linguistic factors (e.g., clausal periphery). It thus offers the potential to enhance current understanding of the complexity of discourse-pragmatic variability.

Blondeau, Mougeon, and Tremblay (Chapter 11) present a real-time trend study of discourse-pragmatic change (see also Aijmer, Chapter 6). The authors investigate the use of consequence markers (French *ça fait que*, *alors*, *donc*, English *so*) in data collected some forty years apart in two Canadian cities – Montreal (Quebec) and Welland (Ontario) – that differ in the status and use of French and English. The real-time perspective enables Blondeau and colleagues to identify the community-specific factors behind the increasing inter-community divergence in the use and distribution of consequence markers: the growing sociopolitical and demolinguistic differences between the two cities. Blondeau and colleagues' study will inspire future studies that trace the

---

[5] The different results in Peterson and colleagues' elicitation and corpus data may also reflect the limitations of elicitation tasks for discourse-pragmatic variation research.

quantitative development of discourse-pragmatic variables across multiple time points, and establish which external and internal factors impact the direction and rate of discourse-pragmatic change in real time. Research of this kind will provide an important context for the design and interpretation of apparent-time studies of discourse-pragmatic change.

In addition to more real-time trend studies, the field will benefit from real-time panel studies that examine individuals' stability or instability in the use of discourse-pragmatic variables over time. Current evidence of post-adolescent linguistic (in)stability is largely derived from studies of phonological and morpho-syntactic variables (e.g., Nahkola and Saanilahti 2004; Bowie 2015; Sankoff 2019; Sankoff and Wagner 2020). Buchstaller (2016) provides rare longitudinal evidence of adults' participation in a discourse-pragmatic change in progress, arguing that adoption or non-adoption of the innovative quotative BE *like* is related to individuals' social trajectories and intergenerational contact. However, Buchstaller's analysis is based on small token numbers in a small speaker sample. Large-scale evidence from analyses of multiple discourse-pragmatic variables is needed to test Sankoff's (2005) proposal that discourse-level features are more susceptible to lifespan change than phonological features, and to explore what the cause for any such differences might be.

Conclusion

In this Afterword, I have briefly outlined some future priorities in discourse-pragmatic variation and change research that emerge from my reading of the chapters assembled in this volume – a volume whose strength lies in illustrating the levels of diversity needed to advance the field. There are no doubt many other directions that the field will and should take over the coming years and decades in order to help it flourish and evolve. One such direction is the integration of multiple theoretical perspectives in investigations of discourse-pragmatic change, as expertly demonstrated by Denis (Chapter 1) in this volume. I look forward to seeing other scholars take inspiration from this volume and celebrate the richness of discourse-pragmatic variability.

References

Acton, E. K. 2011. On gender differences in the distribution of *um* and *uh*. *University of Pennsylvania Working Papers in Linguistics*, 17(2), 1–9.
Adger, D. 2007. Variability and modularity: A response to Hudson. *Journal of Linguistics*, 43(3), 695–700.
Afantenos, S., Asher, N., Benamara, F. et al. 2012. An empirical resource for discovering cognitive principles of discourse organization: The ANNODIS corpus. In N. Calzolari, K. Choukri, T. Declerck et al., eds., *Proceedings of the 8th International Conference on Language Resources and Evaluation (LREC'12)*. Istanbul: European Language Resources Association, 2727–2734.
Aijmer, K. 1985. What happens at the end of our utterances? The use of utterance final tags introduced by *and* and *or*. In O. Togeby, ed., *Papers from the Eighth Scandinavian Conference of Linguistics*. Copenhagen: Københavns Universitet, Institut for Nordisk Filologi, 366–389.
Aijmer, K. 1997. I think – an English modal particle. In T. Swan and O. J. Westvik, eds., *Modality in Germanic Languages: Historical and Comparative Perspectives*. Berlin: De Gruyter Mouton, 1–48.
Aijmer, K. 2002. *English Discourse Particles: Evidence from a Corpus*. Amsterdam: John Benjamins.
Aijmer, K. 2004. Pragmatic markers in spoken interlanguage. *Nordic Journal of English Studies*, 3(1), 173–190.
Aijmer, K. 2011. Are you totally spy? A new intensifier in present-day American English. In S. Hancil, ed., *Marqueurs discursifs et subjectivité*. Rouen: Universités de Rouen and Havre, 155–172.
Aijmer, K. and Simon-Vandenbergen, A.-M. 2009. Pragmatic markers. In J.-O. Östman and J. Verschueren, eds., *Handbook of Pragmatics*, Vol. 13. Amsterdam: John Benjamins, 1–30.
Alvarado Ortega, M. B. 2008. Las fórmulas rutinarias en el español actual, PhD thesis, University of Alicante.
Andersen, G. 2001. *Pragmatic Markers and Sociolinguistic Variation: A Relevance-Theoretic Approach to the Language of Adolescents*. Amsterdam: John Benjamins.
Andersen, G. 2014. Pragmatic borrowing. *Journal of Pragmatics*, 67, 17–33.
Andersen, G. 2015. Pseudo-borrowings as cases of pragmatic borrowing: Focus on Anglicisms in Norwegian. In C. Furiassi and H. Gottlieb, eds., *Pseudo-English: Studies on False Anglicisms in Europe*. Berlin: De Gruyter Mouton, 123–144.
Andersen, G., Furiassi, C., and Mišić Ilić, B. 2017. The pragmatic turn in studies of linguistic borrowing: Introduction to special issue on pragmatic borrowing. *Journal of Pragmatics*, 113, 71–76.

Ando, S. 2005. *Lectures on Modern English Grammar [Genai Eibunpo Kogi]*. Tokyo: Kaitakusha.
Anthony, L. 2018. *AntConc (Version 3.5.7) [MacIntosh]*. Tokyo: Waseda University. www.laurenceanthony.net/software.
Arndt, W. 1960. Modal particles in Russian and German. *Word*, 16(3), 323–336.
Athanasiadou, A. 2007. On the subjectivity of intensifiers. *Language Sciences*, 29(4), 554–565.
Auer, P. and Eastman, C. M. 2010. Code-switching. In J. Jaspers, J.-O. Östman, and J. Verschueren, eds., *Society and Language Use: Handbook of Pragmatics Highlights*, Vol. 7. Amsterdam: John Benjamins, 84–112.
Backus, A. 2014. Towards a usage-based account of language change: Implications of contact linguistics for linguistic theory. In R. Nicolaï, ed., *Questioning Language Contact: Limits of Contact, Contact at Its Limits*. Leiden: Brill, 91–118.
Bailey, C.-J. N. 1973. *Variation and Linguistic Theory*. Arlington, VA: Center for Applied Linguistics.
Bailey, G. 2004. Real and apparent time. In J. K. Chambers, P. Trudgill, and N. Schilling-Estes, eds., *The Handbook of Language Variation and Change*. Oxford: Blackwell, 312–332.
Balteiro, I. 2018. *Oh wait*: English pragmatic markers in Spanish football chatspeak. *Journal of Pragmatics*, 133, 123–133.
Bates, D., Mächler M., Bolker, B., and Walker, S. 2015. Fitting linear mixed-effects models using lme4. *Journal of Statistical Software*, 67(1), 1–48.
Bavelas, J. B., Coates, L., and Johnson, T. 2000. Listeners as co-narrators. *Journal of Personality and Social Psychology*, 79(6), 941–952.
Bayer, J. and Obenauer, H. G. 2011. Discourse particles, clause structure, and question types. *The Linguistic Review*, 28(4), 449–491.
Beeching, K. 2016. *Pragmatic Markers in British English: Meaning in Social Interaction*. Cambridge: Cambridge University Press.
Beltrama, A. 2015. Intensification and sociolinguistic variation: A corpus study. In A. E. Jurgensen, H. Sande, S. Lamoureux, K. Baclawski, and A. Zerbe, eds., *Proceedings of the Annual Meetings of the Berkeley Linguistics Society*, Vol. 41. Berkeley: Berkeley Linguistics Society, 15–30.
Beltrama, A. 2018. *Totally* between subjectivity and discourse: Exploring the pragmatic side of intensification. *Journal of Semantics*, 35(2), 219–261.
Beltrama, A. and Staum Casasanto, L. 2017. *Totally* tall sounds *totally* younger: Intensification at the socio-semantics interface. *Journal of Sociolinguistics*, 21(2), 154–182.
Beniak, É., Mougeon, R., and Valois, D. 1985. *Contact des langues et changement linguistique: Étude sociolinguistique du français parlé à Welland*. Quebec: Centre International de Recherche sur le Bilinguisme.
Bertrand, A. 2014. Exclamatives en -tu, donc et assez en français québécois: Types et sous-types, MA thesis, University of Montreal.
Biber, D., Johansson, S., Leech, G., Conrad, S., and Finegan, E. 1999. *Longman Grammar of Spoken and Written English*. Harlow: Pearson Education.
Biberauer, T., Holmberg, A., Roberts, I., and Sheehan, M. 2010. *Parametric Syntax: Null Subjects in Minimalist Theory*. Cambridge: Cambridge University Press.

Birdsong, D., Gertken, L.M., and Amengual, M. 2012. *Bilingual Language Profile: An Easy-to-Use Instrument to Assess Bilingualism.* Austin: COERLL and University of Texas at Austin. https://sites.la.utexas.edu/bilingual/.

Bittencourt, V. 1999. Gramaticalização e discursivização no português oral do Brasil: O caso "tipo (asim)." *Scripta*, 2(4), 39–53.

Blondeau, H. and Moreno, A. 2018. *On a fait comme "c'est fou là"* ou l'émergence de *comme* et sa concurrence avec *genre* et d'autres formes d'introduction de discours direct dans le français de Montréal. In H. Barthelmebs-Raguin, G. Komur-Thilloy, J. M. Lopez-Muñoz, S. Marnette, and L. Rosier, eds., *Le Discours rapporté: Temporalité, histoire, mémoire et patrimoine discursive.* Paris: Classiques Garnier, 41–58.

Blondeau, H., Tremblay, M., Bertrand, A., and Michel E. 2021. A new milestone for the study of variation in Montréal French: The Hochelaga-Maisonneuve sociolinguistic survey. *Corpus*, 22, 1–16.

Blondeau, H, Mougeon, R., and Tremblay M. 2019. Analyse comparative de *ça fait que*, alors, *donc* et *so* à Montréal et à Welland: Mutations sociales, convergences, divergences en français laurentien. *Journal of French Language Studies*, 29(1), 35–65.

Bloomfield, L. 1933. *Language*. New York: H. Holt and Company.

Blühdorn, H., Foolen, A., and Loureda, O. 2017. Diskursmarker: Begriffsgeschichte – Theorie – Beschreibung. Ein bibliographischer Überblick. In H. Blühdorn, A. Deppermann, H. Helmer, and T. Spranz-Fogasy, eds., *Diskursmarker im Deutschen: Reflexionen und Analysen*. Mannheim: Verlag für Gesprächsforschung, 7–48.

Blum-Kulka, S, House, J., and Kasper, G. (eds.). 1989. *Cross-Cultural Pragmatics: Requests and Apologies*, Norwood, NJ: Ablex Publishing.

Boersma, P. and Weenink, D. 2014. *Praat: Doing Phonetics by Computer [Computer Program]*. Version 5. 3.82. www.praat.org/.

Bolden, G. 2009. Implementing incipient actions: The discourse marker "so" in English conversation. *Journal of Pragmatics*, 41(5), 974–998.

Borkin, A. and Reinhart, S. M. 1978. Excuse me and I'm sorry. *TESOL Quarterly*, 12(1), 57–69.

Bortfeld, H., Leon, S. D., Bloom, J. E., Schober, M. F., and Brennan, S. E. 2001. Disfluency rates in conversation: Effects of age, relationship, topic, role, and gender. *Language and Speech*, 44(2), 123–147.

Bowie, D. 2015. Phonological variation in real time: Patterns of adult linguistic stability and change. In A. Gerstenberg and A. Voeste, eds., *Investigating the Lifespan Perspective*. Amsterdam: John Benjamins, 39–58.

Branca-Rosoff, S., Fleury, S., Lefeuvre, F., and Pires, M. 2012. *Discours sur la ville. Présentation du corpus de français parlé parisien des années 2000*, CFPP2000, New Sorbonne University Paris 3. http://cfpp2000.univ-paris3.fr/.

Brezina, V., Gablasova, D., and Reichelt, S. 2018. *BNClab*. Lancaster University. http://corpora.lancs.ac.uk/bnclab/.

Brinton, L. J. 1996. *Pragmatic Markers in English: Grammaticalization and Discourse Functions*. Berlin, Mouton de Gruyter.

Brinton, L. J. 2008. *The Comment Clause in English: Syntactic Origins and Pragmatic Development*. Cambridge: Cambridge University Press.

Brinton, L. J. 2017. *The Evolution of Pragmatic Markers in English: Pathways of Change*. Cambridge: Cambridge University Press.

Brinton, L. J. 2020. The development and pragmatic function of a non-inference marker: *This is not to say (that)*. In P. Rautionaho, A. Nurmi, and J. Klemola, eds., *Corpora and the Changing Society: Studies in the Evolution of English*. Amsterdam: John Benjamins, 251–275.

Brinton, L. J. and Traugott, E. C. 2005. *Lexicalization in Language Change*. Cambridge: Cambridge University Press.

Brody, J. 1987. Particles borrowed from Spanish as discourse markers in Mayan languages. *Anthropological Linguistics*, 29(4), 507–21.

Brody, J. 1995. Lending the unborrowable: Spanish discourse markers in Indigenous American Languages. In C. Silva-Corvalán, ed., *Spanish in Four Continents: Studies in Language Contact and Bilingualism*. Washington, DC: Georgetown University Press, 132–148.

Brook, M. and Pichler, H. 2021. Orthographic variation reflects constituency variation, am I right or amirite? Paper presented at DiPVaC 5, University of Melbourne, Australia.

Brooks, M. E., Kristensen, K., van Benthem, K. J. et al. 2017. glmmTMB balances speed and flexibility among packages for zero-inflated generalized linear mixed modeling. *The R Journal*, 9(2), 378–400.

Brown, P. and Levinson, S. C. 1987. *Politeness: Some Universals in Language Usage*. Cambridge: Cambridge University Press.

Brunner, L. J. 1979. Smiles can be back channels. *Journal of Personality and Social Psychology*, 37(5), 728–734.

Buchstaller, I. 2006. Social stereotypes, personality traits and regional perception displaced: Attitudes towards the "new" quotatives in the U.K. *Journal of Sociolinguistics*, 10(3), 362–381.

Buchstaller, I. 2009. The quantitative analysis of morphosyntactic variation: Constructing and quantifying the denominator. *Linguistics and Language Compass*, 3(4), 1010–1033.

Buchstaller, I. 2014. *Quotatives: New Trends and Sociolinguistic Implications*. Oxford: Wiley-Blackwell.

Buchstaller, I. 2016. Investigating the effect of socio-cognitive salience and speaker-based factors in morpho-syntactic life-span change. *Journal of English Linguistics*, 44(2), 1–31.

Buchstaller, I. and D'Arcy, A. 2009. Localised globalisation: A multi-local, multivariate investigation of *be like*. *Journal of Sociolinguistics*, 13(3), 291–331.

Buchstaller, I. and Van Alphen, I. (eds.). 2012. *Quotatives: Cross-Linguistic and Cross-Disciplinary Perspectives*. Amsterdam: John Benjamins.

Burchfield, R. W. 1996. *The New Fowler's Modern English Usage*, 3rd ed. Oxford: Clarendon Press.

Bürkner, P.-C. 2017. brms: An R package for Bayesian multilevel models using stan. *Journal of Statistical Software*, 80(1), 1–28.

Bürkner, P.-C. 2018. Advanced Bayesian multilevel modeling with the R package brms. *The R Journal*, 10(1), 395–411.

Buysse, L. 2010. Discourse markers in the English of Flemish university students. In I. Witczak-Plisiecka, ed., *Speech Actions in Theory and Applied Studies*. Newcastle upon Tyne: Cambridge Scholars Publishing, 461–484.

Buysse, L. 2017. The pragmatic marker *you know* in learner Englishes. *Journal of Pragmatics*, 121, 40–57.

Bybee, J., Perkins, R., and Pagliuca, W. 1994. *The Evolution of Grammar: Tense, Aspect, and Modality in the Languages of the World*. Chicago: University of Chicago Press.

Cacchiani. S. 2005. Local vehicles for intensification and involvement: The case of English intensifiers. In P. Cap, ed., *Pragmatics Today*. Frankfurt am Main: Peter Lang, 401–419.

Calhoun, S., Nissim, M., Steedman, M., and Brenier, J. 2005. A framework for annotating information structure in discourse. In A. Meyer, ed., *Proceedings of the Workshop on Frontiers in Corpus Annotations II: Pie in the Sky*. Ann Arbor, MI: Association for Computational Linguistics, 45–52.

Cameron, D., McAlinden, F., and O'Leary, K. 1989. Lakoff in context: The form and function of tag questions. In J. Coates and D. Cameron, eds., *Women in Their Speech Communities: New Perspectives on Language and Sex*. London: Longman, 74–93.

Cameron, R. 1998. A variable syntax of speech, gesture, and sound effect: direct quotations in Spanish. *Language Variation and Change*, 10(1), 43–83.

Campbell-Kibler, K. 2007. Accent, (ING) and the social logic of listener perceptions. *American Speech*, 82(1), 32–64.

Campbell-Kibler, K. 2008. I'll be the judge of that: Diversity in social perceptions of (ING). *Language in Society*, 37(5), 637–659.

Campbell-Kibler, K. 2009. The nature of sociolinguistic perception. *Language Variation and Change*, 21(1), 135–156.

Carlson, L., Marcu, D., and Okurowski, M. E. 2001. Building a discourse-tagged corpus in the framework of rhetorical structure theory. In *SIGDIAL '01: Proceedings of the Second SIGdial Workshop on Discourse and Dialogue*, Vol. 16. Stroudsburg, PA: Association for Computational Linguistics, 1–10.

Carpenter, B., Gelman, A., Hoffman, M. D. et al. 2017. Stan: A probabilistic programming language. *Journal of Statistical Software*, 76(1), 1–32.

Carstensen, B. and Busse, U. 1993–1996. *Anglizismen-Wörterbuch: Der Einfluss des Englischen auf den deutschen Wortschatz nach 1945*. Berlin: De Gruyter.

Castelano, K. L. and Terezinha Ladeira, W. 2010. Funções discursivo-interacionais das expressões *assim, tipo* e *tipo assim* em narrativas orais. *Letra Magna*, 6(12), 1–17.

Chambers, J. K. 2006. The development of Canadian English. In K. Bolton and B. B. Kachru, eds., *World Englishes: Critical Concepts in Linguistics*. London: Routledge, 383–395.

Channell, J. 1994. *Vague Language*. Oxford: Oxford University Press.

Cheshire, J. 1981. Variation in the use of *ain't* in an urban British dialect. *Language in Society*, 10(3), 113–161.

Cheshire, J. 2007. Discourse variation, grammaticalisation and stuff like that. *Journal of Sociolinguistics*, 11(2), 155–193.

Cheshire, J. and Secova, M. 2018. The origins of new quotative expressions: The case of Paris French. *Journal of French Language Studies*, 28(2), 209–234.

Chomsky, N. 1957. *Syntactic Structures*. The Hague: Mouton.

Christensen, R. H. B. 2019. *Ordinal – Regression Models for Ordinal Data*. R package version 2019.4–25. www.cran.r-project.org/package=ordinal/.

Cieri, C., Miller, D., and Walker, K. 2004. The Fisher corpus: A resource for the next generations of speech-to-text. In M. T. Lino, M. F. Xavier, F. Ferreira, R. Costa, and R. Silva, eds., *Proceedings of the Fourth International Conference on Language Resources and Evaluation (LREC'04)*. Lisbon: European Language Resources Association (ELRA), 9–71.

Clancy, P. M., Thompson, S. A., Suzuki, R., and Tao, H. 1996. The conversational use of reactive tokens in English, Japanese, and Mandarin. *Journal of Pragmatics*, 26(3), 355–387.

Clark, H. H. and Fox Tree, J. E. 2002. Using uh and um in spontaneous speaking. *Cognition*, 84(1), 73–111.

Clark, L. and Schleef, E. 2010. The acquisition of sociolinguistic evaluations among Polish-born adolescents learning English: Evidence from perception. *Language Awareness*, 19(4), 299–322.

Coleman, J., Baghai-Ravary, L., Pybus, J., and Grau, S. 2012. *Audio BNC: The Audio Edition of the Spoken British National Corpus*. Phonetics Laboratory, University of Oxford. www.phon.ox.ac.uk/AudioBNC/.

Cortés, L. 2005. La serie enumerativa: Cuestiones de partida. In L. Santos Río, J. Borrego Nieto, J. F. García Santos et al., eds., *Palabras, norma, discurso. En memoria de Fernando Lázaro Carreter*. Salamanca: Ediciones Universidad de Salamanca, 365–380.

Cortés, L. 2006a. Los elementos de final de serie enumerativa del tipo y todo eso, o cosas así, y tal, etc. Perspectiva interactiva. *Boletín de lingüística*, 18(26), 102–129.

Cortés, L. 2006b. Los elementos de final de serie enumerativa del tipo y todo eso, o cosas así, y tal, etcétera en el discurso oral en español. Perspectiva textual. *BISAL*, 1, 82–106.

Costello, A. B. and Osborne, J. 2005. Best practices in exploratory factor analysis: Four recommendations for getting the most from your analysis. *Practical Assessment, Research, and Evaluation*, 10(1), 1–9.

Council of Europe. 2001. *Common European Framework of Reference for Languages: Learning, Teaching, Assessment*. Strasbourg: Language Policy Unit.

Coupé, C. 2018. Modeling linguistic variables with regression models: Addressing non-Gaussian distributions, non-independent observations, and non-linear predictors with random effects and generalized additive models for location, scale, and shape. *Frontiers in Psychology*, 9, 513.

Couper-Kuhlen, E. and Selting, M. 2018. *Interactional Linguistics: Studying Language in Social Interaction*. Cambridge: Cambridge University Press.

Cresti, E. and Moneglia, M. (eds.). 2005. *C-ORAL-ROM: Integrated Reference Corpora for Spoken Romance Languages*. Amsterdam: John Benjamins.

Crible, L. 2018. *Discourse Markers and (Dis)fluency. Forms and Functions Across Languages and Registers*. Amsterdam: John Benjamins.

Crible, L. and Cuenca, M. J. 2017. Discourse markers in speech: Characteristics and challenges for corpus annotation. *Dialogue and Discourse* 8(2), 149–166.

Crible, L. and Degand, L. 2019a. Domains and functions: A two-dimensional account of discourse markers. *Discours* 24, 1–35.

Crible, L. and Degand, L. 2019b. Reliability vs. granularity in discourse annotation: What is the trade-off? *Corpus Linguistics and Linguistic Theory*, 15(1), 71–99.

Crible, L., Dumont, A., Grosman, I., and Notarrigo, I. 2019. (Dis)fluency across spoken and signed languages: Application of an interoperable annotation scheme. In L. Degand, G. Gilquin, L. Meurant, and A. C. Simon, eds., *Fluency and Disfluency Across Languages and Language Varieties*. Louvain-la-Neuve: Presses Universitaires de Louvain, 17–40.

Croft, W. 1990. *Typology and Universals*. Cambridge: Cambridge University Press.

Crystal, D. 1988. Another look at, well, you know ... *English Today*, 13(1), 47–49.
Crystal, D. 2017. *The Story of Be: A Verb's-Eye View of the English Language*. Cambridge: Cambridge University Press.
Crystal, D. and Davy, D. 1975. *Advanced Conversational English*. London: Longman.
D'Arcy, A. 2005. Like: Syntax and development. PhD thesis, University of Toronto.
D'Arcy, A. 2008. Canadian English as a window to the rise of 'like' in discourse. *Anglistik: International Journal of English Studies*, 19(2), 125–140.
D'Arcy, A. 2012. The diachrony of quotative: Evidence from New Zealand English. *Language Variation and Change*, 24(3), 343–369.
D'Arcy, A. 2017. *Discourse-Pragmatic Variation in Context: Eight Hundred Years of Like*. Amsterdam: John Benjamins.
Dailey-O'Cain, J. 2000. The sociolinguistic distribution of and attitudes toward focuser 'like' and quotative 'like'. *Journal of Sociolinguistics*, 4(1), 60–80.
Dajko, N. and Carmichael, K. 2014. But qui c'est la difference? Discourse markers in Louisiana French: The case of but vs. mais. *Language in Society*, 43(2), 159–183.
Davydova, J., Tytus, A. E., and Schleef, E. 2017. Acquisition of sociolinguistic awareness by German learners of English: A study in perceptions of quotative be like. *Linguistics*, 55(4), 783–812.
de Rooij, V. A. 2000. French discourse markers in Shaba Swahili conversations. *International Journal of Bilingualism*, 4(4), 447–469.
Degand, L., Martin, L., and Simon, A. C. 2014. LOCAS-F: Un corpus oral multigenre annoté. In F. Neveu, M. Toke, J. Durand et al., eds., *Proceedings of Congrès Mondial de Linguistique Française*. Paris: EDP Science, 2613–2626.
Delin, J. 1992. Re: 3.174 All's. The LINGUIST List. https://linguistlist.org/issues/3/3-179.html/.
Denis, D. 2016. Oral histories as a window to sociolinguistic history and language history: Exploring earlier Ontario English with the Farm Work and Farm Life Since 1890 oral history collection. *American Speech*, 91(4), 513–516.
Denis, D. 2017. The development of and stuff in Canadian English: A longitudinal study of apparent grammaticalization. *Journal of English Linguistics*, 45(2), 157–185.
Denniston, J. D. 1934. *The Greek Particles*. Oxford: Clarendon Press.
Dessureault-Dober, D. 1974. Étude sociolinguistique de (ça) fait que: "coordonnant logique" et "marqueur d'interaction." PhD thesis, University of Quebec.
Digesto, S. 2019. Verum a fontibus haurire: A variationist analysis of subjunctive variability across space and time: From contemporary Italian back to Latin. PhD thesis, University of Ottawa.
Dines, E. R. 1980. Variation in discourse: And stuff like that. *Language in Society*, 9(1), 13–31.
Diskin, C. 2015. Discourse-pragmatic variation and language ideologies among native and non-native speakers of English: A case study of Polish and Chinese migrants in Dublin, Ireland. PhD thesis, University College Dublin.
Diskin, C. 2017. The use of the discourse-pragmatic marker 'like' by native and non-native speakers of English in Ireland. *Journal of Pragmatics*, 120, 144–157.
Diskin, C. and Levey, S. 2019. Going global and sounding local: Quotative variation and change in L1 and L2 speakers of Irish (Dublin) English. *English World-Wide*, 40(1), 53–78.

Drummond, K. and Hopper, R. 1993. Some uses of yeah. *Research on Language and Social Interaction*, 26(2), 203–212.

Du Bois, J. 1985. Competing motivations. In J. Haiman, ed., *Iconicity in Syntax*. Amsterdam: John Benjamins, 343–365.

Dubois, B. and Crouch, I. 1975. The question of tag questions in women's speech: They don't really use more of them, do they? *Language in Society*, 4(3), 289–294.

Dubois, S. 1992. Extension particles, etc. *Language Variation and Change*, 4(2), 179–203.

Duncan, S. and Fiske, D. W. 1977. *Face-to-Face Interaction: Research, Methods, and Theory*, Vol. 3. Mahwah, NJ: Lawrence Erlbaum Associates.

Duncan, S. and Niederehe, G. 1974. On signalling that it's your turn to speak. *Journal of Experimental Social Psychology*, 10(3), 234–247.

Dupont, M. and Zufferey, S. 2017. Methodological issues in the use of directional parallel corpora. A case study of English and French concessive connectives. *International Journal of Corpus Linguistics*, 22(2), 270–297.

Eckert, P. 2008. Variation and the indexical field. *Journal of Sociolinguistics*, 12(4), 453–476.

Eckert, P. 2012. Three waves of variation study: The emergence of meaning in the study of sociolinguistic variation. *Annual Review of Anthropology*, 41, 87–100.

Egbert, J. and Staples, S. 2019. Doing multi-dimensional analysis in SPSS, SAS & R. In T. B. Sardinha and M. V. Pinto, eds., *Multi-Dimensional Analysis: Research Methods and Current Issues*. London: Bloomsbury Publishing.

Eiswirth, M. 2020a. It's all about the interaction: Listener responses as a discourse-organisational variable. PhD thesis, University of Edinburgh.

Eiswirth, M. 2020b. Increasing interactional accountability in the quantitative analysis of sociolinguistic variation. *Journal of Pragmatics*, 170, 171–188.

Erman, B. 1987. *Pragmatic Expressions in English*. Stockholm: Almqvist & Wiksell.

Erman, B. 1995. Grammaticalization in progress: The case of or something. In I. Moen, H. G. Simonsen, and H. Lødrup, eds., *Papers from the Fifteenth Scandinavian Conference of Linguistics, Oslo, 13–15 January 1995*. Oslo: University of Oslo Department of Linguistics, 136–147.

Erman, B. 2001. Pragmatic markers revisited with a focus on you know in adult and adolescent talk. *Journal of Pragmatics*, 33(9), 1337–1357.

European Commission. 2012. *Special Eurobarometer 386: Europeans and Their Languages*. http://ec.europa.eu/public_opinion/archives/ebs/ebs_386_en.pdf/.

Evison, J., McCarthy, M., and O'Keeffe, A. 2007. "Looking out for love and all the rest of it": Vague category markers as shared social space. In J. Cutting, ed., *Vague Language Explored*. London: Springer, 138–157.

Fellegy, A. M. 1995. Patterns and functions of minimal response. *American Speech*, 70(2), 186–199.

Fernández, J. 2015. General extender use in spoken peninsular Spanish: Metapragmatic awareness and pedagogical implications. *Journal of Spanish Language Teaching*, 2(1), 1–17.

Fischer, K. 2000. Discourse particles, turn-taking, and the semantics-pragmatics interface. *Revue de sémantique et pragmatique*, 8, 111–132.

Fischer, K. 2014. Discourse markers. In K. Schneider and A. Barron, eds., *Pragmatics of Discourse*. Berlin: De Gruyter, 271–294.

Fischer, R. and Pułaczewska, H. 2008. *Anglicisms in Europe: Linguistic Diversity in a Global Context*. Newcastle upon Tyne: Cambridge Scholars Publishing.
Fleischman, S. and Yaguello, M. 2004. Discourse markers across languages. In C. Moder and A. Martinovic-Zic, eds., *Discourse Across Languages and Cultures*. Amsterdam: John Benjamins, 129–147.
Flesch, M. 2019. "That spelling tho'": A sociolinguistic study of the non-standard form of *though* in a corpus of Reddit comments. *EuJAL*, 7(2), 163–188.
Follett, W. 1998/1966. *Modern American Usage*, rev ed. E. Wensberg. New York: Hall & Wang.
Foolen, A. 2008. New quotative markers in spoken discourse. In B. Ahrenholz, U. Bredel, and W. Klein, et al., eds., *Empirische Forschung und Theoriebildung*. Frankfurt am Main: Peter Lang, 117–128.
Ford, C. E. and Thompson, S. A. 1996. Interactional units in conversation: Syntactic, intonational, and pragmatic resources for the management of turns. In E. Ochs, E. A. Schegloff, and S. A. Thompson, eds., *Interaction and Grammar*. Cambridge: Cambridge University Press, 134–184.
Fox, S. 2012. Performed narrative: The pragmatic function of *this is* + speaker and other quotatives in London adolescent speech. In I. Buchstaller and I. van Alphen, eds., *Quotatives: Cross-Linguistic and Cross-Disciplinary Perspectives*. Amsterdam: John Benjamins, 231–258.
Fox Tree, J. E. 2015. Discourse markers in writing. *Discourse Studies*, 17(1), 64–82.
Fox Tree, J. E. and Schrock, J. C. 2002. Basic meanings of you know and I mean. *Journal of Pragmatics*, 34(6), 727–747.
Fraser, B. 1999. What are discourse markers? *Journal of Pragmatics*, 31(7), 931–952.
Fruehwald, J. 2016. Filled pause choice as a sociolinguistic variable. *University of Pennsylvania Working Papers in Linguistics*, 22(2), 41–49.
Fruehwald, J. and Wallenberg, J. C. 2013. Optionality is stable variation is competing grammars. Paper presented at the Twenty-Fifth Scandinavian Conference of Linguistics, Formal Ways of Analyzing Variation Workshop. Háskóli Íslands, May 13–15.
Fujii, K. 2006. *English in America: Its Usage and Pronunciation [Amerika no Eigo: Goho to Hatsuon]*. Tokyo: Nan'un-do.
Fuller, J. M. 2001. The principle of pragmatic detachability in borrowing: English-origin discourse Markers in Pennsylvania German. *Linguistics: An Interdisciplinary Journal of the Language Sciences*, 39(2), 351–369.
Fuller, J. M. 2003. Discourse marker use across speech contexts: A comparison of native and non-native speaker performance, *Multilingua*, 22(2), 185–208.
Fung, L. and Carter, R. 2007. Discourse markers and spoken English: Native and learner use in pedagogic settings. *Applied Linguistics*, 28(3), 410–439.
Furiassi, C. and Gottlieb, H. (eds.). 2015. *Pseudo-English: Studies on False Anglicisms in Europe*. Berlin: Mouton de Gruyter.
Furiassi, C., Pulcini, V., and Rodríguez Gonzalez, F. (eds.). 2012. *The Anglicization of European Lexis*. Amsterdam: John Benjamins.
Gadanidis, T. 2018. Um, about that, uh, variable. MA thesis, University of Toronto.
Galinsky, H. 1967. Stylistic aspects of linguistic borrowing. In B. Carstensen and H. Galinsky, eds., *Amerikanismen der deutschen Gegenwartssprache*. Heidelberg: Winter, 35–72.

Gallois, C., Callan, V. J., and Johnstone, M. 1984. Personality judgments of Australian Aborigine and white speakers: Ethnicity, sex, and context. *Journal of Language and Social Psychology*, 3(1), 39–58.

Gardner, R. 1998. Between speaking and listening: The vocalisation of understandings. *Applied Linguistics*, 19(2), 204–224.

Garside, R. 1993. The marking of cohesive relationships: Tools for the construction of a large bank of anaphoric data. *ICAME Journal*, 17, 5–27.

Giles, H., Bourhis, R. Y., Trudgill, P., and Lewis, A. 1974. The imposed norm hypothesis: A validation. *Quarterly Journal of Speech*, 60(4), 405–410.

Gille, J. 2006. Iraq y cosas así: Conversational appendices in colloquial Spanish. *Moderna Språk*, 100(1), 157–166.

Gille, J. and Häggkvist, C. 2006. Los niveles del diálogo y los apéndices conversacionales. In J. Falk, J. Gille, and F. Wachtmeister Bermúdez, eds., *Discurso, interacción e identidad*. Stockholm: Stockholm University, 65–80.

Gille, J. and Häggkvist, C. 2010. Apéndices generalizadores introducidos por o. *Oralia*, 13, 127–144.

Givón, T. 1989. *Mind, Code and Context: Essays in Pragmatics*. Hove: Psychology Press.

Godfrey, J. J., Holliman, E. C., and McDaniel, J. 1992. Switchboard: Telephone speech corpus for research and development. *[Proceedings] ICASSP-92: 1992 IEEE International Conference on Acoustics, Speech, and Signal Processing*, 1, 517–520.

Goodwin, C. 1984. Notes on story structure and the organization of participation. In J. M. Atkinson, ed., *Structures of Social Action*. Cambridge: Cambridge University Press, 225–246.

Goodwin, C. 1986. Between and within: Alternative treatments of continuers and assessment. *Human Studies*, 9(2), 205–217.

Görlach, M. 2001. *A Dictionary of European Anglicisms: A Usage Dictionary of Anglicisms in Sixteen European Languages*. Oxford: Oxford University Press.

Goss, E. and Salmons, J. 2000. Evolution of a bilingual discourse marking system: Modal particles and English markers in German American dialects. *International Journal of Bilingualism*, 4(4), 469–484.

Graedler, A.-L. 1998. *Morphological, Semantic and Functional Aspects of English Lexical Borrowings in Norwegian*. Oslo: Universitetsforlaget.

Graedler, A.-L. and Johansson, S. 1997. *Anglisismeordboka: engelske lånord i norsk*. Oslo: Universitetsforlaget.

Greenwald, A. G. 1976. Within-subjects designs: To use or not to use? *Psychological Bulletin*, 83(2), 314–320.

Grice, H. P. 1975. Logic and conversation. In Cole, P. and Morgan, J., eds., *Syntax and Semantics 3: Speech Acts*. New York: Seminar Press, 225–242.

Grieve, J., Nini, A., and Guo, D. 2016. Analyzing lexical emergence in Modern American English online. *English Language and Linguistics* 21(1), 99–127.

Guardamagna, C. 2010. When doing is saying: A constructional account of *fare* ('to do') as a *verbum dicendi* in Italian. In G. Bota, H. Hargreaves, L. Chia-Chun, and R. Rong, eds., *Papers from the Lancaster University Postgraduate Conference in Linguistics & Language Teaching, Vol. 4: Papers from LAEL PG 2009*. Lancaster: University of Lancaster, 1–24

Güldemann, T. 2008. *Quotative Indexes in African Languages: A Synchronic and Diachronic Survey*. Berlin: Mouton de Gruyter.

Gumperz, J. J. 1984. *Discourse Strategies*. Cambridge: Cambridge University Press.

Halbe, D. 2013. *English in Business Meetings: A Corpus Study of Directives and Lexis in National and International Settings*. Berlin: epubli Verlag.

Hardie, A. 2018. Using the spoken BNC2014 in CQP web. In V. Brezina, R. Love, and K. Aijmer, eds., *Corpus Approaches to Contemporary British Speech. Sociolinguistic Studies of the Spoken BNC2014*. New York and London: Routledge, 27–30.

Hasselgreen, A. 2004. *Testing the Spoken English of Young Norwegians: A Study of Test Validity and the Role of "Smallwords" in Contributing to Pupils' Fluency*. Cambridge: Cambridge University Press.

Haugen, E. [1953] 1969. *The Norwegian Language in America: A Study in Bilingual Behaviour*. Philadelphia: University of Pennsylvania Press.

Hay, J., Drager, K., and Warren, P. 2010. Short-term exposure to one dialect affects processing of another. *Language and Speech*, 53(4), 447–471.

Hay, J., Warren, P., and Drager, K. 2006. Factors influencing speech perception in the context of a merger-in-progress. *Journal of Phonetics*, 34(4), 458–484.

Heine, B. 2003. Grammaticalization. In B. D. Joseph and R. D. Janda, eds., *The Handbook of Historical Linguistics*. Malden, MA: Blackwell.

Heine, B. 2014. On discourse markers: Grammaticalization, pragmaticalization, or something else? *Linguistics*, 51(6), 1205–1247.

Heine, B., Claudi, U., and Hünnemeyer, F. 1991. *Grammaticalization: A Conceptual Framework*. Chicago: University of Chicago Press.

Heine, B. and Kuteva, T. 2002. *World Lexicon of Grammaticalization*. Cambridge: Cambridge University Press.

Hellermann, J. and Vergun, A. 2007. Language which is not taught: The discourse marker use of beginning adult learners of English. *Journal of Pragmatics*, 39(1), 157–179.

Herring, S. C., Stein, D., and Virtanen, T. 2013. *Pragmatics of Computer-Mediated Communication*. Berlin: Mouton de Gruyter.

Hesson, A. and Shellgren, M. 2015. Discourse marker *like* in real time: Characterizing the time-course of sociolinguistic impression formation. *American Speech*, 90(2), 154–186.

Hickey, R. 2010. *The Handbook of Language Contact*. Malden, MA: Wiley-Blackwell.

Hickey, T. 2009. Code-switching and borrowing in Irish. *Journal of Sociolinguistics*, 13(5), 670–688.

Hilgendorf, S. K. 1996. The impact of English in Germany. *English Today*, 12(3), 3–14.

Hlavac, J. 2006. Bilingual discourse markers: Evidence from Croatian-English code-switching. *Journal of Pragmatics*, 38(11), 1870–1900.

Höglund, M. and Syrjänen, K. 2016. Corpus of early American literature. *ICAME Journal*, 40, 17–38.

Holmes, J. 1986. Functions of you know in women's and men's speech. *Language in Society*, 15(1), 1–22.

Holmes, J. 1995. *Women, Men and Politeness*. London: Longman.

Hopper, P. J. 1991. On some principles of grammaticization. In E. C. Traugott and B. Heine, eds., *Approaches to Grammaticalization, Vol. 1: Focus on Theoretical and Methodological Issues*. Amsterdam: John Benjamins, 17–35.

House, J. 1989. Politeness in English and German: The functions of bitte and please. In S. Blum-Kulka, J. House, and G. Kasper, eds., *Cross-Cultural Pragmatics: Requests and Apologies*. Norwood, NJ: Ablex.

House, J. 2009. Subjectivity in English as lingua franca discourse: The case of *you know*. *Intercultural Pragmatics*, 6(2), 171–193.

Huddleston, R. D. and Pullum, G. K. 2002. *The Cambridge Grammar of the English Language*. Cambridge: Cambridge University Press.

Ilbury, C. 2019. "Beyond the offline": Social media and the social meaning of variation in East London. PhD thesis, Queen Mary University of London.

Irwin, P. 2014. SO [TOTALLY] speaker-oriented: An analysis of "drama SO." In R. Zanuttini and L. R. Horn, eds., *Microsyntactic Variation in North American English*. New York: Oxford University Press, 29–70.

Isosävi, J. 2020. Cultural outsiders' evaluations of (im)politeness in Finland and in France. *Journal of Politeness Research*, 16(2), 249–280.

Israel, M. 2004. The pragmatics of polarity. In L. R. Horn and G. Ward, eds., *The Handbook of Pragmatics*. Malden, MA: Blackwell, 701–723.

Jaramillo, J. A. 1995. The passive legitimization of Spanish: A macrosociolinguistic study of a quasi-border: Tucson, Arizona. *International Journal of the Sociology of Language*, 114, 67–91.

Jefferson, G. 1991. List construction as a task and resource. In G. Psathas, ed., *Interactional Competence*. New York: Irvington Publishers, 63–92.

Jefferson, G. 1993. Caveat speaker: Preliminary notes on recipient topic-shift implicature. *Research on Language and Social Interaction*, 26(1), 1–30.

Jokela, H. 2012. Nollapersoonalause suomessa ja virossa: Tutkimus kirjoitetun kielen aineistosta, PhD thesis, University of Turku.

Jones, M. C. 1998. *Language Obsolescence and Revitalization: Linguistic Change in Two Sociolinguistically Contrasting Welsh Communities*. Oxford: Oxford University Press.

Joseph, B. D. 2001. Is there such a thing as "grammaticalization?". *Language Sciences*, 23(2/3), 163–186.

Kallen, J. 2005. Silence and mitigation in Irish English discourse. In A. Barron and K. P. Schneider, eds., *The Pragmatics of Irish English*. Berlin: Mouton de Gruyter, 47–71.

Kaltenböck, G. 2013. The development of comment clauses. In B. Aarts, J. Close, G. Leech, and S. Wallis, eds., *The Verb Phrase in English*. Cambridge: Cambridge University Press, 286–317.

Kaltenböck, G., Heine, B., and Kuteva, T. 2011. On thetical grammar. *Studies in Language*, 35(4), 848–893.

Kasper, G. and Blum-Kulka, S. (eds.). 1993. *Interlanguage Pragmatics*. Oxford: Oxford University Press.

Kastronic, L. 2011. Discourse like in Quebec English. *University of Pennsylvania Working Papers in Linguistics*, 17(2), 105–114.

Kendrick, K. H. 2017. Using conversation analysis in the lab. *Research on Language and Social Interaction*, 50(1), 1–11.

Kern, J. 2020a. Like in English and como, como que, and like in Spanish in the speech of Southern Arizona bilinguals. *International Journal of Bilingualism*, 24(2), 187–207.

Kern, J. 2020b. Quotatives in English and Spanish among bilinguals. *Sociolinguistic Studies*, 14(1–2), 85–110.

Kilgarriff, A., Baisa, V., Bušta, J. et al. 2014. The sketch engine: Ten years on. *Lexicography*, 1(1), 7–36.

Kilgarriff, A., Reddy, S., Pomikálek, J., and Avinesh, P. V. S. 2010. A corpus factory for many languages. In N. Calzolari, K. Choukri, B. Maegaard et al., eds., *Proceedings of the Seventh International Conference on Language Resources and Evaluation (LREC 10')*. Valetta: European Language Resources Association (ELRA), 904–910.

Kinkade, M. D. 1976. Interior Salishan particles. Paper presented at the 11th International Conference on Salish Languages (ICSL). Seattle, Washington, August 12-14.

Kirk, J. M. 2016. The pragmatic annotation scheme of the SPICE Ireland Corpus. *International Journal of Corpus Linguistics*, 21(3), 299–322.

Kitzinger, C. 2012. Repair. In T. Stivers and J. Sidnell, eds., *The Handbook of Conversation Analysis*. Hoboken, NJ: John Wiley & Sons, 229–256.

Koch, P. and Oesterreicher, W. 1985. Sprache der Nähe – Sprache der Distanz: Mündlichkeit und Schriftlichkeit im Spannungsfeld von Sprachtheorie und Sprachgebrauch. *Romanistisches Jahrbuch*, 36, 15–43.

Kohn, K. 2012. Pedagogic corpora for content and language integrated learning: Insights from the BACKBONE project. *The Eurocall Review*, 20(2), 3–22.

Krippendorff, K. 2004a. *Content Analysis: An Introduction to its Methodology*, 2nd ed. London: Sage.

Krippendorff, K. 2004b. Reliability in content analysis. *Human Communication Research*, 30(3), 411–433.

Krippendorff, K. 2011. *Computing Krippendorff's Alpha-Reliability*. https://repository.upenn.edu/asc_papers/43/.

Kriwonossow, A. 1966. Die Rolle der Modalen Partikeln in der Kommunikativen Gliederung der Aussagesätze, der Fragesätze, der Befehlssätze und der Nebensätze in Bezug auf die Hauptsatzglieder. *Zeitschrift für Phonetik, Sprachwissenschaft und Kommunikationsforschung*, 19(1/2), 131–140.

Kroch, A. S. 1989. Reflexes of grammar in patterns of language change. *Language Variation and Change*, 1(3), 199–244.

Kroch, A. S. 1994. Morphosyntactic variation. In *Proceedings of the Thirtieth Annual Meeting of the Chicago Linguistics Society*, Vol. 2. Chicago: Chicago Linguistics Society, 180–201.

Kunz, K. and Lapshinova-Koltunski, E. 2015. Cross-linguistic analysis of discourse variation across registers. *Nordic Journal of English Studies*, 14(1), 258–288.

Kuznetsova, A., Brockhoff, P. B., and Christensen, R. H. B. 2017. lmerTest package: Tests in linear mixed effects models. *Journal of Statistical Software*, 82(13), 1–26.

Labelle-Hogue, S.-P. 2013. Kids say the darndest things? Discours des préadolescents, changement linguistique et évolution de like discursif par la méthode. MA thesis, University of Ottawa.

Labov, W. 1963. The social motivation of a sound change. *Word*, 19(3), 273–309.

Labov, W. 1966. *The Social Stratification of English in New York City*. Washington, DC: Center for Applied Linguistics.

Labov, W. 1972a. *Language in the Inner City: Studies in the Black English Vernacular*. Philadelphia: University of Pennsylvania Press.

Labov, W. 1972b. *Sociolinguistic Patterns*. Philadelphia: University of Pennsylvania Press.

Labov, W. 2001a. *Principles of Linguistic Change, Vol. 1: Internal Factors*. Oxford: Blackwell.

Labov, W. 2001b. *Principles of Linguistic Change, Vol. 2: Social Factors*. Oxford: Blackwell.
Labov, W., Ash, S., Ravindranath, M. et al. 2011. Properties of the sociolinguistic monitor. *Journal of Sociolinguistics*, 15(4), 431–463.
Labov, W. and Rosenfelder, I. 2011. *The Philadelphia Neighborhood Corpus*. Philadelphia: University of Pennsylvania. http://fave.ling.upenn.edu/pnc.html/.
Lakoff, R. 1972. Language in context. *Language*, 48(4), 907–927.
Lakoff, R. 1989. The way we were; or; The real actual truth about generative semantics: A memoir. *Journal of Pragmatics*, 13, 939–988.
Lambert, W. E., Hodgson, R. C., Gardner, R. C., and Fillenbaum, S. 1960. Evaluational reactions to spoken language. *Journal of Abnormal and Social Psychology*, 60(1), 44–51.
Lappalainen, Hanna. 2008. Kelan virkailijoiden henkilötunnuspyynnöt. Tutkimus rutiininomaisista toiminnoista. *Virittäjä*, 112(4), 483–516.
Laserna, C. M., Seih, Y.-T., and Pennebaker, J. W. 2014. Um ... who like says you know: Filler word use as a function of age, gender, and personality. *Journal of Language and Social Psychology*, 33(3), 328–338.
Lavandera, B. R. 1978. Where does the sociolinguistic variable stop. *Language in Society*, 7(2), 171–182.
Leech, G., Hundt, M., Mair, C., and Smith, N. 2009. *Change in Contemporary English: A Grammatical Study*. Cambridge: Cambridge University Press.
Lehtonen, H. 2015. Tyylitellen. Nuorten kielelliset resurssit ja kielen sosiaalinen indeksisyys monietnisessä Helsingissä. PhD thesis, University of Helsinki.
Leppänen, S., Pitkänen-Huhta, A. Nikula, T. et al. 2011. *National Survey on the English Language in Finland: Uses, meanings and attitudes. Studies in Variation, Contacts and Change in English*. Helsinki: Research Unit for Variation, Contacts, and Change in English.
Leppänen, S., Nikula, T., and Käänta, L. 2008. *Kolmas kotimainen: lähikuvia englannin käytöstä Suomessa*. Helsinki: Suomalaisen Kirjallisuuden Seura.
Lerner, G. H. 1994. Responsive list construction. A conversational resource for accomplishing multifaceted social action. *Language and Social Psychology*, 13(1), 20–33.
Lerner, G. H. 2004. Collaborative turn sequences. In G. H. Lerner, ed., *Conversation Analysis: Studies from the First Generation*. Amsterdam: John Benjamins, 225–256.
Levelt, W. J. 1989. *Speaking: From intention to articulation*. Cambridge, MA: MIT Press.
Levey, S. 2006. The sociolinguistic distribution of discourse marker 'like' in preadolescent speech. *Multilingua*, 25, 413–441.
Levey, S., Groulx, K., and Roy, J. 2013. A variationist perspective on discourse-pragmatic change in a contact setting. *Language Variation and Change*, 25(2), 225–251.
Levon, E. and Fox, S. 2014. Social salience and the sociolinguistic monitor: A case study of (ING) and TH-fronting in Britain. *Journal of English Linguistics*, 42(3), 185–217.
Levshina, N. 2015. *How to Do Linguistics with R: Data Exploration and Statistical Analysis*. Amsterdam: John Benjamins.
Liao, S. 2009. Variation in the use of discourse markers by Chinese teaching assistants in the U.S. *Journal of Pragmatics*, 41(7), 1313–1328.
Lippi-Green, R. 2012. *English with an Accent: Language, Ideology, and Discrimination in the United States*. Abingdon: Routledge.

Lo, S. and Andrews, S. 2015. To transform or not to transform: using generalized linear mixed models to analyse reaction time data. *Frontiers in Psychology*, 6, 1171.

Love, R. 2017. The Spoken British National Corpus 2014: Design, compilation and analysis. University of Lancaster.

Love, R. Dembry, C., Hardie, A. et al. 2017. The Spoken BNC2014: Designing and building a spoken corpus of everyday conversations. *International Journal of Corpus Linguistics*, 22(3), 311–318.

Macaulay, R. 1991. *Locating Dialect in Discourse: The Language of Honest Men and Bonnie Lasses in Ayr.* Oxford: Oxford University Press.

Macaulay, R. 2002. You know, it depends. *Journal of Pragmatics*, 34(6), 749–767.

Maclay, H. and Osgood, C. E. 1959. Hesitation phenomena in spontaneous English speech. *Word*, 15(1), 19–44.

Maddeauz, R. and Dinkin, A. 2017. Is *like* like *like*? Evaluating the same variant across multiple variables. *Linguistics Vanguard*, 3(1).

Malinowski, B. 1923. The problem of meaning in primitive languages. In C. K. Ogden and I. A. Richards, *The Meaning of Meaning*. London: Routledge and Kegan Paul, 296–336.

Marcus, M., Santorini, B., and Marcinkiewicz, M. A. 1993. Building a large annotated corpus of English: The Penn Treebank. *Computational Linguistics*, 19(2), 313–330.

Margerie, H. and Muller, P. 2019. *Excuse me* vs. *(I'm) sorry* as two contrasting markers of interlocutive relations. *CORELA: Cognition, représentation, langage*, 17(2).

Markkanen, R. 1985. Cross-language studies in pragmatics. *Kielikello*, 11, 15–42.

Marnette, S. 2005. *Speech and Thought Presentation in French*. Amsterdam: John Benjamins.

Martin, J. and White, P. R. 2005. *The Language of Evaluation. Appraisal in English*. Basingstoke: Palgrave Macmillan.

Martineau, F. 2019. Réseaux et frontières en français canadien: L'éclairage réciproque des variétés. *Travaux de linguistique*, 1(78), 47–69.

Martineau, F. and Séguin, M.-C. 2016. Le Corpus FRAN: réseaux et maillages en Amérique française. *Corpus*, 15, 1–24.

Maschler, Y. and Schiffrin, D. 2015. Discourse markers: Language, meaning, and context. In D. Tannen, H. Hamilton, and D. Schiffrin, eds., *The Handbook of Discourse Analysis*, 2nd ed. Hoboken, NJ: John Wiley & Sons, 189–221.

Massam, D., Starks, D., and Ikiua, O. 2006. On the edge of grammar: Discourse particles in Niuean. *Oceanic Linguistics*, 45(1), 191–205.

Matras, Y. 1998. Utterance modifiers and universals of grammatical borrowing. *Linguistics*, 36(2), 281–332.

Matras, Y. 2000. Fusion and the cognitive basis for bilingual discourse markers. *International Journal of Bilingualism*, 4(4), 505–528.

Maynard, S. K. 1990. Conversation management in contrast: Listener response in Japanese and American English. *Journal of Pragmatics*, 14(3), 397–412.

McCawley, J. D. 1994. Generative Semantics. In J. Verschueren, J.-O. Östman, and J. Blommaert, eds., *Handbook of Pragmatics Manual*. Amsterdam: John Benjamins, 311–319.

McEnery, T. and Hardie, A. 2011. *Corpus Linguistics: Method, Theory and Practice*. Cambridge: Cambridge University Press.

Mencken, H. L. [1948] 1952. *The American Language. Supplement II*. New York: Alfred A. Knopf.
Mendes, R. B. 2013. Projeto SP2010: Amostra da fala paulistana. http://projetosp2010.fflch.usp.br/.
Meyerhoff, M. 1999. Sorry in the Pacific: Defining communities, defining practices. *Language in Society*, 28(2), 225–238.
Meyerhoff, M. 2014. Variation and Gender. In S. Ehrlich, M. Meyerhoff, J. Holmes, eds., *The Handbook of Language, Gender, and Sexuality*, 2nd ed. Hoboken, NJ: John Wiley & Sons, 85–102.
Meyerhoff, M. and Ehrlich, S. 2019. Language, gender, and sexuality. *Annual Review of Linguistics*, 5(1), 455–475.
Meyerhoff, M. and Niedzielski, N. 2003. The globalization of vernacular variation. *Journal of Sociolinguistics*, 7(4), 534–555.
Meyerhoff, M. and Schleef, E. 2014. Hitting an Edinburgh target: Immigrant adolescents' acquisition of variation in Edinburgh English. In Robert Lawson, ed., *Sociolinguistics in Scotland*. Basingstoke: Palgrave Macmillan, 103–128.
Meyerhoff, M., Schleef, E., and MacKenzie, L. 2015. *Doing Sociolinguistics: A Practical Guide to Data Collection and Analysis*. London: Routledge.
Mihatsch, W. 2009. The approximators French *comme*, Italian *come*, Portuguese *como* and Spanish *como* from a grammaticalization perspective. In C. Rossari, C. Ricci, and A. Spiridion, eds., *Grammaticalization and Pragmatics: Facts Approaches, Theoretical Issue*. Bingley: Emerald, 65–91.
Mihatsch, W. 2018. From ad hoc category to ad hoc categorization: The proceduralization of Argentinian Spanish *tipo*. *Folia Linguistica Historica*, 52(s39-1), 147–176.
Milroy, L. 1987. *Language and Social Networks*, 2nd ed. Oxford: Blackwell.
Mišić Ilić, B. 2017. Pragmatic borrowing from English into Serbian: Linguistic and sociocultural aspects. *Journal of Pragmatics*, 113, 103–115.
Moore, E. and Podesva, R. 2009. Style, indexicality, and the social meaning of tag questions. *Language in Society*, 38(4), 447–485.
Morris, C. W. 1938. Foundations of the theory of signs. In O. Neurath, N. Bohr, J. Dewey et al., eds., *International Encyclopedia of Unified Science*, Vol. 1:2. Chicago: University of Chicago Press, 1–59.
Mortier, L. and Degand, L. 2009. Adversative discourse markers in contrast: the need for a combined corpus approach. *International Journal of Corpus Linguistics*, 14(3), 338–366.
Mosegaard Hansen, M.-B. 1998. *The Function of Discourse Particles. A Study with Special Reference to Spoken Standard French*. Amsterdam: John Benjamins.
Mougeon, R. and Beniak, É. 1991. *Linguistic Consequences of Language Contact and Restriction: The Case of French in Ontario, Canada*. Oxford: Oxford University Press.
Mougeon, R., Frenette, Y., and Gagnon, M.-A. 2018. Genèse, essor et refondation de la communauté francophone de Welland, en Ontario. In F. Martineau, A. Boudreau, Y. Frenette, and F. Gadet, eds., *Francophonies nord-américaines: langues, frontières et idéologies*. Quebec: Presses de l'Université Laval, 263–285.
Mougeon, R., Hallion, S, Bigot, D., and Papen, R. 2016. Convergence et divergence sociolinguistique en français laurentien: l'alternance rien que/juste/ seulement/seulement que/ne ... que. *Journal of French Language Studies*, 26(2), 115–154.

Mougeon, R., Hallion, S., Papen, R., and Bigot, D. 2010. Convergence vs divergence. Variantes morphologiques de la première personne de l'auxiliaire *aller* dans les variétés de français laurentien du Canada. In C. Leblanc, F. Martineau, and Y. Frenette, eds., *Vues sur les français d'ici*. Quebec: Presses de l'Université Laval, 131–184.

Mougeon, R., Nadasdi, T., and Rehner, K. 2009. Évolution de l'usage des conjonctions et locutions de conséquence par les adolescents franco-ontariens de Hawkesbury et Pembroke (1978–2005). In F. Martineau, R. Mougeon, T. Nadasdi, and M. Tremblay, eds., *Le français d'ici: études linguistiques et sociolinguistiques sur la variation du français au Québec et en Ontario*. Toronto: GREF. 175–214.

Müller, S. 2005. *Discourse Markers in Native and Non-Native English Discourse*. Amsterdam: John Benjamins.

Murphy, B. 2010. *Corpus and Sociolinguistics. Investigating Age and Gender in Female Talk*. Amsterdam: John Benjamins.

Murphy, B. 2012. Exploring response tokens in Irish English: A multidisciplinary approach: Integrating variational pragmatics, sociolinguistics and corpus linguistics. *International Journal of Corpus Linguistics*, 17(3), 325–348.

Nahkola, K. and Saanilahti, M. 2004. Mapping language change in real time: A panel study of Finnish. *Language Variation and Change*, 16(2), 75–92.

Neary Sundquist, C. 2014. The use of pragmatic markers across proficiency levels in second language speech. *Studies in Second Language Learning and Teaching*, 4(4), 637–663.

Nelson, G., Wallis, S., and Aarts, B. 2002. *Exploring Natural Language: Working with the British Component of the International Corpus of English*. Amsterdam: John Benjamins.

Nestor, N., Ní Chasaide, C., and Regan, V. 2012. Discourse 'like' and social identity: A case study of Poles in Ireland. In B. Migge and M. Ní Chiosáin, eds., *New Perspectives on Irish English*. Amsterdam: John Benjamins, 327–353.

Nevalainen, T. and Raumolin-Brunberg, H. 2003. *Historical Linguistics: Language Change in Tudor and Stuart England*. London: Routledge.

Núñez Pertejo, P. and Palacios Martínez, I. M. 2014. *That's absolutely crap, totally rubbi*sh: The use of the intensifiers *absolutely* and *totally* in the spoken language of British adults and teenagers. *Functions of Language*, 21(2), 210–237.

O'Keeffe, A. 2004. Like the wise virgins and all that jazz: Using a corpus to examine vague categorization and shared knowledge. *Language and Computers*, 52(1), 1–26.

O'Keeffe, A. and Adolphs, S. 2008. Response tokens in British and Irish discourse: Corpus, context and variational pragmatics. In K. P. Schneider and A. Barron, eds., *Variational Pragmatics*. Amsterdam: John Benjamins. 69–98.

OSF (Official Statistics of Finland). 2015. *Use of Information and Communications Technology by Individuals*. Helsinki: Statistics Finland. www.stat.fi/til/sutivi/2015/sutivi_2015_2015-11-26_tie_001_en.html/.

OSF (Official Statistics of Finland). 2016. *Population Structure*. Helsinki: Statistics Finland. www.stat.fi/til/vaerak/index_en.html/.

Onysko, A. 2007. *Anglicisms in German: Borrowing, Lexical Productivity and Written Codeswitching*. Berlin: Walter de Gruyter.

Oreström, B. 1983. *Turn-Taking in English Conversation*. Lund: Gleerup.

Osborne, J. W., Costello, A. B., and Kellow, J. T. 2008. Best practices in exploratory factor analysis. In J. W. Osborne, ed., *Best Practices in Quantitative Methods*. London: Sage, 86–99.

Östman, J.-O. 1981. *You Know: A Discourse-Functional Approach*. Amsterdam: John Benjamins.
Östman, J.-O. 1982. The symbiotic relationship between pragmatic particles and impromptu speech. In N. E. Enkvist, ed., *Impromptu Speech: A Symposium*. Turku: The Research Institute of the Åbo Akademi Foundation, 147–177.
Östman, J.-O. 1986. Pragmatics as implicitness. PhD thesis, University of California at Berkeley.
Östman, J.-O. 1995. Pragmatic particles twenty years after. In B. Wårvik, S.-K. Tanskanen, and R. Hiltunen, eds., *Organization in Discourse*. Turku: University of Turku, 95–108.
Overstreet, M. 1999. *Whales, Candlelight and Stuff Like That: General Extenders in English Discourse*. New York: Oxford University Press.
Overstreet, M. 2005. And stuff und so: Investigating pragmatic expressions in English and German. *Journal of Pragmatics*, 37(11), 1845–1864.
Overstreet, M. 2014. The role of pragmatic function in the grammaticalization of English general extenders. *Pragmatics*, 24(1), 105–129.
Overstreet, M. and Yule, G. 1997. On being inexplicit and stuff in contemporary American English. *Journal of English Linguistics*, 25(3), 250–258.
Overstreet, M. and Yule, G. 2002. The metapragmatics of and everything. *Journal of Pragmatics*, 34(6), 785–794.
Palacios Martínez, I. M. 2014. The quotative system in Spanish and English youth talk: A contrastive corpus-based study. *Miscelánea*, 49, 95–114.
Palmer, M., Kingsbury, P., and Gildea, D. 2005. The proposition bank: An annotated corpus of semantic roles. *Computational Linguistics*, 31(1), 71–106.
Paradis, C. 1997. *Degree Modifies of Adjectives in Spoken British English*. Lund: Lund University Press.
Partington, A. 2004. "Utterly content in each other's company": Semantic prosody and semantic preference. *International Journal of Corpus Linguistics*, 9(1), 131–156.
Parton, S. R., Siltanen, S. A., Hosman, L. A., and Langenderfer, J. 2002. Employment interview outcomes and speech style effects. *Journal of Language and Social Psychology*, 21(2), 144–161.
Parvaresh, V., Tavangar, M., Rasekh, A. E., and Izadi, D. 2012. About his friend, how good she is, and this and that: General extenders in native Persian and non-native English discourse. *Journal of Pragmatics*, 44(3), 261–279.
Paunonen, H. and Paunonen, M. 2000. *Tsennaaks Stadii, bonjaaks slangii: Stadin slangin suursanakirja*. Helsinki: WSOY.
Peterson, E. 2004. Social appropriateness and language variation: A study of Finnish requests. PhD thesis, Indiana University.
Peterson, E. 2010. Perspective and politeness in Finnish requests. *Pragmatics*, 20(3), 401–423.
Peterson, E. 2017. The nativization of pragmatic borrowings in remote language contact situations. *Journal of Pragmatics*, 113, 116–126.
Peterson, E. and Vaattovaara, J. 2014. Kiitos and pliis: The relationship of native and borrowed politeness markers in Finnish. *Journal of Politeness Research*, 10(2), 247–269.
Peterson, E. and Beers Fägersten, K. 2018. Introduction to the special issue: Linguistic and pragmatic outcomes of contact with English. *Journal of Pragmatics*, 133, 105–108.

Pęzik, P. 2015. Spokes: A search and exploration service for conversational corpus data. In J. Odijk, ed., *Selected Papers from the CLARIN 2014 Conference, October 24– 25,2014, Soesterberg, The Netherlands*. Linköping: Linköping University Electronic Press, 99–109.
Pichler, H. 2010. Methods in discourse variation analysis: Reflections on the way forward. *Journal of Sociolinguistics*, 14(5), 581–608.
Pichler, H. 2013. *The Structure of Discourse-Pragmatic Variation*. Amsterdam: John Benjamins.
Pichler, H. (ed.). 2016a. *Discourse-Pragmatic Variation and Change in English: New Methods and Insights*. Cambridge University Press.
Pichler, H. 2016b. Introduction: discourse-pragmatic variation and change. In H. Pichler, ed., *Discourse-Pragmatic Variation and Change in English: New Methods and Insights*. Cambridge: Cambridge University Press, 1–18.
Pichler, H. 2016c. Uncovering discourse-pragmatic innovations: *Innit* in Multicultural London English. In H. Pichler, ed., *Discourse-Pragmatic Variation and Change in English: New Methods and Insights*. Cambridge: Cambridge University Press, 59–85.
Pichler, H. 2021. Tagging monologic narratives of personal experience: Utterance-final tags and the construction of adolescent masculinity. In K. Beaman, I. Buchstaller, S. Fox, and J. Walker, eds., *Advancing Socio-Grammatical Variation and Change: Sociolinguistic Research in Honour of Jenny Cheshire*. London: Routledge, 377–398.
Pichler, H. In Press. Grammaticalization and language contact in a discourse-pragmatic change in progress: *Innit* in London English. *Language in Society*.
Pichler, H. and Levey, S. 2011. In search of grammaticalization in synchronic dialect data: general extenders in northeast England. *English Language and Linguistics*, 15(3), 441–471.
Pike, K. L. [1954] 1967. *Language in Relation to a Unified Theory of the Structure of Human Behavior*. The Hague: Mouton.
Plümer, N. 2000. *Anglizismus – Purismus – Sprachliche Identität. Eine Untersuchung zu den Anglizismen in der deutschen und französischen Mediensprache*. Frankfurt am Main: Peter Lang.
Pomerantz, A. 1984. Agreeing and disagreeing with assessments: some features of preferred/dispreferred turn shapes. In J. M. Atkinson and J. Heritage, eds., *Structures of Social Action*. Cambridge: Cambridge University Press, 57–101.
Poplack, S., Sankoff, D., and Miller, C. 1988. The social correlates and linguistic processes of lexical borrowing and assimilation. *Linguistics*, 26, 47–104.
Poplack, S. and Tagliamonte, S. A. 2001. *African American Vernacular English in the Diaspora*. Oxford: Blackwell.
Poplack, S. and Torres Cacoullos, R. 2015. Linguistic emergence on the ground: A variationist paradigm. In B. MacWhinney and W. O' Grady, eds., *The Handbook of Language Emergence*. Oxford: Wiley-Blackwell, 267–291.
Popper, K. 1987. Toleration and intellectual responsibility. In S. Mendus and D. Edwards, eds., *On Toleration*. Oxford: Oxford University Press, 17–34.
Prasad, R., Dinesh, N., Lee, A. et al., 2008. The Penn Discourse Treebank 2.0. In N. Calzolari, K. Choukri, B. Maegaard et al., eds., *Proceedings of the 6th International Conference on Language Resources and Evaluation (LREC'08)*. Marrakech: European Language Resources Association (ELRA), 2961–2968.

Prasad, R., Webber, B., and Joshi, A. 2014. Reflections on the Penn Discourse Treebank, Comparable Corpora, and Complementary Annotation. *Computational Linguistics*, 40(4), 921–950.

Prćić, T. [2005] 2011. *Engleski u srpskom: Drugo izdanje*. Novi Sad: Filozofski fakultet.

Preston, D. 2002. Language with an attitude. In J. K. Chambers, P. Trudgill, and N. Schilling-Estes, eds., *The Handbook of Language Variation and Change*. Oxford: Wiley-Blackwell, 40–66.

Preston, D. 2010. Variation in language regard. In P. Gilles, J. Scharloth, and E. Zeigler, eds., *Empirische Evidenzen und theoretische Passungen sprachlicher Variation*. Frankfurth am Main: Peter Lang, 7–27.

Preston, D. 2011. The power of language regard: Discrimination, classification, comprehension and production. *Dialectologia*, Special Issue II, 9–33.

Putnam, M. T. and van Koppen, M. 2011. All there is to know about the alls-construction. *Journal of Comparative Germanic Linguistics*, 14(2), 81–109.

Pya, N., Voinov, V., Makarov, R., and Voinov, Y. 2016. *MvnTest: Goodness of Fit Tests for Multivariate Normality*. R package version 1.1–0. https://CRAN.R-project.org/package=mvnTest/.

Quirk, R., Greenbaum, S., Leech, G., and Svartvik, J., 1985. *A Comprehensive Grammar of the English Language*. London: Longman.

R Core Team. 2013. *R: A Language and Environment for Statistical Computing*. Vienna: R Foundation for Statistical Computing. www.R-project.org/.

Reid, J. 1995. A study of gender differences in minimal responses. *Journal of Pragmatics*, 24(5), 489–512.

Revelle, W. R. 2018. *psych: Procedures for Personality and Psychological Research*. Version 1. 8.12. Northwestern University, Evanston, Illinois. https://CRAN.R-project.org/package=psych/.

Rissanen, M. 2008. From 'quickly' to 'fairly': On the history of *rather*. *English Language and Linguistics*, 12(2), 345–359.

Roberts, I. and Roussou, A. 2003. *Syntactic Change: A Minimalist Approach to Grammaticalization*. Cambridge: Cambridge University Press.

Rodríguez Louro, C. and Harris, T. 2013. Evolution with an attitude: The grammaticalisation of epistemic/evidential verbs in Australian English. *English Language and Linguistics*, 17(3), 415–443.

Romero Trillo, J. 2002. The pragmatic fossilization of discourse markers in non-native speakers of English. *Journal of Pragmatics*, 34(6), 769–784.

Russell, B., Perkins, J. and Grinnel, H. 2008. Interviewees' overuse of the word 'like' and hesitations: Effects in simulated hiring decisions. *Psychological Reports*, 102(1), 111–118.

Sacks, H. 1995. Spring 1970. In *Lectures on Conversation*. Oxford: Wiley-Blackwell, 213–288.

Sacks, H., Schegloff, E. A., and Jefferson, G. 1974. A simplest systematics for the organization of turn-taking for conversation. *Language*, 50(4), 696–735.

Salmons, J. 1990. Bilingual discourse marking: Code switching, borrowing, and convergence in some German-American dialects. *Linguistics*, 28(3), 453–480.

Sankoff, D., Sankoff, G., Laberge, S., and Topham, M. 1976. Méthodes d'échantillonnage et utilisation de l'ordinateur dans l'étude de la variation grammaticale. *Cahiers de Linguistique de l'Université du Québec*, 6, 85–125.

Sankoff, D., Tagliamonte, S., and Smith, E. 2005. *GoldVarb X: A variable rule application for Macintosh and Windows*. http://recombcg.uottawa.ca/lab/software.html/.

Sankoff, G. 2005. Cross-sectional and longitudinal studies in sociolinguistics. In U. Ammon, N. Dittmar, K. J. Mattheier, and P. Trudgill, eds., *An International Handbook of the Science of Language and Society*, Vol. 2. Berlin: de Gruyter, 1003–1013.

Sankoff, G. 2018. Before there were corpora: The evolution of the Montreal French project as a longitudinal study, In S. E. Wagner and I. Buchstaller, eds., *Panel Studies of Variation and Change*. London: Routledge, 21–51.

Sankoff, G. 2019. Language change across the lifespan: three trajectory types. *Language*, 95(2), 197–229.

Sankoff, G. and Wagner, S. E., 2020. The long tail of language change: A trend and panel study of Québecois French futures. *Canadian Journal of Linguistics*, 65(2), 246–275.

Sato, S. 2008. Use of "please" in American and New Zealand English. *Journal of Pragmatics*, 40(7), 1249–1278.

Sayers, D. 2014. The mediated innovation model: A framework for researching media influence in language change. *Journal of Sociolinguistics*, 18(2), 185–212.

Schegloff, E. A. 1982. Discourse as an interactional achievement: Some uses of 'uh huh' and other things that come between sentences. In D. Tannen, ed., *Analyzing Discourse: Text and Talk*. Washington, DC: Georgetown University Press, 71–93.

Schegloff, E. A. 1993. Reflections on quantification in the study of conversation. *Research on Language and Social Interaction*, 26(1), 99–128.

Schegloff, E. A. 2007. *Sequence Organisation in Interaction: A Primer in Conversation Analysis*. Cambridge: Cambridge University Press.

Schiffrin, D. 1987. *Discourse Markers*. Cambridge: Cambridge University Press.

Schleef, E. 2013. Written surveys and questionnaires in sociolinguistics. In J. Holmes and K. Hazen, eds., *Research Methods in Sociolinguistics*. Oxford: Blackwell, 42–57.

Schleef, E. 2019. The evaluation of unfilled pauses: Limits of the prestige, solidarity and dynamism dimensions. *Lingua*, 228, 1–16.

Schleef, E. 2020. Identity and indexicality in the study of World Englishes. In D. Schreier, M. Hundt, and E. W. Schneider, eds., *The Cambridge Handbook of World Englishes*. Cambridge: Cambridge University Press, 609–632.

Schmid, H.-J. 2012. Generalizing the apparently ungeneralizable: Basic ingredients of a cognitive-pragmatic approach to the construal of meaning-in-context. In H.-J. Schmid, ed., *Cognitive Pragmatics*. Berlin: Mouton de Gruyter, 3–22.

Scholman, M., Evers-Vermeul, J., and Sanders, T. 2016. A step-wise approach to discourse annotation: Towards a reliable categorization of coherence relations. *Dialogue and Discourse*, 7(2), 1–28.

Schourup, L. C. 1983. Common discourse particles in English conversation. *Ohio State Working Papers in Linguistics*, 28, i–vi, 1–119.

Schourup, L. C. 1985. *Common Discourse Particles in English Conversation*. New York: Garland.

Schubiger, M. 1965. English intonation and German modal particles: A comparative study. *Phonetica*, 12, 65–84.

Schweinberger, M. 2015. A comparative study of the pragmatic marker like in Irish English and in southeastern varieties of British English. In C. P. Amador-Moreno,

K. McCafferty, and E. Vaughan, eds., *Pragmatic Markers in Irish English*. Amsterdam: John Benjamins, 114–134.

Schweitzer, A. and Lewandowski, N. 2012. Accommodation of backchannels in spontaneous speech. Paper presented at the International Symposium on Imitation and Convergence in Speech. Aix-en-Provence, September 3–5.

Secova, M. 2014. "Je sais et tout mais": Might the general extenders in European French be changing? *Journal of French Language Studies*, 24(2), 281–304.

Shibasaki, R. 2019. From parataxis to amalgamation: The emergence of sentence-final *is all* constructions in the history of American English. In K. Bech and R. Möhlig-Falke, eds., *Grammar – Discourse – Context: Grammar and Usage in Language Variation and Change*. Berlin: Mouton de Gruyter, 221–248.

Shriberg, E. 1994. Preliminaries to a theory of speech disfluencies. PhD thesis, University of California at Berkeley.

Solin, A. and Östman, J.-O. 2016. The notion of responsibility in discourse studies. In J.-O. Östman and A. Solin, eds., *Discourse and Responsibility in Professional Settings*. Sheffield: Equinox, 3–18.

Sorace, A. 2005. Near-nativeness. In C. J. Doughty and M. H. Long, eds. *The Handbook of Second Language Acquisition*. Oxford: Blackwell, 130–151.

Sorjonen, M.-L. 2001. *Responding in Conversation: A Study of Response Particles in Finnish*. Amsterdam: John Benjamins.

Sorjonen, M.-L., Raevaara, L., and Couper-Kuhlen, E. 2017. *Imperative Turns at Talk: The Design of Requests in Action*. Amsterdam: John Benjamins.

Spooren, W. and Degand, L. 2010. Coding coherence relations: Reliability and validity. *Corpus Linguistics and Linguistic* Theory, 6(2), 241–266.

Stange, U. 2017. "You're so not going to believe this": The use of GenX *so* in constructions with future *going to* in American English. *American Speech*, 92(4), 487–524.

Statistics Canada. 2017. *Census Profile. 2016 Census*. Statistics Canada Catalogue no. 98–316-X2016001. Ottawa, Canada.

Stede, M. and Peldszus, A. 2012. The role of illocutionary status in the usage conditions of causal connectives and in coherence relations. *Journal of Pragmatics*, 44(2), 214–229.

Stede, M. (ed.). 2016. *Handbuch Textannotation: Potsdammer Kommentarkorpus 2.0*. Potsdam: Universitätsverlag Potsdam.

Steensig, J. and Heinemann, T. 2015. Opening up codings? *Research on Language and Social Interaction*, 48(1), 20–25.

Stivers, T. 2015. Coding social interaction: A heretical approach in conversation analysis? *Research on Language and Social Interaction*, 48(1), 1–19.

Streiner, D. L. 1994. Figuring out factors: The use and misuse of factor analysis. *The Canadian Journal of Psychiatry*, 39(3), 135–140.

Stubbe, M. 1998. Are you listening? Cultural influences on the use of supportive verbal feedback in conversation. *Journal of Pragmatics*, 29(3), 257–289.

Stubbe, M. and Holmes, J. 1995. You know, eh and other "exasperating expressions": An analysis of social and stylistic variation in the use of pragmatic devices in a sample of New Zealand English. *Language and Communication*, 15(1), 63–88.

SurveyGizmo. 2015. *SurveyGizmo* (Survey Software Website). www.surveygizmo.com/.

Svartvik, J. 1980. *Well* in conversation. In S. Greenbaum, G. N. Leech, and J. Svartvik, eds., *Studies in English Linguistics for Randolph Quirk*. London: Longman, 167–177.

Svavarsdóttir, Á., Paatola, U., and Sandøy, H. 2010. English influence on the spoken language – with a special focus on its social, semantic and functional conditioning. *International Journal of the Sociology of Language*, 204, 43–58.

Sweetser, E. 1990. *From Etymology to Pragmatics*. Cambridge: Cambridge University Press.

Taavitsainen, I. and Pahta, P. 2012. Appropriation of the English politeness marker *pliis* into Finnish discourse. In L. Frentiu and L. Frantila, eds., *A Journey through Knowledge: Festschrift in Honour of Hortensia Parlog*. Newcastle upon Tyne: Cambridge Scholars Publishing, 182–203.

Taboada, M. and Das, D. 2013. Annotation upon annotation: Adding signalling information to a corpus of discourse relations. *Dialogue and* Discourse, 4(2), 249–281.

Tagliamonte, S. A. 2005. *So* who? *Like* how? *Just* what? Discourse markers in the conversations of young Canadians. *Journal of Pragmatics*, 37(11), 1896–1915.

Tagliamonte, S. A. 2006a. "So cool, right?": Canadian English entering the 21st century. *Canadian Journal of Linguistics*, 51(2–3), 309–331.

Tagliamonte, S. A. 2006b. *Analysing Sociolinguistic Variation*. Cambridge: Cambridge University Press.

Tagliamonte, S. A. 2007–2010. *Directions of Change in Canadian English*. Research Grant. Social Sciences and Humanities Research Council of Canada (SSHRCC). No. 410–070–048.

Tagliamonte, S. A. 2008. So different and pretty cool! Recycling intensifiers in Toronto. Canada. *English Language and Linguistics*, 12(2), 361–394.

Tagliamonte, S. A. 2012. *Variationist Sociolinguistics. Change, Observation, Interpretation*. Malden, MA: Wiley-Blackwell.

Tagliamonte, S. A. 2014. Obsolescence and innovation in discourse-pragmatic change: The view from Canada. Plenary at Discourse-Pragmatic Variation and Change 2014. Newcastle University, April 7–9.

Tagliamonte, S. A. 2016. Antecedents of innovation: Exploring general extenders in conservative dialects. In H. Pichler, ed., *Discourse-Pragmatic Variation and Change in English: New Methods and Insights*. Cambridge: Cambridge University Press, 115–138.

Tagliamonte, S. A. and Baayen, R. H. 2012. Models, forests, and trees of York English: Was/were variation as a case study for statistical practice. *Language Variation and Change*, 24(2), 135–178.

Tagliamonte, S. A. and D'Arcy. A. 2004. *He's like, she's like: the quotative system in Canadian youth. Journal of Sociolinguistics*, 8(4), 493–514.

Tagliamonte, S. A. and D'Arcy, A. 2007. Frequency and variation in the community grammar: Tracking a new change through the generations. *Language Variation and Change*, 19(2), 199–217.

Tagliamonte, S. A. and Denis, D. 2008. Linguistic ruin? LOL! Instant messaging and teen language. *American Speech*, 83(1), 3–34.

Tagliamonte, S. A. and Denis, D. 2010. The stuff of change: General extenders in Toronto, Canada. *Journal of English Linguistics*, 38(4), 335–368.

Tanner, J. 2010. Rakenne, tilanne ja kohteliaisuus. Pyynnöt S2-oppikirjoissa ja autenttisissa keskusteluissa. PhD thesis, University of Helsinki.

Tao, H. 2007. A corpus-based investigation of *absolutely* and related phenomena in spoken American English. *Journal of English Linguistics*, 35(5), 5–29.

Terkourafi, M. 2011. *Thank you, sorry* and *please* in Cypriot Greek: What happens to politeness markers when they are borrowed across languages? *Journal of Pragmatics*, 43(1), 218–235.

Terraschke, A. 2010. Or so, oder so, and stuff like that: General extenders in New Zealand English, German and in learner language. *Intercultural Pragmatics*, 7(3), 449–469.

Thibault, P. and Daveluy, M. 1989. Quelques traces du passage du temps dans le parler des Montréalais, 1971–1984. *Language Variation and Change*, 1(1), 19–45.

Thøgersen, J. 2004. Attitudes towards the English influx in the Nordic countries: A quantitative investigation. *Nordic Journal of English Studies*, 3(2), 23–38.

Thompson, S. A. and Mulac, A. 1991. A quantitative perspective on the grammaticization of epistemic parentheticals in English. In E. C. Traugott and B. Heine, eds., *Approaches to Grammaticalization*, Vol. 2. Amsterdam: John Benjamins, 313–329.

Tonelli, S., Riccardi, G., Prasad, R., and Joshi, A. 2010. Annotation of discourse relations for conversational spoken dialogs. In N. Calzolari, K. Choukri, B. Maegaard et al., eds., *Proceedings of the 7th International Conference on Language Resources and Evaluation (LREC'10)*. Valetta: European Language Resources Association (ELRA), 2084–2090.

Torres, L. 2006. Bilingual discourse markers in indigenous languages. *International Journal of Bilingual Education and Bilingualism*, 9(5), 615–624.

Tottie, G. 1991. Conversational style in British and American English: The case of backchannels. In K. Aijmer and B. Altenberg, eds., *English Corpus Linguistics*. London: Longman, 254–271.

Tottie, G. 2011. Uh and um as sociolinguistic markers in British English. *International Journal of Corpus Linguistics*, 16(2), 173–197.

Tottie, G. 2016. Planning what to say: Uh and um among the pragmatic markers. In G. Kaltenböck, E. Keizer, and A. Lohmann, eds., *Outside the Clause: Form and Function of Extra-Clausal Constituents*. Amsterdam: John Benjamins, 97–122.

Tottie, G. 2017. From pause to word: *Uh, um* and *er* in written American English. *English Language and Linguistics*, 23(1), 105–130.

Tottie, G. 2018. Variation and change among pragmatic markers as planners in American English. Paper presented at Discourse-Pragmatic Variation & Change 4, University of Helsinki, Finland, May 28–30.

Traugott, E. C. 1982. From propositional to textual and expressive meanings: Some semantic-pragmatic aspects of grammaticalization. In W. P. Lehmann, ed., *Perspectives on Historical Linguistics*. Amsterdam: John Benjamins, 245–271.

Traugott, E. C. 1995. The role of the development of discourse markers in a theory of grammaticalization. Paper presented at the International Conference on Historical Linguistics XII, Manchester, UK, August 13–18.

Traugott, E. C. 2012. Intersubjectification and clause periphery. *English Text Construction*, 5(1), 7–28.

Traugott, E. C. and Trousdale, G. 2010. Gradience, gradualness and grammaticalization: How do they intersect? In E. C. Traugott and G. Trousdale, eds., *Gradience, Gradualness and Grammaticalization*. Amsterdam: John Benjamins, 19–44.

Treffers-Daller, J. 1994. *Mixing Two languages: French-Dutch Contact in a Comparative Perspective*. Berlin: Mouton de Gruyter.

Trudgill, P. and Giles, H. 1978. Sociolinguistics and linguistic value judgements: Correctness, adequacy and aesthetics. In F. Coppieters and D. L. Goyvaerts, eds., *Functional Studies in Language and Literature*. Ghent: Story-Scientia, 167–190.
Truesdale, S. and Meyerhoff, M. 2015. Acquiring some *like*-ness to others. *Te Reo*, 58, 3–28.
Turnbull, R. J. 2015. Assessing the listener-oriented account of predictability-based phonetic reduction. PhD thesis, Ohio State University, Columbus.
Underhill, R. 1988. Like is like, focus. *American Speech*, 63(3), 234–246.
VanPatten, B. 2004. *Processing Instruction: Theory, Research, and Commentary*. Mahwah, NJ: Lawrence Erlbaum Associates.
Wagner, S. E., Hesson, A., Bybel, K., and Little, H. 2015. Quantifying the referential function of general extenders in North American English. *Language in Society*, 44(5), 705–731.
Wagner, S. E. and Hesson, A. 2014. Listener sensitivity to the frequency of socially meaningful linguistic cues affects language attitudes. *Language and Social Psychology*, 33(6), 651–666.
Waksler, R. 2012. *Super, uber, so* and *totally:* Over-the-top intensification to mark subjectivity in colloquial discourse. In N. Baumgarten, I. Du Bois, and J. House eds., *Subjectivity in Language and Discourse*. Bingley: Emerald, 17–31.
Walker, J. 2010. *Variation in Linguistic Systems*. New York: Routledge.
Wallenberg, J. C. 2013. A unified theory of stable variation, syntactic optionality, and syntactic change. Paper presented at the Fifteenth Diachronic Generative Syntax Conference. University of Ottawa, August 1–3.
Waltereit, R. 2002. Imperatives, interruption in conversation, and the rise of discourse markers: A study of Italian *guarda*. *Linguistics*, 40(5), 987–1010.
Waltereit, R. 2006. The rise of discourse markers in Italian: A specific type of language change. In K. Fischer, ed., *Approaches to Discourse Particles*. Amsterdam: Elsevier, 61–76.
Ward, G. and Birner, B. 1993. The semantics and pragmatics of and everything. *Journal of Pragmatics*, 19(3), 205–214.
Ward, N. and Tsukahara, W. 2000. Prosodic features which cue back-channel responses in English and Japanese. *Journal of Pragmatics*, 32(8), 1177–1207.
Warren, P. 2013. *Introducing Psycholinguistics*. Cambridge: Cambridge University Press.
Waters, C. 2016. Practical strategies for elucidating discourse-pragmatic variation. In H. Pichler, ed., *Discourse-Pragmatic Variation and Change in English: New Methods and Insights*. Cambridge, Cambridge University Press, 41–56.
Watts, R. J. 1989. "Taking the pitcher to the 'well'": Native speakers' perception of their use of discourse markers in conversation. *Journal of Pragmatics*, 13(2), 203–237.
Watts, R. J. 2003. *Politeness*. Cambridge: Cambridge University Press.
Weiner, E. J. and Labov, W. 1983. Constraints on the agentless passive. *Journal of Linguistics*, 19(1), 29–58.
Weydt, H. 1969. *Abtönungspartikel*. Bad Homburg: Gehlen.
White, S. 1989. Backchannels across cultures: A study of Americans and Japanese. *Language in Society*, 18(1), 59–76.
Wichmann, A. 2005. *Please*: From courtesy to appeal: the role of intonation in the expression of attitudinal meaning. *English Language and Linguistics*, 9(2), 229–253.

Wieling, M., Grieve, J., Bouma, G. et al. 2016. Variation and change in the use of hesitation markers in Germanic languages. *Language Dynamics and Change*, 6(2), 199–234.

Wiese, H. and Labrenz, A. 2021. Emoji as graphic discourse markers. In D. Van Olmen and J. Šinkūnienė, eds., *Pragmatic Markers and Peripheries*. Amsterdam: John Benjamins, 277–300.

Wilkinson, S. and Kitzinger, C. 2014. Conversation analysis in language and gender studies. In S. Ehrlich, M. Meyerhoff, J. Holmes, eds., *The Handbook of Language, Gender, and Sexuality*, 2nd ed. Hoboken, NJ: John Wiley & Sons, 141–160.

Wiltschko, M., Denis, D., and D'Arcy, A. 2018. Deconstructing variation in pragmatic function: A transdisciplinary case study. *Language in Society*, 47(4), 569–599.

Wiltschko, M. and Heim J. 2006. The syntax of confirmationals: A non-performative analysis. In G. Kaltenböck, E. Keizer, and A. Lohmann, eds., *Outside the Clause: Form and Function of Extra-Clausal Constituents*. Amsterdam: John Benjamins, 305–340.

Winter, B., and Wieling, M. 2016. How to analyze linguistic change using mixed models, Growth curve analysis and generalized additive modeling. *Journal of Language Evolution*, 1(1), 7–18.

Yale Grammatical Diversity Project: English in North America. *The alls construction*. https://ygdp.yale.edu/phenomena/alls-construction/.

Yli-Vakkuri, V. 2005. Politeness in Finland: Evasion at all costs. In L. Hickey and M. Stewart, eds., *Politeness in Europe*. Clevedon: Multilingual Matters, 189–202.

Yngve, V. H. 1970. On getting a word in edgewise. In R. L. Binnick, ed., *Papers from the Sixth Regional Meeting of the Chicago Linguistic Society, April 16–18, 1970*. Chicago: Chicago Linguistic Society, 567–578.

Zahn, C. J. and Hopper, R. 1985. Measuring language attitudes: The speech evaluation instrument (SEI). *Journal of Language and Social Psychology*, 4(2), 113–123.

Zenner, E., Speelman, D., and Geeraerts, D. 2014. A sociolinguistic analysis of borrowing in weak contact situations: English loanwords and phrases in expressive utterances in a Dutch reality TV show. *International Journal of Bilingualism*, 19(3), 333–346.

Zufferey, S. and Gygax, P. 2020. Roger broke his tooth. However, he went to the dentist: Why some readers struggle to evaluate wrong (and right) uses of connectives. *Discourse Processes*, 57(2), 184–200.

Corpora

AF2013 = Acadian French 2013. Chiasson Corpus.

AF2019 = Acadian French 2019. Hubert-Breton Corpus.

Audio BNC = The audio edition of the Spoken British National Corpus. See Coleman et al. (2012).

Backbone = Backbone Corpus. See Kohn (2012).

BBc = Big Brother Corpus. 2001. www.tekstlab.uio.no/nota/bigbrother/.

BNC = Davies, M. 2004–. British National Corpus. Oxford University Press. www.natcorp.ox.ac.uk/corpus/.

BNC1994D = British National Corpus 1994 – Demographic. www.natcorp.ox.ac.uk/corpus/.

BNC2014S = The Spoken British National Corpus. 2014. http://corpora.lancs.ac.uk/bnc2014/. See Love et al. (2017).

C-ORAL-ROM = C-ORAL-ROM Integrated Reference Corpora for Spoken Romance Languages. See Cresti and Moneglia (2005).

References

CEAL = Corpus of Early American Literature. See Höglund and Syrjänen (2016).
CEN = The Corpus of English Novels. Compiled by H. De Smet. www.kuleuven.be/~u0044428/cen.htm/.
CFPP = Corpus de français parlé parisien. See Branca-Rosoff et al. (2012).
CLARIN = Polish CLARIN infrastructure. See Pęzik (2015).
CLMET3.0 = The Corpus of Late Modern English Texts, version 3.0. Created by H. De Smet, H.-J. Diller, and J. Tyrkkö. www.kuleuven.be/~u0044428/clmet3_0.htm/.
COCA = Davies, M. 2008–. The Corpus of Contemporary American English: 560 million words, 1990–present. www.english-corpora.org/coca/.
COHA = Davies, M. 2010–. The Corpus of Historical American English: 400 million words, 1810–2009. www.english-corpora.org/coha/.
COLT = Bergen Corpus of London Teenage Language. 1993. Department of English. University of Bergen.
DARE = Cassidy, F. G. (ed.). 1985. *Dictionary of American Regional English, Vol. 1: A–C*. Cambridge, MA: Belknap Press of Harvard University Press.
EEBO = Davies, M. 2017. Early English Books Online. Part of the SAMUELS project. www.english-corpora.org/eebo/.
EOA = Earlier Ontario English Collection. See Denis (2016, 2017).
Fisher = The Fisher corpus. See Cieri et al. (2004).
ICE-GB = International Corpus of English (Great Britain). See Nelson et al. (2002).
LOCAS-F = Louvain Corpus of Annotated Speech – French. See Degand et al. (2014).
Movies = Davies, M. 2019–. The Movie Corpus: 200 million words, 1930–2018. www.english-corpora.org/movies/.
Montreal 1971 = Sankoff-Cedergren corpus. See Sankoff et al. (1976).
Montreal 2012: Blondeau, H., Frenette, F., Martineau, F., and Tremblay M. The Hochelaga-Maisonneuve 2012 variationist sub-corpus of the FRAN Corpus (dir. F. Martineau). See Blondeau et al. (2021) and Martineau and Séguin (2016).
NDC = Nordic Dialect Corpus. 2007–2008. https://tekstlab.uio.no/glossa2/ndc/.
NoTa = Norsk talemålskorpus. 2004–2006. www.tekstlab.uio.no/nota/oslo/index.html/.
OED = M. Proffitt (ed.). 2000. *Oxford English Dictionary* [Online], 3rd ed. Oxford: Oxford University Press. www.oed.com/.
OB = The Old Bailey Proceedings Online, 1674–1913. Hitchcock, T., Shoemaker, R., Emsley, C., Howard, S. and McLaughlin, J. et al., eds., version 7.0, March 2012. www.oldbaileyonline.org/.
PNC = Philadelphia Neighborhood Corpus. See Labov and Rosenfelder (2011).
QF2014 = Quebec French 2014. Levey and Prazeres Corpus.
QF2019 = Quebec French 2019. Levey and Kastronic Corpus.
SOAP = Davies, M. 2011–. Corpus of American Soap Operas: 100 million words. www.english-corpora.org/soap/.
SP2010 = Projeto SP2010 Amostra da Fala Paulistana. See Mendes (2013).
Switchboard = The Switchboard-1 Telephone Speech Corpus. Godfrey, J. and Holliman, E. Switchboard-1 release 2 LDC97S62. Web Download. Philadelphia: Linguistic Data Consortium, 1993. https://catalog.ldc.upenn.edu/LDC97S62/.
TEA = Toronto English Archive. See Tagliamonte (2006a).
TV = Davies, M. 2019–. The TV Corpus: 325 million words, 1950–2018. www.english-corpora.org/tv/.
Urban Dictionary = Urban Dictionary. www.urbandictionary.com/.

UNO = Ungdomsspråk i Norden. 1997. http://clu.uni.no/humfak/uno/.
VISK = Hakulinen, A., Vilkuna, M., Korhonen, R. et al. 2004. *Iso suomen kielioppi.* Helsinki: Suomalaisen Kirjallisuuden Seura. http://scripta.kotus.fi/visk/.
Welland 1975 = See Beniak et al. (1985).
Welland 2012–2015 = France Martineau-Raymond Mougeon, and Raymond Mougeon-Mireille Tremblay The Welland variationist sub-corpus of the FRAN Corpus (dir. F. Martineau). See Martineau and Séguin (2016).

Index

abruptness, 6, 15, 17–19, 24, 26, 35–36, 39
accent, 45–46, 56
adjective, 127, 129–131, 134–139, 143–144
adolescent language, 133, 137, 256, 259
age, xix, xxi, 8, 25, 29–30, 42, 44, 48, 50, 52–53, 55, 65–68, 71, 73, 78–79, 127–129, 131–133, 137–138, 143–144, 146, 148, 158, 188, 199, 217, 230, 234, 236, 239–241, 244, 247, 249, 251, 255, 270, 272, 293
age-grading, 128, 234, 240, 247
alors, 90, 231–235, 237–238, 240–241, 243–245, 247–249, 299
alternation, 19, 68, 263
alternative, 20, 88–90, 94–95, 97–98, 101–102, 253, 276, 298
amplifier, 129
apology, 253, 256, 263, 265–270
apparent time, 15, 21, 23, 27, 29, 128, 151, 153, 159–161, 166, 236
audio stimulus, 46–47, 49–50

backchannel, 146, 177, 182–183, 253
be like, xxi, 41, 61, 68, 71, 138, 163, 216, 222, 294, 300
bilingualism, 3, 5, 9, 65, 67, 70, 174, 212, 217, 223, 236, 293–294
booster, 129, 131, 133–134, 136, 138–139, 147, 256
Brazilian Portuguese, 3–4, 61–64, 67, 69, 77–81, 294

(ça) fait (que), 231, 233–236, 238, 240–241, 243–244, 247–249, 299
child language acquisition, xxii
clitic, 153, 156–157, 159, 161–162, 166, 283, 285
colloquialism, 108
Common European Framework of Reference for Language (CEFR), 198–199
como, 62–64, 78, 225
complement clause, 20, 28–34

complementizer phrase, 19
completive adverb, 129
computer-mediated communication, 68, 275, 299
conceptual meaning, 146–147
concession, 88–90, 92–93, 95, 101–102
conjunction, 64, 120–122, 126, 155, 208, 212, 214, 231, 263, 287
consequence marker, 1, 3, 5, 10, 230–231, 233–236, 240, 243–244, 248–249, 299
Constant Rate Effect (CRE), 15–16
conventionalization, 38
convergence, 10–11, 231, 236, 239, 243, 247–249
conversation analysis, xxii, 3, 9, 103, 173, 298
cross-linguistic analysis, 83, 99

decategorization, 215–216
declarative clause, xxi, 125
deductive reasoning, xxi
deixis, 64, 78
diachronic variation. See variation
discourse analysis, xix, xx
discourse annotation, 83–84
discourse domain, 86, 90, 97, 101–102, 294
discourse function, 86, 90, 92, 95–96, 98, 145–146, 151, 163, 165, 254–255, 265, 270
discourse marker, xxi, xxiii, 1, 4, 7–9, 83–84, 88, 91, 94–95, 99, 102–103, 127, 134, 145–147, 153, 156, 216, 222, 228, 232, 248, 252–254, 257–258, 260–261, 267, 269, 273, 294
discourse-pragmatic feature, 2, 4, 7–8
discourse-pragmatic marker, 24
disfluency, 46, 84, 171, 296
disjunct, 132–133
divergence, 10, 77, 84, 99, 163, 231, 236, 238–240, 243, 247–250, 299
donc, 86, 89–90, 230–250, 299
doxastic strength, 6, 23, 26, 28, 30–32, 34–35
doxastic verb, 22
dynamism, 40–42, 48, 52, 55, 58

329

330 Index

Earlier Ontario English Collection, 8, 15, 20, 154
education, xix, 67–68, 78, 197–198, 202–204, 210, 232, 296
ellipsis, 108, 123
embedded clause, 32, 37
emphasizer, 8, 129–131, 133–134, 139–142, 144–145, 147
English
  American English, 8, 109–110, 113, 119, 127, 195, 197, 214, 220, 228, 301, 310, 315, 318, 322, 324–325, 327
  Australian English, 9, 193
  British English, 40, 44, 109, 128, 174, 195, 214, 294–295
  Canadian English, 5–6, 8, 21, 214
  Early Modern English, 126
  Irish English, 174
  present-day English, 109, 120
epistemic meaning, 145, 147
ethnicity, 41–42
ethnography, xix
être comme, 7, 63, 68–77, 80–81, 295
evaluation, 40–42, 44–45, 47, 49, 52–53, 55–57, 135, 140, 249, 266, 295–296
evaluative language, 86
everyday speech. See natural speech
experimental study, 45, 295
extraposition, 24

facework, 33
factor analysis, 49–50
Farm Work and Farm Life Since 1890 (project), 8, 20, 154
filled pause, xxiii, 1, 8, 151, 154, 171, 208, 298
finite clause, xxi
Finnish, 3, 5, 10, 174, 253–254, 272–291, 294
French, 3–5, 7, 10, 18, 61–62, 64–65, 67–73, 76, 78–81, 83, 85, 87–95, 97, 99–100, 102, 195, 209, 213, 230–237, 244–245, 248–251, 294–295, 299, 324
  Acadian French, 7, 62, 65, 67, 70–77, 80–81
  Medieval French, 72
  Multicultural Paris French, 71
  Quebec French, 62–63, 67, 70–76, 81
function. See pragmatic function, discourse function, interpersonal function

gender, xix, xxii, 8, 19, 21, 44, 127–129, 131–132, 138, 148, 155, 158–160, 162–163, 166, 168–170, 174–176, 182–189, 202–203, 217–219, 222, 226–227, 236, 241, 243–245, 247–248, 255, 270
general extender, 212–229, 254, 293–294
  adjunctive, 214–215, 220–221
  disjunctive, 214–215, 220–222, 228
  non-referential, 147, 213, 215–216, 223–226, 229, 293
  referential, 213, 215–216, 223–229
generative semantics, xix
genre, 63–64, 71–73, 81, 108
  fiction, 114, 116, 120, 122
  journals, 122, 252
  magazines, 109, 114, 120, 201
  movies, 109–110, 115, 116–120, 122
  newspapers, 109, 114
  political writings, 121
  religious texts, 122
gradualness, 6, 15–16, 19, 23
grammatical change, 16–18, 36, 71
grammatical person, 28–30, 32–33, 68, 75
grammaticalization, 6, 15–16, 18–20, 22–24, 26, 28, 32, 34–36, 38, 129, 147, 150, 211–212, 215–216, 228–229, 293
Grice, H. P., xix
guises. See matched guise
Gumperz John, xxiii

Hastings County Historical Society, 21
hesitation marker, 24, 86

I guess, xxi, 6, 19, 22–23, 25, 28–29, 31–32, 34–37, 224
I mean, 95, 108, 120, 123–124, 136, 138, 141, 144, 195–197, 200–202, 207–208, 260
I suppose, 4, 6, 19, 22–23, 25, 28–29, 34–35, 92, 171
ideational domain, 86, 94, 98, 100, 103
IFID. See illocutionary force
illocutionary force, 10, 209, 253, 256, 259–262, 267–269
initial, 9, 19, 23–27, 34, 36, 43–45, 50, 109, 121, 126, 151, 156, 159, 162–164, 166, 168–172, 195, 272, 274, 276–277, 285, 287–291, 298
intensifier, 1–2, 5, 127–129, 131–136, 141, 143, 145, 147–148, 237, 274
interaction, xxiii, xxiv, 5, 9–11, 26–27, 30–31, 33, 45, 51, 56, 85, 86, 88, 91, 94–95, 99, 103, 145, 147, 150, 168, 170, 174, 176–177, 180, 182–184, 189, 199, 298
interaction (stat.), 186–187
interactional discourse, 57
interactional linguistics, 103
interlanguage pragmatics, 194
International Pragmatics Association (IPrA), xx, xxii
interpersonal domain, 86, 91, 93–97, 99–100, 102

Index

interpersonal function, 43, 85, 108, 207, 289
is all, 3, 5, 8, 107–126, 213, 299
Italian, 3–4, 7, 61–62, 64, 67, 69, 77–80, 82, 294

(jeg) beklager, 263, 267

kiitos, 10, 253, 272, 274, 276–277, 279–282, 284–291, 294, 299

Labov, William, xix
Lakoff, Robin, xxi
language attitudes, 40
language contact, xxiii, 3, 5, 9–10, 211, 222, 231, 248, 251–252, 273, 275, 290, 294–295
language dominance, 217–219, 222, 226–227, 236, 244, 248–249
lexical meaning, 27, 34, 129–130, 140, 193
lexicology, xxii
linguistic constraint, 8, 23, 68, 75–76, 80, 151, 223, 239, 250, 294
linguistic variation, xix, 17, 83

Malinowski, Bronisław, xix
matched guise, 3–4, 6, 41–44, 295
maximizer, 129–130, 134, 136, 139, 147
maybe, 20–21, 29, 86, 256
meaning. See conceptual meaning, epistemic meaning, lexical meaning, pragmatic meaning, procedural meaning, propositional meaning, semantic meaning, social meaning
medial, 19, 24, 26, 36–37, 43–44
mimesis, 69, 75–76
mixed effects linear regression, 51
mixed-effects logistic regression, 22, 26, 30
modal adverbial, 21, 147
modifier, 8, 132–133, 137–138, 144
modularity, 18
monosemy, 89
morphology, xxii, 69, 272
Morris, Charles W., xx
Multicultural Paris French, 72
multifunctionality, 1, 11, 85, 129, 193–194, 209, 215
multivariate analysis, 10, 74–76

narrative, xxiv, 72, 86, 164
natural speech, 65, 67, 128, 197–198, 273, 296
New Brunswick, 65–66, 73, 76
Niagara, 19–21, 154–158, 232
non-canonical, 62–64, 71, 80
Norwegian, 3, 5, 10, 153, 195, 252–256, 258, 263, 265, 268–270, 294

noun phrase, 8, 64, 127, 132, 134, 143, 212, 278–279, 287–288

obsolescence, 15, 23, 29, 35–36, 235, 247
oh, xxi, 24, 94, 195, 208, 298
operationalization, 176, 183

paradigmatic expansion, 76
periphery, xxv, 11, 36, 214, 289, 299
phonetic reduction, 126, 212, 215–216, 222, 228–229
phonological reduction. See phonetic reduction, phonetic reduction, phonetic reduction
phonology, xxii, 194
Pike, Kenneth, xix
pitch, 45, 69
please, 3, 6, 10, 38, 118, 253–254, 256–264, 269–270, 272–273, 276–277, 287–288, 290, 294
pliis, 6, 10, 253–254, 269, 272–277, 279–291, 294, 299
Poisson regression, 8, 155, 166–169, 176, 183, 185, 187, 189
Polish, 3–4, 7, 9, 83, 87, 95–102, 174, 193, 195, 197–199, 201, 203, 205, 208–209, 294–295
politeness, xxiv, 1, 5, 10, 33, 44, 215–216, 224, 252–254, 256–257, 269, 272–277, 279–282, 284–286, 288–292
politeness marker, 1, 5, 10, 216, 253, 256–257, 272–274, 276–277, 279–282, 284–286, 288–292
polyfunctionality, 7, 87, 90, 93, 95–96, 98–99, 102, 294
polysemy, 7, 87, 93, 95, 102, 147, 294
position, 1, 5–6, 8, 11, 19–20, 23–27, 34, 36–37, 43–44, 87, 109, 111, 125, 127, 140, 145, 151, 155, 159, 161–162, 164, 166, 168–172, 177–178, 195, 211, 272, 274–275, 277, 280–282, 285–289, 291, 296, 298
pragmatic borrowing, 10, 216, 228, 252–254, 269, 272–274, 288, 290, 294
pragmatic function, 1, 4, 16, 43, 108–111, 113, 116–119, 121, 164, 195, 197, 201, 209, 214–216, 223–224, 229, 254, 278–279, 289
pragmatic marker, xxiii, 6–7, 15–16, 18–19, 21–22, 24, 35–42, 44–45, 52, 55, 57–58, 85, 107, 114–115, 123, 125, 150, 152, 193–194, 275
pragmatic meaning, 11, 116, 126, 130, 139, 216, 224, 290–291
pragmatic particle, xxi, xxii, xxiii, xxiv, 1, 43, 289–290
pragmatic shift, 215–216

present-day English, 126
prestige, 40–42, 48, 52, 54–55, 57–58, 296
Principle of Accountability, 3, 9–10, 150–151, 154–155, 164, 170, 173, 182
principle of persistence, 28, 34
procedural meaning, 85, 87
processual model of speech evaluation, 53, 56
pronoun, 22, 24, 64, 110, 121, 132, 264
propositional meaning, 16, 107

quotative constructions, 62, 64
quotative system, 7, 61–62, 65, 67–68, 70, 72–73, 76, 78–81
quotative variation, 67, 70

R (programming language), 49–51, 159, 168, 202, 219, 222
real time, 30, 300
reanalysis, 6, 8, 15, 17, 20, 35–38, 125–126
request, 10, 141, 146, 254, 256–264, 267–270, 273–274, 276–291
responsibility, xxiv, xxv, 6
rhetorical domain, 86, 88, 92–93, 95, 100–101
Romance languages, 7, 64, 94

Schiffrin, Deborah, xxiii
scripted language, 114
Searle, John, xix
second language acquisition, 3, 5, 210
semantic change, 215–216, 228–229
semantic meaning, 102, 209, 295
semantics, xx, xxii, 19, 131
semi-independent clause, 24
sentence grammar, 38
small word. See pragmatic particle
so, 10, 24, 143, 195, 231–236, 238–241, 243–244, 247–249, 274, 299
social meaning, 8, 44, 52–53, 55–58, 128, 139, 150, 272, 278
social salience, 53–55, 57, 296
sociolinguistic factor, 128–129, 137, 200, 203
sociolinguistic interview, 21, 65, 67, 70, 198, 207, 214–215, 221, 299
sociolinguistic variable, xix, 2, 21, 154, 173, 183, 187, 189, 194, 199–200, 202, 231, 248, 250
sociology of language, 40
solidarity, 40–42, 48, 50–52, 54–55, 57–58, 148, 215, 253, 276, 283, 291, 296
sorry, 10, 58, 179, 253–254, 256, 263–270, 294
Southern Arizona, 9, 212, 216–217, 228–229
Spanish, 3–5, 7, 9, 64, 83, 87, 91–95, 97, 99–100, 102, 195, 209, 212–222, 225–229, 253, 293–294

Peninsular (Spain), 87, 213–215, 221–222, 228, 294
US Spanish, 5, 221
specification, 86, 88–90, 92, 94–95, 97–98
spontaneous conversation. See natural speech
standard language ideology, 57–58
survey (method), 41, 44, 47–49, 54, 57–58, 60, 276, 282, 297
synchronic variation. See variation

text linguistics, xix
theory of cooptation, 15
thetical grammar, 38–39
tipo, 62, 64, 78–79, 81
Toronto English Archive, 15, 20–21
totally, 3, 5, 8, 127–148, 224
totes, 128, 137
transformational-generative linguistics, xix
transition-relevance point, 177

uh, 3, 5, 8, 24, 63, 86, 94, 151–158, 163–172, 179, 201, 208, 298
um, 3, 5, 8, 24, 136, 138, 140, 151–155, 157–172, 208, 278, 298
unnskyld, 254, 264–268, 294
urban varieties, 73, 81
usage-based approaches, xx, 210–211
utterance, xxii, 8–9, 36–37, 41, 43–44, 54, 113, 130, 132, 134, 140, 142, 145, 151, 153, 155, 163–164, 170–171, 189, 193, 260–261, 263, 266–268, 289, 298

vær så snill, 10, 254, 257, 260–263, 270
variable context, 21–22, 68, 72–73, 78, 151, 154, 193, 200
variation, 5, 11
variationist sociolinguistics, 1, 61, 200
variety, 21, 43, 49, 57, 65, 67, 70–71, 73–74, 76, 96, 109, 119, 188, 195–196, 200, 202, 208, 211, 213, 216, 252, 294
verb, 18, 20, 22, 34, 37, 68–69, 78, 110, 126, 129–132, 134, 139–141, 200, 258, 263, 274, 278–280, 283–284

wave model of change, 16
well, xxi, 24, 94, 156, 195, 208
Welland, Ontario, 230
Wittgenstein, Ludwig, xix

you know, xxi, xxii, xxiv, 3–6, 9, 40–48, 50–57, 60, 94–95, 97, 121, 125, 138, 140, 142, 155, 157, 179–180, 193–198, 200–210, 214, 224, 274, 282, 288, 295–297

For EU product safety concerns, contact us at Calle de José Abascal, 56–1°, 28003 Madrid, Spain or eugpsr@cambridge.org.

www.ingramcontent.com/pod-product-compliance
Ingram Content Group UK Ltd.
Pitfield, Milton Keynes, MK11 3LW, UK
UKHW020401120325
456051UK00006B/62